THE BRITISH EMPIRE: MY PART IN ITS 'DECLINE'

THE MERCHANT NAVY AND I

John Ayres

The British Empire
My Part In Its Decline

John Ayres

The British Empire
My Part In Its 'Decline'

First published In Great Britain in 2023

Copyright c John Ayres 2023

John Ayres asserts the moral right to
be identified as the author this work

ISBN   (Trade Paperback)

'To be born an Englishman is to be given a first class ticket to life' – Cecil Rhodes

'The past is another country. They do things differently there' – L P Hartley ('The Go-Between')

'Find out what you want to do in life, then find someone to pay you to do it' – Henry Longhurst ('Sunday Times' golf correspondent)

'The best part of being at sea is being ashore' – the seaman's lament

'Our future is the open sea' – Boris Johnson

'You have to stop along the way and smell the roses' - Walter Hagen, US professional golfer.

CONTENTS

INTRODUCTION

INTRODUCTION

This book is about two important institutions:

The British Merchant Navy and the British Commonwealth of Nations.

My contention is that they qualify for celebration.

There is drama in their development in the 1950s and early 1960s. What happened then has had profound influence on where the United Kingdom finds itself today.

My standpoint is, firstly, that I had the opportunity to witness what was going on from both within the UK and other nations. Secondly, I experienced a lifestyle that was uncommon, has disappeared, will never recur and is therefore worth recording. This lifestyle was not without its own moments of drama such as surviving an Atlantic hurricane, when ship's engines were failing. What followed was six months in a Southern Texan town, which was another unique experience.

I believe that there has been continuous incomprehension about the role of the Merchant Navy before, during and after my sojourn. It is, perhaps, encapsulated by a remark of my mother's, where she referred to my 'tuppence ha'penny cargo'. She had not realised that 'my cargo' consisted of food stuffs that were essential in keeping the UK population from starving. It is on a par with the old question to a city centre schoolboy, who, when asked where milk comes from, replied 'Sainsburys'.

Before the 18th Century, the UK was largely self sufficient in food and clothing. The population did not succeed in recovering the numbers lost to the Great Plague of the 14th Century until the early 19th Century. Land under cultivation in the first part of the 14th Century and abandoned after the Great Plague was not cultivated again until the Second World War. During the 18th Century, trade and overseas dominions expanded. This expansion brought new products: sugar instead of honey, cotton instead of flax, coffee and tea and spices to enlarge our cuisine and appetites. As the population increased and people left the land to work in the new industrial towns, the UK imported more food, particularly staples such as wheat. The population continued to increase without a proportionate increase in UK agriculture. From 1822 onwards, there has been an annual deficit in visible imports and exports. As refrigerated ships became available, deficiencies in UK production were made up by imports that included meat, dairy products and fruit. The degree to which we are dependent on these imports is expressed in the calculation that there is never more than six weeks supply of food in the country ready for consumption.

This situation cannot be supported without a means of importing and of exporting (which has to contribute towards paying for imports). The Merchant Navy has provided the means for centuries, often experiencing extreme danger. In modern times, the loss of professional seamen in wartime has been horrendous. 33,000 merchant seamen lost their lives in World War Two. As a proportion of those serving, it was higher than any of the Armed Services.

The number of British merchant seamen is not high as a proportion of the UK population. What they do is unseen for the most part and consequently unknown. This needs to be redressed, hence my memoir. I have set out to describe the life of an Apprentice and Deck Officer. Often mundane, it has its moments of hilarity, drama and sadness. My experiences could constitute a minor addition to the social history of that time. I cannot state that I am one hundred per cent accurate because there is no way of verifying all of my memories. Therefore, whoever may read this should not be surprised if dates and places don't appear to be in the right place. So far as my own travels are concerned, I do not believe that it matters very much whether I went to Melbourne before Adelaide in July 1961 or vice versa. In the same vein, I have expressed opinions and beliefs that others may disagree with or find unacceptable. They are my opini0ns and beliefs as I remembered them and I have no way of verifying them. Accordingly, they are presented in good faith.

What is important is that I was involved in one of the most historically important commercial occupations. We ignore the importance of sea trade at our peril, which importance has long been known.

Four points to consider:

1. 'Hee that commaunds the sea, commaunds the trade, and hee that is Lord of the trade of the worlde is Lord of the wealth of the worlde' – Sir Walter Raleigh

2. 90% of the world's trade is seaborne

3. The UK cannot feed itself. It has relied on imported food for over two hundred years. Since 1822, the UK has imported more goods than it exported. It has depended on services, including shipping, but particularly financial, and overseas investment to balance its trade. In most years, such 'invisible' earnings were more than the deficit. However, returns from overseas investments declined to almost nil between 1914 and 1945 due to the need sell these investments to finance war. Imbalances have been financed by borrowing, hence the National Debt, the interest on which absorbs a proportion of Government revenues.

4. It takes only three weeks from an Asian factory to UK retail distribution.

Wrong decisions were taken in the 1950s about the direction of the UK, both politically and economically. In order to understand why we did not take the right decisions then, we must first understand that the 1950s were a period of great change. More people led prosperous lives, particularly in what is known as the Free, Western or First World. Ownership of homes, cars, TVs, washing machines, refrigerators, fashionable clothes, entertainment and holidays with pay were commonplace. The world had, apparently, recovered from the ravages of two world wars and had embarked on what appeared to be a never ending spending spree. But, it was a world with its own anxieties about nuclear war and was divided into a contest for world leadership between communism and capitalism (state control versus free enterprise). It was also a time when the largest empire ever known, the British Empire, was apparently in terminal decline. I was in the Merchant Navy for seven years between 1955 and 1962. I travelled to parts of this Empire, mostly the 'white' Commonwealth. What did I observe or experience that might be of value to record?

My first observation is that the 1950s was a decade that produced many inventions and achievements, almost wholly through the efforts of the free world. Communism, in the shape of the Soviet *bloc*, produced little or nothing new of any consequence. Here is a list of some of these achievements: first passenger jet aircraft (the Comet); Diners Club Card (the first credit card); transistor radios; colour TV broadcasting; non-stick cookware; superglue; power steering; Barbie; microwave ovens; video tape recorder; heart/lung machine; Velcro; bar codes; programmable music synthesiser; first space satellite (USSR); Fortran computer language; micro chip; polio vaccine; oral contraceptive; solar cells; computer hard disks; pacemaker; radial tyres; modem; lasers; TV remote control; commercially available computer; colour kitchen appliances; hovercraft; antihistamines; discovery of DNA; Leo Fender electric guitar; telephone answering machine; 3-D movies; first successful kidney transplant; optic fibre; 'AA' alkaline batteries; integrated circuits; stereophonic recordings. Apart from the medical advances, it is noteworthy that the bulk of these inventions were related to domestic and/or leisure activities. This reflected the growing power of consumerism in the 'free world', which power was almost wholly absent from the communist world. The United Kingdom was at the forefront of these inventions, hardly an indication of decline.

As I was compiling memories of my time in the Merchant Navy from 1955 to 1962, I came to understand better the great changes that were in progress in those years. These changes virtually eliminated the last elements of the vast European Empires that had dominated the world for a couple of centuries. World trade patterns changed, manufacturing methods changed and a considerable part of the world's population enjoyed widespread material comfort such as had never before been experienced. Overall, the world was better fed. Much has been written and filmed about the 'Swinging 60s' as if this happened without reference to the previous decade. When I look back on my own experience during the 1950s, I am convinced that the 1950s definitely laid the groundwork for the apparent revolutions in attitude, expressions and material comfort we enjoyed in the 1960s.

A crucial element is what I have earlier called the 'virtual elimination of the vast European Empires'. However, I contend that in the case of the British Empire, it was not entirely true and that, although a global financial and military empire centred on London faded away, this empire left a voluntary structure that have could have been put to better use.

The name' Commonwealth' to describe the British Empire was first used by Lord Rosebury in 1890, when he was Prime Minister. The British Commonwealth of Nations was formed by Act of Parliament in 1932 and it still exists today as a voluntary grouping of mainly like-minded nations. There are fifty eight of these nations and they acknowledge King Charles III of the United Kingdom as its titular head. These people, through their Heads of Government, gather together annually for a conference presided over by the Monarch. Every Remembrance Sunday, their representatives in London lay wreaths in a collective ceremony on the Cenotaph in Whitehall. Four of the Commonwealth members (Mozambique, Rwanda, Togo and Gabon) were never part of the original British Empire. Given the vitriol that has been poured over the history of the British Empire, these facts are remarkable, if not miraculous.

What I have endeavoured to show in my narrative is that the 1950s, although during it the UK continued to decline commercially in comparison with other nations, was far from being a period of British imperial decline. It was a period where the empire was continuing to morph into a voluntary collection of countries. It could have been the springboard for developing a community that could have produced great benefit for the world. I would argue that Harold Macmillan's policy of closer integration with Europe destroyed that opportunity. I have expanded my thoughts on this subject at the end of this memoir. My experiences showed that the emotional ties between the UK and Imperial Dominions and Territories was strong. I hope that I have been able to demonstrate that.

In order to describe the life of a merchant seaman, the bulk of the narrative covers my experiences in the Merchant Navy from the time I joined the School of Navigation in January 1955 as a Cadet to obtaining my Certificate of Competency as a First Mate (Foreign Going) and coming ashore in March 1962. I have tried to describe a world and a system of trading that no longer exists. At the time I joined the British Merchant Navy, it still had one of the largest number of vessels in commission in the world. Many of these vessels traded to countries whose external trade was dominated by exports to the UK and which were dependent on manufactured imports from the UK. Although there had been technical progress, essentially the pattern of trade and the navigation and management involving merchant vessels had not changed for a century. I experienced the beginnings of a rapid change, both technically and in patterns of trade, that had already made a profound alteration to my working life in the seven years of my life in the Merchant Navy. Another ten years later and the organisation of shipping companies and their trading patterns with which I had been involved no longer existed. This was a life style unknown to most people. It has disappeared and needs to be remembered. My intention is that this chronicle will make some contribution to an appreciation of a working environment that was, and is, an integral part of the UK's history and economy.

It is my contention that these changes were largely ignored by, or unknown to, the British people, in particular by the Trade Unions. The governing classes were remiss in not explaining effectively the changes that were taking place in manufacture and transport. How many people, even now, understand the concept of 'just in time'? It may be that there was too much emphasis on remedying past mistakes and not enough attention paid to the future. I acknowledge the very real benefits in terms of working conditions and pay that have arisen from working people acting in concert, but there is a downside that has inhibited industrial and commercial progress. Adherence to restrictive practices, combined with reluctance to change and a policy of full employment at any cost, has been a contributory factor to hindering the capacity of the UK both to embrace the opportunities of new techniques and increasing world trade and to increase productivity. Brexit has, at long last and not before time, brought the consequences of these attitudes and practices right into everyday life in the form of distribution shortages and consequent empty shop shelves. Taking the easy option of employing cheap, imported labour and not using technology to improve productivity, combined with inadequacies in education, has proved to be the wrong choice.

I read 'Empire - How Britain Made The Modern World' by Professor Niall Ferguson when it first came out in paperback in 2004 and was profoundly impressed and informed by it. Fortunately, I have kept my copy and recently reread it. I am indebted to Prof Ferguson for helping me to rationalise my vague and unformed ideas. These ideas came to me when I was in the process of producing my narrative. Until I did so, I had not realised that I had been a part, however small and insignificant, in a social, commercial and scientific transformation. Prof Ferguson's argument that the British Empire, as we understood it, declined because the UK could no longer afford it after the costs of two world wars is compelling. Professor Ferguson is not alone in his assertion. Professor Robert Tombs has substantially supported this in his book 'The English & Their History', published in 2014. In the course of this book, I hope to be able to intertwine the changes to which I have alluded with my own experiences, which tend to support Ferguson and Tombs. I contend that there is relevance to the current situation of the UK in that there is an opportunity to reverse the direction that the country took in the last fifty years and to use the lessons learned to our advantage. Hence, my expansion of this chronicle into a more philosophical interpretation of our history and the potential path we should follow.

I have placed technical information and information about ranks and responsibilities into Appendices. So, if you come across a word or phrase that is unknown to you or doesn't make sense, I hope that you can find an explanation in the Appendices.

PART ONE

Where Do We Begin?

Chapter One

Who am I? Am I relevant?

Is it arrogant to consider that I was involved in the changes I have discussed? Was my involvement significant or was I merely an observer who happened to be alive at the time? I would contend that my experiences could be valuable as a source of reference for an updated the social history of the period. Certainly, my lifestyle at that time was not commonplace and an outside view of the countries I visited and the events I witnessed could be valuable. I am acutely conscious that this was also a lifestyle that has disappeared. Terence Rattigan responded to Noel Coward's lament about the trend in post-war playwriting 'Mr Coward had the last of the wine'. Maybe, I had the last of this particular wine, in which case some recording of it could be important.

Am I presumptuous? What in my background would attract the interest of a potential reader? On the face of it, not much. In January 1955, I was a sixteen year old, white, middle class, public school educated son of a local businessman. It might be considered that I was 'privileged' and that my background was too narrow for my views to be of any attraction. If you look further at my background, several circumstances that shaped me were the opposite of privilege.

One of my paternal great-great-grandparents was a weaver in Kidderminster. His wife had been born in Devon in an area noted for domestic weaving. She was probably illiterate. What brought her to Kidderminster and how did she get there? Almost certainly the industrial revolution and the decline of domestic manufacture played a part, but she would not have travelled by fancy horse and carriage. A paternal great-grandfather was illegitimate. He worked in his early teens in a factory, later gaining employment on the railways. By the time my paternal grandfather was born, my great-grandfather had become a provision merchant in Wolverhampton and was flourishing. My grandfather was the third of three sons, but he was privately educated. His father set him up as the licencee of the 'Queen's Arms' pub in Victoria Road, Aston, Birmingham. In the First World War, my grandfather volunteered and became a Staff Sergeant in the Heavy Machine Gun Corps. From there he transferred, as a Private, to the Tank Corps, fought at Cambrai and was subsequently gassed. He never again enjoyed good health because of the damage to his lungs. He moved to Worcester after the war and bought the 'Vaults' pub in Angel Place.

My father was educated at King Edward VI School, Aston, Birmingham, where he was a Foundation Scholar i.e. his fees were paid. He entered into an engineering apprenticeship when he left school but he had to take over the pub licence in 1924, when he was twenty, because my grandfather's health declined and he succumbed to his war wounds in 1927. My grandfather's death left my father responsible for his mother, who was an alcoholic, and the education of his younger sister and brother. My father ran the pub until 1936. He was fortunate to have had a disposable income in the 1930s of £2,500 a year. Unfortunately, he was a gambler, which condition was not helped by the Worcester milieu of the time. He sold the pub on his marriage in 1936, paid off his debts and took the tenancy of the 'Anchor Inn' in Bridge Street, Stratford on Avon.

My maternal grandfather came from Perth and had been a pupil at the cathedral school. He graduated as a dentist around 1910/11 and moved to Manchester, where he set up a practice in Liverpool Road, Eccles, which was not a fashionable district, to say the least.

Simultaneously, he eloped with my maternal grandmother. Her father was a cooper in a factory that produced paraffin from coal. When my maternal grandparents' elder daughter, my mother, married my father in 1936, they too eloped.

I was born in June 1938 in my parent's bed. When asked where I was born, I have a pretentious answer: 'halfway between the theatre and the birthplace'. Both my parents were keen on sport, particularly rugby football, cricket and racing. Well known participants in these sports were customers, if infrequent. More frequent were actors and actresses and other theatre staff, given the proximity of the pub to the theatre. Our principal patronage came via weekend 'trippers' from the industrial Midlands, who provided the majority of our income. Please note that I have not included income from 'tourists', which was minimal.

My father was convivial, liberal minded, a wonderful raconteur and could get an answer from a brick wall. He also read widely, as did my mother, and we took three daily and two Sunday newspapers as well as the local weekly. Consequently, I was exposed to a wider variety of interests and people in my early years than others of my generation.

My parents worked a seven day week, each day starting at breakfast and going on to midnight. We were totally unused to a weekly working regime of five eight hour working days with every weekend free. As I grew older, I helped out more and more with running the pub. In winter, I would rake out four coal fires and lay them, before going to school. At weekends, I chopped kindling for the fires. I cleaned glasses, scrubbed floors and filled up the shelves with bottled beer. In those days, pint and half-pint glass bottles came in wooden crates, each holding two dozen bottles. Each pint bottle crate would weigh over 50 pounds with full bottles. I tapped barrels and cleaned beer pipes. The worst chore was cleaning the outside gents' and ladies' lavatories on a Sunday morning. Invariably, there was solid and fluid waste to be hosed down, then cleansing with Jeyes fluid, then hosing again and brushing the water away into the yard drain. I don't recall any of my contemporaries being faced with these chores. All for half a crown a week pocket money.

Having passed the entrance examination, I went to Warwick School in September 1949. Warwick is an ancient institution that traces its origins back to 914 AD and was reputedly founded by Aethelfrida, our Lady of Mercia and Alfred the Great's daughter. It subsequently received a charter from Edward the Confessor. The school was for centuries a choir school attached to St Mary's Church in Warwick and the original school premises were adjacent to the Church. Links with the Church remained strong. Whoever was the music teacher in my time was also the Organist and Choirmaster of St Mary's and lived in a 'Grace and Favour' house.

In the 1870s, the school moved to specially built premises on Myton Road, which was on the eastern outskirts of the town and on the other side of the River Avon. The school was surrounded by fields with water meadows between the school and the River Avon, which was still the main characteristic of the landscape in my time. The school had thirty two acres of playing fields. Open space and the use of it was a predominant factor in my education. Warwick was about 80% day boy and 20% boarders. The boarders were often the children of service people or parents who worked and/or lived abroad. The father of one of my classmates managed a tea plantation in Assam, not far from Kohima. In my first year, one Sixth Former was American and he was very popular.

When I was a pupil, the school values were firmly Victorian 'muscular Christianity'. We had Chapel every morning, RE classes weekly, conducted by an ordained Anglican priest. There was a brick dais on three levels at the back of the gym and facing the open air swimming pool. On the top level were two benches inscribed with Henry Newbolt's words 'Play up, play up and play the game'. We took part in some kind of strenuous physical activity every day. Intellectual pursuits and sport received equal emphasis. Alumni included John Masefield, a Poet Laureate, Dr Denis Matthews, a noted concert pianist in the 1930s and 1940s and Michael Billington, one of my contemporaries, who has been the drama critic for the 'Guardian'. There were flourishing music, drama, debating and history societies plus a chess club, all of which activities took place outside school hours. We excelled at rugger and cricket. One of my contemporaries gained a double blue at Oxford and another a cricket blue. Two contemporaries were at Sandhurst with one receiving the Sword of Honour. Several 'Old Boys' played cricket and rugby at county level. We also played tennis, athletics, swimming, golf; in fact you could have played anything you wanted to and if you could get enough support. But, those who had gained entry to Oxford or Cambridge and had been awarded Bursaries and Exhibitions received equal applause and drumming of feet when their achievements were announced in the weekly Assembly.

In my final three years at Warwick, my Housemaster and form master was Chris Rieu, also Head of English. He had been awarded the MC in Ethiopia and subsequently fought with the 8th Army in North Africa and Italy. He always had a slight limp from a war wound. He left Warwick coincidentally with my departure, became a celebrated headmaster and the 'Times' published an Obituary on his death. His father, EV Rieu, was a noted Oxford don, who had published a definitive translation of Chaucer's 'Canterbury Tales' and an acclaimed English Grammar, which his son introduced to the school. Dick Seaman was Head of History up to the time I took 'O' levels, after which he became Headmaster of Elizabeth College in Guernsey. Another master, Major 'Piggy' Pearman, had been in the Camel Corps in Arabia during the First World War, and was mentioned in 'The Seven Pillars of Wisdom' by T E Lawrence. He owned a much prized pre-war SS Jaguar, which was a beautiful car. Jack Marshall, head of Junior School, was a useful leg-spinner and had played cricket for Warwickshire in school holidays. The teaching staff was of a very high standard and dedicated. This is exemplified by the time they gave to extra-curricular activities as well as working a six day week. I need to add Lt Col PNG Whitlam TD to this list, although he was not on the teaching staff. He ran the school's administration and the Combined Cadet Force (CCF). He had very high rank for such a position and had been awarded the Territorial Distinction (TD) for long and meritorious service to the Territorial Army. Under him, we had a very efficient cadet force, which was great fun. Our CCF was attached to the Royal Warwickshire Regiment, of which the Colonel-in-Chief at the time was Field Marshall Viscount Montgomery.

Rieu and Seaman encouraged within me an interest in English and History, which interest I had had from an early age. Rieu had flair, humour, intelligence and treated us as though we were thinking adults. He was a tall man who rode to school on his bicycle, which was a 'sit up and beg'. He wore a Homburg hat and I remember how he used to raise it ironically as he passed us as we walked to school from the bus stop in Warwick. A lovely man and I am eternally grateful to him for sharing the width and depth of his knowledge of the English Language and Literature.

Seaman was equally keen on the use of English. He once praised me for a brief verbal description of Sir Humphrey Gilbert's voyages in the late 16th Century. He described my efforts as one of the most grammatically correct and beautiful expositions he had ever heard. Afterwards, he expounded to me his view that learning History was all about 'reading' in the sense of 'read, learn and inwardly digest'. If we did not take the trouble to understand what we read, we would not progress. Dick was a keen cricketer and once spent nearly all of one lesson explaining how to bowl fast: how to grip the ball for different swings and where to place your feet in the final stride. That's what I call a rounded education.

Seaman's successor as Head of History was as rigorous in his demands for clear expression. He once gave me an 'A' for an essay with the comment 'Your conclusions are almost entirely wrong, but this is the best work you have done for me.' Probably reflecting all of the above, the standard of our school debating society appeared to me to be higher than most discussion groups in which I was unfortunate to be a participant in later life.

I cannot continue without a little digression about a remarkable man who, although not contributing to my formal education, did have an effect on how I conducted myself, although I did not realise it until much later in life. He was Derief Taylor, a Jamaican who played cricket for Warwickshire after the Second World War and had become Assistant Coach when I encountered him. Derief had joined the RAF in the war and had been posted to England, where he achieved the rank of Sergeant. He did not return to the West Indies but answered an advertisement in the Birmingham Evening Mail for slow left arm bowlers that had been placed by Warwickshire County Cricket Club. Derief answered the advertisement by attending at the County Ground, Edgbaston, as instructed. The ground was covered in slow left arm hopefuls but Derief prevailed and was appointed. By the early 50s, Derief had retired from playing and had been appointed Assistant Coach under the Head Coach 'Tiger' Smith, who had kept wicket for England in the 1930s. Derief then visited clubs and schools on a regular basis in the summer. He worked long hours, including long summer evenings.

He visited my home club, Stratford on Avon, on Friday evenings to coach any schoolboys who were interested. We were a mixed group, with most showing some talent for the game, except for myself. This was Derief's strength. Interest and enthusiasm were what he was looking for as well as ability. He gave as much time to those who were keen but had little ability as to those who had some. David Cook was our star performer. He was a couple of years older than me and a fellow pupil at Warwick School. He was a fast left arm bowler and a hard-hitting batsmen. He played for Warwickshire a few times as an amateur, as he also did at rugger. It made no difference to Derief and indeed he would spend more time with me at catching practice to make sure that I caught three long hits in succession. One Friday, he placed himself across the nets just as I had bowled an insignificant ball, looked at me straight on and said in his wonderful West Indian accent : 'John, I want to see the word CONCENTRAAATION right across here!' and he pointed to my forehead. Immediately afterwards I bowled the boy out who was batting at the time. This was a lesson that applied not just to cricket but was universal in its application. Without knowing it, I concentrated better and it has become a major factor in my life. I can concentrate so much on the matter in hand that I can become almost totally unaware of my surroundings, to the bewilderment and frustration of my wife. Derief, I salute you with deep affection.

The effects of my marvellous teachers (including Derief) plus my proximity to the Shakespeare Memorial Theatre and constant exposure at home and school to English literature have been long lasting. I cannot abide items that are not well written and bad speakers. What I have continually found exasperating and frustrating throughout my life have been two deficiencies amongst people who were supposedly better educated than myself.

The first is the poor standard of English, particularly written English. The ability to express oneself clearly and succinctly does not appear to have been, or is, a priority in our educational system. I am speaking generally and acknowledge that there are exceptions. I have noticed that those people who have had some study of the classical languages in their education tend to speak and write better English. The outstanding example that I can recall is Quintin Hogg, the 2nd Viscount Hailsham. He had, I believe, obtained a double First in the Classics i.e. Latin and Greek, and subsequently trained and achieved success as a barrister and politician. It was always a joy to hear him speak because his language was so clear and grammatically correct, whilst at the same time being vivid and expressive and without haste. I believe that his qualities of clear expression can be discerned in all those of our writers from Chaucer onwards who would have had an affinity with Latin and/or Greek. There is a discipline in the syntax and sentence construction of those languages that becomes symbiotic in its students and carries through into the writing and speaking of English. When I was a schoolboy, applicants to Oxford and Cambridge had to show evidence of some Latin learning. Maybe we should return to that rigour.

The second is the poor standard of public presentation, which could be considered as a corollary of the first. I have sat and squirmed through so many public and private presentations that have been insulting to the audience. Too many presenters appear to believe that an assembly of slides is sufficient and that rehearsal and learning how to engage an audience are unnecessary. Where a presenter understands that he or she is giving a performance and uses the skills of an actor or stand-up comedian, then the audience is engaged and the presentation is enhanced. Unfortunately, sloppiness and laziness is the general rule.

The above short explanation of my background may help to modify my first description of myself. Wherever I have been, I have tried to be involved, open minded and receptive to new and different ideas, but not always with success.

There is one element of my formative years and early manhood that, I believe, is worthy of consideration. My prep school was co-educational, but from then on my environment was predominantly masculine: the pub environment, sport, secondary school, sea school and the Merchant Navy. There were no female crew members in my time. Until I was 23, I had no experience of women in a working environment. My experience of women was confined to my mother, my sister, bar staff and socialising. After I left the Merchant Navy, I found working with women a strange experience for some time and it took an effort to adjust. Contrary to old stories, a sailor did not have a wife in every port. We spent so much time at sea and our stays in any one particular port were so short that it was difficult to maintain relationships with the opposite sex. Consequently, the sex life of a seaman was very circumscribed and, I suspect, in most instances in my time, non-existent, despite the inevitable bragging amongst adolescents. I cannot tell how this environment affected my development and relationships with women but I have never consciously sought to be superior because I am male.

Nowadays, it is commonplace and politically correct to embrace diversity and display public sympathy for any who declare themselves 'victims'. It could be argued that it has led to giving 'minorities' of all descriptions a disproportionate place in public awareness. It could also be argued that this has been at the expense of the overwhelming majority of the population, particularly young white 'working class' males, who would be considered 'disadvantaged' in any dispassionate consideration. Obviously, I am not, and have not been disadvantaged, but what constituted my background and education was hard won not inherited. Alongside the millions like me, we should not be discounted or ignored. The General Election of 2019 illustrated that there are real grievances amongst those millions. Consequently, I hope that my experiences as here described, and my opinions, will be given the same considerations as others. This liberty is precious and should not be undermined.

CHAPTER TWO

Imperial Attitudes or Sentiment

The title of this book is, obviously I hope, tongue in cheek, and I acknowledge my debt to Spike Milligan for the inspiration of the title. Nevertheless, I probably began my Merchant Navy career with a set of attitudes that young people nowadays would not have. What do I remember of those attitudes? Were they universally held? How has my life and fallible memory made me think that these were my attitudes?

When I joined the School of Navigation in January 1955, World War II had been over less than ten years. The bulk of the then UK population had been alive throughout the war. I believe that we were all very conscious that it had been an Imperial War. We had fought the war as the British Empire. We believed that we fought for the values of free speech, open, elected government and the rule of law against openly barbarous regimes that sought to destroy all that we held dear. Other than UK conscripted service people, most of the Imperial Forces were volunteers and came from India, Northern Ireland, the Irish Free State, Australia, New Zealand, the West Indies, East and West Africa, South Africa, Canada and the Pacific islands. Indian volunteers numbered 250,000, the largest single contingent in the Imperial forces, except for the UK. From the beginning, there were American citizens who crossed the border into Canada and volunteered. The head of the British Army was the Chief of the *Imperial* General Staff, which title still existed when I went to sea. British troops, who fought in the Korean War, fought as part of the Commonwealth Division. The Victory Parade of 1946, in London, consisted of representatives of the armed forces of the Commonwealth.

In 1953, Queen Elizabeth II was crowned Queen of many territories apart from the United Kingdom and was the acknowledged head of the Commonwealth. Much of the globe was still ruled directly from Whitehall. The UK retained the outward appearance of being an Imperial power and the dignitaries attending the Coronation reflected that. Coronation Day itself is imprinted solidly in my memory, largely through the medium of television and the colour documentary that was shown shortly afterwards in the cinema. The solemnity of the crowning ceremony in Westminster Abbey contrasted with the exuberance of the procession through the streets of London afterward, despite the rain. The enthusiasm of the crowds, the smiling Queen in her golden coach, Queen Salote of Tonga defying the rain. London appeared to be the centre of the universe. One could quote Wordsworth and exclaim: 'O what joy it was to be in that moment alive'. This emotion was exhibited in thousands of voluntary street parties throughout the United Kingdom

And then we had the Spithead Naval Review. The whole of the water between Portsmouth, Southampton Water and the Isle of Wight was filled with hundreds of naval ships from many countries, all dressed in row after row with flags and pennants flying from stem to stern. At the head of the review was HMS Vanguard, the largest battleship ever built for the Royal Navy. As the Queen sailed up and down the rows and the vessels dipped their flags in salute, it appeared that the whole world was paying homage to the Queen. We could indeed be excused for believing that the British Empire was a living object of importance to mankind.

Sir Winston Churchill was Prime Minister. He had declared in 1942 that he had not become His Majesty's First Minister to preside over the liquidation of the British Empire. I suspect that he held that view even until and beyond his resignation later in 1955. In that, it is likely that he represented the views of many UK citizens. How much of that was down to sentiment? It has been well documented that the demise of the Empire was expected by prominent people in the later years of Victoria's reign. In fact, it was the consistent policy of successive British governments that laid the groundwork for this and that, often unconsciously, encouraged separatist movements throughout the colonies. This policy was to rule the Empire through officials recruited from the supposedly subject populations, backed by the British Army and locally raised troops. The actual number of British administrators was small. My headmaster claimed that, in 1939, old students of my school administered half of the Empire. India is still administered by a Civil Service run by Indian nationals, which service was founded by the British, who educated a class of Indians to become Civil Servants.

We ate New Zealand lamb, butter, cheese and apples. Our clothes were made from Australian wool and cotton from other Commonwealth countries. We drank sherry from South Africa and bought cocoa from the Gold Coast and bananas from the West Indies. The pound was the reserve currency for the Commonwealth bloc and was freely convertible within that bloc. English was the common language within the Commonwealth and those countries that were self-governing had adopted a UK style of government and the Rule of Law.

My belief at this time was that we were a great Imperial Power. I did not realise the extent to which the cost of two World Wars had ruined the country's finances. We survived bankruptcy in 1945 through a vast loan from the United States, which we did not pay off until 2006. The interest on this loan plus the costs of expanding the Welfare State and the policy of nationalisation undertaken by the post-war Labour government (1945 to 1951) meant that we could not afford an empire, which required a certain amount of armed forces with their attendant expenditure. We had to endure austerity and downsize. In November 1954, just two months before I joined the Merchant Navy, Churchill's Conservative government had signed a Withdrawal Agreement with the Egyptian Government, by which we would withdraw 80,000 troops from the Suez Canal Zone. This number is equivalent to the entire current establishment of the British Army.

I also believed that we had the support of our ally, the United States of America, and were on an equal footing with that country. I had no conception of the real differences between the US economy and foreign policy and ours, or that two World Wars had increased the US economy, whereas ours had shrunk in relative terms. I did not realise until many years later that a significant part of the foreign policy of the USA in the 20th Century was the break-up of the British Empire. Indeed, it had been one of President Roosevelt's main war aims and had been publicly stated. Hence, the US government's insistence that, at the onset of World War II, the UK pay 'cash on the barrel' for armaments, which led to the UK having to sell all its holdings on the American Stock Exchange in order to make these purchases. By the middle of 1941, the UK's resources had been exhausted and the USA offered no credit. It offered instead 'Lend Lease' whereby the USA obtained bases abroad in return for supplying armaments, with the bill deferred until after the war. A consequence of all this was that the UK became bankrupt and a debtor to the USA. As a schoolboy, I had read 'The Turn of the Tide' (the book by Sir Arthur Bryant, which was based on the wartime diaries of the then CIGS, Viscount Alanbrooke) but had not fully appreciated the position of the USA as stated within those diaries, or had forgotten, until I recently re-read it, at which point I finally understood how the USA had become the dominant Western power. Sir Max Hastings' book 'Finest Years Churchill as War Lord 1940 -1945' also contains a first class summary of the UK economy during the Second World War and the uncompromisingly severe attitude of the

USA towards the UK's economic plight. The exploitation of this by the USA contributed substantially to the American economic boom of the war years, which brought the USA out of depression.

The above attitudes were a major part of the belief system of a very naive youth of sixteen as he embarked on what he thought was going to be a great adventure. An adventure where he would be an equal, if not superior, to the inhabitants of any country he visited.

But, are these attitudes so out of date? The late Queen Elizabeth II and our present King Charles III have devoted much time and effort to support and develop the Commonwealth, to the extent that it is now substantially larger than at the time of the late Queen's accession and is still attracting new members. The degree to which Her Majesty succeeded in modernising the old Empire and attracting international support was illustrated by the numbers of foreign dignitaries who attended her funeral, with the attendant pageantry, which demonstrated vividly the continuity of British history. As Her Majesty so clearly demonstrated, continuity is vital in order to maintain a coherent society.

John, Summer 1939, Anchor Inn.

Margaret and Jim Ayres, 1937

Jill (sister), Jimmy (brother) and John, Stratford on Avon 1947

PART TWO

Dream Time And Reality

CHAPTER THREE

'I must go down to the sea again'

I was born and bred in Stratford on Avon, about as far as you can get from the sea in England. Why did I go to sea? I was born in June 1938 and thus qualified to be a 'Munich baby'. At that time, over a third of the world's merchant tonnage was UK registered and we were the world's leading shipbuilder. The term 'Merchant Navy' had only come into official existence in 1928, when King George V authorised the term to honour those members of the Merchant Navy who had given their lives in the First World War. The Merchant Navy has not been a 'safe haven' in wartime. In World War II, 33,000 merchant seamen died as a result of enemy activity. This is a higher proportion of the personnel involved than any of the Armed Services. George V also invested the then Prince of Wales, later Edward VII1, with the title 'Master of the Merchant Navy and the Fishing Fleet'. He retained this title on becoming King. Thus the reigning Monarch became 'The Master of the Merchant Navy and the Fishing Fleet', which title was conferred on both King George VI and Queen Elizabeth II on their accessions, and which, presumably, is one of the present King's titles. The Red Ensign, although in common use beforehand, became the official flag of the Merchant Navy. This ensign had been used in previous centuries by Royal Navy Admirals of inferior rank and experience.

None of this was known to me during my early years.

The Red Ensign, or 'Red Duster', was a commonplace sight throughout the world's oceans and ports. It could be argued that it was a source of 'soft power' that has been underused. Not enough has been done to encourage ship owners to register their vessels in the UK, which registration allows them to fly the Red Ensign on their vessels and thus enhance the UK trade presence. The more of the world's trade that is carried in British 'bottoms', the more the UK earns from its trade in services. This not only covers revenue from cargo but also from financial services such as cargo insurance.

In 1953, after I took my 'O' levels at Warwick School, I went into the Lower Modern Sixth Form and chose English, History and French as my subjects for 'A' levels and dropped French when I went into the Upper Modern Sixth Form. It was unusual in those days to take more than two subjects at 'A' level. It was expected that I would have a try for entry to an Oxford University college. However, I had always had this interest in the sea and the Navy, despite showing no interest or aptitude in Mathematics or scientific subjects, which should be a prerequisite for entering a career dominated by technology. Mr A H B Bishop (my Headmaster) once said to me that if our pub had been called 'The Bugle', no doubt I would have wanted to go in the Army.

I tried twice to get into the Royal Naval College, Dartmouth, but, not surprisingly, I couldn't pass in Maths. The second time, I only needed one or two more marks in the Maths paper and I would have been in the top ten per cent of those passing the written exam. After that, I endeavoured to put the sea out of my mind and tried to concentrate on 'A' levels. Looking back, I realise that I was floundering and without purpose. I enjoyed being in the Upper Sixth with its privileges but was finding it difficult to focus. I was in danger of failing my 'A' levels. To the great credit of Warwick School and its staff, my quandary did not go unnoticed. The Careers Master, Mr Warren, who was also the Geography Master, had a talk with my father. His advice was that I needed to get the sea out of my system and the

Merchant Navy was an option. A number of Old Warwickians had joined the Merchant Navy over the years, including John Masefield, who actually ran away to sea and then entered 'HMS Conway'. Since the Second World War, several had gone to the School of Navigation at Warsash, near Southampton, as a Merchant Navy Cadet. This school specialised in training boys to be Merchant Navy Officers.

Accordingly. in early December 1954, I was despatched to Warsash for two days for an appraisal. I travelled alone by train and was met at Southampton Station by a school representative with a car. My knowledge of the School of Navigation was almost non-existent and I had done no preparation beforehand. Neither was I encouraged to do so. The appraisal was part written and part oral. Candidates lived with the cadets for two days i.e. shared their living accommodation and meals. Most of the Cadets lived in 'cabins' of six and the senior cadet in the cabin was known as a Junior Leading Cadet (JLC). Some cabins did not have six cadets and, therefore, had a spare bunk. Candidates used the spare bunk. The JLC of the 'host' cabin showed the candidate round the school and was responsible for looking after him. If I remember correctly, on the first day I arrived late morning, was shown round, had lunch and then there were written exams. Evening meal was at 7 p.m. and I was surprised that cadets and the Mess Officer were in full uniform and bow ties. After dinner, all cabins and occupants were inspected by the Officer of the Day, who was also the Mess Officer. Cadets were inspected for smartness and cleanliness, and that included the candidates. I don't remember much about the next day except that at some time in the day I was 'interrogated' by one of the School's Officers, a Mr McKillop, who had the honorary rank of Lieutenant-Commander. Sometime after dinner that day, I was summoned to the home of the Director of the school for a final examination. His name was Captain G W Wakeford. He lived in a substantial house in the grounds called 'Salterns'. The JLC, in whose cabin I was accommodated, advised me that if Wakeford asked me for my worst impressions, I should tell him 'the bogs' (of which more later). There were three of us waiting to be seen. Later, I understood that what we went through was his usual practice. We were kept waiting for at least half an hour in this rather drab, small room. Then this imposing man arrived dressed in naval evening wear and with medals on his breast. He admonished us for not standing up when a superior officer entered. None of we candidates knew who he was or why we should defer to him. But, as I discovered, that was essential Wakeford. He called us into his study one by one. I don't think I was in there more than ten minutes when he told me that I had been accepted. But he did ask me for my worst impression, to which I gave the advised answer. He agreed and expressed his desire to rebuild with marble halls. He then ushered me out and I had to find my way back to the school in the dark without waiting for the other candidates. I don't know how I did it because I was in a bit of a daze, there were no lights and the walk was about a quarter of a mile. When I got back to the cabin, everybody was in bed asleep but the JLC woke up and asked if I had got in and was pleased that I had. I do not know what percentage of applicants succeeded, but I did not see the other two applicants when I joined in the following January.

Captain G W Wakeford OBE and Mrs Wakeford.
Director, School of Navigation.

My parents picked me up the next day. As it was December and I would be starting in January, we had to order my kit straightaway from Miller Rayner, a naval tailor, in Southampton. This came to about £100, a lot of money then, when the average weekly wage was less than £10.

This kit was compulsory. It included an oilskin full length coat, wellington boots with added tops that came to the groin and an oilskin souwester. The souwester is a waterproof floppy cap, with an all round brim, which can be turned down so that rainwater is diverted over the oilskin coat. Although they were called oilskins, they were not made of oiled leather, which was the original material. The original material would crack with age. These newer coats and hats were made of a shiny plastic that was superb in keeping you dry. The coats had a double opening with a Velcro closure. The wellingtons were more like waders and you could fold down the upper thigh covering. In wet weather, you never got wet.

Then came more personal stuff: underwear, pyjamas, dressing gown, toiletries, swimming gear, sports gear and any other personal items you wanted. It all fitted into a tin trunk.

At Warwick, we had to wear semi-stiff, detachable collars. Now I would have to wear starched, stiff, detachable collars. These were uncomfortable and caused irritation, particularly in hot weather. Furthermore, they dirtied quickly, so that you needed a considerable supply. This was very impracticable when you were at sea for long periods. Fortunately, stiff paper collars became available later on. They were inexpensive and throw away. In addition, they were more comfortable to wear and lasted longer before becoming grubby. Gradually, stiff collars went out of use, to the relief of all.

I was now, at least materially, equipped for an adventure that many others had experienced. These are a few of the notable people who had been at sea as merchant seamen:

- James Cook.
- Joseph Conrad, novelist.
- Gerry Fitt, founder of the SDLP.
- Charles Howard, GC, Earl of Suffolk and Berkshire, bomb disposal hero.
- Gareth Hunt, actor ('New Avengers', 'Upstairs and Downstairs').
- Freddie Lennon, John Lennon's father.
- Kevin McLory, screen writer ('Never Say Never Again', 'Thunderball')
- John Masefield, poet laureate.

- Arthur Philip, founded Sydney, first Governor of New South Wales.
- John Prescott
- Ken Russell, film director ('Tommy')
- Captain Webb, first to swim the Channel
- Tommy Steel

First Uniform, School of Navigation, January 1955.

Looking at my cap in the above photo, reminds me that one issue during my stretch at Warsash was the shape of the naval uniform cap. It was made of soft material that would not stand up straight on its own. It had to be kept upright by a copper circle inside, which was known as a 'grommet'. We were supposed to have the grommet fitted at all times so that we all had a uniform shape. What many of us tried to do was to adjust the grommet so that it was not a perfect circle and made the cap crown lower at the sides than at the front and the back. This was known as 'yobbing' and it was a mark of pride to have a 'yobbed' cap and get away with it. You have to express your individuality in some way. Shortly before I left Warsash, Billy Blyth, the Drill Instructor, likened my working cap, unfavourably, to a German railway worker's. I felt I had won!

The No.1 uniform was made of an expensive cloth known as 'doeskin'. It was very silky to the touch and had a long nap. This nap had to be brushed in only one direction, downwards. Otherwise, the nap stood up and looked scruffy. The trousers were not easy to press because care had to be taken not to destroy the nap.

There was no legal requirement for Merchant Navy personnel to wear uniform. It had become the custom for shipping companies to insist on uniforms for Officers. The uniforms were of the same design and material as Royal Navy uniforms, although cap badges and insignia of rank varied between shipping companies. Ratings did not wear uniform, except on passenger liners where they came into contact with passengers and where stewards directly served Officers on any ship. All sea going personnel provided their own clothes and there were no uniform allowances. Considering that shipping companies insisted on uniforms being worn, the lack of uniform allowances was intrinsically unfair because of the cost of provision. Additionally, standard uniforms were not practical in some working environments e.g. working in a cargo hold and wearing white tropical rig.

CHAPTER FOUR

WHAT IS THE MERCHANT NAVY

Before we progress further, it will be helpful to understand what the Merchant Navy is and isn't. The British Merchant Navy is amorphous. It is not a homogenous unit. It is not a military unit. It is, essentially, a civilian organisation. The term 'Merchant Navy' encompasses all activities connected with sea transportation of goods, passengers and services. It is regulated by Merchant Shipping Acts and international regulations, not by the Mutiny Act. Shipping Companies are regulated for governance by the Companies Act in the same way as any registered corporation.

Nevertheless, there is an element of 'serving' and a pride in having served in the Merchant Navy. National recognition is demonstrated by the inclusion of Merchant Navy representatives at the Annual Royal British Legion Festival of Remembrance at the Albert Hall and the laying of a wreath at the Whitehall Cenotaph on Remembrance Sunday. Those of us who have spent time in the Merchant Navy have served the Sovereign in his or her capacity as 'Master of the Merchant Navy'.

Concerning ranks in the Merchant Navy, there is no specific, legal rank of 'Officer' or 'Captain'. Legally, the senior officer of a ship is called the Master and all the Deck Officers below him are Master's Mates (more usually known as Mates). This goes back hundreds of years. The rank of Captain is a military rank in origin. In the Middle Ages, 'Captains', who were always military men, were appointed to command ships in war time. These ships were often merchant ships which had been requisitioned by the Crown. They retained the original crew, including the Master and his Mates. The 'Captain' very often had no experience of handling ships at sea and the Master and Mates continued to sail the ship whilst the 'Captain', and any soldiers he brought with him, decided where the ship was to go and led the fighting. As time went on and ships were built specifically as warships, the Royal Navy retained the rank of 'Master' and he was responsible for navigation and sailing. He was inferior in rank to the Royal Navy Captain and Lieutenants but they were expected to defer to him in matters of sailing and seamanship.

Similarly, Engineer and Radio Officers qualify as engineers or radio operators. It has become the custom for shipping companies to denominate their qualified seamen, engineers and radio operators with the rank of Officer. The Master is called 'Captain'. Below him there is the Chief Officer, Chief Engineer Officer and Chief Radio Officer. All other 'Officers' are defined by number i.e. 2nd Officer or 2nd Engineer Officer.

I repeat that there is no standard Merchant Navy uniform or any legal requirement to wear one. Shipping Companies have adopted the Royal Navy uniform as standard and require their Officers to wear uniform. Each company has its own cap badge. Rank is usually demonstrated by the number of gold stripes worn on the uniform. Some companies wear stripes on the lower sleeves, as is the custom in the Royal Navy. Others stipulate that stripes are worn on epaulettes. In other words, the uniform is a company livery.

Ratings do not wear uniform and provide their own working clothing.

The point is the title of 'Captain' in the Merchant Navy is an 'honorific'. The master would be known as 'Captain Ayres' or whatever as a mark of respect. It also makes it easier for civilians to understand who is in charge. Similarly, the First Mate was usually known as the Chief Officer, the Second Mate as Second Officer, the Third Mate as Third Officer and the Fourth Mate as Fourth Officer. To become a Master, or Captain, of a vessel on foreign and deep sea service you had to pass three examinations, as follows:

Certificate of Competency as Second Mate (Foreign Going). You had to finish your apprenticeship before you could take this examination. Passing it entitled you to serve as a Second Officer, but it was more usual to serve as a Third or Fourth Officer before you took your next exam. The subjects you had to take, and pass in every subject, were: navigation, chartwork, seamanship and ship handling, signals, mathematics (mostly geometry and spherical trigonometry), physics, ship construction, cargo handling, meteorology, astronomy and English (just to prove you were literate) and an oral exam, conducted on a one-to-one basis by an examiner. The pass marks for each subject varied: 50% for English, 90% for navigation, chartwork and signals and 100% for the oral. I am not aware that there is a series of examinations in other professions that require such high pass marks.

Certificate of Competency as First Mate (Foreign Going). You needed eighteen months sea time as a Deck Officer before taking this exam. Passing this exam meant that you could serve as a First Mate or Chief Officer but holders of this Certificate usually served as Second Officers before they took their next exam. The subjects included physics (mostly magnetism and electricity), navigation, cargo handling, ship handling and seamanship, first aid and oral. Not as many subjects but the exams were harder and the pass marks required were similar.

Certificate of Competency as Master (Foreign Going). This was essential if you were to command a ship. It means that only Deck Officers can become Masters. After you gained this certificate, you would most likely become a Chief Officer and, eventually and hopefully, a Master. The subjects included Maritime Law, Navigation, Mathematics, Ship Handling and Oral.

Certificate of Competency as Extra Master (Foreign Going). There is no requirement to have this qualification to be a sea officer, but it is essential if you wish to pursue a career ashore but still be connected to the Merchant Navy such as an examiner, lecturer, surveyor, maritime lawyer or judge, consultant. I can't recall what the subjects were but believe they included advanced maths (specifically differential calculus), law and ship construction.

The manner in which shipping companies manned their vessels, at Deck or Engineer Officer level, ensured that, in the case of death or other incapacity, there was always a subordinate Officer on board with the right qualification to step into the vacancy. This was important in order to satisfy the Merchant Shipping Act and maritime insurance.

I believe that the titles of these Certificates have been changed so that they reflect changes in tertiary education and provide a relationship with other qualifications. I am not sure what the present names are but I believe that they are linked to degree status. For instance, a Second Mate's Certificate is equivalent to a Foundation Degree, a First Mate's Certificate to a BSc, the Master's to an MSc and the Extra Master's to a Doctorate or third Degree. I got a First Mate's Certificate, the equivalent of a BSc, although subsequent experience and professional qualifications means that I have the equivalent of an MSc.

CHAPTER FIVE

MERCHANT NAVY TRAINING

What Was Available?

Merchant Navy Officer Training Schools

HMS Conway. Founded 1859 in Liverpool by Liverpool shipping interests to provide deck officers for their ships. Originally based at Rock Ferry, Birkenhead, on a 19th Century ship of the line named 'HMS Conway'. The ship was moved to the Menai Straits, between Anglesey and North Wales, in 1939 to an area safe from bombing. 1953: established ashore at Plas Newydd, Anglesey, the home of the Marquis of Anglesey. School closed down in 1974 when government funding, via Cheshire County Council, was withdrawn. Alumni include John Masefield, Captain Matthew Webb, Sir Clive Woodward and Sir Ian Duncan Smith. Cadets were automatically enrolled in the Royal Naval Reserve for the period of their membership of the foundation.

HMS Worcester. Founded in 1862 by London shipping interests as a reaction to the founding of HMS Conway. HMS Worcester was the popular name although its proper name was the Thames Nautical Training College. It was originally established at Greenhithe on an old ship of the line named 'HMS Worcester'. This ship was replaced by the Royal Navy several times. Worcester cadets were automatically enrolled in the Royal Naval Reserve for the period of their membership of the foundation. In 1968, the school was incorporated into the Merchant Navy College at Greenhithe.

Pangbourne College. Founded in 1917 as 'The Nautical College, Pangbourne' by the owners of a shipping company, Devitt and Moore, to provide officers for the Merchant Navy. Students were known as cadets and were automatically enrolled in the Royal Naval Reserve for the duration of their stay at the school. The school changed its name in 1968 to Pangbourne College and embraced a more traditional secondary education curriculum.

All three were essentially boarding schools and provided a general education as well as training for a career at sea. Although orientated towards the Merchant Navy, a proportion of cadets from these schools went into the Royal Navy. Many cadets did not pursue a sea career on leaving. These schools were run as naval establishments with uniforms and naval discipline. Their reputations were first class, but they were expensive, and, therefore, exclusive. Boys started at these schools aged thirteen or fourteen and stayed until they went to sea at seventeen.

The School of Navigation (later known colloquially as 'Warsash') was founded shortly before the Second World War at a country house outside Southampton. The founders believed that there were insufficient training places for Merchant Navy officer cadets. The founders believed that there should be training for boys who only decided to go to sea when they left school at sixteen and who wanted to train as Deck Officers. Warsash has never had the same relationship with the Royal Navy as the other schools described above. Its cadets were not enrolled in the Royal Naval Reserve.

It was not necessary to go to sea school to get into the Merchant Navy as a cadet. You could join as an apprentice at sixteen or seventeen if you could find a shipping company to take you. But, during your apprenticeship you were unlikely to receive formal training. It would be on the job training and correspondence courses. Some shipping companies had their own cadet ships or other means of formal training, but all too often training depended on the enthusiasm and skills of the ship's officers, who themselves were not educated to train.

An apprenticeship lasted four years. The legal requirement was that you had to serve 3 years and nine months of 'sea time', i.e. be on the books of a ship engaged in deep sea trade. Therefore, allowing for leave, it took about four years before you could take your first examination to become a Deck Officer. Boys who went to sea school got exemptions from that sea time, in other words the 'sea time' requirement was reduced. Boys at Conway, Worcester and Pangbourne received 12 months redemption and those at Warsash got nine months. The difference of three months was because the Warsash course was for a year (three terms of three months each), whereas at the other school you got, effectively, four months for each year you spent at the school. It was considered by the Ministry of Transport that the Warsash course was more intensive as regards sea training.

The best shipping companies tended to prefer boys who had been to sea school.

Worcester, Conway and Pangbourne had a problem as the 1950s turned into the 1960s. Fewer boys were presenting themselves for entry as cadets in their early teens. These schools had followed the old naval tradition of enlisting boys to go to sea at twelve or thirteen years of age. The Royal Navy abandoned recruitment at those ages and Warsash never recruited cadets before they had reached sixteen. Eventually, Worcester, Conway and Pangbourne could no longer attract boys at a young age and they either adapted (Pangbourne), amalgamated (Worcester) or faded away (Conway). Only Warsash remains of these four as a Merchant Navy cadet training establishment and Warsash does not now take cadets at age sixteen. Apprentices now serve two years at sea before entering a college for a year's academic naval education. Consequently, sea schools are nowadays more in line with university education.

Captain G W ('Whalley') Wakeford was the first Director of the School of Navigation. The School was attached to the then University College of Southampton, which became the University of Southampton after the Second World War. Wakeford had previously served with the New Zealand Shipping Company. Because of Wakeford and his wife, Pearl, Warsash gained an international reputation and attracted cadets from several countries. He was very deservedly awarded an OBE in the 1960s but died relatively young in 1966. It has continued to expand and is now known as the Warsash Maritime Academy and is part of Solent University.

During this narrative, I will, at times, be critical of Wakeford. He was not an easy man and lacked a sense of humour. In my time, he was respected by the cadets but not necessarily admired. However, his achievement in establishing a pre-eminent maritime educational establishment with an international reputation has to be acknowledged and applauded. His vision encompassed a regime that covered the spectrum of a Merchant Navy Officer's training from initial cadet training to obtaining an Extra Master's Certificate. Hence, the establishment of residential courses for all the examinations required to become a Master Mariner and beyond. I believe that this is still unique inasmuch as that there are other establishments that offer officer examination courses, but they are not residential, as far as I know.

CHAPTER SIX

The School of Navigation, University of Southampton, Warsash.
Organisation and Routine

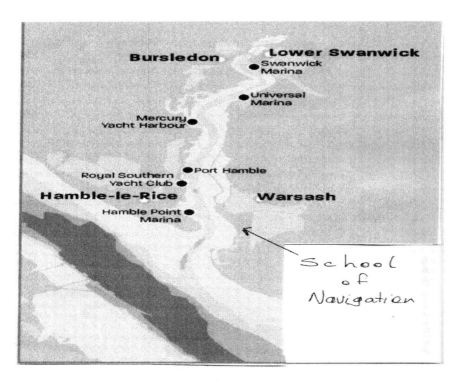

School of Navigation

I joined as a Cadet in January 1955. A Cadet is the lowest of the low, especially a Junior Cadet. You know nothing and are treated accordingly. The Cadet School at Warsash had a reputation for toughness. Wakeford was proud to refer to it as 'the English Belsen'. His view was that our experience should be tougher than anything we were likely to experience at sea. This only applied to the Cadet School. When you joined as a Junior Cadet, we were told that it was no disgrace to decide that being at Warsash was a mistake. We were told not to run away but to advise our Divisional Officer, who would provide the train fare home. In retrospect, this regime included aspects, such as regular formation and small arms drill and petty disclipinary procedures that had nothing to do with the operation of a merchant vessel. There was too much slavish copying of Royal Navy routine.

In addition to Merchant Navy courses, Warsash had a flying school with a primitive simulator, which was for aspiring airline pilots.

By this time, the School of Navigation was established in its third and final site at Warsash. It had originally been built as an ammunition store, then an RAF barracks and prison before becoming a location for Combined Forces Operations in the Second World War under Lord Louis Mountbatten (later Earl Mountbatten of Burma). It had also contained the clubhouse for the Brigade of Guards Yacht Club, which was the mess for the RAF signals unit within Combined Ops during the war. The location on the east bank of the estuary of the River

Hamble is fabulous, with superb views across Southampton Water and the Solent to the New Forest and the Isle of Wight. The main entrance was situated on Newtown Road, a mile south of the cross roads in the village of Warsash.

Cadets came from all over the world. In my time, we had New Zealanders, Australians, South Africans, Greeks, Burmese and even a Swiss. The Greeks tended to be older and more worldly wise because they had already put in sea time. The Burmese were funny and enjoyed a laugh. They were so much smaller than us and had very flexible joints. We hid one in a drawer once and the Officers were concerned he had gone missing!

Organisation of the Cadet School

Officers:

Captain Superintendent (Captain Stewart).

Divisional Officer in charge of Starboard Watch (Lt Cdr Pierce).
Divisional Officer in charge of Port Watch (Lt Cdr Clubb –nicknamed 'Jacko').
Both these Officers carried the honorary rank of Lieutenant-Commander.

Lecturers for the various subjects.

All the above had been Captains or Chief Officers in the Merchant Navy and several had an Extra Master's Certificate. In my time, all had seen war service in the Merchant Navy or Royal Navy Reserve and several had been decorated. Lt Cdr Pierce had been an Officer on a Clan Line ship that had been in the 'Pedestal' convoy, which relieved Malta in August 1942. Obviously, he survived but the losses from German and Italian aircraft, submarines and surface vessels was horrific. Although the above, with the exception of the Captain Superintendent, took classes, I have never been aware if any received any formal training in education. I will come back to this later.

Drill Instructor. A retired Senior NCO with the honorary rank of Lieutenant. In my time, he was Billy Blyth, who had been in the Durham Light Infantry. He was always known as 'Mr Blyth'. As well as drill, he organised rotas for guard duty and boat crews. He was getting on and had what are known as 'Cunard feet' i.e. he had become very flat footed because of fallen arches and could not march. But he was an excellent drill instructor. 'Cunard feet' were so-called because Stewards in the Cunard Line spent so much time on their feet that eventually something had to give way. Cunard ran the great transatlantic liners like the Queen Mary and Queen Elizabeth and the first class passengers required twenty four hours service.

Mr Blyth was also a highly skilled cabinet maker. He made a mahogany wardrobe once for the Director. His workshop adjoined the boathouse, which was always damp. When he installed the wardrobe in 'Salterns', the central heating dried the wood out too quickly and the frame warped so that the doors would not close.

There was a maximum of 120 cadets, divided into two watches (Port and Starboard) or into the Boat Section.

Cadet Ranks, in order of importance:

Chief Cadet Captain (CCC). He was responsible for discipline, a bit like Head of School.
Senior Cadet Captain (Boats) (SCC Boats). He was responsible for boat drills and rotas and was second in rank to the CCC.
Senior Cadet Captain (SCC) (Port or Starboard Watch). Responsible for discipline, watches, drill and cleanliness.
Junior Cadet Captain (JCC) (Port or Starboard Watch). Deputy to the SCCs described above.
Senior Leading Cadets – three in each watch. Each SLC was responsible for two cabins.
Senior Leading Cadet (Boats). Deputy to SCC Boats.

All those holding the above ranks would be in the Senior Term.

Junior Leading Cadets (JLC). Each responsible for one cabin.
Junior Leading Cadet (Boats). Supported SCC Boats and SLC Boats.
JLCs were always from the Intermediate Term.

Junior Leading Cadet (Bugles). He sounded the bugle for reveille, morning run, ablution time, breakfast, divisions, class times, lunch, dinner and any other activities. In other words, he was the school timekeeper. He could be a Senior or an Intermediate.

Senior Non-Executive Cadet. A Senior who had not been promoted.
Intermediate Non-Executive Cadet. An Intermediate who had not been promoted.
Junior Cadet. All those in the Junior Term.

Non-Executive Cadets shared cabins with JLCs and Juniors. Sometimes this could be awkward if a Senior Non-Exec did not co-operate with his JLC, who outranked him although the Senior Non-Exec was in a higher term.

Accommodation

The buildings left a lot to be desired. Cadets were housed in an old, two-storey brick building. The building was divided into three sections: the Port and Starboard Watches at either end, each with their own entrance and staircase, and the class rooms, which were in between on the ground floor. We were either in cabins of six (JLCs, Senior and Intermediate Non –Exec Cadets and Junior Cadets) or in cabins of two (Senior Executive cadets). We slept in two-tiered bunks, with the junior of the cabin mates always on the top bunk. There were two drawers under each bunk tier and each cabin mate was allocated one drawer. We each had a wardrobe. The furniture was a wooden table with six wooden chairs. The cabins were on two floors. The ground floor had two cabins with concrete floors and a rug. The remaining space on the ground floor was taken up by store rooms. If I remember correctly, our oilskins and wellingtons were kept in one of the store rooms. The first floor had four six-berth cabins and three two-berth cabins, all with wooden, uncarpeted floors. Each cabin had two sash windows. The Chief Cadet Captain and the Senior Cadet Captain (Boats) had their own cabins in a separate block. The Chief Cadet Captain had an en-suite shower and toilet. What luxury! The Divisional Officers had a maisonette each at each end of the block. The six berth cabins were known as either Port 1,2,3,4,5 or 6 or Starboard 1,2,3,4,5,or 6

The accommodation block also housed the classrooms (one for each term). The mess room (where we ate) was in a separate block of old Nissen huts, that also housed the kitchens and a separate mess for students studying for certificates. Other buildings included:

A 'library', which had been the RAF signal unit mess for Combined Operations during the Second World War. It had several rooms, of which one was reserved for Senior Executive Cadets but rarely used. It had large windows giving views over the Solent. It had originally been the Head Quarters of the Brigade of Guards Yacht Club. It was not much used. My father was stationed there when he was seconded to Combined Ops.

The Guard Room. Each cabin took its turn as 'Guard' for a period of twenty four hours from Reveille to Reveille. There were six bunks. More later about Guard Duty.

Buildings for students studying for certificates: class rooms and accommodation. Some of the accommodation was a quarter of a mile away.

Boathouse, workshop and pier.

The Director's house: the 'Salterns, which was a large detached house on the highest ground of the property and set in a large sloping garden of about half an acre. This house was about halfway between the main entrance and Warsash village.

The entire property consisted of about 50 or 60 acres and included some woodland.

The school had access to the foreshore, which was a strip of land between the River Hamble and the higher ground. It was partly shingle and partly scrub and was tidal. The foreshore was open to the public along its whole length, but a fence separated the school's part of the foreshore from the public areas. The school kept its smaller boats beached on the public foreshore. The main school was on higher ground. The foreshore enclosed a small lagoon in the school grounds. There was a drainage lock for the lagoon on the foreshore, which lock the cadets maintained.

The school sailing ship, 'Moyana', was moored in the River Hamble and access was via boat from the pier. 'Moyana' was a 19th Century ketch and used for sea training.

The Cadet building had central heating but we were not allowed to sleep with closed windows unless the rain was being driven in. This was sensible because it kept the air in the cabins fresh, especially in summer. Adolescent boys smell. It wasn't a hardship. There were no curtains. The ablutions block was separate and extremely primitive. It was unheated. There was no glass in the windows and we had tin bowls for washing and shaving. The bowls were placed in a long, zinc-lined trough and there were hot and cold water taps above the trough. You emptied the bowl into the trough when you had finished. Showers, baths and loos were at the rear of the block. The block had concrete floors covered in duck boards. It was one of Wakeford's boasts that one day we would swap all this for marble halls. It did come to pass but way beyond mine and Wakeford's time.

All the above is now history. The School of Navigation is now called the Maritime Academy and is part of the Solent University. Although the Warsash site is a campus within the University regime, the buildings have changed out of all recognition and I understand that cadets are now accommodated in Halls of Residence in Southampton. Cadets are now sponsored by shipping companies and they start their apprenticeships at sea before going to sea school. Consequently, what I have described above and in the following pages is social history and not what is presently available.

Into The Lion's Mouth

All of we Juniors took time to settle in. The regime was tough, demanding and you had to get stuck in straightaway. There was no induction period. I remember that in my first letter home after the first week, I wrote 'I hate this place'. In my next letter, a week later, I stated that I was now enjoying it. Looking back on these first weeks reminds me of a song by Allan Sherman, a noted American comedian. The song was about being sent to a Summer Camp and a boy's first letter home saying how much he hated it. The Song began 'Hello Mudder, Hello Fadder, here we are at Camp Frenata.' and was set to the music 'Dance of the Hours' by Poncielli. It then went on to the next letter where he had started enjoying the swimming and the games. It encapsulated exactly how I felt in those first weeks at Warsash.

Arrival was unsettling. All the Juniors were told to be at Southampton Railway Station at a certain date and time and in uniform. I cannot remember the exact time but it was dark. Most of us had travelled by train from Waterloo Station, London. We were met and marshalled at the station by senior cadets and led outside. I seem to remember that there was a certain amount of shouting and exhortations to get moving. Then, we were loaded onto Army trucks fitted with benches along the sides and driven to Warsash. I think that our trunks had been sent on earlier, because we just had hand luggage. We could not see where we were being driven, so were somewhat disoriented by the time we arrived at Warsash. We were assigned to our cabins and left to our new JLCs to be sorted out. We were shown our bunks and where and how to put away our clothes in our wardrobe and drawer. Everything was regimented, even socks had to be folded in a certain way. This did not bother me much because it was not too different from my mother's regime. The other Juniors in my cabin were a Greek and another English boy. The Greek was about two years older and, despite poor English, seemed to have no difficulty in following instructions. On the other hand, the English boy was lost. His mother had obviously done everything for him and he had no idea how to fold and put away his clothes. He was the one I had to help with shoe polishing. I remember he spent all his time at Warsash as a Non-Exec. Looking back, those who did not get promoted tended to be those who had been, in my view, molly coddled at home. After putting away our possessions, it was dinner and then bed. No time to reflect before we were plunged straightaway into the Daily Routine.

Daily Routine.

Here is the rigorous routine that we had to acclimatise ourselves to with the minimum of explanation.

0615. JLC (Bugles) blows 'Reveille'. This is a tune on a bugle that signals it is time to get up. All cadets, except the Guard Commander, put on singlet, shorts and plimsolls.

0630. Bugle call for morning run. All cadets, without exception, assemble outside for morning run. The run took place every morning from Monday to Saturday, unless it was raining hard. We ran in ice and snow. Nobody was allowed to wear warm clothing – shorts, singlet and plimsolls only. You ran a quarter of a mile up the road to where the day's Guard Commander stood, went round him and back to the school. When it was dark enough in the winter, some cadets tried to hide in bushes that lined the road and join the others on the way back. The Divisional Officers were wise to this and would wait in ambush to catch transgressors, who would be disciplined and punished. There was no incentive to run slowly or walk because of the day's timetable. You could not afford to be late.

After the run, Seniors and Intermediates went to their ablutions. Everyone had to shave and shower every day. Juniors cleaned cabins and rolled back bedding, including the Senior Execs cabins. It was particularly hectic for Juniors on a Monday because that was when bed linen was changed and bed linen and clothes were sent to the laundry (we had no facilities or time for washing clothes). It all had to be collected and bagged and the pillows and blankets arranged in what were known as 'folds'. Seniors and Intermediates changed into Rig of the Day after ablutions. Rig of the Day was normally a blue, soft collar shirt, woollen black tie, navy blue battle dress, gaiters and boots, which we wore for Morning Divisions. Those on the boats rota or similar activities would wear blue cotton working trousers and plimsolls, but they would wear Rig of the Day if their activities started after Divisions.

0710. Junior ablutions. By this time most of the hot water had gone and the showers were cold. One of the Senior Execs would be responsible for seeing that no Junior missed a shower. January 1955 was one of the coldest Januarys on record with snow on the ground for a week or more and a biting northerly wind. Juniors had less than ten minutes for all this because they had to change for breakfast.

0730. Breakfast. We ate well and were served by young women from the village. We would have cereal (cornflakes or porage), kippers or bacon and eggs, toast, marmalade and tea or coffee. The mess had tables down each side at right angles to the adjacent wall and a long table down the middle. The Officer of the Day (a Divisional Officer or Senior Student Lecturer) sat at the top of the long table and the SCC or JCC of the Day at the bottom. The Senior Execs always sat at the top of the long table. Each cabin had its own table on the sides or a share of the long table.

After breakfast, bunks were made, except on Mondays, cabins cleaned and all made ready for Morning Rounds at 0830. Each Watch SCC would conduct these rounds in his own watch and would be accompanied by his senior executive cadets. The object was to make sure all was clean and tidy, especially the cadets. Some Juniors had never had to do any domestic chores before they left home. I had to teach one of my fellow Juniors how to polish his shoes! We ironed creases in our trousers and the Juniors did this, in their own time, for themselves, the Intermediates and the Seniors. This was done under the stairs, where the ironing board and iron were kept – one board and one (non-steam) iron for 60 Cadets! A wet cloth was placed on the trousers so that the steam helped to make the creases. I had ironed at home and was rather good at this, so Seniors would ask especially for me to iron their creases. This helped relationships with other Junior cadets as it relieved them from this chore. Conversely, I was spared other chores. I continued to do my own creases in my Intermediate and Senior terms because I could not find anybody who did as good a job as myself.

0855. Bugle call for Morning Divisions. Divisions were taken by the Officer of the Day (OOD). We paraded in our watches, one on each side of the parade ground, which flanked the main building, and facing each other. The parade ground was known as 'The Quarter Deck' and you had to salute it each time you crossed or passed it. This perpetuated an old Naval tradition. There was a flagstaff at one end. The Guard stood at the head of the parade, with the CCC in front. SCCs and JCCs stood behind their respective watches. The Officer of the Day stood opposite the guard, so the whole body formed a rectangle. Sometimes, the Captain Superintendent would take the parade.

0900. Bugle call: 'Colours'. The CCC called the parade to attention. The guard marched to the flagstaff and raised the school flag to the accompaniment of another bugle call. Officer of the Day and Cadet Captains saluted. The Guard then marched back to its place. The Officer of the Day inspected the ranks. If the OOD was dissatisfied with a Cadet's appearance, the Cadet could be disciplined and punished. Was it a useful way of spending this time? Perhaps it was all part of a regime to instil 'team spirit' and co-operation. Whatever, it had no bearing on our lives afterwards, especially as we did not, for the most part, meet again and spent the rest of our sea time in regimes that did not indulge in this or similar activities.

0915. Morning lessons. Mostly, lessons would be in the classrooms. For Juniors, the morning class on their first day was also the first opportunity for the Divisional Officers to address their charges and explain the routine and what to do if you wanted to leave. There were plenty of lessons outside. Seamanship lessons were taken by the Officer in charge of boats (whose name, apart from 'Jeff', I cannot remember) and the Boatswain, known as the Bosun. He was a Dutchman called Koeman and had served in the Dutch Merchant Navy. He taught knots and rope and wire work (splicing and joining etc) and how to look after small boats. Billy Blyth would take us for drill in the morning. It was known as Command Training and we were marked on our ability and progress. We learned marching and rifle drill and how to drill others, firstly in small sections and then a watch and, finally, if you were good enough, the whole school. My experience in the Combined Cadet Force at school meant that I did well at Command Training. In any group of people, there are uncoordinated people who cannot march or handle weapons. We had our share of those. They create amusement but it must be galling if you are the uncoordinated one. But, the same criticism could be laid against Command Training as that against Morning Divisions.

Our lessons were almost wholly concerned with a sea officer's training. We received no general education at all, with the exception of English, but even here it was perfunctory. The English lessons, once a week, were presided over by a retired mathematician, who was a ballistics expert. His curriculum consisted of setting essays or of writing a letter for employment while he wrote increasingly complicated ballistics problems on the blackboard with algebraic formulae that were incomprehensible to us. No examination of literature that might have relevance to our career choice i.e. no Masefield and no Conrad. No geography training related to the countries with which we might trade. No consideration of world trade or economics that might have been useful. I now find it unbelievable that we were not even educated about the other departments on a merchant vessel: engineering, radio and steward's. One would have thought that instilling a rudimentary knowledge of diesel and steam propulsion and of how to victual a crew of sixty would have been beneficial. On reflection, our training was too narrow and did not properly prepare us for the world into which we would soon enter. This restriction of training continued right through my subsequent apprenticeship.

On a Monday there would be Captain Superintendent's Rounds. He inspected cabins whilst the Cadets were at lessons. He was accompanied by the Cadet Officer of the Day. Captain Harry Stewart had a fearsome reputation and people were scared that he would find something wrong and feared the consequence. He did not overawe me. He was severe in his bearing and appeared aloof but I found him easy to talk to and with a very sensible approach. He had been very ill just before I joined. Prayers had been said for him and I think he had to hold himself very carefully and ration his energy. You will notice that we spent an awful lot of time and energy in cleaning and tidying our cabins, in many cases to excess. There was a good reason for this as I will explain later. Captain Stewart was well aware of this and I think that, privately, he wanted us to take a more pragmatic approach. One morning, during rounds, he said to me 'You boys spend more time on your little cabins than my wife does on the whole of our house, yet our house always passes muster and she does it alone'. People used to think he was out to find trouble, but I never found that. He just wanted to see that all was 'shipshape and Bristol fashion' and nothing was out of place. He was one of the fairest minded men I have ever met and I remember him with affection.

I have mentioned how hectic the early morning period could be, especially on Mondays. One Monday, when I was a Junior, I awoke early and decided to get up and start clearing up early.

Unfortunately, our Divisional Officer was on the prowl and must have heard me. The next thing is my JLC, a Yorkshireman called Thwaites, is on a charge of abusing his position by making me get up early. This was a serious charge because there had been instances of bullying and the Authorities took a very serious view. Captain Stewart conducted the enquiry and I was called to give evidence. I told the truth and he said: 'So, you absolutely exonerate JLC Thwaites?' 'Yes, Sir!' Case dismissed. Stewart then said 'when you are a Non-Executive Intermediate, you won't have to worry so much about time on a Monday.' Thwaites and the SLC who accompanied us both said that I would be promoted at the end of term. They were right. Anyway, I liked Thwaites, he was a good chap.

1230. Lunch. Three courses, always cooked. Mail would be distributed after lunch and for Junior Cadets it was usually a quiet time, unless their JLCs decided otherwise.

1400. Afternoon lessons. These were very often outdoors, the idea being that there must be some physical activity every day. It usually meant putting rowing boats called 'whalers' into the water and rowing (known as 'pulling' in the Royal and Merchant Navies). This was hard work because the boats were large, wooden and heavy and designed for use in a seaway. They were also designed for sailing. We would sail if the weather was right. Sometimes, we were involved in maintaining the grounds and foreshore. The lagoon had originally been a barrier between the school and the foreshore but the cadets before us had, over several years, built a causeway. It was all done manually without machines and used techniques that the Romans had used. First of all, 'fascines' were laid on the bottom of the lagoon in a line to represent the eventual causeway. These 'fascines' were bundles of long sticks with each bundle fastened together with twine. (The word fascine was originally the Roman 'fasces', from which derives the word 'Fascist'. The symbol of Mussolini's Italian Fascist Party was an axe within a fascine.) Then rocks were laid on the fascines. The fascines stopped the rocks from sinking into mud. Once the height of the rocks was above water, the rocks were covered in shingle and the shingle tamped down. The shingle came from the foreshore and cadets brought it in by wheel barrow. It was hard work. We finished it in my first term. The causeway was nicknamed the 'Burma Road' after the infamous Japanese death railway in Thailand and Burma.

One bitter January afternoon, some of us had to clean out the drainage lock that led from the lagoon to the river. We had our bare hands in freezing cold water.

Another activity was preventing erosion from the foreshore. During the war, a lot of concrete blocks, each about eight feet long and two feet high, had been left lying around on the foreshore. We pulled these blocks into positions where they would protect the foreshore shingle. We put ropes around a block and pulled the ropes so that the block rolled over and moved forward. Sometimes we could find wooden rollers, which was a great help. Otherwise, we might make twenty yards in an afternoon. Apart from building us up physically, it taught us how to work in a team.

One other way to combat erosion was to move shingle from a spit, where there was no erosion, to endangered spots. Again, we moved the shingle in wheelbarrows. This was usually a Saturday afternoon job or as a punishment job. These activities would be done by squads, or sections, of us, not the whole school at once.

In retrospect, it is very noticeable that we employed no mechanical means to move objects or when engaged in any other manual activity. It was all manual labour, which cost the school nothing.

When we moved between various locations, it was done at the double, no walking, except for moving from the accommodation to the mess. We would always move in a squad of three per line and 'doubled' in time. Nobody was allowed to lag.

We played sport on at least one afternoon a week and had cricket and rugby competitions between watches. We ran school rugby and cricket teams, which matches we played on occasional Saturdays. I think there were no more than three or four other schools that we played. Captain Wakeford had no interest in sport and any fixtures we had were due to the enthusiasm of Lt Cdr Pierce.

1700. School day finishes. Big clean up of cabins. This meant thorough dusting including pulling out drawers and dusting all the surfaces underneath, tops of wardrobes, around windows, even light bulbs. The wooden floors were polished using 'bumpers'. These were heavy wooden blocks with a handle that was fixed to the block by a swivel. A cloth would be placed around the bottom of the block and the bumper pushed backwards and forwards over the floor. It brought up a sweat even in the winter. Cabin cleaning was a job for the Juniors. An Intermediate Non-Exec would do the Senior Execs cabins. What did the Senior Execs do? They supervised and wanted everything right because they had pride in their watch. It all went into the reckoning for Best Watch at the end of term. The Senior and Intermediate Non-Execs cleaned the corridors and the staircases. The staircases had black and white horizontal tiles on each step and they had to be cleaned and whitened each evening. The Non Exec responsible usually took great pride in his cleaning and woe betide anybody who stepped on the 'Whites' before Evening Rounds. As we went down the staircase, the cry would go up 'Mind the Whites!'

Then a wash and change before Dinner. We dressed for Dinner every night, except for Sunday. No 1 uniform with wing collar and bow tie, shirts with double cuffs and cuff links. That day's Guard did not dress but wore battle dress because they had to be immediately available for emergencies (which never arose in my time). On Visitor Nights, we wore starched shirts with stiffened fronts and wing collars. Starched shirts did not have buttons, instead they had gold studs. The studs were in two parts, a male and female, as were the collar studs. The male stud was on the outside and usually had a jet inlay. You put your shirt on, then pushed the male stud through the button openings to hold the edges together and screwed it into the female stud. I think there were four studs to each shirt. Then the cuff links, collar studs and bow tie. The bow ties were not made-up, you had to learn how to tie one. Then a cummerbund round the waist which covered the join between the top of the trousers and shirt. One of the problems with a starched shirt is that the front is very stiff, like a board. When you sat down the shirt front tended to bow out. To help keep it flat, there was a tab at the front that you could fasten over a trouser button. Finally, a short, white jacket called a 'bum freezer. It was about the size of a waistcoat. You had to put a brass or gold button in to fasten the front and then there were epaulettes to be fastened on the shoulder, which showed your rank. You can imagine the time this took. Fortunately, Visitor Nights were always on a Saturday, when there was more time to prepare.

As Juniors never had as much time as the others, they were often tying their bow ties as they made their way to dinner. I learnt very quickly to tie a bow tie without a mirror.

1800. Sunset Ceremony. The Guard paraded and lowered the school flag to the accompaniment of a bugle.

1900. Bugle Call for Dinner. This was more formal than the other meals and was often four or five courses – soup, fish course, main course, pudding, cheese and biscuits, coffee. So, we had three substantial meals a day but we didn't put on weight because we used up so much energy each day. Before each meal, after all the Cadets were assembled, the Officer of the Day would process from the door and up one of the aisles between the long table and side tables to the top of the middle table. He would then say 'Grace' and we sat down. One of the Senior Student Lecturers was very tall and had a long stride. When he was the presiding Officer, we would count his strides from door to table to see if he broke his record for the shortest number of strides. Mostly, our counting was 'sotto voce', but, sometimes, with over 100 cadets sounding out, it was audible. He didn't seem to mind or feigned oblivion. He was nicknamed 'Kiddlydonks', although I never found out the reason.

We didn't have alcohol, except on Visitors Night, when wine would be served to the visitors and all at the top table and to the Cadet Officer of the Day at the bottom of the long table. Port would be served to the top table and the Cadet Officer of the Day at the end of the meal and a loyal toast drunk. The Senior Officer present would say 'Mr Vice' and the Cadet Officer of the Day would propose the toast, which always went ' My lords, ladies and gentlemen (or lady and or gentleman depending on who was present), the Master of the Merchant Navy, The Queen'. The port was drunk and the other cadets drank their water. This was done sitting down because toasts at sea have traditionally been drunk sitting down. This concession was granted by William IV because when he was the Duke of Clarence and served in the Royal Navy, he became very conscious of the difficulty of standing up and drinking a toast in a turbulent sea, particularly when all the diners had been well-refreshed.

Visitor Nights were only about two a term. Once a year, the President and Secretary of the Southampton University Students Union came. In my year, the Secretary was a girl and I think she was a bit overwhelmed by being the only female in a room of 120 males, all with loads of testosterone and no outlet. Anyway, she got through it all right and seemed to enjoy it at the end. Usually, visitors were people distinguished in the Merchant Service in one way or another.

After Dinner, Mondays to Fridays, there were evening rounds conducted by the Officer of the Day (OOD). The Chief Cadet Captain and SCC Boats accompanied the OOD. On Saturdays, the Chief Cadet Captain, accompanied by the Senior and Junior Cadet Captains, conducted Rounds. There were no rounds on Sundays.

The object was to inspect the cabins and the cadets for tidiness and cleanliness. The impression given by each cabin went towards deciding best cabin of the week. Occupants of best cabin could 'go ashore' on the next Tuesday evening. The award of best cabin was decided on the Saturday evening after the Chief Cadet Captain's Rounds. So you can see why there was so much enthusiasm about cleaning and tidiness. Some of the Senior Executive Cadets got a bit carried away at times. The SCC Boats in my Senior year was apt to take drawers and wardrobes apart and leave clothes on the floor. I remember getting very angry with him because it was bullying behaviour and throwing his weight around to no purpose. He was an arrogant sod.

When I became a JLC, I was assigned Port 6 cabin on the ground floor. The floor was concrete. As the ground floor cabins were also darker that than those on the first floor, it was difficult to impress those who awarded Best Cabin of the Week. I decided to polish the floor to create a better impression. So, I got some floor polish and we set to work with a bumper. We got a lovely sheen. Unfortunately, on his rounds the next Monday, Captain Stewart stepped onto the rug which slid away underneath him. End of experiment, although he did see the funny side of it.

Most Officers of the Day were pretty perfunctory but some took too much of an interest. One in particular, who was a vain man anyway, always inspected the Cadets' dress minutely. If he found something he disliked, perhaps a bow tie wasn't straight, he would not only make a fuss about it but blame the JLC of the cabin and get him punished. One OOD was 'Frankie' Thiele, the Flying Instructor. He had been a fighter pilot in the Second World War and had piloted a Gloster Meteor, the first jet aircraft in service with the RAF, from Manston Aerodrome in Kent when my father was stationed there. He had a resplendent RAF moustache was very affable and more inclined to engage the Senior Cadets in interesting conversation than the other Officers.

This insistence on formality and accommodation inspection struck me as excessive at the time and from what Captain Stewart said to me, I suspect that he thought the same. A weekly inspection would have sufficed. It all chimed in with what Wakeford wanted and, I suspect, continued throughout his time as Director. As I look back, I still cannot believe that it served any useful purpose other than satisfying one man's vanity and wasting our time.

Once Evening Rounds were over, our time was our own until bedtime, which was announced with a bugle call 'Lights Out' at 2200. Then, we turned in

On Saturdays, there were no classes but there was a routine programme of activities in the morning that you took turns to do:

Boiler suit washing. Each week, you would have one of your white overalls, or boiler suits, washed. This clothing was used for dirty jobs like wheel barrowing shingle or boat cleaning. Part of one watch would wash the suits in the ablutions. We would be dressed in our other boiler suit and wellies. The suits were first of all soaked in hot soapy water, then rubbed through by hand, then rinsed, then wrung out and, finally, put out to dry, often on the grass if it was dry enough. This was usually enormous fun because if you put boys and hot water together, it will get everywhere and we all ended up getting soaked because we splashed each other. Of course, boiler suits could have been included in the normal laundry, but I suspect that we did it because the Authorities could save money and provide work for otherwise idle hands.

Boat maintenance. This was mostly cleaning but sometimes sanding and varnishing.

Grounds maintenance i.e. wheel barrowing shingle or moving concrete posts.

On Saturday afternoons, you could opt for activities such as cricket, rugby, sailing, tennis or swimming. But, it was not an option to do nothing because you would be ordered to do something. We would finish about 1600 on Saturdays.

Sunday

No run. No Morning Rounds. Church parade at 1030. Best uniform with stiff collar. March to 'Hook with Warsash' Church. We made up about half the congregation. The village girls would attend because there were so many of us and there weren't enough boys in the village. After the service, march back to school.

If you wanted to, you could 'go ashore' immediately on return from church or go after Lunch. There would be a shore leave parade to make sure you were properly dressed and neat and clean. We had to wear uniform ashore. In summer we wore 'whites': starched white shirts and starched white cotton shorts. Always a uniform cap. I always felt that uniforms made us too conspicuous and a target for undesirables. This was the 1950s and the powers that be felt they had to control us at all times. We could not be trusted. We were allowed to go to Southampton but not to Portsmouth, because it was felt that Portsmouth was a 'sailors' town' with too many temptations. I ignored this and sometimes went to Portsmouth to visit my grandparents, aunt and uncle and cousin. I was never caught. Fareham was a popular spot because it was the nearest town with a direct bus service and the cinema was open on Sunday. We had to be back for 2130.

We could not get into trouble ashore because our money was limited. Our parents sent a fixed amount of money at the beginning of each term to be doled out as pocket money each week. The doling out was a copy of an old Naval custom. We paraded in order of seniority and went, in turn, to a table, on which was the money to be doled out. The table was presided over by a Divisional Officer. Each Cadet, on presenting himself to the table, doffed his cap, held it out and the Officer placed the coins on top of the cap. Seniors got more than Intermediates and Intermediates got more than Juniors. Everybody in each term had the same amount. I cannot remember the weekly amount but it barely paid for a bus fare to Fareham or Southampton plus a cinema ticket or a cup of tea at a cafe. Most of us relied on parents sending additional money by post. Hence our letters invariably read 'Am well, please send five'. It was a requirement to write home each week, although there was no censorship. The whole thing was just another example of useless formality and an attempt to make us look and appear 'Naval'. What was the point?

Some cadets were invited out to Sunday lunch on designated Sundays. Local families could 'adopt' one or two cadets for lunch and invitations were eagerly awaited. I was never a lucky one. I was adopted once, but the family never turned up!

Other activities during the week.

Guard Duty.

Each cabin did at least one week's guard duty a term. As the term was thirteen weeks long and there were only twelve cabins, some poor sods had to do two Guard Duties per term. It was mainly symbolic but was utilised to get us accustomed to taking responsibility and being uncomfortable during the process. The Guard Room was less comfortable than a cabin, particularly the bunks, and could be cold in the winter.

Guards were changed on a Monday. Before breakfast on a Monday morning, the new guard would take their bedding, including mattresses, to the Guard Room plus everything you would need for the coming week: e.g. clothing, toiletries and books. You were not allowed into your normal cabin for that week.

Duties of the Guard.

Colour ceremony at Morning Divisions.
Sunset Ceremony at 1800.
Generally 'guarding' the premises. Quite what we were supposed to guard was never disclosed. The main entrance to the site was entirely open with no fences or gates. There were other ways an intruder could gain access without being seen. As far as I was aware, there were no alarm systems. No one accessing the premises were stopped and questioned. Indeed, the only time one of the guard would be 'on guard' outside the Guard Room with an unloaded rifle and fixed bayonet was between close of classes to lights out, with a break for dinner. So the concept of a guard was purely ceremonial and served no educational purpose.

Each 'guardsman's shift lasted an hour and the cadet 'on guard' had to ring a brass bell every half hour from close of classes to 'lights out'. The number of strokes each time the bell was rung indicated the time. As follows:
Four strokes for 1800 – the start of the second 'Dog Watch'
One stroke for 1830
Two strokes for 1900
Three strokes for 1930.
Eight strokes for 2000, the end of the second 'Dog Watch' and the start of the 'Evening Watch'.
One stroke for 2030
Two strokes for 2100
Three strokes for 2130
Four strokes for 2200.

The ringing was referred to as 'One bell of the Dog Watch', 'Two bells of the Dog Watch' and so on. This was how crews were traditionally kept aware of time. At sea, it was discontinued with the advent of reliable clocks and watches.

On board the old sailing ships, the crew was split into two 'watches', Port and Starboard. One watch would be on duty for four hours and was then relieved by the other watch, who stood for the next four hours and so on throughout each twenty four hours, Sunday to Sunday, 365 days a year. The watch times were split as follows:
Midnight to 0400 – the midnight or graveyard watch
0400 to 0800 – the morning watch
0800 to 1200 – the forenoon watch
1200 to 1600 – the afternoon watch
1600 to 1800 - first Dog Watch. During this time in the old sailing ships, half the ship's company had their supper.
1800 to 2000 – second Dog Watch. Those who had had their supper relieved the other half of the ship's company for supper.
2000 to midnight – the Evening Watch.

These times are still observed today, although merchant seamen are no longer split into two watches and do not work four hours on and four hours off. If on watch, they now work four hours on and eight hours off. There are also crew who only work in the day. This also applies in the Royal Navy, although their organisation is still closely linked to the traditional.

Occasionally, the Guard would be 'turned out' during the night to carry out an inspection of the grounds. This was largely done to accustom Cadets to disruption in routine, but we still had valuable equipment around the grounds and young men armed with rifles and fixed bayonets could be a deterrent. However, the Guard would make so much noise that any intruder would have had plenty of advanced warning.

At 0600 the Guard Commander got up, dressed and made his way up New Town Road to the point where the morning run turned round. He stood there until all the runners had reached him and turned for home. He carried the guard room keys with him. The lock was a self-locking Chubb or Yale and the guard locked the door behind them after leaving for the run. The Guard Commander handed the keys to the first member of the guard to reach him during the run. This Guardsman then had to sprint back to the Guardroom to unlock it so that no time was lost in rolling up bedding, tidying up and, on Mondays, moving gear back to the cabin before washing and dressing before breakfast.

Other than the above regime, the Guard provided no useful function. Another useless 'Naval' exercise, which had no equivalent on any ship I sailed on.

Duty Boatman and river activities.

A feature of Southampton Water, which includes the tidal reaches of the River Hamble, is that it has four high tides a day. This is because the Isle of Wight splits the tidal current that flows up the Channel from the west on the flood. Part of this current comes up the Western Solent between the Needles and Bournemouth and the other part goes round the Isle of Wight to the south and then comes up the Eastern Solent between Ryde and Portsmouth. The western current reaches its high water mark about ninety minutes before the eastern current. The result is that Southampton Water has enough depth for the greater part of the day to enable the largest vessels to access Southampton Port. It makes Southampton very attractive to shipping companies and explains why it has huge container, ferry and cruise traffic.

Warsash owned a number of craft, apart from 'Moyana', and some were permanently moored in the Hamble. How did people get to them? There was a concrete and metal pier about 200 yards long from the boathouse on the foreshore out into the Hamble. It had to be that long in order for the pierhead to provide access to water no matter the state of the tide. The pierhead had a shelter. There were steps from the end of the pier into the water. Therefore, we could get out on to the water at any time. If you wanted to get to one of the vessels, you went by dinghy. This could hold four people easily and six at a pinch. It was propelled by oars and was operated by the Duty Boatman. The Duty Boatman was a cadet and each day (except for Sunday) there would be a different cadet, assigned by rota. As each term lasted about ninety days, normally each cadet would be Duty Boatman twice in his year.

Anybody who wanted to reach a vessel or come ashore hailed the boatman. The boatman was always stationed in the middle of the river. He was not allowed to moor to the pier or a buoy.

This was all right when the tide was not running at 'slack water', but for most of the time the boatman was rowing against the stream in order to keep his position.

Sometimes, this ebb and flow was accentuated by the passage of large vessels in Southampton Water. All vessels displace their own weight of water. Therefore the larger the vessel, the more water is displaced. When the liners Queen Elizabeth and Queen Mary, each weighing over 80,000 tons, moved through Southampton Water, the displaced water was pushed in front of them and a 'hole' was left in the water behind them. Some of the displaced water entered the Hamble, thus raising the water level significantly. After the liners had moved past the Hamble, the displaced water rushed back into the hole made by the liners. It was like a flood and ebb tide in quick succession.

The boatman was there after breakfast until lunch, then after lunch until 5 pm. It was very tiring but on a day of good weather, you were out of the classroom and there was always something interesting to see. Every now and again, one of the Officers would give the boatman a task, not because there was any need but to see how competent the boatman was. Captain Stewart tested me one day. He ordered me to row to a buoy without looking round. As I had been brought up on the Avon, this was easy for me. You just line up two landmarks over the stern with your destination and keep them in line until you reach your destination. Which I did. He then asked where I had learnt to row, so I guessed I passed.

When I was a Junior, I was one of a crew sent to clean the 'Moyana'. The leader of the crew was a Senior Cadet Captain. When we had finished, he hailed the Duty Boatman and told us all to get in the dinghy. There were seven of us, far too many, but you had to obey orders. So, off we went and soon water was coming over the side (the 'gunwale').We should have just bailed the water out and rowed slowly, but our leader was an idiot and kept the boatman rowing as hard as he could. The dinghy filled up and we kept going further under. Eventually a motor boat came to our rescue. As it was February, the water was cold.

We would sail or 'pull' the whalers. 'Pulling' is the naval term for rowing when the boat has fixed seats or benches for rowing. Whalers were originally designed to catch whales and would have carried a harpoonist in the bow. They were heavy boats and were pointed at the stern as well as the bow. A whaler had tow masts, both of which could be dismounted when not needed. The main mast had a mainsail and a foresail. The main sail was gaff rigged and the fore sail was triangular. The after mast carried a triangular sail aft of the mast to aid steering. We had a lot of fun with them and the Hamble is a safe environment. You can't get lost.

Discipline.

One hundred and twenty adolescent boys are not always going to behave or will 'forget' to do what they have been told to do or what is ordered by routine. If you transgressed, these were the punishments:

Overtime.

You could be placed on overtime for transgressions such as inappropriate dress, untidiness, not cleaning your cabin properly, being late for a work party, not saluting an Officer. You would be assigned tasks to be carried out in your own time. These would usually be arduous tasks such as wheel barrowing shingle from the foreshore to the

Burma Road or other places. Overtime was usually one or two hours. If you had accumulated more than two hours, it would be spread over more than one overtime session. I once got two hours overtime because I had not heard the Reveille bugle and was woken up by the Duty Officer and, because I was a Junior Cadet Captain, setting a bad example. The fact that it had been blowing a gale and the bugle was difficult to hear was no excuse. Normally, I shared a cabin with SCC (Port) but at the time he was ill in sick bay, so I was running the watch on my own at that time. Had he been there, he would have woken me. Perhaps my hearing problem goes back a long way.

I seemed to be a regular on overtime. Billy Blyth took the overtime parades and allocated work. I remember him once saying 'it doesn't seem to matter what you give Ayres, he always comes up smiling'. But, I did once deliberately not put my name in the Punishment Book. On the last Sunday but one of my last term, I had lunch at the home of my friend Bunny Hayward in Hillhead, with drinks at the 'Osborne View' beforehand. He had been one of my Juniors when I was a JLC and was now a JLC himself. It was a lovely, sunny day and we went for a walk after lunch. We were in uniform but without our caps on. Towards the middle of the next week, Bunny and I were summoned to the office of one of the Lecturers. He informed us that we had been seen and reported. We did not know who had reported us, neither were we informed of the reporter, but presumably he or she was not one of the staff. Otherwise, it would have been reported directly to the Divisional Officer. So, most likely a self righteous member of the public. The Lecturer told me to book us both in for an hour's overtime in the Punishment Book. It was unlikely that I would serve that hour because it was so close to the end of term and I did not see why Bunny should suffer next term. So I disobeyed his order and told Bunny that I would not put our names in the book. I never heard anymore about it, but what kind of person would go to the lengths of reporting us? What a small mind.

Drill.

This was for more serious offences. If you were given one or two hours drill, you would parade in battledress, gaiters and boots and rifle and bayonet. You would then carry out rifle drill on the double. This would be for offences like swearing or bullying a junior. It was rarely given. I remember that Captain Wakeford gave one cadet two hours drill for playing tennis in someone else's tropical kit (white shorts and shirt) without permission. If you wanted to borrow kit, you had to get an Officer's permission. Bit extreme, but he was like that.

Demotion.

Executive cadets could be reduced to non-executive rank for offences such as mis-treatment of Juniors or generally misbehaving. In my Junior term, the Junior Cadet Captain of my watch was demoted because he proved totally unreliable. He had became an habitué of the 'Rising Sun', a pub on the Warsash foreshore. One of my best friends, John Tait, was a Junior Leading Cadet and had an insubordinate Greek as one of his Juniors. To teach the Greek a lesson, John made him run to the pier and back one evening in his mess kit. It was a hot evening. The Greek snitched on him and John was demoted in a humiliating ceremony. He was paraded in front of all the cadets and the CCC removed his badge of rank from his uniform. Obviously, it was done to deter us from misbehaving and there had been a serious spate of bullying in the previous year. I thought that it was all a bit extreme. The other Greeks felt the same and sent their fellow countryman to Coventry. Fortunately, it didn't harm John's career and he was promoted to SLC in his senior year.

Sent down.

This was the most extreme. It never happened in my time. Obedience to orders was drummed into us as a most heinous offence. We always assumed that if you disobeyed an order, you would be expelled. If you transgressed, were in your Senior term and had already got a position with a shipping company, the fear was that the school would recommend the shipping company to withdraw their offer.

Punishment could be commuted or written off. During the Summer term, Warsash would have an official visit from the Lord Mayor of Southampton. We would provide a Guard of Honour, he would inspect the cadets on parade, we would march past and then he would be given lunch. After lunch he would be asked by the Chief Cadet Captain to look at the Punishment Book and write off some punishments. At the time, I had been booked for two hours by my Divisional Commander, Lt Cdr 'Jacko' Glubb. My punishment was one of those written off. Jacko was not pleased but he did not oppose my promotion to Junior Cadet Captain.

CHAPTER SEVEN

SCHOOL OF NAVIGATION

Other Activities.

The 'Moyana'

Moyana

'Moyana' was a sailing vessel. It took cadets on training trips in the English Channel.

It was a gaff-rigged ketch with a diesel engine. A 'ketch' has two masts, a main mast and a mizzen mast (behind the main mast). The steering wheel is behind the mizzen mast. If the steering wheel is in front of the mizzen mast, the vessel is known as a 'yawl'. The main mast carried two triangular foresails, which were situated between the main mast and the bow (the front end). The main sail was in two parts. The main part was shaped like a shoulder of mutton with the lower part being the longest side. One side ran up the mast and was the shortest side of the sail. The highest side of the sail was attached to a wooden beam called a 'gaff'. The gaff was attached to the main mast by a ring so that it could be hauled up and down. When hauled up tight, the gaff would be at an angle of about fifty degrees to the horizontal. The gaff enabled the sail to be kept taught and, therefore, more efficient.

The mainmast extended higher than the gaff, so there was a triangular space between mainmast and the gaff. Another sail could be placed there.

The mizzen mast had a triangular sail with a lower boom. This sail helped to keep the vessel stable for steering.

All the sails were red, This colour was applied by a liquid called 'barking', which acted as a preservative.

The accommodation had cabins aft for the captain and senior officers. There was a chart room forward (in front) of these cabins and a mess room and galley (kitchen) forward of that. Next to the galley was the diesel engine. The crew's quarters were in the bow and consisted of a dozen bunks and storage spaces. Cadets made up the crew. The crew space was cramped, poorly ventilated and filled with the smells of the galley and diesel fuel. Being in the bow, the effects of pitching in a seaway (up and down motion) were exaggerated. It was unpleasant and many cadets were sea sick.

'Moyana' was moored in the Hamble. Each week, Billy Blyth selected a 'Moyana' crew and posted the names on a notice board. No cadet was advised individually and it was each cadet's responsibility to check the notice board. No excuses were accepted for not checking work rotas. Most weeks, the crew were only required to carry out maintenance on selected days, particularly in winter. In Spring, Summer and Early Autumn, 'Moyana' went on Channel cruises for four or five days.

I went on one cruise in the summer of 1955 under the command of Captain Stewart. We sailed first of all across the Solent to Cowes and were manoeuvring to anchor when a yacht flying the flag of the Royal Yacht Squadron nearly ran us down, although it was our right of way. As Captain Stewart said, resignedly: 'one rule for the Royal Yacht Squadron and one rule for the rest of us'. Next day, he wanted to make Cherbourg, but there was insufficient wind and it was in the wrong direction. On that night, several cadets were ill. One kept retching non-stop. One of the Officers came forward and asked him to retch a little more genteely! Nobody could sleep because of him. Shortly after he went on deck and was sick over the side. Unfortunately, he was sick over the windward side i.e. into the wind. The wind carried his vomit right aft and all over Captain Stewart.

We sailed into Weymouth and I went ashore and had a drink in a pub run by a man known to my father. The publican had been a professional footballer for Aston Villa and England. If we had gone to Cherbourg, I would not have met him.

The year after I left, 'Moyana' took part in the first International Tall Ships Race, which finished in Lisbon. 'Moyana' won. However, she met bad weather on the way home, sprang a leak and sank in the Channel. The crew were rescued by a Clan Line ship.

Tony 'Norm' Robb was a Junior in my Senior year and later joined me as an Apprentice with the New Zealand Shipping Company. He was not in the race crew for 'Moyana' but was in the crew that sailed 'Moyana' to the race start. It was not his first acquaintance with shipwreck. His family were Service people and were stationed abroad in the early 1950s. The family had finished their posting and Norman and his mother were coming home on the 'Empire Windrush', which was a troopship operated by the New Zealand Shipping Company on behalf of the Ministry of Defence. She had also been used to transport the first of the West Indian immigrants to the UK in the late 1940s, hence the name 'Windrush Generation'. The ship was built at Blohm und Voss in 1930 for Hamburg Sud, a German shipping line. She was originally built to carry German emigrants to Argentina but found more profitable business with inexpensive cruises. The UK claimed her as a war prize in 1945 and converted her to a troopship. The management was contracted to the New Zealand Shipping Company Limited.

The 'Windrush' had started for home in Yokohama, Japan, in February 1954, and was carrying men who had been wounded in the Korean war. She also called at Singapore, Hong Kong and Aden. The number of passengers and crew was over 1,500. This voyage had been plagued with mechanical breakdowns and 'Windrush' was weeks behind schedule. She had passed through the Suez Canal and stopped at Port Said. On the evening of March 28th 1954, she was north of Algiers. There was an explosion in the engine room which killed the 3rd Engineer and three others and started a fire that quickly went out of control. All the electrical generators were out of action and there was no sprinkler system. The lifeboats were supposed to be lowered with electrical power, which was now non-existent. It was possible to lower some lifeboats manually with the women, children and wounded aboard. The other lifeboats were just let go and the rest of the passengers and crew jumped into the water. Everybody got into lifeboats safely and there were no further casualties. I guess that because the passengers were all service families, discipline was strong. The Chief Officer was the last to leave the ship. He and the Ship's Carpenter were subsequently amongst those decorated for their efforts.

Because the incident happened so near Algiers, help came quickly and everybody was ashore the next day. The ship was taken in tow by 'HMS Saintes' and headed for Gibraltar but sank within 15 miles of starting the tow in several thousand feet of water. The official enquiry concluded that there were two possible causes for the incident. The first was that there was corrosion in the funnel and that a metal plate, or plates, came away and brought soot into the engine room. The plates and soot would have been hot and could have come into contact with oil and caused an explosion. The second cause could have been an oil pipe fracture. Given that the ship was now twenty four years old and had previous form with mechanical unreliability, these conclusions were not unreasonable, but there was no physical examination because she sank in deep water. Norm was convinced that it was a bomb planted by Egyptian extremists in Port Said, possibly the Muslim Brotherhood. He was definitely conscious of a violent explosion. Maybe, the timing was set for when 'Windrush' had passed the Straits of Gibraltar, was in the Atlantic and rescue would have been more problematical. Given that 'Windrush' may not have been travelling at her normal speed of 15 knots because of engine trouble, the alleged bomb fortunately went off where rescue was speedy and effective.

Whatever the cause, 'Windrush' passed through Suez and Port Said at a time of considerable unrest and accompanying agitation by the Egyptians with the object of 'encouraging' the UK to withdraw her troops from the Canal Zone. An agreement was signed with the Egyptian Government in October 1954 whereby the UK agreed to withdraw troops from the Canal Zone, i.e. just over six months after the 'Windrush' incident. Was there a connection and the UK did not want to make waves? Certainly, there were Egyptian extremists, notably the Muslim Brotherhood, who were carrying out violent acts against UK troops and diplomatic personnel during the early 1950s. The parents of another of my cadet colleagues, Stuart Crawford, fell foul of the Muslim Brotherhood, which organisation still exists. The cadet's father was a diplomat stationed in Cairo and his wife was with him. They went to a night club within Shepheard's Hotel one evening when the Brotherhood set fire to it. As the customers ran out of the club, they were mown down by machine gun fire. This tactic has been used in other places since by Muslim extremists.

Dancing.

All cadets in their Junior Term were taught ballroom dancing on Saturday nights after dinner. This was at the instigation of Wakeford, who was keen to ensure that we learnt a few social graces. The instructor was called Jimmy Grist and he was a professional ballroom dancer who took part in competitions. Jimmy was in his 50s at this time. He brought with him a young female partner. The sessions lasted about an hour. We learnt the basic steps of the quickstep, waltz and foxtrot. No Latin steps as there wasn't time. If you were lucky, you had a chance to practice with the female professional, but mostly we followed Jimmy's steps and practiced on our own. Very weird but it worked and gave you confidence that you could get round the dance floor. A girl at a dance in The Bluff, New Zealand, once asked if I was a professional! Jimmy would stay on for another half an hour if any of the Intermediate and Senior cadets were interested in more advanced moves.

Judo.

Wakeford also had this idea that we might end up in dangerous situations and would need to be able to defend ourselves. So, the Juniors were instructed in so-called 'Judo' one evening a week. The instructor was a professional wrestler and he taught us self defence more than anything else. Firstly, how to fall so that you fell on a relaxed back. This is the basis of clowning and slapstick comedy. Then we advanced to basic holds and throws, which I still remember and have used on occasions for a bit of fun. I doubt any of us had cause to use any of the moves we were shown to defend ourselves.

About twice a term, a 'Judo Team' was selected to demonstrate what we had learnt during the Visitor Nights I have mentioned above.

Director's Evenings.

These were a nightmare and I only had to endure it once. Wakeford would hold dinners at his house, to which two or three cadets were invited, along with outside guests, in order to instruct us how to behave socially. Full mess kit, so it was uncomfortable to start with. He was dreadfully pompous and full of himself. He would pontificate about wine, particularly port. As I was a publican's son, I knew that he talked rubbish. At least, it was an opportunity to get a drink!

Hair cuts.

When I started at Warsash, we had weekly visits from a local barber called Nippy Knipe. He charged one shilling (five pence in decimal currency). We would get our hair cut about every three weeks, so it was quite a bite out of our weekly pocket money. Wakeford decided that in order to cut the cost, he would get one of the catering staff to cut our hair on the basis that it was traditional for the ship's cook to cut hair at sea. The results were disastrous, particularly on a Greek called Mavrophoros. Poor bugger looked as if he had been through a meat grinder. Captain Stewart asked me at the time if I had any complaints and I complained about the new hair cut regime. He took one look at Mavrophoros and stopped the regime on the spot. Nippy was back next week.

Sport.

There was not much opportunity for sport although Warsash had an excellent sports field. We played rugger and cricket matches between watches and my watch, Port, always won. We would also play against the Second Mates. These were people just out of their apprenticeships who were studying for their Second Mate's Certificate. Obviously, they were scratch teams and not much opposition. We played two or three schools at cricket and rugger, but they were always better than us. The thing was that they were 'away' matches so we had a chance to get off campus. Naturally, competition to be on the teams was keen. I captained the rugger team in my Senior Term but only because I think nobody else wanted to do it.

Royal Navy Training at HMS Excellent.

Each Senior Term spent five days at 'HMS Excellent' in Portsmouth. 'Excellent', also known as Whale Island, was the Royal Navy Gunnery School. It is a shore establishment i.e. it is not a ship, but every Royal Navy establishment is always known as 'HMS Something or Other'. It still exists but I suppose that it is called the Surface Weapons School or something like that. In Portsmouth, the main naval base was, and is, 'HMS Nelson' and another establishment, 'HMS Vernon' at the Gunwharf, was the torpedo and underwater weapons school. 'Excellent' ran courses in gunnery, small arms and fire fighting ('HMS Phoenix' at Horsea Island). Whilst we were there we held the rank of Midshipman local, acting and unpaid. In other words, the lowest of the low. At least, we had lunch in the Wardroom, which is what the Officers' Mess in the Navy is called.

We did not live at Excellent but were bussed in every day. This meant an early start and breakfast as we had to be at Excellent ready to go by 0800 and it took us nearly an hour to get from Warsash to Portsmouth. In those days, the road between Portchester Castle and the bridge onto Portsea Island ran along the north shore of Portsmouth Harbour. The foreshore was covered by old motor torpedo boats, motor gunboats and launches. The engines and weapons had been stripped out. Many were occupied by families who had no other homes. This area was later filled in and accommodates retail and industrial estates.

Just as at Warsash, at 'Excellent' we 'doubled' everywhere i.e. we ran at about 200 paces a minute in formation. Not easy to do and keep formation. Each day we experienced a different gunnery operation.

To start with, we were introduced to the four-inch gun trainer. This was an obsolete weapon but it was used to train seamen to operate as a team. The gun was on an open platform, which was slung on motorised 'gimbals'. This was a series of pivots that enabled the gun to 'pitch' and 'roll' to simulate movement at sea. First of all we were divided into teams of six or seven and taught how to load the shell, fire and eject the used shell whilst the platform was stationary. A four- inch shell weighs several pounds. Once we had 'mastered' that sequence and could operate without injuring ourselves, we went into a 'live' sequence'. We put on waterproof clothing and anti-flash headgear. All big guns have a flash back from the muzzle and gun crews wore anti-flash headgear and goggles to protect skin and eyes. Then we mounted the platform and the motor was started. The platform rolled all over the place and we then loaded, fired and ejected. All the time we were doing this, the training crew threw buckets of water over us and set off fire crackers to simulate actual firing conditions. It was great fun. One of our teams was going great guns (sorry!). It looked as though they could set the fastest time of the week. We weren't the only trainees there. There were several RN detachments, amongst whom there was an unofficial competition for the fastest time. The loader of this team was Mavrophoros, who was big and powerful. He had to put the shell in its cradle and push the shell off its cradle into the breech and then shut the breech. To do so he had to shove his arm up to his elbow in to the breech. On the run to establish the fastest time, his overall got caught as he was pushing the shell in and we lost time.

The dome attack was interesting. This was a large dome used for anti-aircraft fire training. It had an anti- aircraft gun in the middle of the building. A film of aircraft attacking a ship was projected onto the inside of the dome. The gunner could operate a motor that made the gun swivel round and move up and down whilst firing. Very difficult and not many people could attain the necessary standard. We were told that by then, 1955, aircraft were so fast that unless the aircraft was attacking your ship you had no chance of shooting it down. We nearly did not make the dome attack. Each day, a different cadet was appointed to be the team leader. The team leader marched and doubled in front of the squad and was responsible for leading the squad from one lesson to another. I was chosen that day and our first lesson was at the dome attack. I did not know where it was although I had been given a plan of the area with the dome marked on it. What nobody told me was that one of the paths we had to use had been blocked off and there were no signs to tell us about a diversion. We formed up on the Quarterdeck in front of the Wardroom. At certain times of the day, a Marine drummer would stand in front of the Wardroom and blow a bugle call to indicate the time of day or that a certain event was about to take place i.e. lunch break. He was required to salute an Officer or Officers as they passed him. On this morning, there stood the drummer, who saluted as we doubled past. As I could not find my way to the attack dome, we had to go round the Wardroom block and cross the Quarterdeck again. The drummer was still there and duly saluted us. Again, I could not find my way and went round the Wardroom block again. As we entered the Quarterdeck and the drummer saw us, he could not contain himself, burst out laughing and ran away. He could not salute us with a straight face. By this time, one of the training Petty Officers had been sent to find us and guided us to the attack dome.

We did some small arms firing. We used .303 Short Lee Enfield magazine rifles. Again, these were obsolete for war but excellent for target shooting. We fired at targets up to 300 yards away with live ammunition. To my surprise, I found that I was quite good at it whereas I was useless with the .22 rifles we had used for target shooting in Warwick School CCF. The Chief Petty Officer small arms trainer instructed us how to treat our weapon as follows 'Think of it as your girl friend. The more you cuddle it, the more it will do for you.' And he was right. The ranges, at Tipner, are still in use and visible, to the right, from the motorway bridge as you cross from the mainland onto Portsea Island

The fire fighting day at 'HMS Phoenix' on Horsea Island was shambolic. There were a number of blackened buildings with no windows. We had to find our way through virtually blindfold whilst smoke was pumped through. We wore asbestos helmets with a 'transparent' visor. You could see hardly anything in broad daylight. One of us led whilst we followed with an arm on the shoulder of the man in front. We just went round and round inside this building because the team leader couldn't see where he was going. I hope they teach modern fire fighters better. We did learn a lot about different types of fire and how to put them out.

Our last day was on the Friday. On each Friday morning, the Royal Navy holds Divisions. Wherever they are in the world, ships' crews and shore establishments parade formally, on Friday mornings, in front of their Commanding Officers and are inspected. This tradition goes back to the 17th Century. In shore establishments, the company will march past their commanding officer. At 'Excellent', Divisions take place on the Quarterdeck, usually in the open. If the weather is not suitable, Divisions take place in the Drill Shed, which is a large shed open on the side facing the Quarterdeck. It is at least one hundred yards long, so can accommodate up to 200 seamen. We cadets formed up at one end of the shed. A Naval band was formed up in the middle. All the formations faced the open side. A Captain took the parade with the orders being given by a Lieutenant in charge of the parade. He called the parade to attention. His command was not very clear and we, being unused to it, were still standing at ease. There was a deathly silence. Then we heard the crunching of boots on gravel and an irate Chief Petty Officer stood in front of us. In very clear tones, so that everybody heard, he told us: 'When the Officer calls the parade to attention, that includes the Merchant Navy Cadets. Atten- shun!!' Red faces all round. Then happened what our predecessors told us would happen. In order to march past, the Divisions had to do a left turn. The order was shouted out: 'Divisions will move to the left in threes. Left Turn!!!' To our credit, we carried out the order perfectly. The trouble was that not all the RN seamen knew their left from their right. Some turned left, some turned right and others did not move. It took several minutes to get us all in the right direction. Apparently, this happened often. Then we marched past, halted and the parade was dismissed. We redeemed ourselves with the march past and our instructor was all smiles.

One of the latest destroyers, 'HMS Daring', was in port whilst we were at Excellent and we had a look round. Everything was enclosed. After the Second World War all new warships had enclosed bridges and gun turrets. The Navy no longer fought in the open but had to be protected from nuclear and chemical weapons. 'Daring' had the latest anti-aircraft guns called STAG (Stabilised Tagometric Anti-Aircraft Gun). No matter how much the ship pitched and rolled, the gun was always on a stable level platform and it 'locked on' to the target via radar. A gunnery AB (Able Seaman) demonstrated it for us and finished with: 'That's it. I'm f...... chocker and I'm f...... off'. 'Chocker' is a Naval expression for being fed up. I think he was past his 'smoko' (break time) and we were a nuisance.

There was a Russian Naval squadron visiting Portsmouth that week, and after we had visited 'Daring', we marched round to have a look at the cruiser 'Sverdlovsk' and go on board. A look from the dockside was all we got, because as soon as the Russians saw a squad in officer's uniforms marching towards them, a couple of their officers ran down the gangplank yelling 'Niet' at the tops of their voices. 'Sverdlovsk' was at the centre of a diplomatic incident a few months later on another visit to Portsmouth. She had brought the then Russian leaders Marshall Nikolai Bulganin and Nikita Kruschev to Portsmouth at the start of a State visit to the UK on what was described as a 'charm offensive'. The Secret Intelligence Service commissioned a retired frogman, Lt Cdr 'Buster' Crabbe', without proper authorisation, to have a clandestine look at 'Sverdlovsk's' hull in order to obtain an idea about the ship's anti-submarine location devices. Crabbe never returned and his headless body was found a considerable time later. This incident did not contribute positively to what was intended as a charm offensive, in which objective the visit failed.

That day we were shown a film about atom bombs that had not been shown to the public and we were told not to discuss it. Alarming! What a day we had! And what an introduction to the Cold War!

Thus ended my week in the Royal Navy.

Sunset Ceremony.

In November 1955, the Senior Term was invited to HMS Collingwood at Fareham to observe the Sunset Ceremony. HMS Collingwood is the training school for naval electrical and communication equipment. Sunset, or lowering of the colours, is observed on all UK ships, including the Merchant Navy. If you have a bugler to play 'Sunset', then all well and good. Most merchant ships made do with a whistle although some used a recording of a bugle player. On important occasions, sunset becomes an elaborate ceremonial and can be emotional. This was the first big occasion Sunset Ceremony I had witnessed.

The ceremony took place on an enormous parade ground with a tall mast on one side. If my memory serves me right, it would have been seventy or eighty feet tall. About ten feet below the top of the mast was a spar, which was a length of wood horizontal to the ground and fastened to the mast at its centre, so that about fifteen feet of the spar projected from the mast on either side. The spar was circular in cross-section. The top of the mast was covered by a gold painted wooden button. The mast was secured by rigging on two sides that ran from the point on the mast where the spar joined it to securing points on the ground several feet from the bottom of the mast. The rigging was in the form of several rope or wire ladders, so that it could be climbed. It was similar to the rigging you see in pictures of old sailing ships.

The Commanding Officer (CO) of HMS Collingwood stood on one side of the parade ground ('quarterdeck') with his guests, Officers and Senior Petty Officers behind him. We sat on benches to one side of the official party. There was another, shorter mast to one side of the CO. This mast was flying the 'White Ensign', the official flag of the Royal Navy.

A naval band was already in place on the parade ground and played throughout the ceremony. The ratings marched on to the parade ground in sections known as 'divisions'. They all bore rifles. Some were dressed in the naval costumes of the Nelson era and carried muskets. They were all ordered into line so that they faced the CO. They then 'presented arms' in a general salute. Next, there was a march past and the CO took the salute.

After this, the mast was 'manned' by ratings in white sailor caps, blue tops and white trousers. About a hundred ratings climbed up the mast so that they were equally spaced up the rigging and along the spar. One rating climbed up to the button and stood on it. He was known as the 'button boy'.

At the same time, the ship's guard marched to the mast that carried the flag. The 'colour party' section of the guard prepared the ensign for lowering by releasing the halliards but still holding them tight so that the ensign did not come down or flutter uncontrolled.

As the sun set, we were called to attention, a bugler played the sunset call, Officers saluted and the ensign was lowered in time to the bugle call so that by the time the call had finished, the ensign was in the hands of the 'colour party'. The ensign was then disconnected from the halliards and folded up and the guard marched away to the edge of the parade ground. The bugler then sounded the 'Last Post' whilst the band played the Evening Hymn. The ratings dismounted from the mast.

It might be hard to understand, but it is an emotional moment. I have been present at several Sunset Ceremonies and none of them has failed to be emotional. I particularly remember one on board 'HMS Tiger' in Manila, capital of the Philippines, in 1977. I was there as part of a British marine equipment business drive and 'Tiger' was there with three destroyers 'flying the flag'. We were invited to witness the ceremony along with senior Philippine naval officers, diplomats and the captain of a Thai cruiser that was in port. We had enjoyed a few drinks beforehand, but it was very emotional because it was so far from home and I felt so proud of the show that our boys put on. The Marine band was fabulous.

Speech Days and Visits.

I have mentioned above visits by the Lord Mayor of Southampton, the President of Southampton University Students Union and other dignatories. There were always lots of visits by other people who did not get formal attention but were shown round by nominated cadets.

In the Summer Term, we had two events on the lawn at 'Salterns', the home of the Director, Captain Wakeford. One was a garden party for local dignatories. The other was a ball with a big marquee and a dance band. All the local dignatories attended the ball plus whatever girls the cadets could muster. Invitations were sought after. Wakeford had a charming wife, Pearl. She took a shine to me and asked that I be her ADC at the garden party. I had to attend her all afternoon as she socialised and I carried her cine camera. She sent me a lovely thank you letter afterwards, which I still have.

The ball took place on the last Monday of term (we broke up on a Tuesday, don't know why). At the last minute, I had an order to report in full mess kit at Salterns to be ADC to Captain Wakeford. I had to wear a golden, tasselled cord over one shoulder and across my breast. You see them even now when Naval Officers are in full dress. It ruined my evening. I had to attend Wakeford all the time and hardly got a dance. Instead, I took a drink whenever I could from a bottle of sherry that was on a table where Wakeford greeted guests. I was barely standing at the end.

On Speech Days, the last day of term, we would get a visit from somebody distinguished in the Merchant Navy, Armed Services or education. There would be a formal passing out parade. Parents of cadets from all terms were invited. The Senior Term marched past the speech giver, who took the salute in front of the accommodation block, whilst the Intermediate and Junior Terms, lined the opposite side of the Quarter Deck. Then the Senior Term and parents retired to a room for the prize giving and speech. The prizes were always the same:

Chief Cadet Captain: a book called 'The Last of the Windjammers'.
Senior Cadet Captain Best Watch: a sea adventure book
Junior Cadet Captain Best Watch: a sea adventure book. I won this but can't remember the book, except that it was partly based in East Africa and had very racist language. Too unpleasant to want to keep.
Senior Cadet Captain Boats: a book.

Then the speech. In my year it was given by the Director of the Mates' and Masters' Courses at Warsash. He had been a Master at sea. He started off by saying that he had no idea what to say when asked but somebody advised him to talk about his early days at sea. He then talked about joining his first ship, where part of the cargo was lavatory bowls, which were loaded to huge hilarity from the 'wharfies'. On his last voyage as captain he went to Vanuatu in the Pacific, which is famous for vast quantities of 'guano', the droppings of sea birds. Guano was then a major source of phosphate for fertiliser. He pointed out that his career would seem to have gone backwards rather than forwards, so how could he offer advice to cadets just starting out? His speech was short and continued in much the same vein. My dad thought it was one of the best he had heard, and he had experienced many. It went down well with the cadets but Wakeford did not appear to like it. He sat with a stony face.

A State Occasion

Every October, the Missions to Seamen organised a service at St Paul's Cathedral for seamen. Missions to Seamen was a non-denominational religious charity that provided recreational, educational and accommodation facilities for British seamen in ports all over the world. Representative bodies of all three services and the Merchant Navy attended this service, including cadets from HMS Britannia (Dartmouth Royal Naval College), HMS Worcester, HMS Conway, Pangbourne and Warsash. Jacko Clubb was in charge of our party and I remember his words before we left Warsash early on a dark morning 'Make sure that you have all pumped ship before we leave'.

The Warsash contingent was made up of the Senior Term, so we were the equivalent of a platoon in the parade. We lined up in Fleet Street before marching down Fleet Street in column of threes and up Ludgate Hill to the Cathedral. We marched to the beat of a Guards band and one other band. There were huge crowds in the street. We were not told beforehand that it was a State Occasion and that this year the Queen and the Duke of Edinburgh were attending the service. So, the bands started to play, we marched off and the crowds were cheering and waving Union Jacks. It was very exhilarating. We were placed in rows in the cathedral and I was at the end of one row next to the aisle along which the Queen would process. As she passed, all the people in each row turned towards the Queen and bowed their heads. I had never seen such a beautiful woman and the occasion has burned itself in my memory. Shakespeare wrote these lines for John of Gaunt in Richard II: 'There is a divinity that doth hedge a king'. I was close enough to touch the Queen and, at that distance, you really feel the aura. Unforgettable.

I am not sure about the date for this next memory, but it is possible that it was in the afternoon after the Missions to Seamen Service. Whatever, around about this time, we attended a lecture in London by Alan Villiers, a noted sea adventurer and author. He was a qualified sea officer and had won the DSC when in command of a large landing craft during the Normandy invasion. He was extremely well travelled and later commanded a replica of the 'Mayflower' to commemorate the original Pilgrim Fathers' journey to America. He wrote many books and this illustrated lecture was based on a book called 'Indian Ocean' and concerned a voyage he had made a few years earlier in an Arab dhow from, I think, Aden to Zanzibar and back. He had a somewhat eccentric speaking style, a bit staccato and at times offhand. He would just throw away facts and was nonchalant about challenges he faced. Having reached Zanzibar, whose name is exotic enough, he concluded his lecture by saying 'and then we went back the way we came' or words to that effect. Nevertheless it was enthralling and the still photos were sensational when projected on a large screen. Definitely a larger than life character.

Carl Rosa Opera

In my Junior term, we were offered the chance to see the Carl Rosa Opera Company in Southampton. Carl Rosa were a touring company and I had previously seen them at Stratford. About half a dozen of us saw an evening performance of Gounod's 'Faust'. Whatever the quality of the performance, it was a very welcome break from normal routine. We never had a similar opportunity in my year. As with the Celebration Dinner (see below), this was such an unusual occurrence that, despite its normality for the rest of the population, it stood out for us.

Celebration Dinner

Senior Term, Warsash. December 1955.

My Senior Term decided to have a celebration dinner before we left Warsash. This would be a first and we were very apprehensive as to whether or not we would be given permission. To our surprise, permission was granted, and, unbelievably, we were left to organise it ourselves and no Officers would be present. We considered several venues and decided on the 'Dolphin', a somewhat ancient hostelry in Below Bar, Southampton. We were never asked how we were going to fund this but it must have been obvious that our weekly pay would not cover the cost. Maybe the Warsash staff had always known that our parents sent us extra money. We turned up in our finery and enjoyed a decent dinner and wine. I cannot remember how we got there or got back. There were over thirty of us, so going by bus could have been difficult if we wanted to travel together. I think we organised a coach there and back, which, again, would have added to the cost.

This event may seem nothing to later generations, but to my knowledge this was the first time that the cadets had organised a social occasion on their own, and not only that but outside the campus. We certainly felt that it was a big occasion. I can only hope that we were trail blazers and that succeeding terms followed our example.

CHAPTER EIGHT

Choosing a Shipping Company.

During the Senior Term, I had to choose with which shipping company I wanted to serve my apprenticeship. Most cadets had a good idea which one they wanted, usually based on the type of trade and which countries the companies traded with. Passenger liner companies and oil tankers were at the bottom of the list because they would not provide the breadth of experience required for examinations.

Initially, I was undecided. My Divisional Officer, 'Jacko' Clubb, had been a cadet and officer with the New Zealand Shipping Company. This company was a subsidiary of the Peninsular and Oriental Navigation Company (P&O). P&O was a prestige company and traded with the Middle East, India, Pakistan, South East Asia, China and Australasia. The name 'Peninsular' in its title came from its initial trading with the Iberian peninsula, Spain and Portugal, which were then also stopping points on the voyage east. The New Zealand Shipping Company (NZS) traded with Australia and New Zealand. P&O was what is known as 'pukka' and NZS was considered to be even more pukka. Pukka meant the maintenance of high standards in terms of dress, behaviour and standards of maintenance. It certainly provided a better standard of living for its crew than other shipping companies. All the accommodation was covered and surrounded in teak decking, whereas other companies had noisy, metal decks. Each officer had his own wash basin in his cabin, which was not common.

For some reason, NZS felt that not enough cadets from Warsash had applied recently for apprenticeships. I never understood this because its two cadet ships were disproportionately crewed by Warsash graduates. Whatever, Jacko gave the Senior Term a lecture on the 'finest shipping company in the world'. His lecture had its desired effect because four others and myself applied. They were John Tait, Peter Matthews, 'AN Other' and Peter Huguenin, who was Swiss. We went up one weekday to London for our interviews. The New Zealand Shipping Company had its offices in an imposing Edwardian block on Leadenhall Street, just a few doors down from P&O, the parent company. This was one of the only three times in seven years that I entered the head office. It had dark, oak panelling and we were led into a waiting room on the first floor. There were five people on the interviewing panel and I only remember the name of the panel chairman, Captain Moncrief. He was the Marine Superintendent of the company i.e. he had responsibility for the day to day running of the fleet and personnel. The panel were all middle-aged men and sat behind a large table with a green baize cloth covering it. I was placed on a chair in front of the table. It was the first time that I had faced such a situation. It was very intimidating and I felt in a daze for most of the interview, as though I was in another world. I was told that they had four places reserved for Warsash cadets. I was also told that Huguenin had already been eliminated because he was Swiss and NZSC only recruited British nationals. That was tough on old 'Huge' as he was competent and his choices would be limited. I was asked why I wanted to go to sea and why I was a Junior Cadet Captain and why the other applicants had not attained that rank. What does a seventeen year old answer to that? Anyway, a couple of days later all four of us were told that we had been accepted.

Before we left Warsash, the four of us were sent a letter from NZSC, via Captain Wakeford, advising that two of us would be joining 'MV'Rakaia' and two would be joining 'M V Durham'. Both ships were cadet training ships. Rakaia was in the UK and would be sailing before Christmas. Durham was still at sea, homeward bound, and we could not join her until sometime in January. We were offered a choice of which one to join. Captain Wakeford, without consulting us and before we had seen the letter, replied on our behalf that he was sure that we wanted to get to sea as soon as possible and would prefer to join Rakaia. He sent a copy of his reply for us to sign that we approved. All four of us were appalled at his presumption. Naturally, we would prefer to spend Christmas at home. We had no idea when we might do so again. Wakeford sent for us and read us the Riot Act and pushed a pen across the table for us to sign. We refused, he blustered but there was nothing he could do. I remember that he made a comment that there was no room for sentiment in the Merchant Navy. We sent our own letters expressing our desire to spend Christmas with our families. We had stood up to a bully and won. NZSC chose John Tait and AN Other for the Rakaia and Peter Matthews and I for the Durham. NZSC made the original mistake by asking us to choose. They should just have made the assignments and told us that was that.

A week later, in December 1955, I had passed out of Warsash, carrying with me two volumes that were to prove invaluable: the 'Bosun's Manual' and 'Nautical Tables', the latter of which contained logarithms and other tables that reduced the need for lengthy calculations in navigation.

PART THREE

The Maritime Environment

CHAPTER NINE

Working Environment in the UK Docks

Soldiers unloading in Royal Albert Dock during a dockers' strike. Note absence of mechanical handling.

Unloading meat in the Royal Albert Dock

Before I continue with my own experiences, I believe that it would be important to understand how merchant ships were loaded and unloaded (discharged) in the UK during the 1950s and early 1960s. I cannot offer a comprehensive view because my experience was mostly limited to London, the Bristol Channel ports and Liverpool. However, I believe that what I observed holds good for the whole of the UK port industry in that time.

London.

My experience in London covers only the Royal Albert Dock, which was part of a complex of three London docks known as the Royal Docks: Victoria Dock, King George V Dock and

Royal Albert Dock. They are on the north bank of the river and east of the development now known as Canary Wharf.

The Thames is tidal, which means that the river level varies with the tide. At low tide, there was not enough water for deep-water ships to navigate the river and to moor. The answer, in an era of growing trade and ever larger ships, was to build 'docks' that always contained enough water for ships to berth alongside and load and discharge without sitting on the bottom of the river. These docks were dug out by hand. They were connected to the river by locks. When there was enough water in the river, a ship entered the lock. The riverside gate was shut and the dockside gate was opened and the ship proceeded to her berth. For ships leaving the dock, it was done in reverse.

UK docks had warehouses alongside the berths, with enough space between the dockside and warehouse to enable cargo to be unloaded before being shifted into the warehouse. On the other side of the warehouses were railway lines. Ships would discharge on to the dockside, port workers called 'dockers' would move cargo into the warehouses and then onto trains or lorries on the other side. It was mostly manual work. Dockers, known professionally as 'stevedores' and to we sailors as 'wharfies', would load cargo in the holds into nets or onto wooden trays and these nets and trays would be lifted out of the hold and onto the dockside. In London, cranes were used but in many ports worldwide there were no cranes. Each cargo ship was fitted with 'derricks'. These are long, hollow metal tubes about one foot in diameter that are connected to derrick posts. These posts, about two feet in diameter, are placed on the deck, one at each corner of the holds. There are either two derricks or four derricks per hold. The derricks have a short post at the bottom end at right angles to the line of the derrick. This post fits into a 'pintle', a steel belt with a hole that was fitted on the bottom of the derrick post. This allows the derrick to swing in an arc once it has been raised. There would be a block at the top of the derrick post and one at the top of the derrick. Through these blocks were passed ('riven') wire ropes that enabled the derrick to be raised from its horizontal secured position to the height that was needed to operate. Another block was also fitted at the top of the derrick through which another wire rope was riven. One end of the wire was connected to a winch on the deck, the other had a hook on the end to attach to cargo nets. To load or discharge, one derrick would be positioned over the dock. Another would be positioned over the opening ('the hatch') to the hold. The cargo hook was attached to the ends of both derrick wires. To discharge, the hook was lowered into the hold, the cargo net was hooked on and the winch attached to the inboard derrick would haul the cargo out of the hold. Once clear of the hatch, the winch for the out board derrick would wind up its wire and the winch for the inboard derrick would slacken off. The cargo would then swing over the ship's side and would be lowered onto the dockside. To load, it was all done in reverse. Apart from the use of power, this was how ships had been loaded and unloaded for centuries. If cargo was crated, it had to be manhandled into the hold and manhandled out. Each net or tray would only carry about a ton. Given that a ship could carry thousands of tons, this method was time consuming and was also labour intensive.

When I joined NZS, there was not much mechanical handling equipment in use in the UK. There were fork lift trucks but they were few and far between. Stevedores moved cargo in and out of the warehouses using heavy duty sack trucks and, occasionally, electric flat trucks (see picture above of unloading SS Trevelyan). It was very hard work and they had to work fast. Much of the cargo we carried was in sacks and boxes that could be lifted by hand. Frozen or chilled carcasses would be loaded, carcase by carcase, into a net. Car parts would be crated and would be delivered to the dockside by lorry or train and then lifted onto the ship. In South Wales, Liverpool and Glasgow, we loaded sheet metal, lengths of metal and ingots. Sheet metal and ingots came on trays. Longer lengths and wire would be lifted by slings.

The UK ports were slow to introduce improved methods of materials handling. The main reasons were historical and the power of the unions, particularly the Transport and General Workers Union, the biggest union in the country. Dock labour had traditionally been supplied by stevedoring firms, who contracted with the ship owners. Dock workers worked for the stevedore firms, not the ship owners. Up to the Second World War, dockers worked on a daily basis. They turned up at the dock gates for work and were hired for that day. It meant that favouritism and nepotism ruled and many men received little or no work. There was no continuity of work. It was grossly unfair and demeaning. The National Dock Labour Board was formed in 1947 to ensure continuity of work, fair employment and that there were no delays in providing labour. As long as the docker had signed on with the Dock Labour Board, he was guaranteed a minimum wage, even if the stevedore firms still contracted with the ship owners to provide labour. The trouble was that the Dock Labour Board was a Quango and a monopoly and this system promoted inefficiency and over supply of labour. I recall that dockers would often sit in the holds playing cards. This was an accepted practice whereby one half of a gang would do the first half of a shift and the other half would do the remaining half. They also resisted change and were encouraged in this by the unions, who were more interested in rates of pay and full, even over, employment than the efficiency of the system. Hence, fork lift trucks were a rarity in the UK docks when I started, but were common place in the USA. The world was changing and new ships were being built that required different methods of cargo handling, particularly containers. London would probably have lost out in any case because the new, larger ships required deep water ports that could be worked at any state of the tide. But still they resisted and Rotterdam began to attract trade from London. London was what was known as an *entrepot,* a port where cargo would come from all parts of the world and then be transferred to other ships for delivery elsewhere. Rotterdam built a new port, Europort, to handle the new types of trade. Eventually, trade disappeared from the traditional UK ports and new container ports were built: Tilbury, Immingham, Felixstowe and Southampton.

On the other hand, working conditions were appalling. The work was hard and often resulted in accidents. There was no training and little or no safety precautions. The dockers provided their own clothing, which was always their oldest clothing and not cleaned. Dockers could work with chemicals one day and with food the next without changing their clothes. Protective clothing and equipment and 'Hivis' jackets were unknown. Dockers could not always rely on the unions to protect them and deal with their grievances.

The attitudes that hastened the decline of UK docks were commonplace throughout industry. Industries that I later worked in, particularly the printing industry, were rife with restrictive practices and resistance to change. Other industries and professions that resisted change to their disadvantage were ship building, coal mining, telecommunications, service industries, the NHS and teaching. It is no coincidence that in all cases the unions were over-powerful and that mining, telecoms, NHS and teaching were government monopolies. It took privatisation to restore technical progress. Unfortunately, where there is still a government monopoly and strong union representation (NHS and teaching) the old attitudes remain, principal amongst which is a sense of entitlement.

CHAPTER TEN

The New Zealand Shipping Company (NZS)

From now on, I will use words, terms and expressions that are common at sea but incomprehensible to a landlubber. Rather than explain everything in the narrative and bore you, I have included these in Appendices:

Appendix 1: Glossary of Naval Terms.
Appendix 2: Ranks and Responsibilities in the Merchant Navy
Appendix 3: Navigation

NZS History.

Pre-P&O Years

The New Zealand Shipping Company Limited was incorporated in 1873 in Christchurch, New Zealand, by a group of local farmers and merchants, who were dissatisfied with the country's existing shipping facilities and their inability to cope with the country's rapidly expanding trade. The company was initially administered from New Zealand, with input from a 'Board of Advice' in the City of London.

The new company began by purchasing four second-hand, iron sailing ships. At first, competition from existing shipping companies, particularly the Shaw Savill and Albion Line, was keen, but following a brief rate war, an agreement was made to establish uniform and viable rates of freight i.e. a cartel. These cartels were commonplace in the shipping world and were known as 'Conferences'.

In 1877, NZS was operating seventeen sailing ships under its own flag as well as a large number of chartered vessels. In 1879, the joint charter of a steamship with Shaw Savill demonstrated that, at the outset at least, a regular steamship service would have to be subsidised. Accepting this, the New Zealand Colonial Government provided for a subsidy of £30,000 on its joint contract with Shaw Savill and Albion and NZS in 1884. This contract ran for five years but was not renewed. Refrigeration was introduced and the second cargo of frozen meat from New Zealand was carried in 1882 in one of the company's sailing ships,

Mataura, fitted with cold-air refrigerating machinery, which machinery was supplied by a company called Haslam.

The company was reorganised in 1880 and financial control of NZS was transferred to London. In 1889, Edwyn Sandys Dawes (later Sir Edwyn Dawes, 1838-1903) acquired a controlling interest in NZS. It was the start of a connection between the company and the Dawes family which was to last until 1970.

Additionally to its United Kingdom trade, NZS made strategic alliances with other shipping companies, either as shareholders in a company or partners in a consortium, which were involved in trading with other companies and countries. An early example of this was the New Zealand & African Steamship Company (1902-1911), formed to take care of trade with South Africa. A Canadian connection, the Canadian-Australian Royal Mail Line (1901-1910), was a joint venture between New Zealand Shipping and the Union Steam Ship Company of New Zealand.

A much more significant corporate development came when NZS absorbed the Federal Steam Navigation Company in 1912 and with it a firm foothold in the neighbouring Australian trade. Federal Steam had been founded in 1892 when one Allan Hughes (d.1928) had acquired the remaining assets of Money Wigram & Sons Ltd (owners of the Blackwall Line of high-quality sail powered passenger 'frigates'), which had failed to make the transition to steam power. Federal Steam ships continued to fly the same house-flag and adopted the same English county names used previously by Money Wigram's ships.

The P&O Years

In September 1916, the Peninsular and Oriental Steam Navigation Company acquired a controlling interest in NZS. In spite of the change in ownership, both NZS and Federal continued to enjoy considerable autonomy with the latter's founder, Allan Hughes, becoming chairman of NZS in 1920.

The company continued to pursue joint ventures and, in partnership with Ellerman's and Port Line, the three companies formed the Montreal, Australia and New Zealand Line (MANZ) which operated from 1936 to 1971. MANZ carried cargoes between Australasia and the East Coast of the United States and Canada, which trade was also served by the American and Australian Steamship Line (1956-1971). In 1954 the Avenue Shipping Company Ltd was founded to augment the NZS and Federal Steam fleets when needed; otherwise its ships operated on tramping services. At the same time, NZS commissioned three vessels specifically for the MANZ Line trade: Whangaroa, Wharatane and Wharanui, henceforth known as 'Wh' ships.

NZSC made no attempt to advise new recruits of its history and current operations. Everything we learnt came from information passed on by fellow shipmates. Consequently, when we joined we were totally unaware that we might be involved with the MANZ Line, which meant a long period of fifteen months on one secondment. Would we have joined if we had known more? Were we at fault in not asking more questions? We were only 17 at the time.

Crusader Line (1957-1967), a joint service from New Zealand to the West Coast of the United States and to Japan (in partnership with Shaw Savill, Port Line and Blue Star) was another Pacific venture. Crusader would later become containerised as Crusader Swire Container Service, part of Overseas Containers Ltd (OCL). Finally the Dolphin Line (1967-1971) was a joint service formed of conventional cargo ships to supplement the OCL service; the partners were NZS, Scottish Shire and Clan Lines, Shaw Savill and Ocean Steamship Company.

The advent of the container ship (the Australian trade was one of the first to be containerised in the late sixties with the New Zealand trade following much later) and the rapid development of air travel presaged the end of the passenger/cargo liner in the 1960s and the conventional cargo liner in the 1970s. The subsequent absorption of New Zealand Shipping Company, Federal Steam Navigation Company and Avenue Shipping Company into the General Cargo Division of P&O in 1971 was seen as a natural development. The evolution of these changes was apparent during my time in the Merchant Navy. The changes in working practices that were evolving were a major factor in my decision to leave the Merchant Navy. As we shall see in the narrative that follows, the lifestyle that I enjoyed when I joined had changed considerably by the time I left.

For all practical purposes, in my time, NZS was actually two companies with a common management: the New Zealand Shipping Company and the Federal Steam Navigation Company. Officers and crew moved between ships of both companies as though they were one company and the Officers' uniform was the same for both companies. It was impossible to tell one company's ships from the other apart from the names and that NZS ships had yellow funnels whereas FSNC ships had red and black funnels with the company's badge on each side of the funnel. NZS ships had Maori names, usually of places although the passenger liners reflected female and male titles of tribal chiefs. FSNC ships were named after English counties that did not end in 'shire' i.e. Durham, Essex, Sussex.

Trade was predominantly with New Zealand and Australia plus some Pacific Islands. Outward bound, that is from the UK, we carried general cargo. Some of it was heavy – particularly from the Welsh ports and Liverpool. Heavy items would be tinplate, steel plate, iron ingots and steel wire. These would be loaded in the bottom holds. Other cargo included car parts in crates, known as 'CKD' or cars knocked down, TV and radio sets, alcohol and clothing. Coming home with imports, it would be frozen meat (mainly lamb), cheese, butter, wool, hides and fruit.

NZS had offered me an apprenticeship. This meant that I had to sign up for a period of three years and three months sea service. In return, NZS would train me to be a Deck Officer and educate me to pass my first exam for a Second Mate's Certificate Foreign Going. Both parties signed what is known as 'Indentures', which laid out the obligations of each party. I had to bind myself to good behaviour, including not frequenting 'taverns and alehouses'. It was all rather quaint but at the end of my apprenticeship, NZS had to sign a declaration attesting to my good behaviour and sobriety. The document was on parchment, which made it long lasting. We had a signing ceremony at the flat of my dad's best friend, Chris Rookes, who opened a bottle of champagne to celebrate. I signed, my dad signed and then Chris Rookes signed as a witness. We posted the signed document back to NZS together with a cheque for £120 from my dad. The £120 was evidence of my sincerity. For each year of my apprenticeship that I completed, my dad got a portion of the money paid back. At the end of my apprenticeship, NZS sent the balance of the money to my dad and the Indentures to me, which were annotated with the ships I had served in, the length of time served in each ship and a note as to my good behaviour and sobriety. I then presented this document to the

Ministry of Transport Examiners as proof that I had served my apprenticeship. I still have the Indentures.

My pay for my first twelve months would be ten guineas per month (£10.50) and all found. I did not have to pay for food and lodging but had to supply my own clothing and equipment. My pay went up every year by about £1.50 per month until I was earning £18 a month in my fourth year

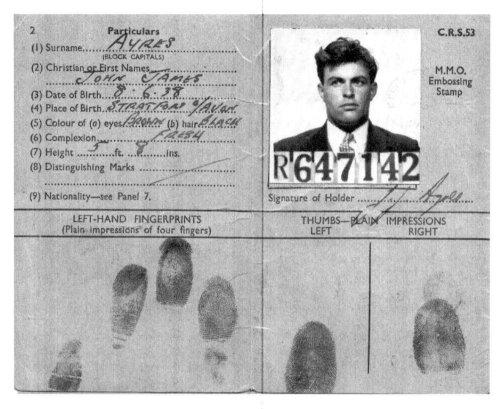

All merchant seamen had to have an identity card. Its purpose was twofold. Firstly, it confirmed that you were a bone fide seaman and exempt from National Service. Secondly, some countries, particularly the United States, required such a card. I don't recall ever being asked to produce it, even when I was 'marooned' in Galveston Texas, for 6 months. The one illustrated is a replacement for the first one issued. I was appointed as 4th Officer on the 'M V Whangaroa' in June 1960. This ship traded between Australasia and North America. Before we left the UK, one of the shipping clerks in NZS asked to see our cards to ensure we had them when visiting the USA. I had mislaid mine and the above was produced in a hurry. I was never asked to produce it.

I have relied almost exclusively on my memory for the events during my voyages. I believe that I have captured the essence of the events I have described even if the chronology and the places are not absolutely accurate. For instance, where I have said that the sequence of ports we visited was A, B, C and D, it maybe that it was actually A then C then B then D. Unless I have been absolutely sure, I have been vague about dates and have limited myself to mid-

April or such like. Additionally, any photos that I took on my old box Brownie have not survived, so that most of what I can reproduce are stock photos and those supplied by friends.

I had to wait until mid-January 1956 to be summoned to join a ship, which was the 'Rangitoto' in Royal Albert Dock, London. This dock still exists and is near what is now London City Airport. It is no longer used for shipping. NZS ships docked at Royal Albert Dock when loading or unloading cargo or passengers in London. The company had an office in the docks. 'Rangitoto' was one of five passenger liners that NZS owned : 'Rangitane',' Rangitoto', 'Rangitiki', 'Rangitata' and 'Ruahine'. The passenger liners traded exclusively between the UK and New Zealand and carried passengers and cargo. Rangitata and Rangitiki were over twenty years old but the others were built post-war with Ruahine being the youngest. They were all gradually taken out of service by the end of the 1960s and never replaced.

My first ocean going voyage was to be in the 'MV Durham', a cadet training ship, but she was not in port. So, I was berthed in the Rangitoto for a few days and had nothing to do apart from compiling a list each day of all the shore workmen who were on board carrying out repairs. These people included diesel engineers, boilermakers, sheet metal workers, painters, carpenters, joiners and lino fitters. All the public passenger areas were covered in a particular type of patterned lino. The high heels of lady passengers played havoc with this lino, which was replaced after every voyage. Getting the list of workmen was a thankless task because you had to chase all the different foremen all over the place, including the dockside, and you never got a complete answer. I think it had to be done for insurance purposes in case one of the workers was involved in an accident and there would have to be proof of where and when he was employed. Note 'he' as women were not employed on the docks at this time, except workers in dock offices.

RMS Rangitoto at Lyttelton South Island, New Zealand

CHAPTER ELEVEN

First Voyage.

My first voyage was not on the 'Durham'. She had still not arrived and the company decided that there was no point in letting us rot in London with nothing constructive to do. We were learning nothing. There were four of us apprentices on the 'Rangitoto' waiting to move to the Durham, together with three or four officers returned from leave and awaiting their next berth. One of these was John Hutson, who had just been Fourth Officer on the 'Rangitoto'. 'Hutty' was a very handsome man and I was told that he had been an unwilling victim of female attention during his last voyage. He was continually harassed to the point of young female passengers hammering on his cabin door to be let in whilst he was trying to sleep after coming off watch. This, as I later learned, was an example of a syndrome where passengers on ocean liners cast their usual inhibitions aside. It was as if being at sea was divorced from normal life and they could let their carnal desires have free rein. This syndrome has been the subject of a number of books, in particular one that had been recently published at that time: 'The Captain's Table' by Richard Gordon, who had also written the 'Doctor' books, which themselves were made famous in films starring Dirk Bogarde and James Robertson Justice, amongst others.

One of the apprentices waiting with me was Henry McCutchan. He was a farmer's son from Polegate in East Sussex. He was a younger son, so there was no place on the farm for him. His father had been married late in life to a Frenchwoman much younger than himself. His father was in his seventies when he had his two youngest children, Henry and his younger sister. The powers that be had decided that there was no point in us hanging around 'Rangitoto' with nothing to do. We were carrying out some duties such as reading the draft and keeping a log of workmen carrying out onboard repairs. Hardly a full time occupation and we spent much of our time in the West End of London. Henry and I were dispatched to the 'Cumberland', which was going, firstly, to Falmouth in Cornwall for dry docking and hull painting, and then to the Bristol Channel ports for loading. The Cumberland was a twin screw ship i.e. it had two propellers, each powered by a separate diesel engine.

Henry McCutchan and Scot Gilchrist

Proceeding down the Thames, I experienced the sensation of 'bumping along the bottom' for the first time. Where there is not much space between the bottom of the ship and river or sea bottom, it feels as though you are bumping along. Moving vessels create a vacuum as they disperse their weight. What happens is that the vessel appears to go up and down as it travels.

It was blowing a gale with snow flurries in the Channel. Henry and I stood watch for our first time and learnt how to take bearings of lighthouses and prominent points and then plot the bearings on a chart to 'fix' our position. This had to be done every twenty minutes in coastal waters and would be used as evidence if there ever had to be an enquiry following a collision or shipwreck.

The Chief Officer also gave me my first chance to steer the ship. The ship was steered from the 'bridge' by a wooden wheel, which was a circle connected to an axle by spokes. The axle was connected by cable to the controls of a steering engine positioned over the rudder at the stern of the ship. The steering engine operated hydraulically, which meant that the minimum amount of force was needed by the helmsman. In front of the wheel was a magnetic compass, which was a legal requirement, in case the ship's electrical system failed. On the front of the bridge above the windows was a gyro compass repeater. This is more accurate than the magnetic compass and is the one used to set a course and steer. In Merchant Navy ships, the ship was physically steered by an experienced seaman, known as the 'Quartermaster' when he is on duty. The Master usually decides the course to steer. The Quartermaster's job is to keep the ship on the designated course and to alter course as instructed by the Master, the Pilot or the Officer on watch. If you want the ship to go to 'port' i.e. left, then the wheel is turned to the left. Vice versa to go to the right i.e. starboard. Once the course is set, it requires constant vigilance by the Quartermaster to maintain course by small movements of the wheel to right or left. The calmer the sea and the wind, the easier it is to steer. There are times when it is possible so to balance the wheel that no correction is necessary for several minutes. This rarely happens. So, I had my first attempt whilst butting into a south-westerly gale with snow and the ship pitching and rolling. Shades of John Masefield and a 'dirty British coaster with a salt-caked smokestack butting down the Channel in a mad March gale'. Turning the wheel requires some force because of the tension on the steering cables. I managed half an hour before the Chief Officer decided I had done enough for the first time. Usually, the Quartermaster is changed every two hours, which is a long time to stay on your feet and concentrate. These days, ships have stabilisers and automatic steering. Courses are maintained better, which saves fuel, and there is a saving on manpower.

Two days after leaving London we arrived in Falmouth, which is at the mouth of the River Fal. It was a fishing port and had a ship's repair yard with a dry dock. It is the first deep water port on the eastern side of the Atlantic and was, therefore, the first port to be attempted by vessels in distress. This led to the development of the repair yard and a service base for deep-water tugs. The passage to Falmouth was my initial introduction to how slow sea travel is. We averaged about 15 knots per hour, or just over 16 mph. The Cumberland was a 15,000 ton ship and it requires a huge amount of diesel fuel and power to drive such a ship. If you try and make such ships go faster, the extra engine size and extra fuel needed makes them uneconomic. We went into dry dock at Falmouth and were there for about two days whilst the ship's hull was scraped free of barnacles and repainted. Henry and I were introduced to one of the characters in Falmouth. He was a Scotsman known as 'Jock' and he kept a famous pub called the 'Chain Locker'. He was only about five feet tall and explained that his lack of height was due to him walking from Scotland and being' worn down' en route. He claimed that he was six foot tall when he left Scotland. His pub was full of ships' memorabilia. Jock maintained that all we seamen would eventually marry in Falmouth and end up as 'artists' i.e. painting ship's bottoms in the dry dock.

When we left Falmouth, we sailed round Land's End and up the Bristol Channel to Avonmouth. This is the deep sea port for Bristol. Deep sea ships cannot get up the Somerset Avon to Bristol. We left the 'Cumberland' and were sent home for a short leave before joining the Durham in London. However, Durham was late and we were berthed in a variety of ships and carrying out menial duties until the Durham arrived.

From 'joining' the Rangitoto' in January until joining the Durham, we berthed in Officers' quarters, took our meals in the Officers' saloon and relaxed in the Officers' Lounge. This was a luxury that I did not enjoy again for over three and a half years. As with most adolescents, I did not appreciate this at the time.

CHAPTER TWELVE

M V DURHAM

The M V Durham was owned and operated by the Federal Steam Navigation Company. This company was a sister company to NZS and was operated by exactly the same management as NZS.

She was a 10,000 gross tonnage ship, which means that that was the amount of cargo that she could carry, not her actual weight. Merchant ships are always designated by the cargo carrying capacity in contrast to the Royal Navy, where the weight actually does mean the weight of the ship (this is known as 'displacement'). A ton of cargo was usually defined by the amount of hold space required. Lighter cargo took up more space and was charged by the amount of space required for carriage. If the actual volume of a particular cargo was less than 100 cubic feet per ton, then it was charged by weight e.g. steel and tinplate.

Durham was a twin screw motor vessel. She was fitted with two 'Sulzer' diesel engines, each driving one screw (propeller). Sulzer is a world famous Swiss company, which manufactures large diesel engines. Their marine engines were considered to be the Rolls Royce of marine diesels. Electricity was provided by a separate diesel generator. Another diesel engine provided power for the ship's pumps and the refrigeration pumps. She was built at Workman Clark in Belfast in 1934. The Durham was built from steel originally ordered for the 'Queen Mary' by Cunard at John Brown's Shipyard, Glasgow. Cunard had delayed the building because of the depression in the early 1930s. John Brown sold some of the steel ordered for the Queen Mary to Workman Clark. This steel was thicker than the usual steel used for shipbuilding, so Durham was very strong in comparison with other merchant vessels. She was fitted out as a cadet training ship and operated as such until the outbreak of World War Two. All the cadets were scattered throughout the fleet at the beginning of World War Two. It was considered too risky to have all the company's future officers in one ship with the possibility of being sunk. NZS lost over half of its fleet in the war, nineteen ships in total, and by the time I joined nearly all of the fleet was post-war built.

In the war, Durham had been the target of Italian human torpedoes in Gibraltar in 1942 and had been beached. It is believed that this was shortly after she took part in a convoy to relieve the siege of Malta. This convoy brought supplies to Malta just in time to enable the island to hold off starvation and continue fighting the Luftwaffe and the Regia Aeronautica (the Italian Air Force). The convoy was attacked by surface ships, submarines and aircraft. A later convoy called 'Pedestal' took place in August 1942. More than half the merchant ships were lost along with many of the Royal Navy escorts, including the aircraft carrier 'Eagle'. I believe that the film 'Malta Story', starring Jack Hawkins and Alec Guinness, covered that part of the war and included scenes illustrating the 'Pedestal' convoy.

Durham was eventually refloated and sent back to John Brown's for refitting. Meanwhile, NZS had bought a second-hand ship, M V Rakaia, and fitted her out as a cadet ship. She was a temporary replacement that lasted for over twelve years! Durham had been re-commissioned about two years before I joined and NZS kept both cadet ships in operation until a new cadet ship, the 'Otaio', was built and commissioned in 1958.

Durham had six cargo holds and each hold was divided into three decks. The bottom two decks were constructed to carry frozen cargo: meat, butter and cheese. These holds were insulated with rock wool between the ship's side and wood panelling. Refrigeration was carried out by a network of brine filled pipes, which were secured to the wood panelling. Brine is very salty water and has a lower melting point than fresh water. The brine was regularly pumped round the system from the refrigerating plant in the engine room. This type of refrigeration became obsolete shortly after the Second World War. It was replaced in newer ships by cold air blowers, which cooled down the holds more quickly and eliminated concerns about leaks. The top deck carried un-refrigerated cargo, except for No 3 Hold, where there were lockers fitted in the top deck. These lockers could carry chilled cargo e.g. apples and chilled beef. They were also used to carry alcohol, tobacco and cigarettes because they could be locked, hence the name 'lockers', which refers to any compartment in a ship that can be secured.

I joined Durham in early March 1956 in the Royal Albert Dock. I became a 'tripper', an apprentice on his first voyage. Once again, I was the lowest of the low. There were several other trippers: Peter Matthews (from Warsash), Scott Gilchrist and Hugh Perks (known as 'Reg') from HMS Conway,), Henry McCutchan, Robert 'Mackie' McGregor and Glenn Smith. Mackie's father was the Dockmaster in Falmouth i.e. he managed the repair yard.

The establishment was thirty cadets but we were four short. We were organised into Port Watch and Starboard Watch. I was in Starboard Watch. The senior apprentice was known as the Cadet Captain, who was John Rankin on my first trip. Under him were the Port Watch Captain and the Starboard Watch Captain. Our quarters were what would usually have been the after end of the top deck of No 6 hold. You entered this space from the after deck via a small deckhouse, which was aft of the hatch with doors on two sides. On top of this deckhouse was a magnetic compass and emergency steering wheel, so that the ship could be navigated from that position if the bridge was damaged beyond use. A companion way led down to the forward end of our quarters. The quarters ran around the ship's side. The centre of the space was a hollow steel square that led down into the steering engine. There was a corridor that ran around this structure.

It is easiest to describe the cadets' accommodation if I start with the ablutions. These ran across the after part and contained showers, wash basins and washing machines. We washed and ironed our own clothes, but not bedding, which was carried out by stewards in the ship's laundry.

The trippers were divided into two cabins that contained six berths and each cabin had a cadet senior to us in charge. These cabins were immediately forward of the ablutions, one on each side, Each cabin had one porthole in the ship's side. There was a small square between these cabins, bounded on the forward side by the structure described above and on the after side by the ablutions. The other cabins were on the port side. The Cadet Captain had his own cabin and wash basin. The Watch Captains shared a cabin with a wash basin. There were five other cabins, each with three berths. Each cabin contained double bunks with drawers underneath, wardrobes, a desk and a bench seat. It was cramped.

Lounge and cabin. These pictures are from the 'Otaio', MV Durham's successor, but those in the Durham were almost identical. Apprentices were especially posed in uniform for a brochure.

Under the companion way was a small larder with a kettle, where we could brew up. If you turned right at the bottom of the companion way, you came to our cabins. Turn left and there were two rooms: one was our lounge with tables, chairs, bench seats, a piano, a record player and a small library; the other was the school room. You might ask: where did you eat? Our mess was amidships on the starboard side. Halfway along the working alleyway was a companionway leading down into a space that contained a small vestibule, a pantry and our mess room. We also used the mess room for parties. This was the domain of the Pantryman, who was part of the Chief Steward's crew and reported directly to the Cook. Our food was delivered from the galley above via a dumb waiter in the vestibule. The pantry had a hot plate and warming oven, cupboards and a sink. The Pantryman dished out the food. He was assisted by a 'Peggy'. The Peggy was always one of the trippers and the trippers did a week's stint on a rota. The Peggy's job was mostly to clear up the tables, wash the dishes and clean the deck. Washing up for thirty people three times a day plus 'smokos' took up much time and was drudgery. A 'smoko' is a naval term for a work break when there was time for a drink and a smoke.

Our food was plentiful and nutritious but uninspiring and indifferently cooked. We knew exactly what food we were going to get on any particular day. In those days, refrigerated space for crew food was minimal. We only had fresh milk and fresh greens and fruit in port or for a few days after sailing. We had powdered milk, baked beans, root vegetables, canned green vegetables and tomatoes, canned fruit and condensed milk. Root vegetables were mashed, except with Sunday lunch, when we had roast potatoes with roast chicken. Fresh, crusty bread and butter were served at every meal and we ate three cooked meals a day. Breakfast was the best meal. We usually started with cereal or porage, and the cook could not mess up cereal, followed by bacon, sausages, scrambled powdered egg, occasionally kippers, toast and marmalade.

Lunch and dinner were almost identical menus. Sometimes we had soup followed by a roast or a stew and a pie or canned fruit for dessert. Cheese was available as an extra. The stew was always lamb and always greasy and you had to skim the top before serving. For us, the cook used the cheapest and fattiest cuts. Once you had cut the fat off the stewed meat, there wasn't much meat left. On Sundays we had 'centipede chicken', so called because it was always chicken legs, we never had breast. Chicken breasts were reserved for the Captain's and Senior Officers' tables. Salads were non-existent except for some weekends in port, when the galley staff wanted time off from cooking. Meals were washed down with tea, which was our staple drink. Tea was always served in mugs and we brewed up before work in the morning, then tea at breakfast, morning smoko, lunch, afternoon smoko, dinner and in the evening. If you were on watch at night, you made cocoa. Cocoa has long been a favourite in both the Merchant and Royal Navies for all ranks. It had to be made hot, sweet and thick enough to stand a spoon in it. You mixed cocoa powder, condensed milk and sugar and then added hot water. It was great for a cold night on the bridge.

The ship's domestic consumables and deck and engine room consumables were supplied by Duncan Wallet Ltd, a ship's chandler. A ship's chandler was a marine provision and hardware merchant. Duncan Wallet was owned by P&O. Wherever possible, P&O kept all its operations 'in house'.

Fellow Crew Members

Durham carried about ninety crew members.

Apprentices.

I was berthed in the starboard 'tripper's' cabin with Henry McCutchan, Peter Matthews and Scott Gilchrist. An apprentice on his second trip, called Warwick Lewis, was put in charge of us and berthed with us. Warwick and I struck up a partnership on the rugger team. He was fly half and I was scrumhalf. We spent hours discussing how to work together and then hours practicing ashore whenever possible. We became very effective together.

The other 'trippers': Glenn Smith, Mackie and Reg were berthed in the port cabin. I can't remember how 'Reg' got his nickname, but it may have been because a Reg Perks had opened the bowling for Worcestershire for the past twenty years or more, had played for England, and was a friend of my father. Bob MacGregor reckons that he was named after Reg Harris, a world champion professional cyclist. Reg had no sporting interest but the name stuck.

Other apprentices on their second trip were 'Dinghy' Lane and 'Jack' Hawkins, both of whom had been at Warsash with me, but in the term ahead of me. Other cadets I can remember were Peter 'Headdown' Barr from Portsmouth, Malcolm 'Ginger' Eglon from Yorkshire and Davey Pounder from Hartlepool. Davey's father was a sea captain and he only saw his family for a few weeks each year. Davey had a wicked sense of humour and he and Ginger were inseparable. Sadly, Davey died at the age of 22 from choking on a piece of steak. 'Monty' Banks was an apprentice on his third trip. He had been transferred from the Rakaia and eventually became one of my best friends. Cedric C Hufflett ('Huffie') was also on his third trip and was the rugger captain. 'Pongo' Eastwood was on his fourth trip when I started. Tony Batt was, I think, a second tripper and a jazz aficionado. Charles Turner was on his fourth trip and his family lived near Henry McCutchan. Charles and Pongo were bosom friends. Geoff Morris, a Yorkshireman, was on his second trip.

I recall that John Rankin called all the trippers to a meeting and told us very sternly that we not only had to work hard but to work quickly.

I can't remember other names and lost contact with all my shipmates shortly after leaving the sea.

Crew members with most connection with the Deck apprentices.

My first master was Captain Albert 'Dig' Hocken. He was in his late fifties and had a reputation for eccentricity. I think he was called 'Dig' because he called everybody 'Dig'. Dig was a teetotaller but did not enforce his ideas on any one. He was keen on sport and always took time off to play golf whenever he could. He used to sunbathe in the nude on a reclining board. He was married late in life to an Australian, Melbe Downer. She was a member of a powerful political family: one Australian Prime Minister and several Cabinet Ministers and MPs. They were members of the Australian Liberal Party, equivalent to the UK Conservative Party. Melbe was a charmer and used her connections in both Australia and New Zealand to attract the most desirable young ladies to our parties and dances. She was a member of the Primrose League and the Navy League and an organiser of the Ladies of the Harbour Lights of Adelaide. Melbe always joined the ship as soon as we arrived in Aussie or NZ and stayed with us until we left for 'home'.

Captain 'Dig' Hocken, taken on the 'Otaio'.

Dig left us when we were in Galveston for repairs in the spring of 1958. He was replaced by Captain Barnett. Barnett was much younger and more sociable with his Officers than Dig. Barnett was in the Royal Navy Reserve and had served on warships during the Second World War. On one of his postings, his Captain was a Bowes-Lyon and a kinsman of the late Queen Mother. Barnett recounted a conversation he had had with Bowes-Lyon, who stated: 'The problem with you Merchant Navy types is that you don't realise that you are expendable.' This was somewhat inappropriate because the Merchant Navy suffered over 30, 000 fatalities in the Second World War, which was a higher proportion of those serving than in any of the Armed Forces. I suppose the point is that we Merchant Navy types will avoid danger where possible. It is ingrained in our culture.

Chief Officer: On my first trip, John Beavis was Chief Officer He was a man with a big smile and a sense of humour. After that trip, he was promoted to Master and left us. For the next two and a half trips we had a man called Frankie Field, who lacked social graces and was difficult to get on with. He was to be married after his second trip with us and when we were in the Channel on our way home, his future mother-in-law telephoned the ship via radio. She proceeded to lay down the law to him about what he had to do for the wedding and in no uncertain terms. For whatever reason, the radio officer had linked the call to all the repeater speakers in the ship. We heard every word to our enormous enjoyment. He left us in Galveston, Texas (see my Fourth Trip). The next Chief Officer was Rollinson, who stayed for the rest of my time on the Durham and was much more amenable. He was firm but fair and could enjoy a joke. He even called in on our pub with his wife when he was on leave.

The first Second Officer we had was Dick Hannah. He was tall and imposing but we had little to do with him. On my first trip, we carried two dogs as cargo. As he was the Cargo Officer, Dick had to exercise them round the boat deck every day. They had their kennel on the boat deck and it stank. Dick was already drinking too much. He used to take what purported to be a flask of water on watch. One night, one of the apprentices took a swig only to find it was pure gin. He left after my first trip and was promoted to Chief Officer on another vessel, before joining 'Otaio' when she was commissioned. Desmond Jones, who had been the Training Officer, was the Second Officer at the beginning of my fourth trip. I do not recall the names of the Second Officers for the rest of my time on the Durham.

The Third Officer. Charles Treleavan was my first Third Officer. He was tall, well built and very keen on rugger. He played second row and organised the ship's rugger team. Whenever possible, we trained ashore after work several days a week. He was succeeded on my second trip by a guy who was somewhat vain. He grew a beard and continually stroked it. John Needham succeeded him on my third trip.

The Fourth Officer. John Needham was the Fourth Officer on my first trip and had been Cadet Captain on the Durham's previous voyage. He was a very earnest person and had taken his Second Mate's Certificate three weeks after leaving Durham and had taken no leave. His appointment to the Durham was his first after passing his exam. He was a nice enough guy, but I always thought that he was a bit uncertain about himself with regards to his rank in relation to us. He became Third Officer on my third trip and then Instructional Officer on my fourth, after which he was posted to the other cadet ship 'Otaio'. So, he spent the first five or six years of his sea life on a cadet training ship. He had no experience of working with a deck crew entirely composed of experienced seamen. I always thought that that was a mistake. David Evans, who had served his time on the Rakaia, succeeded him as Fourth Officer on my third trip. More of David later.

Instructional Officer ('Schoolie'). He was responsible for our academic training and his rank was equivalent to Second Officer. I do not believe that the Schoolie received any training in educational techniques. The Schoolie on my first trip was called Nash. Accuracy was his watchword and he was somewhat austere. He was always immaculately dressed. He looked as though he used more starch in his white shirt and shorts than the rest of us put together. Because of that and he was very thin, he was known as 'Auntie Hatrack'. Desmond Jones succeeded him on my second trip and became the Second Officer on my fourth trip. 'Dainty Desmond' was a much more cheerful character and tried very hard to establish a relationship with the cadets and you felt you could confide in him. John Needham succeeded Des, when Des became Second Officer.

Deck Crew

We spent much of our time performing the duties of seamen. Because we carried these out, the Durham did not need to carry a full complement of deck crew as required by the Merchant Shipping Act. We did have a couple of Able Seamen. There were two Junior Ordinary Seamen, known as 'Peggies', on their first or second trip, whose main duties were cleaning and serving food to the Petty Officers. Our contacts with other members of the crew were principally with the Deck Petty Officers, who taught us what we needed to know as seamen and who supervised our work. They were: the Bosun, Lamptrimmer, Ship's Carpenter, Physical Training Instructor ('Pete') and Training AB.

My first Bosun was Charlie Nicholls, a Norfolk man with a wicked sense of humour. Schadenfreude was probably invented by him. I learnt so much from him. He was transferred to another ship after my third trip and his replacement was a Londoner who became a real friend and teacher. Our Lamptrimmer was a native of Stornaway in the Outer Hebrides. When he was drunk, usually on the last day in port, he was incomprehensible. But, he taught us all we needed to know about paintwork.

The Ship's Carpenter, a Scouser, always had one apprentice as his assistant, known as 'Chippy's Mate', who was appointed by rota. In that way we learned about his duties. On my third trip, he was replaced by a little Irishman, who was a real character. He made me think that leprechauns really existed.

My first 'Pete' was ex-RAF and a highly intelligent man. He was obviously vastly over-qualified intellectually for the job. His duty was to keep us fit and physically occupied in our spare time. He was keen on basketball and arranged matches ashore and to see the 'Harlem Globetrotters' during a tour they made of New Zealand. He used his time in New Zealand to search out other job opportunities and got a job as a lecturer at Wellington University. His successor, on my second trip, was ex-Royal Marines and a bit too full of himself at first. He thought that he could institute a regime of physical training similar to the Royal Marines Commandos. He was astute enough to abandon it very quickly because it simply did not fit. As it was, he was very enthusiastic and joined in vigorously with games like deck hockey, which was quite dangerous.

The Training AB taught us essential seamanship techniques: rope work, wire work and canvas sewing principally. My first training AB ('Bob') had been captured by a German naval raider early in World War II and then sent via a prison ship to a prisoner of war camp in Germany. His experiences were hair-raising and made his hair go white overnight. He and his fellow prisoners were made to disguise the prison ship during the hours of darkness. This meant being lowered on a stage over the ship's side and painting it whilst the ship was travelling at full speed and pitching and rolling with the waves. He was with us for a couple of trips. He was replaced by 'Topper' Turner, who had been an AB on my first trip. He stayed with us until I left the Durham.

'Bob', my first Instructional AB

Doctor. It is a legal requirement for ships with ninety or more crew to carry a doctor. We had a doctor, Colonel Campbell, a retired Army medico, and this was his way of getting round the world for free. His rank was equivalent to Chief Officer. He gave us lectures on first aid and keeping healthy. We were a very healthy lot and did not take up much of his time. He did experience one or two incidents out of the ordinary. The Captain's Steward had a tattoo on his forearm and he was concerned that it was too obvious when he served at table. I don't know how he did it, but the Doc carried out procedures that reduced the prominence. The other incident was more amusing, but not to the perpetrator. One of the Stewards was homosexual. He reported to the Doc one morning with a painful and embarrassing problem. He had pushed a wineglass into his rectum and could not get it out. The Doc managed to retrieve the wineglass. The Doc probably also treated some cases of sexually transmitted diseases, but I was unaware if he did.

PART FOUR

The First Two Years

CHAPTER THIRTEEN

First 'Durham' Trip

First Trip.
Front Row: Scott Gilchrist, Hugh 'Reg' Perks, Bob 'Mackie'McGregor, Henry McCutchan, Peter Matthews, John Ayres, AN Other (known as 'Cowboy').
Second Row: 'Pongo' Eastwood, Charles Turner, AN Other, John Rankin Cadet Captain, AN Other, AN Other, 'Monty' Banks.
Back row: Davey Pounder, Cedric Hufflett, Warwick Lewis, AN Other, Pete 'Headdown' Barr, 'Jack' Hawkins, Geoff 'Moonbeam' Morris, AN Other, Glenn Smith, Tony 'Dinghy' Lane, Tony Batt, Malcolm 'Ginger' Eglon.

March 10th 1956 to September 3rd 1956.

In this chapter, there will be much along the lines of 'what did we have for breakfast?' I have done this to show what we did on a daily basis as apprentices with the expectation that I won't have to repeat it in the chapters concerning later trips.

Before we left London, we were taken on two interesting outings designed to increase our knowledge. The first was to a rope works in Deptford, where we saw how rope was made from raw sisal grass. The rope shed was several hundred feet long. I believe that this site is now on the tourist trail and is near to Greenwich. Secondly, we went to the Whitechapel Bell Foundry. This is world famous and we were fascinated to see how bells were cast. Every ship has to carry a bell in the bow area. It is still used to ring out the time at night and the lookout uses it to warn the bridge of any lights or other objects he sees. One ring if the light is to starboard and two if it is to port.

Just a short description of how we were paid. This was a time before employers paid salaries directly into bank accounts. People were either paid weekly or monthly in cash or by cheque.

This was impractical for seamen. It would mean carrying large amounts of cash on board for weekly or monthly payments and would mean payments when men were at sea. The opportunities for loss and other problems were too great. Traditionally, seamen were paid off at the end of each voyage with accumulated pay less deductions for items purchased on board, principally cigarettes, alcohol, clothing and postage. How as provision made for those with dependants or wishing to save? The answer was 'Remittance'. Each seaman decided at the start of each voyage how much money he wished his wife, for instance, or parent to have paid by the shipping company. A Remittance Order was signed by the seaman and sent to the recipient. Each month, the recipient presented the Order, by post, to the shipping company who then paid the agreed amount to the recipient. In this way, married me ensured that their wives and children had sufficient living expenses and others could save for study leave etc. It was cumbersome but it worked and I always had money in hand on leave or for study.

Seamen were also entitled to an issue of cigarettes, tobacco and alcohol at duty free prices. This was usually limited to a weekly supply ordered from the Second Steward. If I remember correctly, we were allowed 200 cigarettes a week and spirits or beer depending on your rank. Only Officers were allowed spirits, all other ranks had to make do with cans of beer, usually McEwans in the case of NZSC. Apprentices were the lowest in the pecking order, limited to 2 cans of beer a week, if over 18. The cigarette and tobacco allowance was equal for all ranks. A bottle of gin cost 8 shillings and 6 pence (42 pence in decimal) and 200 Players cigarettes about the same. A double gin and tonic ashore then cost about the same as a duty free bottle. Most of us contrived to save enough cigarettes to take home to loved ones on leave.

We left London in March 1956 bound for Fiji and New Zealand. We carried sheet metal, wire, crated vehicles and a host of other items that were not manufactured in New Zealand. At that time, New Zealand had a serious balance of payments problem and the government placed severe limits on imports. The policy of the NZ government was that imports must be paid for by exports, which were primarily agricultural with little or no added value. New Zealand had a very small manufacturing capacity virtually limited to woollen clothing and dairy products. There was some coal mining providing coal for energy along with hydro-electric power. New Zealand had to import all its oil-based products, which made the balance of payments worse and which imposed severe limitations on electricity supply. In the 1950s there were frequent power cuts. New Zealanders had a higher standard of living and wages than the UK and full employment but there was not the variety of activities that were current in the UK. No TV, limited number of theatres and so on. But, it has a wonderful climate, crops grow well and bigger than in the UK, awesome scenery, including the Southern Alps, and a long and varied coastline. New Zealand is about the size of the UK and its population was then just over 3 million. There was so much space for everyone and it encouraged an outdoor life and an emphasis on sport.

After we left the Channel, we sailed south westwards across the Atlantic. Our first port of call was to be the island of Curacao in the Caribbean off the coast of Venezuela. This island is part of the Dutch Antilles, a series of small islands and what was then known as Dutch Guiana on the north coast of South America (it is now known as Surinam). Curacao had an oil refinery processing crude oil from Venezuela, which then produced the cheapest crude oil in the world and still has the largest reserves. The New Zealand Shipping Company ships always bunkered here on the outward journey and sometimes on the inward. We carried enough fuel for some twenty thousand miles of ordinary sailing. To reach Curacao, we sailed past the Azores in mid-Atlantic and then made for a gap in the Caribbean Leeward Islands chain between Guadeloupe and Dominica. This was not the most direct route but the best for the prevailing currents and weather. Note that ships with engines take just as much notice of weather and sea conditions as sailing ships.

By the time we had passed the Azores, the weather was warm and sunny, so much so that I got sunburn on my back. No suntan lotion in those days! We spent our days in three ways:

Classroom.

The cadet ship had two principal purposes. One was to train the apprentices in the culture of the New Zealand Shipping Company and its trade. The other was to educate the apprentices to take their first exam at the end of their apprenticeship: Certificate of Competency as Second Mate (Foreign Going). Not all the apprentices had been to sea school, so this education was their first introduction to maritime subjects. The school room regime was rigorous and we were penalised by loss of privileges if we did not give our all. There was no room for slackers and it would have been unfair on the others if one apprentice did not try. The subjects covered were: maths (Including spherical trigonometry), physics, astronomy, navigation, chartwork, signals, English, meteorology, ship construction and mechanical drawing. The 'schoolie' would also set us home work, which had to be presented weekly.

I can't remember at what time of day we attended class, but our class time was fixed and the time allocated to the other duties was always subordinate to the classroom time, except for those on 'watch'. Classes were Monday to Friday whether we were at sea or in port.

Deck Work

Superstructure maintence. Each outward voyage, we washed the main superstructure paintwork with 'sougi'. Sougi is caustic soda diluted with water. You need a strong solution to clean outdoor paintwork at sea. Salt in the atmosphere is very harmful to paint. Sougi is a marvellous cleaner and removes all kinds of dirt and grease. It also keeps your hands clean and seamen would use it sometimes before the end of a voyage to get rid of any ingrained dirt and grease, although I would not recommend constant use. We repainted the white superstructure on the outward journey and sometimes on the homeward. We used four inch brushes, which are hard work to use all day. The paint was known as 'Dense White', was leadless and came in five gallon tins. It was thick and had to be diluted with 'thinners', usually white spirit. This was the Lamptrimmer's job and he sometimes did not use enough thinner, which made painting hard work. The thinned paint was poured into painting 'kettles', which were saucepan shaped and made of metal with a carrying handle. They could carry about a pint and a half of paint. These were our paint pots.

Other superstructures and metal, painted objects. We would also clean regularly the deckhouses between holds, anchor windlass, winches, after deckhouse, railings, bulwarks and mooring bitts. Painting these depended on the time available.

Deck maintenance. We regularly scrubbed and 'holystoned' the wooden decks. The Bridge, Boat deck, the Officers' deck, the after deck and the working alleyways were covered in teak decking. The latter two were battered and grimy after loading and unloading. We used sand, 'holystones' (which were the same as 'bumpers' but with a stone instead of a wood base) and plenty of sea water using hoses attached to hydrants that were strategically placed around the ship. These hoses would also be used for fire-fighting, if necessary. Sometimes, we used sand and canvas cloths, scrubbing away on our knees.

Scot and Geoff Morris: holystoning

We would also be employed on other maintenance jobs such as replacing worn out rope and wire. In the Pacific, on the outward journey, we would 'black down' the running rigging, of which more later.

Throughout my time, there was little regard for Health and Safety. Except for lifejackets, there was no provision of protective clothing. If you worked aloft, i.e. in a 'bosun's chair', or over the side on stages, there was no safety harness or lifeline. The only time I recall any additional safety measures was the provision on deck of horizontal ropes at waist level to hold onto during exceptionally bad weather. Robert Louis Stevenson referred to them as 'Long John's earrings' in Treasure Island. Our first Training AB (Bob) advised us to have one hand for the ship and one hand for ourselves. Damned good advice, as we learned.

c. Watches.

If you were on the watch rota, you worked four hours on and eight hours off. Therefore, those on watch were divided into three groups or 'watches'. As the three watch system only required twelve people, those not on the watch rota worked during the day: 7 a.m. to 5 p.m. We rotated the watches weekly, so you would expect to do at least one watch every three weeks. Each watch was led by, usually, an apprentice on his last trip. He would assist the Officer of the Watch and, accordingly, learn his duties and skills. He stood the full four hours of the watch and was excused other duties during his week on watch. The rest of the watch was composed of three others who would rotate as quartermasters (two hours per watch), lookouts (night time only) and any other duties needed. They would usually be drawn, one each, from the third, second and first trippers. If you were on watches but not otherwise required, you would work on deck.

I was taught a salutary lesson whilst on lookout before we got to Panama on my first trip. I was first lookout on the 'Midnight Watch' and had just taken over from the second lookout on the Evening Watch. One of the duties of the Officer on Watch immediately on being relieved at night was to inspect the decks, which he did by walking round the decks fore and aft. This was to ensure that all was secure and that nothing had been broken or come adrift. Mostly, this was just routine but it was essential if the weather was bad, providing that it was not so bad that you could not go on the foredeck. The lookout was in the bow next to the ship's bell. There was a vertical pipe that came out of the anchor locker and which was capped at the open end. It was sited so that you could sit on the top of the pipe and still see over the bow. I was sat there when the Third Officer (Charles Treleaven) made his rounds after being relieved. I did not hear him approach or see the beam of his torch, so I was startled when I heard his voice 'Are you comfortable', to which I replied 'Yes, Sir!' Bollocking followed. No sitting on watch as you were less likely to fall asleep when standing. Only the Master was allowed to sit whilst on watch. There was a wooden armchair with long legs on every bridge so that the occupant could see clearly through the wheelhouse windows. This was the Master's chair and woe betide anybody who had the temerity to use it. The Master had this concession if he was required to stand watch for long periods, for example if we were in a very busy shipping lane, there was fog or other bad weather. In those circumstances, the Master would often be on watch for several hours, so the chair was a necessity. This was when he earned his money and his experience mattered.

Every Sunday morning we had a church service, led by the Captain. We paraded on the boat deck in best uniforms, were inspected and then moved to our lounge where we held a short service: a hymn and a couple of prayers. Before breakfast on Sunday, we washed down all the outside decks with hoses and brushes. This hygiene routine is standard in all UK and American ships and goes back several centuries. There was no deck work or classwork on Sundays. After church parade, the day was ours free, unless we were on watch. It was a time for deck sport, writing letters and 'make do and mend' i.e. repair damaged clothes. I became an adept sewer and once made a complete working shirt out of two otherwise old shirts that had rotted across the back. I was complimented by the Bosun on my work, particularly my neat stitching.

One morning every week, we had boat drill. All crew members were allotted to a lifeboat. We had four lifeboats, one on each side, that were each fitted with a mast and sail and could be rowed. Each lifeboat carried basic stores and equipment to keep the crew alive for a short time: water, hard biscuits and boiled sweets were the basics, plus a bailer to scoop unwanted sea water out. Each crew member kept his lifejacket in his cabin. The stores and equipment do not appear substantial but there was a limit on space and in most cases shipwrecked seaman did not have to wait long for rescue. Also, the lifeboats were intended as more of a refuge than a boat designed for a long voyage. Once launched, the accepted procedure was for the lifeboats to stay together and not move away from the last position of the ship. The further you moved away, the less likely that rescue ships would find you.

The capacity of the lifeboats was such that the lifeboats on each side could carry all the crew. If the lifeboats on the port side, for instance, could not be lowered, then the starboard lifeboats could carry everybody. This came about after the 'Titanic' tragedy. The 'Titanic' had enough capacity in all of its lifeboats for all the passengers and crew. Unfortunately, after hitting the iceberg, the 'Titanic' was no longer on an even keel. The ship had leaned over on one side, what is known as 'listing'. This meant that the lifeboats on the other side could not be lowered. The result was that there was only enough lifeboat space for half the passengers and crew. Following this tragedy, the regulations were changed so that the lifeboats on each side have to have the capacity to carry all the ship' occupants.

Each lifeboat was commanded by a Deck Officer. That was the law under the Merchant Shipping Act. At sea, the drill was short: mustering each crew at the correct boat, checking all were wearing their lifejackets and then hoisting out the boats on the davits, of which there were two to each boat, at the bow and the stern. Davits are like a small crane and are pivoted on the deck so that the head (top) of the davit can be swung out and over the ship's side. The boats were stored on chocks on the deck. The boats were attached to the top of each davit by a block and tackle. When the boats were swung out over the side, they could be lowered. At sea, we only lowered as far as the Officers' deck and then raised them, swung them inboard and secured them. Lowering and raising was electrically powered but could be done manually if there was electrical failure.

In port, the boats were lowered to the water with the crew on board. Then we practiced rowing the boats, raising the mast and sailing. It was OK doing this with experienced seamen and a crew of apprentices, who knew what they were doing. Other crew members, stewards in particular, were often useless and showed no inclination to learn what to do. They did not seem to understand how important it was. Similarly with fire drill, which we did every two or three weeks at sea. We had very primitive equipment, just powerful hoses, sprinklers and hand held extinguishers. We had no really effective breathing apparatus. It consisted of an asbestos helmet attached to an air hose. There was no pump for the air hose and we had no protective clothing.

The weather was uneventful and got hotter and hotter. As soon as we were past the Azores we wore tropical uniform, which was our standard uniform until we were between Fiji and New Zealand. For a tripper, everything we did was new and absorbing and there was always a lot of skylarking, particularly in the showers after work. Water, water, everywhere! This was not always good news for the trippers who had the job of keeping the ablutions area clean. Every evening, the Chief Officer inspected all our quarters. Trippers, as well as cleaning their own cabins, cleaned all the 'public' areas on rota: ablutions, lounge, kitchenette, classroom and corridors. Consequently, we had less free time than others.

In our free time, we played deck cricket and deck hockey, using a puck similar to an ice hockey puck. We rigged up nets on the starboard side of Nos. 4 and 5 hatches. There was enough space for a full length wicket and runs were scored by the batsman hitting the ball past lines painted on the wooden deck. The ball was made of line wound tightly round a solid core. It was very hard and came off the deck at awkward angles. We wore pads but no other protective gear.

On Saturday nights we had a film show. The screen was rigged over the chippies' shop between hatches 4 and 5 and we brought up chairs to sit on, with the Officers sitting above us at the end of their deck. That was when we drank our beer ration – two cans a week. Generally, the films were of good standard. I remember we once had 'Richard III' with Laurence Olivier. Usually, the films were exchanged by the agent in one port or another, but sometimes the exchange gave us films we had seen before. On one occasion, we exchanged films and a library at sea when we met another NZS ship, using what is known as a 'Breeches Buoy'. The lounge had a record player, but you could not use it at sea because the vibration from the engines and propellers was too much – the needle jumped all over the records. There were no CDs, tapes or digital players then. Some people had a radio but you needed a long wire to try and fasten it to the ship's metal rigging, which then functioned as an aerial. More often than not, we were too far away from land to pick up radio signals and there were no satellites.

You soon realised how isolated you were at sea. No radio contact when you wanted it and no newspapers. Occasionally, the Chief Radio Officer would put together a news bulletin from items he had gleaned on watch, but even these were skimpy, far from comprehensive and lacked detail. If anything broke, you either mended it there and then or did without. Sometimes this isolation was awesomely beautiful, particularly in the Pacific night when there is no cloud and the sky is full of stars and the sea is like oiled silk. We often had dolphins playing with us. They would do acrobatics and jump across in front of the bow. Sometimes we would see whales. In the right season, there would be meteors (shooting stars). But, it was rare to see another ship and if we were passing islands, we were never close enough to see people or animals. Passage is slow, merchant ships travel at economical speeds so as not to use more fuel than is necessary. The Durham travelled between 320 and 340 miles a day.

And so after ten days we had crossed the Atlantic, passed through the Dominica Passage and into the Caribbean. Winter is the best season in the Caribbean. It is drier and cooler and there is no worry about hurricanes. A day after the Dominica Passage, we reached Curacao. The bunker station where we refuelled is on the north of the island and some distance from the main town, Willemstad. It isn't much of a harbour, just a jetty with pipelines. Once we had berthed, and it was night time, there was nothing for the deck crew or stewards to do. Bunkering was operated and overseen by the Engineers. It took several hours and we were gone by breakfast. On a cliff nearby was a little stone fort. The legend is that the 17th Century pirate, Henry Morgan, kept women there for his pleasure and that several leapt to their deaths rather than succumb. Henry Morgan was a very successful pirate and, generally, operated with the connivance, if not active financial support, of the Government. Eventually, he became Governor of Jamaica and was knighted by Charles II.

Then we sailed along the coast of Venezuela and Colombia for a day or so before arriving at Panama. This was the first exotic place I had been to. Panama lies in an east/west direction between Colombia and Costa Rica. After the break-up of the Spanish Empire, it became part of Colombia in 1813. It is about three hundred and fifty miles long (east to west) and twenty miles wide (north to south). It seceded from Colombia in 1903 with support from the USA, who then proceeded to build the Panama Canal at the narrowest section of the country between the Caribbean and the Pacific. On completion of the canal in 1914, the USA wanted a safe area so that no outside body could interfere with the operation of the Canal. The Americans saw the construction of the Canal as a major strategic enterprise. It enabled the USA to move its Navy from the Atlantic to the Pacific, and vice versa, without going round Cape Horn and provided better sea connections between the Pacific West Coast and the Mexican Gulf and Atlantic coasts. The USA negotiated a treaty with Panama that established a Canal Zone along the length of the Canal with a width of several miles. It was administered as a sovereign area by the USA. The Panama Canal Company did not employ native Panamanians. Most of the manual labour came from the British West Indies. All the Canal Pilots were American.

We arrived at the port of Colon in the afternoon and anchored. Colon is the Spanish name for Columbus. Columbus (or Columbo) is an Italian name and Christopher Columbus came from Genoa. We had to wait until the next morning for a convoy to go through the canal. I was on the four to eight watch at the time and received a call from the Fourth Mate to go up to the bridge. All of a sudden, the heavens opened and it rained as I have never seen rain before. It hit you physically and I was wet through before I got to the bridge. Fortunately, I just had on a pair of swimming trunks under my oilskin coat and a pair of wellies. I soon learnt that it rained like that regularly almost every afternoon in Panama.

The process of anchoring has a definite procedure. It is not just a case of dropping an anchor to the bottom wherever you want to stop. Each ship has two anchors, one on each side of the bow. Usually, they are what is known as 'bower anchors'. A bower anchor consists of a central, cast iron stock and an attached 'bower'. At the top of the stock is a large eye, to which the anchor chain ('cable') is fastened by a shackle. The bottom of the stock has a horizontal hole through which the 'bower' is placed. The 'bower is a length of cast iron with an arrow head shape at right angles at each end. Thus the bower can swivel around the bottom of the stock and stick into the sea bottom. You need to ensure that the ground will hold i.e. that the anchor will not 'drag'. A mixture of sand and gravel is ideal.

When not in use, the anchor is secured outside the bow at the upper end. The construction of the anchor allows the bower to swivel so that it is snug on the bow. The cable leads through a hawse pipe in the bow bulwarks and is then would around a windlass with the cable on the other side of the windlass leading through the deck into the chain locker below.

When anchoring, the Master commands the ship, assisted by the Officer of the Watch. The Chief Officer is stationed at the bow and responsible for the lowering of the anchor and securing the cable after the procedure. The chippie mans the windlass. The Chief Officer may decide to be assisted by other crew members such as an apprentice, an AB or an Officer not on watch. The ship proceeds at dead slow until it almost reaches the desired position. The engines are stopped and then put into slow astern to stop the ship. Ships have no brakes, so going astern is the best way to slow and stop forward movement. Once in the correct position, the Master signals to the Chief Officer to let go. The Chief Officer orders the chippie to release the anchor, which he does by releasing the windlass brake and gravity then lowers the anchor to the sea or river bottom. When the anchor hits the sea bottom and the cable is vertical, the Chief Officer signals the Bridge that the cable is 'up and down'. The Master then orders 'dead slow astern'. This pulls more cable from the locker and the weight and velocity of the ship encourages the bowers to swivel and grip the bottom, thus making the anchor secure. When enough cable has been 'paid out', the engines are stopped and the anchor brings the ship to a stop. The ship is held secure both by the anchor digging into the surface and the weight of cable that has been paid out. If the anchor was left 'up and down' the chances are that the anchor would not have bit into the sea bottom and the ship would have been in danger with no engines working. There also has to be enough cable to allow the ship to 'swing' with changes in the tide, current or wind. Consequently, care has to be taken not to anchor too close to other vessels.

'Up anchor' is the reverse process. The vessel goes dead slow ahead until the cable is up and down, engines are stopped and the anchor is winched up and secured.

Whilst at anchor, the Officer of the Watch takes frequent bearings on shore objects to check that the anchor is not dragging and the ship remains stationary, allowing for the swing because of tide, current and wind.

At Colon, we received our first mail of the voyage. Generally, we received mail at all ports. Before sailing, we were given a list of ports, with dates, we expected to call at, and the names and addresses of the shipping agents at each port. We passed this onto our families and friends so that they could keep in touch by air mail. Air mail had comprehensive world coverage by this time and we could be confident of receiving recent letters. On arrival at port, we handed in our mail to the Chief Steward's office. The Second Steward was responsible for stamping and dispatching. The cost was taken from our pay at the end of the voyage.

In the morning, a Canal Pilot came on board. He took complete control of the ship. It is the only part of the world where the Pilot is superior to the Master. Normally, when a Pilot comes aboard, this entry is made in the log: 'To Commander's Orders and Pilot's Advice'. Legally, this means that the Pilot advises the Master on what to de next and the Master gives the necessary order. In practice, this is a clumsy procedure and the Pilot will pass orders directly to the relevant member of crew eg. changes of course to the quartermaster and changes in engine speed to the Officer of the Watch. The Officer of the Watch keeps a movement log to record the Pilot's orders and the passage past landmarks.

With the Pilot on board, we joined a convoy and entered the first series of locks. The Canal is not level. It is actually two canals, one on the Caribbean side and one on the Pacific. In the middle is a lake, Lake Gatun. This lake is artificial and was formed by damming the Rio Chagres as part of the construction of the Canal. At its formation, it was the largest man-made lake in the world. It is about ninety feet above sea level, so you have to go through a set of locks to reach the lake and then another set on the other side. These locks are an engineering marvel and run entirely by electricity. Power comes from a hydro-electric plant at the dam that formed Lake Gatun. The ship is towed in to the lock by electric locomotives, called 'mules', on each side of the lock. There are three locks in each set. The first lock is filled with water up to the level of the second and the ship is then towed into the second lock. The process is repeated to go from the second to the third lock. Once the third lock has filled up, the gates open and the ship sails into the lake. There you wait while the convoy going in the opposite direction passes you and you can proceed to the other side of the lake and commence the same operation in reverse. This brings you to the Pacific side. You have to go in convoy because the locks are not in pairs. You can either have ships going down or up, but not both at the same time. It is a very impressive operation.

Panama Locks

During the Canal passage, the ship is moving slowly or stationary whilst the main engines are operating. It becomes very hot in the engine room because there is no draw of air through the funnel and the fans cannot cope. Therefore, all engine room crew get an issue of lime and rum to thin the blood.

We were not allowed to work on deck during the canal passage, therefore we were limited to watch duties and the classroom. It meant that we had more free time than usual. We tried to fish when anchored in Gatun Lake, but without success. It was reputed to be crocodile infested, but we never saw any.

In 1977 the USA was forced by international pressure to give up the Canal Zone and pass ownership to Panama. US President Carter signed a treaty that gave the Canal Zone back to Panama in 1979 and the Canal itself on December 31st 1999. I suspect that the US government no longer wanted the responsibility and expense of maintenance. If I remember correctly, there were concerns that the Panama Canal Company was no longer a going concern and the Canal was not wide enough or deep enough to accommodate the larger ships that were being built. There has been continual discussion about building a larger canal through Guatemala, which was the original idea before the Panama Canal was built. Nevertheless, the Canal has been the principle source of revenue for Panama since 1999.

During my sea time, I experienced and heard a few stories about the Panama Canal. Here are three of those that I think are the most interesting:

First Story: We used old bunting to clean and polish brasswork. Bunting is the coarse material used to make flags. Scott Gilchrist and I were cleaning the bridge brass work during our first passage of the Panama Canal on the Durham. Some of our old bunting was a torn-up 'Stars and Stripes', the national flag of the USA. Americans have an attachment to the Stars and Stripes as their national symbol that we do not have with regard to the Union flag. It is the equivalent of the Queen to some extent in their hearts and minds. When the Canal Pilot saw what we were doing, he went berserk. 'I don't care what you do with an old flag, burn it, trash it but, PLEASE, don't use it for cleaning brass. That's sacrilege'. I have rarely seen anyone so upset without resorting to physical violence.

Second Story: This concerns the most famous ballet dancer of my age, Dame Margot Fonteyn. She had married one Roberto Arias, a member of a prominent Panamanian political family. In 1959, the Arias family had been thrown out and exiled. They planned an armed coup and Margot went out to give support. The coup failed and Margot was arrested along with her husband. Her husband had been badly wounded and was now paralysed from the waist down. Eventually, he and Margot were released and allowed to leave Panama. She had reportedly been picked up by the Panamanian Army whilst trying to escape through the jungle. The papers at the time had made it a big story worldwide. On the next canal passage I made after the event, I asked the pilot for the full story. He said that she had never been in the jungle. She had been arrested in the bar of the Panama Yacht Club because the Arias had bungled their attempts at bribery.

Third story: This concerns a certain Captain 'Montgomery-Smythe' and was told to me by an engineer, who had been on a ship captained by Montgomery-Smythe. We were both on the 'Whangaroa' when he told me the story. 'Monty' was a glutton and grossly over-weight. He was also vainglorious. He had hyphenated his middle name and his surname to sound more important. He was not a nice man. On this occasion, his ship had just taken on board the Panama Canal Pilot. The pilot climbed up to the bridge, extended his hand and said 'Good Morning, Captain Smith'. Monty replied 'The name is Smythe' to which the pilot responded 'Smith or Smythe, Shit or Shite, it's all the same to me, Cap!'

For some unknown reason, we berthed overnight at Cristobal, the port of Panama City, the capital of Panama. We had no cargo to deliver there. Cristobal is the Spanish form of the Italian Christoforo (Christopher). Our shipping agent and Dig Hocken arranged for us to have a tour of Panama, which is reputedly the oldest European-founded city in America and where half the country's population live. A coach was arranged to take all the cadets who were not on watch. We set off in the evening with the Fourth Officer as chaperone. Well, the tour we had was not what Dig thought he had arranged. The tour guide decided that what a group of virile young men wanted was not the normal sightseeing tour. The first stop was a bar on the outskirts of the city. It was large, empty and uninviting. If I remember correctly, it had a dirt floor. The chairs were fold-up metal frames with wooden slats for the seat and back, such as you used to see around town bandstands, outdoor cafes and the like. Two women appeared and offered us drinks. One was a large, black lady and the other was a very skinny Native American woman. Their ages were indeterminate. They offered their 'services' somewhat crudely. We declined despite the urging of the tour guide. We returned to the coach and the guide obviously thought we needed something more sophisticated. We pulled up outside this large villa which had a large neon sign 'Villa d'Amor' (The House of Love). In we went and were surrounded by a bevy of gorgeous women. The Villa d'Amor was, we were told, the premier brothel in Panama and was legal. It was explained to us at some length that all the 'ladies' had regular medical examinations and were guaranteed clean. However, it was a Monday and the girls did not work on Monday although the establishment was open for drinks. In any case, we could not have afforded the girls. After a couple of drinks, we were ushered out and ferried back to the Durham. Thus ended our life enhancing tour of Panama.

Next day we entered the Pacific. This is the longest leg of the voyage to either Australia or New Zealand. It takes three weeks. The course steered is decided by the Master. Usually, if you are going from East to West, the course is more or less south-westerly, depending on whether the ship is going to Sydney, Brisbane, Auckland, Wellington or Christchurch (South Island, New Zealand). This general direction took advantage of favourable currents and good weather. Going in the other direction, i.e. from West to East, the course follows what is known as a Great Circle. This is the shortest distance between two points on the globe known as the Earth. The course is firstly eastwards and takes you into the Roaring Forties, an area between 40 degrees South Latitude and 50 degrees South Latitude. The Roaring Forties are so called because a westerly gale blows nearly all the time and the sea is very rough. But, with the wind behind, you make good speed and after about a week, the ship gradually steers more to the North East and warmer and calmer latitudes until Panama is reached. The Great Circle route is not used for the East/West passage because you would be heading into the wind and waves all the time.

On this trip, Dig Hocken decided to sail close to the Galapagos and then past the Marquesas Islands, which are roughly mid-Pacific. We did not see the Galapagos because we passed them at night. There was much excitement about the Marquesas because UK ships rarely visited. We passed close enough to see a waterfall. Then it was on to Fiji.

In the tropical regions the Pacific lives up to its name. Long, sunny days and quiet nights. Very little cloud so that the night sky is brilliant with stars. Calm seas with a slight rolling swell that could be quite soporific. There was little difference between day and night temperatures, largely because of the constant sea temperature, which was around 85 degrees Fahrenheit. We had no air conditioning and relied on 'scuttles', which we pushed through the portholes, to improve air circulation. These were like old-fashioned coal scuttles without a bottom. They were supposed to catch any breeze generated by the speed of the ship. As we were at the stern, which curved inward, the effect was minimal.

Any painting we had not finished was completed before we started on the big maintenance job. This was called 'blacking down' and consisted of overhauling and repairing the 'running' rigging needed for cargo work, the wire 'springs and the 'standing rigging'. We would allocate two or three days for this work. All the rigging needed for the cargo derricks was taken down and spread on the decks. We inspected all the wire cabling to see if repairs or replacements were needed, then we 'blacked down' the wire. This involved spreading a preserving mixture along and into the wire. This mixture consisted of fish oil, tar, candle wax and whatever other ingredients the Lamptrimmer could think of. It was very messy and, where the decks were wooden, the decks were covered with canvas tarpaulins. Also, when wire is used frequently, it frays and the sharp, frayed parts can inflict nasty gashes. There were wire cables that we could not 'send down'. These were those used for the standing rigging that supported the masts and the block and tackle that were attached to the 'heavy derrick'. This was a derrick mounted at the rear of the base of the foremast so that we could lift a heavy piece of cargo that the normal derricks could not. A normal derrick had a safe working load of 2.5 tons, whereas the heavy derrick could lift ten times that. Blacking down this equipment meant sending somebody aloft in a 'bosun's chair'. This was a piece of wood about 18 inches long and six inches wide with two holes at each end. Rope would be rove through the holes at each end and then joined above the wood to form a triangle. The top of the triangle was then joined to a halliard, which itself was rove around a block high up in the rigging so that the chair could be hauled up and down. It was always a senior apprentice, dressed in a boiler suit, who would do this job. His reward would be an extra can of beer. His white boiler suit would be black by the time he finished. There was no way it could go in the washing machine and scrubbing was no good. What we did to clean it was to tie a line to it and throw it over the stern and let the ship drag it through the water. The friction got most of the blacking off but the boiler suit was never pristine white afterwards.

The fore deck was all that part of the main deck between the superstructure and the bow. It was metal and painted red. You've guessed it, here was another painting job. However, this time the Chief Officer and the Bosun decided that it would be a good idea to remove all the accumulated paint and start afresh. We did not use paint stripper or use mechanical means. Why use labour saving methods when you have young and healthy apprentices to do it? So we set to on a job that actually took three trips to complete. The process is called 'chipping' and you use a 'chipping' hammer. This is a hammer whose head is shaped like two blunt chisels. You hammer away at the paint and the paint eventually gives up and chips off. One of us took turns to help the process by banging the deck with a sledge hammer, which is called a 'maul' at sea. The sun was overhead, temperature in the high eighties and dust everywhere. After we had cleared several square feet, the Lamptrimmer gave us fish oil to spread over the bare metal. After the oil had dried, we then painted it with 'red lead' (a rust resistant) and finished up with two coats of red paint.

This first Pacific crossing introduced me to a facet of Durham life that was to last until my fourth trip and led to a prolonged stay in Galveston, Texas, in 1958. We had to stop the engines twice because one or two of the cylinder liners cracked and needed replacing. This was a big job and took several hours to carry out. Until November 1957, it never happened in bad weather during my time.

We played lots of deck cricket on the Pacific stretches because the weather was so good and organised matches: Port Watch v Starboard Watch, Apprentices v Officers, Apprentices v Ratings. Dig Hocken fancied himself as a leg spin bowler and revealed himself as a genius at cheating. He always bowled from so wide of the crease that the batsman could not see him until the ball arrived in front of him. Totally illegal. And if Dig called 'Howsthat' you had to be out. Also, when he was batting, he could never be out unless the ball knocked his wicket down and, even then, he would cry 'No Ball! This was my introduction as to why the Master was often referred to as 'God' in the Merchant Navy. The Master's position and decisions could not be questioned. It allowed Masters to get away with outrageous behaviour, indulge their prejudices and accentuate their eccentricities.

Another game was deck hockey or 'shinty'. We played it in the same netted area alongside Ns 4 and 5 hatches where we played deck cricket. We used a puck like an ice hockey one instead of a ball. It was a vicious game, made even more so by the confined space and we had no shin pads or other protective gear. Life as an apprentice was not for the faint-hearted.

All NZS ships had a demountable swimming pool. It was a canvas cube supported by a metal frame. Once in warm waters in the Pacific or Indian Oceans a pool would be erected on the foredeck alongside No 2 hold and filled with sea water. Although it was not large, we did play water polo on occasions. My experience was that it was more used on the Durham than on the other ships I sailed on.

And so, we wended our slow, slow way across the Pacific until we reached Fiji in mid-April.

CHAPTER FOURTEEN

ON THE COAST

'On the Coast' was a generic term meaning time spent in Australasia and nearby territories.

Fiji

Fiji is an archipelago 1,000 miles north of New Zealand. It is part of a great sweep of islands that stretches southwards down the western pacific from the Aleutians in the north, through Japan, the Philippines and then southeast and eastwards through the Solomon Islands, Fiji, Tonga and Samoa to Tahiti and Pitcairn. Together with Papua New Guinea, the Solomon Islands, Tonga and Samoa, Fiji forms the geographical area known as Melanesia. The area is volcanic and prone to earthquakes and is not for nothing known as the Pacific Ring of Fire.

Fiji was then a Crown Colony and was ruled by a Governor, appointed by the Queen. He had an elected, advisory council to support him. The soil is fertile and the climate is agreeable. It does not require much effort to exist through fishing and gathering. Hence, the original inhabitants had developed a relaxed life style. Coconut palms are plentiful and the products (coconut milk, coir and copra) are exported in large quantities.

We were due to berth at Suva, the capital, which is on the largest island, Vita Levu. Immediately before arriving, we prepared the hatches for cargo work. This involved removing the outer layers of canvas covering the hatches and raising the derricks so that cargo could be worked. This was a practice carried out before arrival at any port, except for London. On leaving port, we reversed the procedures to make the hatches and cargo gear secure for sea.

On arriving at or leaving port, we were allotted either to the forward berthing party or the after berthing party. The forward party was in the charge of the Chief Officer and the Second Officer commanded the after party. The Third and Fourth Officers were stationed on the bridge to support the Master and the Pilot. Before arrival, the two parties prepared the hawsers and wire springs for making the ship fast to the wharf. Hawsers and springs were laid out along the deck so they would flow easily without obstruction. Heaving lines would be attached to the free ends. A heaving line is made of lighter material with a large 'knot' at one end to give it weight. The heaving line was then coiled so that a coil was in each hand of the thrower. On the command of the Officer, the thrower 'heaved' the two coils towards the berthing party on the dockside. The dockside party then hauled on the heaving lines until either the hawser or the wire spring had passed through the 'leads' and was clear of the ship and hauled onto the dockside. A 'lead' is a hole in the bow bulwark through which a hawser can pass. It is in line with a winch to enable the hawser to be paid out or hauled in. Each hawser and spring had an 'eye' at the end, which the shore party could place over a bollard. The ship's parties wound the onboard hawser or spring around an electric winch or windlass, which then hauled in the slack. The hawsers and springs were then permanently secured to on board bollards known as 'bitts'. This required, first of all, removing the hawser or spring from the winch or windlass. If the winch or windlass was just put into reverse to release tension, the hawser or spring would go slack. To avoid this, a 'preventer' was wound round the hawser or spring between the windlass/ winch and the lead. The other end of the preventer was secured to the deck. The windlass/ winch was then put in reverse and the preventer 'nipped' the hawser/spring, thus keeping it taut . In the old sailing ships, the person who handled the preventer, was a boy seaman known as a 'nipper'. This is the origin of 'nipper'. Once the hawser/spring was nipped, it was taken off the windlass/ winch and secured around a bitt. The nipper then released the preventer. On leaving port, the shore party released the hawsers and springs on command from the Bridge. The deck parties then hauled them in and stowed them.

At some ports, particularly those where space was tight, tugs would be used to manoeuvre the ship into the right berthing position or to facilitate departure. This involved additional work for the berthing parties, who had to pass towing hawsers to the tug or tugs.

Suva is not a large town, mostly one main street with smaller streets off it and then countryside. Most of the shops were run by Hindus. In the late nineteenth century, European colonists decided to grow sugar cane but they could not persuade the native Fijians to work on the cane farms. So, they imported Hindus from India. As had happened elsewhere, the immigrant's descendants took on businesses in which the natives were not interested. Consequently, all the commercial activities were in Hindi hands and the Fijians were left with their landholdings and Stone Age lifestyle. Eventually, this led to conflict about how Fiji should develop when it became independent in the mid-1960s. As the Fijian Defence Force and its officers were predominantly formed of native volunteers, the native population ruled the roost for a time until a concensus was achieved, but not until after a civil war. But, that was long after our visit.

There was one substantial hotel, The Grand Pacific. The writer, Somerset Maugham, had described it as 'a large morgue with everything and everything'. It was still like that when we visited. I went in once and it was like a tropical old peoples' home – all cane furniture and no atmosphere. I found a bar at the side, which was actually reserved for the natives. I sat down and was immediately surrounded by native Fijians with huge smiles on their faces. They were surprised and delighted that a white man had come to their bar. Fijians are by nature friendly and hospitable. The Queen had recently visited and they were so pleased that she had been. Fijians are very loyal to the monarchy and Fijians still volunteer for our Army.

At Suva, I experienced for the first time the saying 'had to get used to his land legs'. For any ladies reading, I have experienced the earth moving. During a long sea voyage on a ship without stabilisers, the seafarer adjusts to the ship's movement without realising it. On going ashore after a voyage, the seafarer is unused to a solid platform and experiences the odd sensation that the earth is moving. Gradually, the sensation subsides and is felt more acutely by 'first trippers', to whom it is a new experience. On subsequent voyages, the mind expects this phenomenon and adjusts quickly. Seafarers who have spent long years at sea, and particularly on small vessels, habitually walk with an exaggerated gait ashore, with the body above the waist moving from left to right and back with each step. It is known as 'the western ocean roll'. It is often difficult to walk alongside such people without them barging into you. I remember the wife of my dad's barman saying that she always walked behind him or in front. He had spent over twenty years in the Royal Navy as a signalman, often on small ships.

On one trip ashore, we met a 'beach comber'. Essentially, a beach comber is a bum and this man was also a 'remittance man' i.e. his family paid him to live abroad because he was an embarrassment. Anyway, he got us an invite to an evening 'kava party'. Kava is a root from which an aromatic drink is made by immersing the root in water and then squeezing it. The drink is supposed to be mildly hallucinogenic. The Pacific Islanders make a great thing about holding these parties. Guests have to bring presents. It was suggested that we bring cigarettes.

We took WD and HO Wills 'Gold Star'. These were made in Fiji, sold in paper packs of five, were dirt cheap and tasted awful. Anyway, the fags were enough to guarantee our entry. We sat on the ground cross-legged in the open. The drink was in a large earthen bowl and was ladled out into coconut shells cut in half. It was a bit like the old Hollywood westerns where the pipe of peace is passed round at Native American gatherings. We did not have individual coconut shells. One shell was passed round and you took a large sip. This went on for about an hour and I was getting bored. In any case, we had to get back to the ship by 9.30 pm and made our excuses and left. Legend has it that you are a bit shaky when you get up. None of us were affected and I suspect that the shakiness has more to do with sitting cross-legged for a long time.

The shipping agent organised a coach trip for us to see what the interior of the island looked like. Despite the palm trees, it reminded me of the Cotswolds. We stopped at a clearing where there were a number of round mud huts with palm leaf roofs. Families lived here and showed us round. Everything was sparse but very clean. The head man demonstrated how to open a coconut. He had a length of wood with a sharpened point stuck in the ground. He rammed the coconut onto the pointed wood, which opened up a hole. Then we drank the milk through the hole. It was delicious and fresh. Then he held the coconut in one hand and used a cleaver to cut it open with one cut. If I had tried, I would probably have cut my arm off. It was very impressive. The huts were on a hill with a stream and a natural pool at the bottom. We had lots of fun jumping in and out and the water was lovely and warm.

Ceddie Hufflett, Coconut Gatherer

We played our first rugger match as the ship's team against a club called 'Suva Spitfires', some of whose players had, reputedly, recently represented Fiji against the All Blacks. Some people remember the Fijians playing bare footed, but I think they have confused this with watching some children playing a few days later. They dwarfed us and we were beaten but not by much. It had rained heavily and most of the pitch was ankle deep in water, so the match was foreshortened. I recall that Charles Turner scored a try and he seemed to skim over the water as he ran.

Next day, we played cricket on the same ground. It had miraculously drained but the wicket was coir matting because of the state of the ground. We watched some children play rugger once. They were aged about six or seven and most of them did not have boots, but they were very enthusiastic and could run fast.

Before I left home for this voyage, I knew that I would be visiting Fiji. My mother and her friends wanted me to bring home coral and grass skirts. I never saw a grass skirt in Fiji but coral was on sale. It came in a variety of delightful pastel hues. I bought some in a gift shop. It was sold in a basket made of leaves, possibly palm, maybe rush. Several of us bought such baskets. The colour faded to a dirty white before I arrived back home. We did not realise that coral is a living organism and that it had died soon after we bought it. I hope that this trade has been outlawed. Coral is endangered and must not be considered a trinket. I am ashamed now of my ignorance.

Fijians are naturally big and often run to fat. The traditional hair style for men and women piles the hair on top of the head and adds about six inches to their height. The smallest member of our crew was a pantry boy called Henry Bones. He was on his first trip. He went ashore on our last night but didn't turn up for work in the morning. Nobody knew where he was and we were preparing the ship to leave. He turned up mid-morning in a very groggy state. He was helped along the wharf by a Fijian policeman. This guy was over six feet to start with plus his traditional hair style, so he was about seven foot tall overall and weighed fourteen stone or so. He wore a military-style jacket and a traditional Fiji skirt. The skirt was white with a blue hem. The hem was zigzagged. He also had the biggest grin you ever saw. Henry was not much over five foot and would trouble the scales to make seven stone. The contrast was so great that everybody fell about laughing. He was lucky that the police had found him because the ship would have left without him.

Fijian Policemen

On our last night, we went to a dance. It was mostly Fijians and one large girl took a fancy to Glenn Smith. He couldn't get rid of her and had to run off with her chasing him down the street crying 'Come back, white boy, I love you!' Fijians are pretty relaxed when it comes to sex, as are many Pacific Islanders.

We had crammed a lot into a few days and were sad to leave. It had been a great experience and the exotic location and people had made a great impression on a boy fresh out of England. It was very beguiling.

NEW ZEALAND

The original New Zealanders were South Sea Islanders (Polynesians), who discovered New Zealand about 1,000 years ago. They arrived in dugout sailing canoes fitted with outriggers. The Polynesians were wonderful seamen and navigators. They travelled long distances with amazing accuracy by their knowledge of the stars and wind and sea conditions. All without the benefit of technology.

It is not sure if these people arrived complete with wives and families or if men arrived first and then went back for their families. One issue still to be solved is that Polynesian journeys tended to be with the wind. Their craft were not well adapted to sail against the wind. Whatever their origins, they liked what they saw and settled. They would have arrived first in North Island and it would have been the biggest land mass they had ever seen and also with hills and mountains of an unaccustomed height. There was a continual cloud mass over the high ground, so these people called New Zealand 'Aotearoa', the 'Land of the Long White Cloud'. They called themselves 'Maori', which means a native of that place. They flourished and numbered several hundred thousand by the time that Captain Cook became the first European to set foot there and chart its coastline.

The first British settlers arrived in the late eighteenth and early nineteenth centuries. Unlike the Australian penal settlements, all these settlers were volunteers. There was tension and the Maoris defended their land tenaciously and violently. These so-called 'Maori Wars' ended with the Treaty of Waitangi in 1840. The Maoris accepted the sovereignty of the UK in return for the retention of their own property and equal rights. There is some doubt that the Maoris entirely understood the terms of a written treaty because they could not read or write. Whatever, it established a consensus between the Maoris and the Europeans and a recognition of equal rights that has lasted, although there have been tensions. The Maoris have always had equal voting with the Europeans and there has been a Maori Prime Minister. There has been much intermarriage which makes it difficult at times to determine if a person is Maori or European. Just look at photos of the All Blacks. Whatever, they are all 'Kiwis'

The population of New Zealand in the mid-1950s was just over 3 million and I believe was composed equally of Maoris and Europeans.

New Zealand has the distinction of being way ahead of other countries in the granting of voting and pension rights. Women were granted the vote in 1893. It was the first country to do so and twenty five years before the UK did the same. Additionally, the voting age for women was the same as for men from the outset. Also, in 1898, the right to an Old Age Pension was established in the Old Age Pension Act. In 1938, the NZ Parliament passed the Social Services Act, which established a universal health service. However, the medical profession insisted on continuing to charge those who could afford it and it took several bouts of legislation before universal access, which was free at the point of delivery, became available in the 1990s.

We always found wonderful hospitality in New Zealand and Australia. The ethnic link between the UK and NZ and Aussie was very strong. UK ships were known as 'home' boats. Our ties were strengthened because the activity of the 'home' boats was so tied up with their economic well being. The produce we exported for them provided their bread-and-butter. During my time, these links weakened as the Southern hemisphere nations found more markets in Asia and the Americas. Also, immigration brought more people from other countries and helped to weaken emotional ties with the 'home' country, particularly in Australia. As we shall see, future decisions by several UK governments further weakened these ties.

Working cargo in New Zealand and Australia

In the UK, port areas were fenced and there were security gates. In most ports we visited Down Under, the wharves and jetties had open access and had no warehouses. As cargo was unloaded it was taken out of the port immediately by road or train. In the UK, most ports had warehouses that were close to the ships so that no damage would be caused by rain etc. As the weather Down Under tended to be drier and warmer, there was no such need. There were railway lines along the wharves and jetties that allowed railway wagons to get up close to the ship's side for loading and unloading. This was essential when loading freezer cargo. The frozen meat, butter or cheese would be delivered in insulated wagons and loaded directly from the wagons into the hold. The cargo would be offloaded from the railway wagons into cargo nets and then hoisted aboard.

What was notably different about cargo work Down Under, and in the USA and Canada, was the standard of personal hygiene of the wharfies compared to the dockers in the UK. In the UK, dockers turned up in dirty clothes, even when unloading food. In New Zealand and Aussie, the wharfies turned up in clean clothes every day and wore coverings over their footwear when walking over stowed meat. There was a saying in Aussie: 'As dry as a Pommie's bath towel!' It was very noticeable how much cleaner people were Down Under. In summer in the 50s and 60s, the London Underground stank.

Our first port of call in New Zealand was the capital, Wellington. Wellington is situated at the southern tip of the North Island. New Zealand has two main, inhabited islands, named North Island and South Island. Wellington harbour is a sunken volcano with Wellington on the north side. The entrance is through the 'heads', a very narrow passage from the western entrance to the Cook Strait, which is the body of water between the North and South Islands. The passage is lined by steep cliffs and there are dangerous rocks underwater. It is made more difficult by the prevailing westerly winds. The latitude of Wellington is about 41.5 degrees south, which puts it in the path of the Roaring Forties coming across the Tasman Sea. Wellington is known as 'Windy Wellington'. But it is a very safe harbour because of the high ground surrounding it on all sides with Mount Victoria dominating to the north. It was autumn when we arrived, so it was windy. It is spectacular and I think it is more so than Sydney.

As was the normal and legally required practice at every port of call, we took on board a 'Pilot'. The Pilot always boarded at sea, in this case outside the heads. He then advised the Master on the courses to steer and the speeds to maintain until we berthed. The main berth is

Custom House Quay, which can take several ocean going ships. Ships can come and go at all stages of the tide because of the deep water. When we arrived, the 'Ruahine' was there. She was the newest of the NZS passenger liners and was a very good-looking ship. Very graceful. The NZS passenger liners only went to the main ports in New Zealand: Auckland and Wellington on the North Island, and, occasionally, Lyttelton, the port of Christchurch, the biggest city on the South Island.

Before I go further, let's get out of the way the routine we followed in port in Aussie, NZ, Canada and the USA. As we approached port, the ship had to be prepared for cargo working. The derricks were raised from their supporting 'crutches' and all the hatch tarpaulin covers were removed except the lowest one. Normally each hatch would be covered by removable boards and three canvas tarpaulins on top. In the UK, this work would be done by dockside labour because of union agreements that soaked up surplus labour. There was no such labour available abroad so we did it ourselves. If the position of the derricks had to be changed, the 'wharfies' would not touch them and we would be called out to change them no matter the time of day or night. A small party of two or three apprentices would be given the job of swinging out and lowering the companion ladder, which enabled people to access and leave the ship.

An immemorial problem for ships has been the attraction of ships for rodents, particularly rats. The spread of the 'Black Death' and other plagues has been mistakenly attributed to ship borne rodents. In any case, a rodent infestation is not wanted, particularly where food stuffs are concerned. Consequently, measures are taken to prevent rats from boarding. These principally consist of fastening rat guards to the mooring lines. These guards are galvanised circles, which are fashioned into a funnel shape so that the outer edges are nearer the shore than the central hole. A segment of the circle is cut out so that it can be placed over the mooring line. These are very effective and I never experienced a problem with rats during my time.

Before we left port, we would secure the hatches with the hatchboards and covered with one or two tarpaulins if it was a short journey to the next port. Otherwise, for deep sea we covered the hatches with three tarpaulins. This operation made the hatches watertight. Next we lowered the derricks and secured them on their supports. The last job was to bring the companion ladder aboard.

Whenever we were 'on the coast' we carried out work that could not be done at sea. Obviously, we could not work on deck because cargo was being worked. We concentrated on hull maintenance. Most of the time, we painted the hull. If we were lucky, we were able to hire metal rafts that were big enough to hold a dozen or so of us. We moored the raft alongside and painted the hull black above the waterline using long handled rollers. The ship was painted red below the waterline. We had to be careful that we maintained the correct line between the black and the red. We did this by chalking a length of line, stretching it along the dividing line and then pulled the line away from the hull in the middle and let go. As the line came back and hit the hull, it left a distinct chalk line that we could follow. We also painted the white draft markings on either side of the bow and stern. These markings were so sited that they could be read from the dockside. The markings were numbers, each one six inches in height with the smallest number lower down. There was a six inch gap between the numbers. Thus between the bottom of one number and the bottom of the number above or below the distance was one foot. The draft was then read by observing where the water surface 'cut' the number. If the water surface was three inches above the number '10', then the draft was 10 foot 3 inches. It was, and is, very important to take these readings twice a day in order to ensure that the vessel was correctly balanced i.e. the bow draft should be the same as the stern draft.

Regulations also stipulated how deep the vessel could be loaded. The amount of cargo that could be loaded varied depending on geography and the season. Thus, we could load less in Winter North Atlantic than Summer. Above and below the waterline mentioned in the above paragraph was what is known as the 'Plimsoll Line'. This was placed, on each side, midway between the bow and the stern. There were thick marks in white paint showing the maximum depth for various seasons and regions. These were as follows, reading from top to bottom:

'TF':   Tropical Fresh Water
'T':   Tropical
'F':   Fresh Water
'S':   Summer
'W':   Winter
'WNA': Winter North Atlantic

Vessels can be loaded deeper in fresh water than in sea water because sea water is denser than fresh water. The vessel will ride higher in the water in sea water. The markings also indicate the element of risk, with TF being considered less risky than WNA because the weather was generally better. The worse the expected weather, the greater the need to have more 'free board' i.e. the distance between the waterline and the deck.

All this came about because of the activities of Samuel Plimsoll, an MP in the 19th Century. He was alarmed at the number of vessels lost at sea because they were overloaded. It was not unknown for ship owners to deliberately overload vessels in the hope that they would capsize in bad weather and they could claim off the insurance. This would especially happen with older vessels carrying heavy but inexpensive cargo. It is a cynical world, my masters. In 1876, Plimsoll carried the Unseaworthy Ships Bill through Parliament. This regulated the weight of cargo that could be carried by region and season. All vessels had to have their sides marked with the 'Plimsoll Line', so that it could easily be seen that the vessel complied with the law. This measure was one of the most important safety measures ever enacted and seamen ever since have cause to thank Samuel Plimsoll.

Roller painting from a raft

We could not always get hold of a raft and some parts of the hull we could not reach from a raft. Then we went over the side in 'stages'. A stage is a long length of wood similar to a scaffolding plank. At each end, there was a cross piece. A length of rope was passed round each cross piece and then taken back about a metre above the stage and fastened to itself to form a triangle. Each triangle was attached to another heavy line. So, there was a line at each end which went to a block on deck and then back down to the stage. This enabled those on the stage to lower the stage as required. Apart from a line that stretched horizontally from one lowering line to another, there were no lifelines. We were not secured by harness in case we fell. We wore no hard hats or 'hi-vis' clothing. So much for Health and Safety in those days. The worst job was cleaning the ship's name on the bow. There was an inward curve so that the bow gunwale overhung the hull. It was difficult to 'warp' (pull) the stage close enough in so that we could put enough pressure on the brass letters to clean and polish. We only did this once, on my second trip in Port Chalmers. Scot Gilchrist and I were ordered to this job. Scot was several inches shorter than me. We had to hold on to the stage with one hand and lean out to do the job. In fact, we only kept our balance by sitting across the stage and gripping the stage tightly with our thighs. The problem was that as we stretched our bodies out, we could not help pushing the stage further away from the hull. It was a nightmare and very scary. We were about thirty feet up from the water. The Chief Officer, Frankie Field, didn't help. He leaned over the bow and said that I would do a better job if I wasn't so shitty scared. Well, I was but what I wanted was encouragement. But that was typical of Field and nobody regretted it when he left us.

Our school work continued all the time in port. There were other duties. Those apprentices on their First, Second and Third trips took it in turns to man the companion ladder. This was an adjustable staircase, situated amidships with the top being a square of wood that jutted out from the main deck. The steps were at an angle of about 45 degrees leading down to the bottom plate. The sides of the steps were secured to a pintle at each end. This enabled the steps to swivel up or down as required. The bottom of the ladder was a horizontal board with holes pierced in it to allow rain water to drain through. It was attached to two metal posts, one on each side, with a cross piece joining them at the top. A block and tackle was attached to the cross piece with another block secured on a beam that jutted out from the Officer's deck. The quartermaster used the block and tackle to raise or lower the bottom of the ladder as needed. This was done by hand, no motor. As the ship unloaded or loaded it went up or down in the water. Also, the ship would rise or fall according to the tide.

The person manning the ladder was called the 'quartermaster' and each turn, or watch, lasted for four hours. The primary job was to ensure that the bottom of the ladder was just above the level of the dock so that people could come and go without hindrance. Therefore, the quartermaster had to be vigilant and it was heavy work. The ladder was manned 24/7.

Every morning at 8, the watch on duty would hoist and break out the flags to a bugle call. On the Durham, the bugler was one of the Junior Ordinary Seamen. If there was nobody who could blow a bugle, the Officer of the Day would blow a whistle. Normally, we would fly the flag of the country we were visiting (known as the 'courtesy ensign') on one side of the foremast and the company's house flag on the other. The Merchant Navy ensign, the 'Red Duster', would be flown on the stern post. At sunset the reverse would occur. Both ceremonies would be overseen by the Officer of the Day (3rd or 4th Officer). These ceremonies were carried out on all UK merchant ships. When we were at sea, we flew the 'Red Duster' at the mizzen mast and no other flags. Before entering port, we hoisted and flew the courtesy ensign and the house flag plus the 'Yellow Duster'. This last was a square yellow flag that stated that we were healthy and required 'free pratique' i.e permission to enter port without hindrance. Before leaving the port, the 'Blue Peter' flag was also flown as a notice that the ship was about to sail and that all who had no further business on board should leave and that all crew who were ashore should repair on board. These practices are hundreds of years old and I believe rather charming.

Apprentices on their fourth and fifth trips would assist the Officer of the Day and would wear uniform. The first duty of the day was to read the 'draft'. This told you how much of the ship was below the waterline and whether the bow was higher than the stern and vice versa. The Second Officer needed this information to verify his loading programme. After that, the duties were as decided by the Officer of the Day: overseeing 'bonded' cargo (alcohol, tobacco, coinage), listing in a book what was loaded and unloaded, listing other shore workers carrying out maintenance and repairs, and generally making sure that cargo work was carried out in a regular and safe manner. In some ways this was one of the most valuable parts of our training.

CHAPTER SIXTEEN

The Social Side Of The Voyage.

Our social life was prescribed. NZS considered itself to be 'in loco parentis' and enforced a strict regime in the hope that we would be controlled and kept out of trouble. We had to go ashore in uniform and paraded for inspection before we were allowed ashore: 6 pm on a weekday, midday on Saturdays and Sundays. Trippers had to be back by 9.30 pm. Given the distance to the nearest cinema in some ports, it was sometimes impossible to see a film. Second trippers had to back by 10, Third by 10.30 and Fourth and Fifth by 11. If you had a written invitation, you could get an extension. The more adventurous and rebellious of us circumvented this regime by sneaking off in civvies and coming back when we wanted. The worst that would happen is loss of shore leave if caught. Every now and again, the Officer of the Day would carry out a search of our quarters to see if we were all where we should be. I think that this was more to satisfy Head Office than any real desire on the part of the Officers. In any case, most of these searches took place so late that those of us who had been 'naughty' were back on board anyway. Guess whether I conformed or not?

A major problem with this regime was that we were very prominent when ashore in uniform. All kinds of undesirables tried to strike up acquaintances with us. I was walking across a pedestrian crossing in Wellington just below the Houses of Parliament, in broad daylight when a man came up to me and asked me if I 'was fit'. The rules were actually putting us in harm's way. The ship's Officers were in agreement with us that the situation was untenable. Gradually, the rules on uniform were relaxed, firstly for the senior apprentices, and later we were allowed ashore for longer. It was an age when 'paternalism' and deference were commonplace. I doubt that teenagers today would stand for it. It was a regime that none of our parents would have instituted.

Here is a bizarre comparison with the attitude of the Armed Services. We once carried a Royal Navy cadet when we were coasting in the UK. He was about to graduate from Dartmouth and was part of a programme to educate RN Officers about life in the Merchant Navy. He was not allowed to go ashore in uniform. In fact, in the RN uniform is only required when on duty. He was totally bemused that our Company regulations required us to go ashore in uniform and agreed that it was essentially unsafe.

In New Zealand at this time, people rarely worked after 5 pm and never over the weekend, except for shop workers and essential services. New Zealanders thus had a great deal of free time that they spent very much outdoors or visiting neighbours and friends. Cinemas were open seven days a week. Only Auckland and Wellington had any kind of professional theatre and there was not always a production on show. It meant that we did not work much over the weekend. We worked Saturday mornings and could go ashore in the afternoon. Sundays were the same as at sea, except that we could go ashore after midday. NZS always tried to get its ships at sea over the weekend because it cost more to keep them in port on a Saturday or Sunday without working.

Wellington
Custom House Quay, the commercial shipping berth, is in the middle of the picture.

The main streets of Wellington were wide and had trams. The Governor General's Residence and the NZ Houses of Parliament were situated on a small hill just behind Custom House Quay. It was very open in aspect. At the far end of Custom House Quay was a cafe that served the best salads I have ever had. It specialised in salads and they were made of all kinds of fruit and vegetable. The idea of different kinds of lettuce, grapes, oranges, apples, shredded carrot, kiwi fruit and mango in a salad was revolutionary to me. Otherwise, Kiwi restaurant food in those days was very unadventurous. Soup, steak, roasts and puddings were the order of the day. I don't remember the Kiwis eating much fish although the waters were teeming with them. Salmon was plentiful but they preferred it out of a tin. The South Island had a profitable shrimp and crayfish industry but it was all exported to New York restaurants and presented as Lobster Thermidor. Deer had been introduced and its meat was available, but nobody ate venison.

Our PTI was keen on basketball and he arranged a couple of matches with local teams in Wellington, which I believe we lost heavily. It may have been at this time that we went to see the Harlem Globetrotters basketball team. The Globetrotters are, essentially, a show business operation that tours the world. They recruit black basketball players who are not only skilful to a high degree but who also possess personality and a spirit of mischief. They always took with them on tour one or two other teams, who were there as foils to the brilliance of the Globetrotters. The Globetrotters clowned around a lot and were thoroughly entertaining.

The PTI did make a mistake in organising what we thought was going to be a basketball match against a girl's school. It turned out that it was netball match, a game none of us had played before. Somehow we won, but more because of our physicality than any skill. After the match, the girls provided refreshment and made it quite clear that they wanted to arrange dates with us. One guy was, literally, cornered by several girls and only extricated himself with difficulty. Quite a role reversal for us, but we escaped without entanglement.

The Third Mate started the training regime for our rugger team in Wellington. Wherever we could find a ground, we practiced for an hour or so two or three times a week in whatever port we were in. We ran to the ground and back. We were very rough to start with but gradually we found a blend and a winning formula. We could not have chosen a harder environment in which to play. Rugby is the Kiwis' national sport and to become an All Black is everything. Their whole rugger regime is structured to produce the best national team. Children start to play competitively at six or seven in leagues. But they do not play in age ranges as we do in the UK. They play in teams according to their weight. So, you would have under six stone leagues, under seven stone leagues and so on. As kids, they are never intimidated by kids bigger than themselves. This allows them to play freely without fear of being overwhelmed. The end result is an All Blacks team that plays totally unafraid of the opposition and a huge belief in their own ability. No wonder that they are the best in the world. We struggled at first but gradually gave as good as we got and it was our dedicated training that helped.

Durham 'First XV:
Back Row: Charles Turner, Charles Treleaven, Pete Barr, 'Monty' Banks, AN Other, Peter Matthews, Geoff Morris, Glen Smith, Warwick Lewis.
Front Row: Henry McCutchan, Davey Pounder, John Ayres, Charles Cedric (Ceddie) Hufflett (Captain), AN Other, 'Pongo' Eastwood, Bob McGregor.

Durham carried boats for 'relaxation'. We had two whalers and two dinghies. We used the whalers for rowing and sailing. In the Royal and Merchant Navies rowing is called 'pulling', which is a more accurate term. Whalers are heavy wooden boats which have pointed sterns as well as bows. They were originally designed for the whaling industry. The 'mother' whale ship could not get close enough to a whale to get a harpoon in. The harpoonist stood in the bow of the whaler and threw his harpoon into the whale. The harpoon was attached to a very long length of greased line, which followed the harpoon and the whale. The idea was to tire the whale out, bring it alongside the whaler, kill it and tow it to the mother ship for processing. The oars were long and heavy. The rowers sat on wooden thwarts (benches) across the boat. It is hard work. The NZS cadet ships had a reputation for whaler racing and we challenged other ships whenever possible. We practiced regularly.

Whaler under full sail.

This time in Wellington, we had no chance of races but we did get an afternoon's sailing in. Unfortunately, half a gale was blowing. This was fine with the wind behind, but we got blown into Evans Bay on the west side of the harbour and couldn't get out. Whalers are not good at what is called 'tacking' i.e. sailing zigzag against the wind. We had to moor the boats at the Evans Bay Yacht Club and hitch a ride back on land. The whalers were eventually brought back towed behind motor boats. Great embarrassment.

Whilst in Wellington, we trippers had our first introduction to the then draconian licencing laws of New Zealand. All pubs shut at 6 pm and were closed all day Sunday. The reason for this stemmed from the First World War. There were problems with departing troops indulging themselves plus concerns that drunkenness was affecting productivity. Additionally, departing service men had built up tabs, which never got paid. It became illegal to run up a tab in a pub. Drinks had to be paid for at the same time as they were served. A similar situation had developed in the UK, which itself instituted statutory opening and closing times for the first time. In the UK these regulations did not become relaxed until the 1960s.

A custom developed known as the 'six o'clock swill'. When people, predominantly men, left work, they visited the pub before going home. They drank as much as they could in the hour or less available. Pubs would have full glasses of beer lined up on the counter before 5 o'clock so that bar staff did not have to waste valuable drinking time filling up glasses and keeping the punters waiting. Glasses were filled by hoses, not by beer engines, because all draught beer was kept cooled and under pressure. Nobody sat down and most bars were pretty primitive and all had a foot rail at the counter. Everybody went home happy. As the pubs were open all day Saturday, there was considerable drunkenness on that day and there was always a noticeable police presence. Beer was relatively cheap. You bought draught beer in three sizes: a 'schooner' was the largest, probably a bit more than half a pint. I can't remember what the other two sizes were, but they were smaller. It did not matter what size you bought, the price was the same: six pence on average (two and half pence in decimal). This price meant that beer was within the buying capacity of we apprentices. The glass sizes and prices were similar in Australia, although the Aussie pound was only worth about twelve shillings (60 pence decimal) of an English pound.

Stand-alone restaurants could not obtain a licence. If you wanted to go out for dinner and wanted a drink with your meal, you took your booze with you in a paper bag. The restaurant would then charge 'corkage' for providing the service of pulling the cork out and opening the bottle. All of Kiwi society complied with this. I remember seeing a newsreel at the cinema of an awards evening at a Wellington night spot. All the guests arrived in their best togs and carried the all too recognisable paper bags. The only exceptions to this were hotels which had a restaurant. They could serve drinks with meals to bone fide visitors and hotel residents. If you were staying in a hotel with a licence, you could drink in the hotel private bar as long as it was open. Some hotels let you 'sign in' the hotel register so that you could claim to be a resident and get a drink. Obviously, some hotels had more 'residents than they had rooms. I can remember having Sunday lunch at the Wellington Hotel with a bottle of wine when I could afford it. A little bit of civilisation.

Australia also had the same regime and in both countries there developed the practice of the 'sly grog'. A number of pubs allowed their customers to stay after 6 or to have an arrangement whereby they would be admitted later. Wherever we went, we found 'wharfies' or other people associated with the port who would introduce us to the local 'sly grogs'.

Over the years there were a number of referendums offering a relaxation of the licencing laws. Until after my time, they tended to fail because of an unholy alliance between married women, temperance societies and brewers. The married women did not want their husbands to have an excuse to come home later and the brewers were making good profits from the 'sly grog'. The change to later closing times started in New South Wales in the late 1950s, probably because of the influx of immigrants from Southern Europe who could not understand the licencing regime and who persuaded the New South Wales government to change. Once one area had changed, the resistance to change began to crumble and the relaxation was speeded up by the expansion of the tourist trade in the 1960s and 1970s with its consequent growth in eating establishments, which demanded to be able to satisfy tourists. But, it was fun while it lasted if you knew how to beat, and work with, the system.

After a few days in Wellington, we went south to Lyttelton, which is the port of Christchurch. Christchurch is about halfway down the east side of South Island. It is the third largest city in NZ and is the capital of Canterbury province. Much of the eastern side of South Island is rolling grassland, ideal for sheep. It is where 'Canterbury Lamb' comes from. Christchurch is like a large English country town and has a cathedral. Otherwise, it was very boring for an adolescent. The port of Lyttelton is on the other side of a hill. A railway tunnel had been built through the hill and was the quickest way between the two towns. We had the first of our on-board parties in Lyttelton, with the girls organised by Melbe Hocken, the Captain's wife, who had joined us in Wellington from her home in Adelaide. A continuing attraction for New Zealand girls was our supply of music. Because NZ was short of foreign currency, imports were severely restricted, particularly items associated with entertainment. We brought the latest long playing records with UK and American pop music and musicals, which were unattainable in NZ.

Next we went south to Port Chalmers to finish unloading. Port Chalmers is the port for Dunedin, which is a city largely populated by people of Scottish extraction, as is most of the southern half of South Island. Over half of UK emigrants to New Zealand and Australia in the nineteenth and twentieth century were Irish, Scots or Welsh. Dunedin is the principal town of the province of Otago. It lies at the western, innermost part of Otago Harbour, which is a sunken volcano and is about 14 miles long. Port Chalmers is about halfway between Dunedin and the Pacific on the north side of Otago Harbour. It is very sheltered. In the late 19th Century and early 20th Century, it was an entry port for immigrants to New Zealand. A quarantine station was established on an island in the harbour near Port Chalmers and called Quarantine Island. It is now a nature reserve.

Port Chalmers is a small town, perhaps 5,000 inhabitants and it was too far from Dunedin for a night out. The surrounding cliffs had ships' names painted at the top, but Durham's name was not there. One night, some of the apprentices, including Henry McCutchan, took a stage up to one of the cliffs, hung the stage over the top of the cliff and painted the ship's name there. It was foolhardy but we were immensely proud.

Our berth was a long jetty that could take ships on each side. On the other side of the jetty was a 'Port Line' ship. Port Line was a subsidiary of Cunard and a great commercial rival of NZS. Their ships had very distinct, rounded superstructures and steeply raked bows making them look streamlined. The Cunard group was obsessed with speed and tried to get every extra knot out of their ships. They also took great pride in their appearance. Some of our lot decided that this ship was ripe for a bit of piracy. One night, the Port Line ship was raided and the raiding party made off with the ship's bell, a couple of flags and other paraphernalia. It was obvious that we had done it and the Chief Officer paraded us with our 'trophies' for a dressing-down, but we could see that he was secretly highly amused and proud of us. Anyway, he had to take the trophies back and apologise to their Chief Officer. He had a very long lunch. We heard via bar gossip that the Port Line crew were pissed off that they had been bested by a bunch of kids barely out of school. It was rumoured that they were going to raid us. We had an Engineer Cadet, Tom, who increased the pump pressure on our hoses so that we could blast them away. We kept watch all night but nothing happened and we sailed away.

There was a New Zealand navy frigate in port. She was part of the New Zealand Antarctic Expedition, which had permanent stations in the Antarctic. As it was now winter, she was here on leave and refitting. The use of Port Chalmers as a base for Antarctic expeditions was well established by this time. It is the nearest sheltered, deep water port to the Antarctic and with access to fresh water and supplies. Captain Scott sailed from Port Chalmers on the 'Terra Nova' in 1910 on his last and tragic expedition to Antarctica. We were berthed at the same jetty that the 'Terra Nova had used, but on the opposite side. The port has undergone considerable reshaping since my time into a container port. Therefore, the layout we knew has disappeared.

We challenged the frigate to a rugger match. The nearest ground was in Dunedin and we could not have chosen a worse day for the weather. The wind blew and it hailed. It was very, very cold but both sides stuck it out and we lost narrowly, although in the conditions we played in it was a bit of a tossup which team had the best luck.

Whilst in Port Chalmers, I had an alarming and embarrassing experience. I was quartermaster one afternoon, in charge of the companion ladder. There is a big rise and fall of the tide in Port Chalmers. At low water, the mooring lines slacken off and the ship can drift off the wharf. This makes it difficult to get on and off the ship because the bottom of the companion ladder can be too far away from the jetty. This means that the Officer of the Day has to keep a close eye on the ship's moorings to make sure that the ship is tight in to the jetty. On this particular day, the ship had drifted about three feet away from the jetty. The 3rd Officer, Charles Treleaven, did not notice this, I could not leave my post to warn him and none of my shipmates were around so that I could send a message. Consequently, I had to keep lowering the ladder. The 3rd Officer then realised the situation and decided to haul in the forward mooring lines without warning me. The result was that, as the ship moved closer to the jetty, the bottom of the ladder was caught between the jetty and the ship. The side frame of the ladder cracked and had to be replaced. I came in for some very severe criticism, despite my explanation. However, I received no official reprimand or punishment, so I imagine that the 3rd Officer had to take his share of the blame. I can only surmise that because I never heard the outcome of the 3rd Officer's interrogation. The chippie was able to repair the damaged side and no more was ever heard of this incident, possibly to save face on the part of the 3rd Officer, who never apologised or explained anything to me. However, as he ran the rugger team and I was an integral part of it, we retained an amicable relationship and I was sorry when he left at the end of the voyage.

I won a bet with a pub owner in Port Chalmers. Can't remember the name of the pub but it was halfway up the main street of the left hand side. A conversation had turned to Roger Bannister, the first man to run a mile in under 4 minutes. The question was why Bannister never won an Olympic medal. I had the answer. In his book 'The First Four Minutes', Bannister explained why he did not win a medal in the 1500 metres at Helsinki in 1952, the only time he raced in the Olympics. He had trained expecting two races – a heat and a final. The organisers added a semi-final. This extra race had taken the edge off Bannister's performance and he finished fourth. The publican disputed my explanation and we struck a bet. Next day, I produced Bannister's book and he paid up. A bit unfair as I knew I would win, but a couple of quid was my week's spending money.

Nelson

The next port was Nelson at the north end of South Island. It has a very mild climate and we were in shirt sleeves even though it was winter. The climate is quite soporific and Nelson was known in my time as 'Sleepy Hollow'. Nelson is a sheltered harbour, with mountains shielding it from the Roaring Forties. It is near Marlborough Sound, which is the area that first grew vines in New Zealand in commercial quantities. Its Sauvignon Blanc is now world famous but sheep, dairy and apples were the main agricultural products in my day. Here we started to load frozen meat, wool and hides.

Nelson has one of the top public schools in New Zealand, Nelson College. Nelson is where Rugby Union started in New Zealand. The game was brought there by a master at the college, David Munro, after a trip to the UK. The first recorded match in New Zealand occurred in May 1870 when Munro organised a match between the Nelson Club and the College. Since then, over 20 former students have played for the All Blacks.

We arranged a rugger match against the College and we started to understand what we were really up against in terms of New Zealand rugby. We were well beaten by 39 points to 3. This was when a try was only worth three points. I think they scored nine or ten tries against us. I scored our only try from a scrum on their line. The whole school and a few locals turned out to watch. We played the school again a few days later. They only put their second team out, but I noticed several in the team who had played against us for their first team. They beat us again but there were only a few points in it.

Our stay at Nelson gave us the opportunity to earn extra money. Nelson was our 'turn-round' port for this voyage. It was where we finished unloading and started loading. Usually, at these ports, the shore organisation employed ship's crews to clean the holds and prepare for new cargo. We did this work in the evening after our normal work. We were paid at NZ rates of hourly pay, which was much higher than our 'salary'. Pay for this overtime meant that we did not need to sub for the rest of the trip.

Because we had carried general cargo and were taking home frozen cargo, the holds had to be thoroughly cleaned. The first job was to remove all the 'dunnage'. Dunnage is wooden planks, laid on wooden battens, used to cover the hold floor and to separate cargo when necessary. You cannot lay cargo on a metal floor because it will be contaminated by condensation. Most of this dunnage would have been laid in New Zealand and Australia on the previous trip, but it was no longer clean enough for a food cargo. We bundled up the dunnage into 'slings' and it was hoisted up and over the ship's side into waiting lorries. NZ and Australia are very particular about the hygiene of imported organic material and the regulations stated that used dunnage had to be incinerated.

However, human nature being what it is, the 'availability' of free building material was too tempting an opportunity to be missed. A foreman carpenter in Adelaide told me on my last voyage that it was still valuable building material and he and his mates had deals with the waste disposal companies to hang on to the timber. At one time, he had a large collection at his house when he heard that government inspectors were noseying around. So, he got all his mates round with several crates of beer and they put up an extension over the weekend. He had a wooden bungalow, like many Aussies, so it was easy to disguise the origins of his material.

After clearing the dunnage, we swept up and washed down with hoses. The last job was to clean the bilges, known as 'bilge diving'. The bilge covers were taken off and we mopped them out. It was uncomfortable work rather than nauseating because any liquid was just a mixture of water and oil. After we had finished, new dunnage would arrive and was laid down by shore carpenters. We were then ready for loading. Because this took some time, our stay in a turn-round port was always at least a week. These ports tended to be small and, because everybody knew everybody, we had a good social life in these ports, particularly in NZ.

Our official voyage dance was held in Nelson at the National Party Club rooms. The National Party is the NZ equivalent of the Conservative Party. All the apprentices, plus any ship's officers who wanted to, attended. Melbe Downer arranged the girls although some of us brought girls we had already met. Melbe was a member of the Primrose League, which was very active politically 'Down Under'. This meant that she had access to well-to-do families all over both countries and these families were happy to deliver their daughters to us in her safe-keeping. Life-long friendships did happen and I know of at least one marriage as a result of Melbe's activities. We had a live band. These events were often the social highlight of the year in the ports where we held them and this was no exception. Apparently, I distinguished myself by swinging on a chandelier, or so Monty Banks always claimed for years afterwards. As far as I remember, there was no chandelier, but I do remember that there was a galleried landing above the room and I think I hung off the banisters for a dare.

There was also a party on board and this illustrated how isolated New Zealand was in terms of entertainment, in this case up-to-date gramophone records. At the end, one girl said she was not going home until we played 'Shine On Harvest Moon' one more time.

We had an inter-watch pulling race in Nelson, which was the only pulling event we had on this trip because it was winter. Can't remember who won.

There was pub in Nelson called the 'Rising Sun'. The landlord was called Fisher and had been the Middleweight Boxing Champion of New Zealand. He was in trouble because of some licencing infringement, 'sly grog' as like as not. He had an alliterative sign outside which read 'Fisher Fighting Fit Fights for ..' can't remember the rest. Anyway, I was intrigued and went in. It turned out to be very convivial as he had a lot of friends who made an effort to spend money in his pub. I remember having a snooze on a park bench afterwards.

Timaru

Next port was Timaru, which is halfway between Christchurch and Dunedin. Timaru does not have a natural harbour, it is all man-made. The location of Timaru occurred because it is halfway along the Canterbury coastline between Christchurch and Dunedin and adjacent to the sheep grazing country, and the graziers needed a port to export their produce. There was always a swell from the Pacific. We berthed at a long jetty, which led directly to the main street. As with most small ports 'Down Under', the jetties were completely open with no security gates. Anybody could walk on them and the townspeople would often do so to have a look at the ships. As it was on the edge of the Canterbury Plain, Timaru had a slaughterhouse and freezer works. Exports were predominantly sheep-related: wool, meat and hides.

We were there for about a week. Timaru has a High School, well-known for its sporting prowess. A former pupil, Jack Lovelock, won the 800 metres at the 1936 Olympics. The Silver Medal winner was Godfrey Brown, an old boy of my school. We had an excellent practice ground for rugger and played Timaru High School. We lost narrowly and were obviously improving. Also in port was a New Zealand navy frigate, HMNZS Pukaki. We played their team and it was our last match of that voyage. When we got back, the Bosun asked how much we lost by. We had great pleasure in telling him we won, so we ended our sporting season on a high.

Our last port on this trip was to Wellington to finish loading before heading home. North Island is rich in dairy produce and we loaded cheese and butter as well as lamb, wool and hides.

In 1956, the Springboks rugby team toured New Zealand. They were unsociable and, as a result, unpopular. They kept themselves very much to themselves, which was a characteristic of South Africans during the apartheid era. They did not want to be involved in conversations with people who disagreed with them. This was particularly so with the Springboks, most of whose players were Afrikaaners, the descendants of the original Dutch settlers, who were the most fervent believers in apartheid. They believed that their reading of the Bible assured them of racial superiority.

In late-July, the Springboks played Wellington province at the Basin Reserve in Wellington on a Saturday afternoon. The Basin Reserve is a stadium to the north of Wellington city centre and divides the main road. It was owned by Wellington Cricket Club and staged test cricket matches as well as big rugby matches. This is common 'Down Under'. Eden Park in Auckland, Sydney Cricket Ground, Melbourne Cricket Ground and the Adelaide Oval all host big rugby or Australian Rules football matches. We wanted to go but were too late to get tickets. Half a dozen of us hired taxis and the drivers took us on spec to the back of the stadium. Up a steep slope was a fence that was partly torn down. Up we went, through the fence and found a precarious vantage point. Wellington won, much to our delight.

Many stadiums Down Under at that time did not have enough stand space for big matches. The practice was to put up temporary stands, which is why we were able to get into the Wellington/Springboks match. The stands often left space in between and enterprising people put up stands outside the ground that still provided a view. These were colloquially known as 'Scotsman's Stands'.

Shortly after we left Wellington for home, New Zealand played South Africa in the last Test match at Auckland. New Zealand won, thanks to a remarkable try by the New Zealand wing forward, Peter Jones. He scored a try where he started from near his own line. After the match, he was interviewed by Winston McCarthy, who commentated on rugby football for New Zealand radio. Peter did not realise that his comments were live on the PA system and on radio. McCarthy asked him how he felt, to which Jones replied: 'I am absolutely buggered!'

A couple of days, before we left, several of us were in a bar when a couple of coppers entered and made a beeline for us. The legal age for drinking in NZ is 21. We were in uniform and obviously under age. The coppers interrogated us, sniffed and tasted our drinks and then let us go. I don't think they were going to report us because we were leaving soon. But it put the wind up us. It made me realise even more how much we stood out because we were in uniform. I determined to break the rule as often as I could in the future.

Geoff Morris has written a memoir of this time called 'Serendipity'. He states that we also went to New Plymouth and Auckland on this trip, but I have no memory of this. Just goes to show that memory can be so fallible.

CHAPTER SEVENTEEN

Homeward Bound

We left Wellington in late-July bound for Panama on a modified great circle course. If you traced our course on a map, you would see that it would take us on a curved course through the Roaring Forties and then north-eastwards past Easter Island to Panama. The first week through the Roaring Forties was very uncomfortable. We had a gale behind us all the time with towering seas. The ship pitched and rolled continuously. We rigged life lines between our quarters and the main superstructure to give us something to hang onto. We were not allowed on the main deck forward of the superstructure because we were taking water over the bow regularly. This meant that lookouts could not be sent to the bow. The lookout stood on top of the bridge deckhouse next to a magnetic compass. The rolling of the ship was exaggerated at that elevation, 40 or 50 feet above the water line. Steering the ship was hard work because you had to compensate for the pitching and rolling, which tended to push the ship off course. Days and days of this make you very tired because you have to spend so much energy just staying upright. No work on deck was compensated by more work in the classroom.

Navigation was not accurate because of the lack of sun and star sights. Thick cloud was the norm. It meant that we had to navigate by 'dead reckoning'. This involves calculating the ship's position by estimating the course and distance from the last position. As the ship was affected by 'set' (ocean currents) and 'drift'(wind speed and direction), neither of which could be accurately determined, the position was only an approximate one, made worse if the previous position had been calculated by dead reckoning. However, this is how navigators had worked for centuries before reliable compasses and chronometers and we were never far out. In the vast expanse of the Pacific, it did not matter but was much more of a hazard in a busy shipping lane.

I saw my first albatross. They are fantastic to watch. They swoop and follow the ship without appearing to use any energy. Their huge wing span allows them to get tremendous lift from the wind. One of them landed on top of the foremast and hitched a ride for a while. He didn't offer to pay.

We had a passenger on this trip home. He was a Lieutenant-Commander RN and had taken a sabbatical to sail from England via the Panama Canal to New Zealand. His boat was wooden and twenty feet long. It had a mast and two sails: a jib and a mainsail. There were no electronic aids, no automatic steering and no electricity. Sail handling and steering was all done manually. He set out with a companion but they had a row over a woman in the Canary Islands that ended in fisticuffs. Exit companion and he sailed on alone. I do not know how long it took him but it was an amazing feat. NZS gave him a passage home on condition that he worked his passage. He joined us on deck work and shared drinks with the Second Officer. He was very affable and approachable, far more than our officers. He did not, of course, have to be concerned about our discipline or status in the hierarchy. He gave us a talk about his journey when the weather got better and he was a good presenter. He confided that he would like to do it again, but in a smaller boat!

After a week or so in the Roaring Forties, we turned north eastwards towards the Tropics and warmer and calmer waters. We went past Easter Island, but at night and we saw nothing. I think it was on this trip that we passed Rakaia, she being outward bound, before we reached

Panama. I remember that it was in the tropics. It was most unusual to pass one of the other company ships on an ocean passage, but to pass our fellow cadet ship was as rare as hen's teeth. There was some excitement before hand, particularly amongst those cadets who had started their sea life on Rakaia before being transferred to Durham on her re-commissioning. We passed as close as we could whilst observing a safe distance. We lined the decks and waved but had made no particular preparations. In fact, we just stopped whatever activity we were engaged in. Rakaia, on the contrary, had lined up all the cadets in uniform and presented as formal an appearance as possible. Some of our cadets expressed dismay that Rakaia had got one over us and looked smarter than us, but most of us thought that they had been too formal in what should have been a friendly and fortuitous meeting. If formality was to have been the order of the day, then Rakaia should have dipped her ensign to us as our captain was senior to theirs. Whatever, it was enough to have been present on such an uncommon occasion.

Next, we traversed the Panama Canal, bunkered at Curacao, passed through the Windward Islands and sailed home across the Atlantic. Most of our cargo was to be unloaded in London, but we paid a call first to Dunkirk. We were there about a day and had a chance of a run ashore. You could see bullet holes in the house walls from the Dunkirk campaign. Henry McCutchan and I went ashore together. His mother was French and he spoke perfect French. It was a Sunday with not much going on. We went into a boulangerie and Henry introduced me to the delights of French baking. It was the first time I had eaten 'pain epice'. Lovely.

We paid off in London at Royal Albert Dock on September 3rd 1956 and went on leave after a trip lasting just under six months. We were paid what was due from our pay after subs, remittances and anything we had spent on board. We were all paid in white five pound notes. These 'fivers' were made of thick paper that crackled as you folded it. It felt like real money. At the height of the British Empire, fivers were accepted as currency anywhere in the world. We were also given rail vouchers to pay for a third class ticket home and back again after leave. For those seamen who lived far away, e,g. in the Hebrides, this concession was very important. It was a relic of the war. Attlee's Labour government had wanted to abolish this privilege but Winston Churchill made an impassioned plea that it was part of the acknowledgement of the sacrifices that merchant seamen had made in the two world wars. We had enough money to share a taxi to a main line station and pay the extra to exchange our voucher for a first class ticket. Such luxury because you could sit in the first class dining car and be waited on whilst the countryside passed by.

As this was my first leave, it was my first experience of how little impact my absence had made. People would ask me 'Have you been away?' or 'You're back, when are you going away?' Very few had any interest in where I had been. It helps me to understand the frustration of ex-Servicemen who return to their original home areas and find themselves isolated. I did have a more humorous experience on a leave a year later when I met an old friend called Eric Rudd. Eric was a brewing chemist who worked for Flower & Sons. He was a bachelor, lived with his sister and devoted his leisure time to Stratford Rugby and Cricket Clubs. He was the team secretary at both clubs and was responsible for seeing that selected players were informed, make sure they turned up and juggle replacements if anybody 'cried off'. I was walking across the canal bridge one Friday when he passed by on his bike. It was the first time I had seen him since I got back. Never mind 'Hello' or 'How are you?' it was 'Glad to catch you. We're short of a scrum half for the first team tomorrow. Can you play?'

During this leave, one of the senior Durham cadets, Pongo Eastwood, paid me a visit. I don't know why as he was a couple of years ahead of me. Anyway, we had a very convivial lunch at the Swan's Nest, after which we took a rowing boat from Sonny Rose's boathouse. Pongo was somewhat the worse for wear after our lunch and did not impress any watchers that merchant seamen could handle small boats.

CHAPTER EIGHTEEN

Second DurhamTrip.

6th October 1956 to 13th March 1957

On this trip, I was still berthed in a Trippers' cabin but as the Apprentice in charge. I had to 'break in' the new boys and ensure that they carried out their duties in respect of hygiene etc.

We embarked on another trip to New Zealand and the prospect of Christmas to look forward to. My indentures stated that this trip began on October 6th, which may have been the official date in the Ship's Log but we certainly joined before then. When I look back at my trips, I am certain that my time on board each ship began before the official date. My leaves were not that long! What makes me sure in this instance was that I have a document that lists our trip to the Meteorological Office HQ at Dunstable. The Met Office is part of the Ministry of Defence. Part of the Second Mate's Exam is a paper on Meteorology and this trip was interesting in itself and definitely of value academically. Apart from the use of computers, my view is that not much has changed in how these people go about their forecasts. They came across as supreme professionals. The Director of the Met Office joined us for lunch and endeared himself by ordering gin and tonics all round.

One of the last voyage's trippers, Hugh 'Reg'Perks, did not return. We never knew what discussions took place between him, his parents and NZS, but I guess that it was a mutual decision to end his indentures. Looking back, it now seems obvious that Reg was in the wrong environment. Reg never fitted in and was always at the back end of any activity. His personal hygiene was awful. He seemed to wear the same T-shirt for weeks on end. He had been at 'HMS Conway' with Scot Gilchrist and both had enjoyed the sailing opportunities there. Sailing vessels were Reg's keenest interest and there was little opportunity for expanding his interest whilst serving in a deep sea merchant vessel.

Once he had left, Reg proved that he was a formidable character and determined to make his way in life on his own terms. As such, he should be regarded as an inspiration. I lost touch with Reg as soon as he left, but have since subsequently learned, thanks to Peter Matthews, that he had a distinguished life. The standard Merchant Navy career could not supply Reg with the experience that he wanted i.e. to be in touch with traditional seamanship, in particular life on Thames barges. After NZS, he became a mate on a barge until he had to do his National Service. He chose a commission and served ten years in the Gurkhas. He subsequently became a Lecturer in Medieval History whilst retaining his interest on Thames barges, on which he wrote two books. Reg was always sustained by his deep Christian faith. Reg will forever be an example of not forcing people into convention and allowing us to forge our own destiny.

We had a largely uneventful voyage across the Atlantic and through Panama. There was a major incident in the Pacific because of engine trouble. We had one stop in the Pacific to change cylinder liners and then another, more serious one. The second time lasted almost a day. Dig Hocken decided that we would make use of the time by practicing lifeboat drill and getting the boats in the water so that we could both row and sail them. Having done so, it became obvious that we were going to be 'hove to' for longer than expected. So, we hoisted the lifeboats on board and lowered the whalers and dinghies. The weather was lovely and we made the most of it sailing and pulling. It was a lovely break from routine. On top of it all, we went swimming. Imagine that, swimming in the middle of the Pacific with the sea bed thousands of feet below you? Not an experience many have had, well not voluntarily anyway.

Second 'Trippers': Bob, Henry, John, Scot, Peter. Somewhere in the Pacific, 1956 or 1957. Contrast with later picture: 2022 Reunion (Page 259)

This stop gave the Chief Officer a chance to put a new type of prototype motor lifeboat through its paces. Officially, it was called a 'Rescue Boat' but we came to call it the 'Crash Boat' because it sounded more dramatic. It was the same length as the other lifeboats but had an aluminium hull. It was covered by a 'turtle deck'. A turtle deck is curved so that water will run straight off. RNLI lifeboats have turtle decks. It had a small wheelhouse about two-thirds of the way along from the bow and behind this wheel house was an engine compartment containing a diesel engine. The boat was designed to be very resistant to rolling over and to be watertight. The engine was started by compressed air. We used it extensively and it proved itself highly practical, especially as a means of keeping lifeboats together and providing weatherproof housing for an emergency radio. The only problem was that the compressed air generally failed and the engine was started by hand cranking. After one trip with us, it became standard issue very quickly throughout the company's ships.

We had a new Chief Officer, Frankie Field. He had the knack of rubbing everybody up the wrong way. He also made himself look ridiculous. He habitually carried a clipboard with him, which we called his 'finalising board' because he was always going to finalise something. One hot day, he appeared on deck dressed just in his swimming trunks, plimsolls, uniform cap and clip board. He had an unprepossessing figure, 'skinnymalink' comes to mind. Everybody wanted to laugh. It was his insistence on wearing his uniform cap that made him look so absurd. This is a problem with sea officers. Isolation and increasing seniority accentuates their eccentricities. When we arrived in New Zealand he really got on the wrong side of the deck ratings. It is a long tradition that, after a sea voyage, the deck ratings are given the first day in port off so that they can go ashore and have a blast. He wouldn't let them and they did not serve him willingly afterwards.

Whatever, he didn't really spoil what was probably the happiest trip I had apart from my first trip as Fourth Mate. Summer 'Down Under' is heaven if you like an outdoor life. As you will see as I open our social diary, the next two months were blissful.

Literally 'old sweats': Chippie, Donkeyman, Bosun, Instructor AB, Lamptrimmer.
They taught us everything about life at sea. Taken on my third trip, I guess.

Wellington.

We arrived in Wellington about November 21ˢᵗ. On the 24ᵗʰ, there was a cricket match
between the Apprentices and the Officers, which we won. That night, some organisation
called the Wellington Navy League gave a dance for us. The dance itself was not up to much
but several of us paired off with some nice girls and we had several invitations for dinner and
nights out at the pictures or dancing. I particularly remember a girl called Sue Ellison. She
lived in a part of Wellington called Khandallah, which we nicknamed the 'Indian District'.
Districts of Wellington were named after their relationship with the first Duke of Wellington,
after whom Wellington is named. What was really nice about meeting these girls was that we
were able to meet up with them again on subsequent trips without having to worry about
commitment. We always wondered what they did with their boyfriends when we were in
port. One possible answer was that New Zealand boys were terrible at asking girls up to

dance. In those days, there was always at least one dance hall with a live band in every town. Invariably, the girls would sit in a row of chairs along one wall and the boys in a row of chairs along the opposite wall. If you asked a girl to dance, you had to walk across the floor with all the girls' eyes on you. Lots of New Zealanders chickened out and never asked a girl to dance the whole night. That meant that any boy who was keen always got a dance partner. The same applied in Ireland at the time.

The next day, the soccer team played the crew and drew 1-1. Two days later we played Wellington YMCA at basketball and lost 55-28, which was not bad as we had had few opportunities to practice. The same day some cadets played Marsden Girls School at tennis and won 4-1.

Now, this next event was interesting. There was a small population of Pitcairn Islanders in Wellington and the men mostly worked on the docks as carpenters. They were skilled at woodwork. They also had a reputation for whaler pulling. They challenged us to a whaler race and the course was to be over 7 cables. A 'cable' is 100 fathoms or 600 feet. 10 cables equals approximately one nautical mile. So, the race was over about 1,400 yards, which is a long way to pull. Our team, of which I was not a part, won by 7 lengths, which is a big margin.

The next day, we had a pulling and sailing regatta against the local Sea Cadets. The pulling race was over 5 cables and we put out two crews and I was in the second crew. We came first and second. The first crew was four and a half lengths ahead of our second crew and on that basis our second crew would have given the Pitcairners a close race. We did not do so well at sailing. Our officers came first, the Sea Cadets second and the apprentices came last. Experience, not brute force, told here.

We finished our sporting time at Wellington by going to the YMCA and playing tennis.

Whilst we were in Wellington, the regime of going ashore in uniform started to relax. Those apprentices on their last trip could go ashore in blazer, tie and flannel trousers, although the blazer had to have a Merchant Navy badge on the breast pocket and there was still an inspection by the Duty Officer before being allowed ashore. Gradually, this privilege extended to all apprentices during my time, except for 'trippers', together with doing away with the formal inspection. Eventually, we just informed the Duty Officer we were going ashore and were logged out. Even when I became a Deck Officer, all the Officers logged out when going ashore and logged in when returning on board. This was sensible in case of an emergency and the ship having to move suddenly, so that it was known who was on board and who wasn't.

Before we left Wellington, Lloyds of London carried out one of its periodic surveys. These surveys are essential if the ship owner wishes to retain the highest grading that Lloyds can offer, which was A1. These grades had a significant impact on insurance premiums and Lloyds of London is one of the foremost marine survey organisations. On this occasion, the survey concerned the security of hatches. As well as sufficient covering that was well secured by wedging the tarpaulin coverings along the hatch sides, the requirement was that all hatches had to be able to be secured by wire lashings. These were lengths of wire that criss-crossed the hatch coverings and that could be secured and tightened to prevent the tarpaulins from lifting and tearing off in bad weather. Each hatch had to have its own lashings and bottle screws. We had sufficient lashings for two hatches and did not often use them. Peter

Matthews, Henry McCutchan and I were assigned by the Chief Officer and Bosun to ensure that it would appear to the surveyor that we had the right quantity of equipment. The surveyor, accompanied by the Chief Officer and the Bosun, started at No 1 hatch and proceeded down the starboard side until he had finished his inspection at No 6 hatch. Two of us were stationed at No 1 hatch on the port side with enough lashings and bottle screws to hand. The other of us was at No 2 hatch with the other set of lashings and bottle screws. When the surveyor had finished with No 1 hatch, we doubled round the deckhouses with the first set of lashings and presented them at No 3 hatch. After No 2 hatch, we doubled down the port working alleyway and presented the second set of lashings at No 4 hatch. We repeated the exercise for Nos 5 and 6 hatches. All went well, although I cannot believe that the surveyor did not know what was going on. I cannot recall that we ever used the lashings for real.

The Bluff.

We left Wellington to sail to the Bluff, which took several days. We discharged cargo, loaded wool and took on fresh water. This fresh water was very sweet but light brown in colour because of the amount of peat in the environment.

The Bluff is the southernmost town on South Island and is the port for Invercargill, the principal town of the province of Southland. The coastline is rugged and just east of the area along the south west coast known as Fiordland, which is now a cruise destination. The Bluff is a small town about half the size of Farnham.

We were in Bluff for about a week. We had an inter-watch sailing race and Starboard won because Port Watch was disqualified after touching a buoy. Two days later we had a sailing race against 'HMS Cockade', a Royal Navy frigate. The Navy whaler capsized at the start of the race. It was a windy day and they had not taken a 'reef' in i.e. roll the sail down a bit to shorten the sail area. They had to be rescued by our Crash Boat. We completed the course and won. What a humiliation for the boys in blue. They also showed us over their ship but did not offer us any beer. Our basketball team also beat YMCA Invercargill. Then to complete our superiority over the Navy, we beat 'HMS Cockade's' whaler pulling crew by 10 lengths over 5 cables.

My mother had given me the address of some friends who had emigrated to New Zealand and lived in Invercargill. I went over there for dinner one night and their teenage son gave me a lift back in his car. In those days, a New Zealander could get a driving licence at 15 because so many people who lived on the land needed to drive machinery at a young age. His car radiator ran out of water and overheated. We scooped some water out of a pool by the side of the road after we had broken the ice. This was in summer time! It often froze at night in summer in the far south. Needless to say, we did not do any sea bathing at The Bluff.

Timaru.

Timaru was our turn-round port for this trip, so we knew that we would be there for a good stay. We were there from just before Christmas to mid-January. Because it was our turn-round port, we had plenty of cash in our pockets with which to enjoy Christmas, which was my first Christmas away from home. The weather was warm and mostly dry all the time and we made the most of it: cricket, sailing, pulling, basketball, table tennis and dancing.

Nobody worked in Timaru between Christmas Eve and the day after New Year's Day. Timaru is also a holiday resort and had a good dance hall called the 'Elizabeth Tea Rooms' at the northern end of the beach. There seemed to be a dance there every night to a live band. One of our stewards fancied himself as a dancer. He was thin and had red hair – he was by no means good-looking. He couldn't get a dance partner at all one evening. Every girl he asked said 'No'. The problem was, and still is I guess, that if more than one girl turned you down, then none of the other girls would get up. He must have asked about ten girls without success and then stamped up and down the floor crying out 'Why won't anybody dance with me?' It was made worse for him because we apprentices had no problem.

The wharfies had a cricket team and they invited us to play against them. We led on the first innings, had lunch at a pub and then rain ended play, so we ended up playing darts in the pub all afternoon. This pub was a notorious 'sly grog' and I became a regular. The pub landlord said that he would get a cricket team to play us on a Sunday afternoon. It started with a coach trip into the country and we played in a field which had a pitch mown but the rest of the grass was about six inches high. It made it difficult to score unless you could hit the ball high and safely. Unfortunately for us, the opposition had a big hitter. He had played first class cricket for Canterbury Province. He hit our bowling all over the place and then bowled us out for next to nothing. This was our first introduction to 'casual cricket' Down Under. Every time a wicket fell, everybody retired for a drink. Given that we did not get many of them out but we were all out, it still meant that we drank about 15 beers each during the match before we got seriously stuck in afterwards. Happy Days!

We made friends with the Timaru Yacht Club and the Rowing Club. Our dinghies came second and third in a sailing regatta and the Rowing Club let us join in rowing practice in their boats. One of the Rowing Club members had a father who was a sheep shearer. The last weekend of our stay he invited us to go with him whilst he visited his dad up country. The Canterbury Plain is a vast area of rolling grassland. We had no idea where our friend's dad was. We just kept going until we saw his tent, admired the view, which included the Southern Alps, had a brew and then came back.

Also in port was 'HMNZS Pukaki', on leave from the Antarctic. We beat them in a pulling race. Our first crew beat our second crew (with me in the second) by eight lengths and our second crew were ten lengths in front of the Kiwis. Our officers then beat the Pukaki officers. However, I reckon that the Pukaki crew had enjoyed Christmas and the hospitality of the Timaru people even more than we had. Wherever we went, we were not allowed to put our hands in our pockets. The Pukaki had hired a few bicycles and the Navy boys were a hazard when they cycled along the wooden wharf from their ship into town. One evening, a drunken sailor came from town at full speed but didn't stop at his ship. He just kept going and disappeared over the end of the wharf into the sea.

Timaru had a velodrome, which was suprising considering its small size as a town. There was a cycle meeting there and one of the contestants was Reg Harris from Cheshire. He was then the world professional sprint champion. The velodrome track was steeply banked and all the cyclists tried to get a commanding position at the top of the banking. In the sprint races at that time only the last lap counted. Harris was a master at holding a stationary position at the top of the banking. His opponents had to compete with him to stay still, but they couldn't. When they were off balance, he swooped and left them behind to complete the last lap in front. That kind of tactic is illegal now.

Reg Harris

There was also an athletics meeting at the same venue and we were supposed to have a Kiwi competitor, Murray Halberg, who had competed at the Melbourne Olympics. Unfortunately, he was ambushed and plied with too much beer. As a result, he was too 'crook' to run, much to the amusement of the crowd.

One of the sights in New Zealand during the summer was the sight of young men riding motor bikes dressed only in their shorts and barefoot, particularly in smaller towns and rural areas. New Zealand had also introduced an annual vehicle check known as a Certificate of Fitness or Warrant of Fitness. It was the Kiwi equivalent of the MoT and was introduced years ahead of the UK MoT. It was not uncommon for the police to pull over young drivers and riders to check their Warrant, which did cause resentment. As the population was small, it was easy for the police to identify offenders and they kept a close eye on them.

All good things have an ending and all too soon we had to leave Timaru. Several hundred people and the town band came to see us off. It was an acknowledgment that we were not only important materially to the town but that there was a strong emotional link as well. As we started to move away, the band played 'Now Is The Hour' or 'Po Atarau' in Maori. This was the last trip before retiring for Tom, one of the greasers. He stood at the top of the companion ladder and sang and cried his heart out and the crowd joined in.

I was touchingly reminded of this event whilst watching the BBC programme 'VJ Day 75 – The Nation's Tribute'. Sheridan Smith sang a Vera Lynn medley, including 'Now Is The Hour'. I immediately went back to that moment in Timaru and cried, whilst my wife held my hand. This memory reinforces my view that the Commonwealth is a living and breathing entity, which we should cherish and develop both emotionally and economically.

Lyttelton

We went to Lyttelton for a few days and lost a basketball match against the Royal New Zealand Air Force. Then on to Wellington before going home.

Wellington.

On the Sunday after we arrived we were inspected by the Chief of Staff, Royal New Zealand Navy, Rear-Admiral J E W McBeath CB, DSO, DSC. Then we had a lecture on the 'Merchant Navy in the Event of War' by an RNZN Captain. It was all very necessary at that time because the Cold War had intensified after the Hungarian uprising against Russia and the Suez Crisis. We had a moan because it was on our day off.

Sue Ellison and a friend of hers, who was dating one of my colleagues, 'Jack' Hawkins, arranged a trip to Paraparaumu. This is a lovely beach with light surf about 50 miles north of Wellington. You have to climb to get out of Wellington and we followed the Hutt Valley and into an area known as Wairarapa. As we climbed there was a big notice at the side of the road: 'Beware Of The Wind'. It always provoked a laugh amongst the locals but the wind could make the climb awkward. We had a great day out and I tried my hand at surfing for the first time since Croyde Bay in Devon on a holiday when I was fifteen.

The Evans Bay Yacht Club invited us to their regatta on our last Saturday and our whaler came third in a big field. That evening, we held the voyage dance at the 'Roseland Cabaret', which was a very swish place and the buffet was marvellous. One of the best dances I have ever been to. We followed up with a leaving party on board.

We left a few days before the end of January after what had been a memorable stay. Looking back at our social life, it is hard to see where we found the time to work.

We arrived home in the middle of March and went on leave for nearly a month. My dad was supposed to go on a coach trip to Twickenham to see England play Scotland in what was the last match of what was then the Five Nations Championship. He was not well and he gave me his ticket. England won and, in so doing, won the Grand Slam for the first time since the 1930s. It was my first England game and I can remember most of the England players' names. Reg Higgins scored the winning try in the right hand corner next to the old Adrian Stoop stand and right in front of me.

CHAPTER NINETEEN

Third Durham Trip

14th April 1957 to 4th October 1957

This time we were headed for Australia and the older hands told us that we would not have such a good time as we had in New Zealand. My memory is not so strong with detail about this trip. Certainly, there was nothing out of the ordinary during our outward journey. Even a couple of stops to change cylinder liners seemed ordinary. So, I will move on from London, Avonmouth, Newport, Cardiff and Panama to our arrival in Sydney.

Australia.

Australia is divided into six states (Queensland, New South Wales, Victoria, South Australia, Western Australia and the island of Tasmania) and one Territory (Northern Territory, which is administered as a Federal territory). It is a federal state with the capital of the Federal Government being in Canberra. Canberra, like Washington DC, Ottawa and Brasilia, was chosen as a capital site in order to avoid antagonisms between state capitals. There is great rivalry between Sydney and Melbourne in terms of sport, trade and culture. The choice of Canberra as the capital of Australia resolved forever the competing claims. Each state has its own government with a two chamber system as we have in the UK, although both chambers are elected. The Federal Australian Government is organised in the same way. The King is the Head of State and is physically represented by the Governor General. This person used to be appointed by the Monarch Queen acting on his or her own. Nowadays, the incumbent is a person recommended by the Australian Government and subsequently appointed by the Monarch. Each State has its own Governor. The positions of Governor General and Governors are very much like the Monarch's. They do not govern but have the right to fire Prime Ministers and appoint new ones, but always in consultation with the governing parties. There has always been a strong republican element in Australia, which element was originally supported by Irish immigrants and their descendants and the descendants of the original convict immigrants. Their ranks have been increased by immigrants from non-UK countries who had either no experience of a monarchy or a bad experience. In a couple of referendums, the population voted to remain a monarchy but republicanism remains strong.

Australia is huge and has considerable variations in climate. What it does not have is adequate rainfall. Much of Australia is desert and there are periodic droughts, which acerbate the tendency of the 'bush' to catch fire and wreak havoc. There are enormous areas of grassland, a proportion of which has been turned into arable farming. Australia has large mineral deposits: gold, silver, lead, opals and coal. It exports beef, lamb, cheese, butter, wool, hides, iron, steel, coal, wheat and precious metals. Although Australia is a major wine exporter now, it exported hardly any wine during my trips. The reality was that Australia had a low reputation as a wine producer even though it had been producing wine for a hundred years. Nearly all the wine was for domestic production. It had a gold rush in the mid-1880s as big as the Californian Gold Rush of 1849. It is a prosperous country with a high standard of living made more attractive by a climate that encourages outdoor pursuits.

Sydney.

The approach to Sydney by sea can be dramatic. The entrance to Port Jackson, which is the correct name for Sydney Harbour, is through Sydney Heads, a narrow channel between two cliffs. We arrived at dawn and there had been a mist. The sun shone on the mist and it turned the whole of Port Jackson, and the surrounding shore line, pink. It was a wonderful sight and a great introduction to one of the greatest natural harbours in the world. Sydney Harbour is huge and has numerous bays and inlets, each with their separate villages and townships. It is these indentations that separate Sydney from the other great harbours, such as Wellington, Poole, Southampton, New York and San Francisco. The indentations have created a greater length of shoreline so that there is more space for waterfront properties than in other similar areas.

The harbour is actually the estuary for the Parrammata River. Sydney Harbour Bridge joins central Sydney and the northern suburbs at the narrowest point of the harbour. Ferries also connect central Sydney with the northern suburbs. The main surfing beaches are outside Sydney Harbour: Bondi to the south east and Manley to the north east.

Normally, merchant ships go to open berths on a man-made island on the inland side of the bridge, which is a bus ride from Sydney centre. This time we berthed in Rushcutters Bay opposite the Woolomoloo Naval Base and were within a short walk of the city centre. This area has been substantially redeveloped and is now the site of Sydney Opera House.

Sydney is the largest city in Australia and New Zealand and completely different from any other city in those countries. It is the capital of New South Wales State. It is very cosmopolitan. The Australian Government encouraged immigration from countries with a Caucasian population after the Second World War. Thousands of Brits took advantage of the low price of a passage subsided by the Australian Government. For years, you could emigrate by buying a ticket for £10 on a passenger liner. Also migrating were Italians, Greeks and Spanish. They tended to settle in Sydney and Sydney had shops selling Continental European food and goods. This led to a varied selection of cafes and restaurants not available elsewhere in Australia and New Zealand. It also led to the increasing influence of the Roman Catholic Church. New South Wales was the first state to relax the First World War drinking laws. In my time, pubs could open to 10.30 pm and restaurants could obtain a drinks licence. This developed an after work society (theatres and clubs) unique to that part of the world. All in all, Sydney exuded an atmosphere of excitement.

The Royal Australian Navy's flagship at the time was an aircraft carrier, 'HMAS Melbourne', and she was berthed opposite us in the Naval Base. Melbourne was originally an RN ship called 'Majestic' and was the first of the 'Majestic' class. Completed in 1945, she never saw RN service and the Australian Government bought her in 1947, after which she went through extensive conversions, including one of the first angled flight decks, and only entered service in 1955. She dwarfed us and carried over 1,300 crew. We challenged them to a whaler race. It was a bit like David and Goliath, with the same outcome. Our two crews (I was again in our second) absolutely smashing their crews. The race was in Rushcutters Bay and Melbourne had all her crew lining the decks cheering their whalers on. We really felt we had achieved something and Dig Hocken went around with a big grin on his face for days afterwards. We were never invited on board Melbourne, although it had been common practice when we met ships of the Royal New Zealand Navy in port. Aussies are bad losers.

We played a rugger match against Parramatta School, which is in the eastern suburbs. Parramatta is one of the top public schools in Australia. It ranks with Geelong Grammar, where the King, when Prince Charles, spent a term about ten years later. The setting and the weather were ideal. The main school buildings are elevated and the principal sports field is at the bottom of a slope, which provided a natural grandstand. I can't remember if we won or lost, but it was close. Melbe Hocken had bought a 16 mm film camera and shot extensive film on this trip, including this match. I played open side wing forward in this match and the film clearly shows me off-side at a lineout although the ref did not spot it. I do not know what happened to that film and I have made attempts to find a copy, including contacting a member of the Downer family, but without getting a reply.

We also played a soccer match against a newly formed club in Sydney. It was mostly English ex-pats and a few European immigrants. Soccer was very much a minority sport in Aussie. The most popular sports were cricket, Rugby League, Rugby Union, Australian Rules football, tennis and swimming. The pitch had no grass and was very hard clay. We were made very welcome and there was plenty of free beer in the clubhouse afterwards. I hope that this club kept going because they were so friendly and enthusiastic.

Social and sports clubs in Australia, and particularly in Sydney, were wealthy institutions compared to their British equivalents. The Aussie gaming laws allowed one armed bandits in private clubs. Consequently, these clubs had enhanced incomes. This was reflected in vastly superior facilities compared to the UK. The main clubs were those associated with the RSL (Returned Servicemen's League) and Rugby League. The RSL is the equivalent of the Royal British Legion, but with more political 'oomph' because of its wealth. Similarly, Rugby League clubs had sufficient income to attract the best players, including those enticed from Rugby Union.

Because it was winter, we did not visit any beaches this trip.

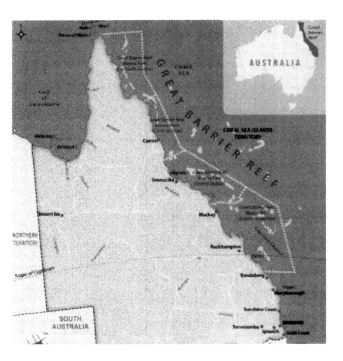

Brisbane

Up the coast we went to Brisbane. Brisbane is the capital of Queensland and is on the Brisbane River, which runs into Moreton Bay, just south of the Great Barrier Reef. We were berthed practically in the middle of the city. The climate in winter is very pleasant, often in the seventies although we did not wear tropical whites. The older apprentices introduced us to 'Cloudlands'. This was a huge ballroom on top of a hill and you had to climb a long set of steep steps to get to it from the main road. The dance floor could probably accommodate several hundred people at once. I remember that it had a roped off area for those who wanted to jive.

Whilst in Brisbane, those of us on our third and fourth trips took exams to obtain our Lifeboat Certificates and Efficient Deck Hand Certificates (EDH). In order to sit my first professional exam, I had to have a lifeboat certificate. The Merchant Shipping Act also requires each ship to have a minimum number of EDHs. Durham did not carry enough deck ratings, so the apprentices had to obtain EDH Certificates. As senior apprentices left, so the more junior had to obtain an EDH Certificate, otherwise Durham could not sail. The EDH Certificate was not a requirement for a Deck Officer. It just suited NZS for its Apprentices to have the Certificate and save money. The average wage of an Apprentice was then about £15 a month compared with £36 a month for an EDH, plus an EDH could earn overtime.

There was another NZS ship in Brisbane and it was arranged that there would be a lifeboat exam held on that ship. We took with us some stewards and engine room ratings who were interested. The numbers were made up of ratings and stewards from the host ship. It was a verbal and practical exam. The examiner questioned us individually about lifeboats: construction, equipment and stores. Then we started to launch the two lifeboats that were on the side overlooking the water. At this point, one of the stewards from the host ship asked to be excused because he had to go and make the Officers' tea. The examiner let him go saying 'You wouldn't have passed anyway'. I guess the steward was one of those drafted in to make up the numbers. Just goes to show how people can be very short-sighted. Knowing how to handle a lifeboat is, potentially, lifesaving. I would have made it compulsory for all sea-goers to obtain a Lifeboat Certificate after a minimum number of years of service, otherwise they could not continue at sea. We lowered the boats, sailed them and rowed them and then hoisted them up again. All the apprentices passed and it would have been a huge shock if any one hadn't. The exam was not difficult. It just needed a little bit of practice and application.

A couple of days later, we were back on the same ship for our EDH exam, which, as with the lifeboat exam, was solely a practical exam. We had to demonstrate our skill with rope and wire splices. It so happened that the Second Officer, who had organised the exam, was not only a Warsash man but also an Old Warwickian. When I was doing my specimen wire splice, he kept a close eye on me and advised me by lifting his eyebrows or nodding and shaking his head. Once again, we all passed.

We launched the dinghies and whalers because the sailing is easy in Brisbane River and the water traffic was low because it was winter. I remember two lovely lazy afternoons sailing dinghies in a light wind.

Des Jones, the 'Schoolie', organised a trip to Coolangatta for some of us who had no other duties. I did not go. Coolangatta was an incipient tourist resort, mainly because it offered year round surfing with an equable climate. Over the years it became known as the 'Gold Coast' and became a major resort area with many organised outdoor activities. It has housed the Commonwealth Games. Everybody who went thoroughly enjoyed themselves.

Monty Banks (on the rightt) and AN Other. Sailing in comfort

Scot and 'Dinghy' Lane working on a dinghy. The only true sailors amongst us?

Cairns

From Brisbane, we travelled about two hundred and fifty miles north to enter the Great Barrier Reef and the tropics. For the following day and a half we sailed through exceptionally calm waters inside the Reef. This is the world's largest coral reef and is now in great danger from climate change. Coral is very sensitive to temperature changes and will die if the water is too warm, which warmth creates too much carbon dioxide. Then, all we were aware of was a chain of low, green islands to starboard. A couple of days later we were in Cairns in North Queensland. Cairns is a small town set in a sunken volcano. Its wharfies had the reputation of being the most bolshie in Australia, which means that they were very bolshie. They whinged about anything. One bloke moaned to me that the rope he had to handle was a bit frayed and he could not pass it through a hole in a piece of wood. He did not take kindly to me telling him to put some hair round it.

We took the whalers out to Green Island on the reef, or was it Magnetic Island? Can't remember but it was lovely sailing weather – light breeze and a calm sea. The winter weather in North Queensland is perfect. There is no tide either in the Barrier Reef, so the water level is constant. You don't really see much on the Reef islands and few are inhabited. The swimming on the inside of the reef is great, if you are careful about the sharks. Everything we took we brought back, no rubbish left.

After my time, the tourist trade developed with glass bottomed boats and scuba diving allowing visitors to appreciate the abundant marine life.

Townsville

After Cairns, we travelled back south to Townsville, about half a day's sailing and still within the Great Barrier Reef. Townsville is larger and more important than Cairns. It lies up a creek and the surrounding countryside is flat. Apart from sheep and cattle, sugar cane is grown. Italians were encouraged to migrate here to work the sugar fields. I noticed that a lot of men wore white gloves at dances. It can be very humid and those working in the sugar fields would get their hands cut. A combination of sweat and sugar cane residue meant that men could leave unpleasant stains and smells on ladies' frocks. So the custom grew for men to wear white gloves when dancing and it stuck, even for those not involved in sugar production.

The berths were about a half hour's walk from the town and you walked partly past sugar cane fields.

Townsville had an Olympic sized outdoor swimming pool and diving pool called the 'Tobruk Pool'. It was used by the Australian Swimming Association as winter training quarters. At that time, Australian swimmers, especially the girls, were world beaters. During our visit, Lorraine Crapp was training there. She had won two golds and a silver at the 1956 Olympics in Melbourne and had broken fifteen world records in training for the Olympics. We watched her training a couple of times and she really put the effort in. She paid us a visit on board one afternoon, but she was shy and a bit overwhelmed by being in the company of thirty adolescent males. But she smiled her way through. She was about average height and build, a completely different physique from today's champion swimmers.

Lorraine Crapp in training

Our visit coincided with 'Bush Week'. This is an annual event when the station owners and their people come in from the bush to have a week's holiday during the town's annual show. A 'station' is an Aussie and a Kiwi word for a ranch or farm. In this part of the world, these stations can consist of tens of thousands of acres of poor quality grazing. At that time, the cattle were worked by men on horseback. These men, mostly young, were known as 'jackeroos' and were the Aussie equivalent of American cowboys. Their life was hard and isolated. For eleven and a half months of the year they never left the station and never spent their pay.

Townsville puts on an agricultural show and there is a race meeting. If you ever get a chance to see an old Robert Mitchum film called 'The Sundowners', it encapsulates exactly what Bush Week is. I had heard about the gambling that went on but could not believe it until I saw it. There was a lot of 'two up' where a man places two coins on a piece of wood and throws the coins over his shoulder. Bets are placed on how the coins fall: heads, tails or evens. It is illegal, takes place outside, usually behind buildings, and there would be lookouts posted to alert the players to the police arriving. Another game, customarily played in a bar, was to bet on the last two or three of the numbers on a bank note. I could not believe how much was gambled in this way. There was quite a lot of drunkenness. At the end of the week, most of the jackeroos went back to their stations penniless.

There was a big dance organised one evening. It actually took place in a large shed with a corrugated iron roof and was attended by the Town Mayor and Council. The occasion was a visit by that year's 'Miss Australia', June Finlayson. The sponsor of 'Miss Australia' was an underwear manufacturer whose main brand was 'Hickory Bras'. Not exactly a glamorous name. Having won the event, 'Miss Australia' had to go on a tour to promote the bras. 'Miss Australia', who was a pretty brunette with too much makeup and a sticky out skirt, arrived, gathered the women around her and proceeded to extol the virtues of Hickory Bras. She then stood on one side whilst the band played the first dance. After a couple of dances, she was still standing there and I asked her up to dance. I expected her, or her minder, to say 'no'. To my surprise, she said yes and was obviously glad that somebody had taken the courage to ask. The problem was she couldn't dance and had no conversation. It was like pushing the furniture round.

The next event demonstrated how adept Aussies are at creating a spontaneous occasion. If I remember correctly, some of us were invited to a Rugby League match. I think it was in Townsville, but it could have been Cairns. There were no stands. Several spectators turned up with flat bed trucks and pickup vans. These were reversed, in a line, close to one of the touchlines. Spectators then climbed up and used the vehicles as grandstands. Beer was plentiful. A memorable social occasion.

I committed a very reprehensible act in Townsville. I went to the races on our last day in port. The racecourse was some distance from town and you got there by train. There was no platform, you just got down by the side of the track. It seemed as though all the town was there and the women were got up in their finery, despite the heat. It was sort of their equivalent of Ascot or Derby Day. I won what was called 'The Tote Double'. For a bet of a pound, I won over sixty. Naturally, I celebrated and fell amongst thieves, all people whom I had met during our stay and were out for a good time. The celebration continued after we got back to town. We were due to sail at six the next morning. I was listed as 'quartermaster' for the 12 to 4 watch in the morning. That is, I was on security watch on the companion ladder. I had arranged a late pass until 11 pm. Somehow, I staggered up the road from town to the ship and got back on board just in time to report back at 11. We were still working cargo. I knew I had the Quartermaster watch, changed and went to sleep on a bench in the apprentices lounge. The 8 to 12 Quartermaster woke me up for my watch and I staggered on deck. The 4th Mate was just finishing supervising the last of the loading and securing hatches. He instructed me to make sure that I woke my relief at 3.45 am and that he had to wake the officers, senior ratings and apprentices at 5.30 am. Well, I couldn't keep awake and went to sleep again. When I woke, it was quarter past six. So, I woke my relief, told him he had to wake everybody up and went to bed. In fact, the Pilot had come on board at six and woken up the Chief Officer. The result was that we left port an hour late. When we were clear of port, the

Captain called a meeting of the apprentices and gave us a lecture on the effects of 'too much bloody booze'. Everybody knew he was referring to me. I had my shore leave stopped indefinitely, which was very fair. I could have been kicked out, but somehow Head Office never found out. I never did anything like that again, although I did have late nights when it didn't matter.

Rockhampton, South Queensland.

What a place to begin my 'sentence'! The town of Rockhampton is nearly forty miles inland from the sea. It's 'port' is situated on a mudflat 32 miles from town and is itself a few miles up a creek. The only way out from the port is along a single track railway that is only used for freight. The port was one long wooden dock. On the 'landside' was a collection of huts. These huts were used to house the wharfies, who contracted to work the ships in port. They were brought from Rockhampton by the railway and stayed in the huts until the ship left. I can't remember how long we were there for, but it was less than a week.

We launched the Crash Boat some distance out before berthing because we would be berthed with the starboard side to the wharf and the crash boat was on the starboard side of the boat deck. This had become, or became, standard practice after this occasion, so that we always had use of the Crash Boat for work or leisure during our stays in port. It was our experiences with this experimental craft that led to it being installed in every vessel in the fleet.

Whaler sailing: Geoff Morris, Tony 'Dinghy' Lane, Pete Barr. Pater Matthews, Scot Gilchrist.

We could sail in the creek and we played football on the mudflats. Dig Hocken and Melbe practiced golf shots on the mud. He even let some of us use have a go, including (surprise, surprise) me. Whatever had happened in Townsville, I was allowed to work myself back into favour and it wasn't difficult because I enjoyed my life as an apprentice.

Henry McCutchan and Bob McGregor have told me recently that we, together with Peter Matthews, went on board a China Steam Navigation Company vessel that was also in port. Apparently, we were regaled by the officers and I ended up singing a Shakespeare soliloquy. I have absolutely no recollection of this. Bob also said that the China Steam Navigation captain was the best recruitment officer that China Steam could have put in place. He and Peter joined China Steam after obtaining their Second Mate's Certificate and enjoyed their time with that company. In light of subsequent events, perhaps I have should have joined them. Had I done so, this book would have had a very different ending.

Melbourne

Our next port of call was Melbourne and we were there about ten days. It lies at the north end of Port Philip Bay, named after Captain Philip, the leader of the first penal colony in Botany Bay. The bay is enormous, about the size of Surrey. The entrance is through a series of sandbanks in the south west corner. There are towns on the bay, such as Geelong, that have no physical connection with Melbourne. If you watched the TV serial 'The Cry', you will get an idea of what the countryside is like –somewhat flat and uninteresting.

Melbourne is the capital of the state of Victoria, is built along the Yarra River and is inland from the bay. It was named after Lord Melbourne, Queen Victoria's first Prime Minister. The harbour area is called Port Melbourne and is a collection of jetties on the east side of the Yarra estuary. You went into Melbourne by tram. The main street is Flinders Street. At the intersection of Flinders Street and Collins Street is Flinders Street railway station. Next to it is a pub called 'Young and Jackman's'. Visiting this pub used to be a rite of passage. The first floor bar housed, and still does, a famous nude portrait behind the bar called 'Chloe'. It was painted in 1875 in Paris and subsequently exhibited there. It is very large, about eight and a half feet tall and four and a half feet wide. There is a tragic story behind the painting. The model, Marie, was Italian and came to Paris to make her name. She was, reputedly, a lover of the painter, but he married her sister. A year after her portrait was painted, she committed suicide. Anyway, the painting was bought by an Australian and has been on display in the pub since 1908.

Chloe

Melbourne had two good theatres and a number of restaurants but it is not as cosmopolitan as Sydney. In fact it rivals Adelaide as the most English of all the Aussie cities and big towns. It does have the Melbourne Cricket Ground (the MCG). It is still, I believe, one of the largest sports stadia in the Southern Hemisphere. It can hold over 90,000 people, which is a lot for a city population of less than1,000,000 when it was built. It is filled regularly for the final of the Australian Rules Football Cup, is the home of the Victoria Cricket Club and a test match venue. In 1956 it hosted the Olympic Games. Just outside Melbourne is Flemington Racecourse, the venue for the Melbourne Cup. This meeting is the biggest meeting in Australia and everybody dresses up, which can be uncomfortable as it is staged in November when the temperature can be in the high 20s or low 30s.

After a few days in Melbourne, Monty Banks, then Cadet Captain, invited me into his cabin. He said: 'Trog (my nickname on the Durham), I've had a word with Frankie (the Chief Officer) about you. Everybody is pleased about your attitude and I said that it would not be a good idea if you had no shore leave before we face the long trip home. It might not be good for your morale. You've got your shore leave back provided you behave yourself'. I suspect that there was a bit of self-interest here because Monty and I were friends and often went ashore together. He wanted his drinking companion back. A couple or so days later, he had arranged a night out with some friends he had picked up on previous trips, one of whom, Tom Smeaton, was now at Uni. We went ashore without parading and in casual clothes. We expected to be out all night. We had a few drinks, went to a party and ended up in Tom's student digs playing cards until four in the morning. This was good behaviour! Good old Monty!

We did not have a trip dance but we had a big party on board with the galley providing a sumptuous cold buffet. I had been introduced to a girl called Caroline a couple of days before and she came and was good fun. In fact, it turned out to be such a good party that we were allowed to extend the time into the early hours. Caroline lived in the district of Toorak, in Orrong Road. This was where Barry Humphries (Dame Edna Everage) was born and brought up. It is possible that Barry's dad built Caroline's house because he was a house builder. I like these connections.

Adelaide

This was our last port of call before going home and we were not there long. Adelaide is the capital of South Australia and was named after the wife of William IV, Queen Victoria's uncle. It is up river from the sea and the river is not deep enough for deep sea ships. A port was built on the coast of the Spencer Gulf called Port Adelaide. To access Adelaide, you caught a bus. I remember the bit about the bus because one of the apprentices senior to me, Jack Hawkins, went into Adelaide and got a driving licence. There was no practical test in South Australia then. All you had to do was answer seven verbal questions out of ten. Jack told me that he read the Aussie Highway Code on the way in on the bus and got eight right. The benefit was that the licence was recognised in the UK as long as you were a visitor. Back home, you just gave an Aussie address for the insurance and so on.

Melbe Downer was a native of Adelaide, but because we were there for only a few short days, there was no opportunity for her to organise a big party.

Our journey home was westwards across the Great Australian Bight to Cape Leeuwin, the south western extremity of Australia and then north west across the Indian Ocean to Aden and Suez.

Aden

Aden is a port at the eastern entrance to the Red Sea. It is part of Yemen but the province of Aden was at that time a Dependency of the British Empire. It was developed originally as a coaling station for ships travelling through the Suez Canal to India and beyond and later as an oil bunkering stop. There was a permanent Army and RAF garrison there. It is very hot and humid. I tried to write a letter but my sweat poured over the paper and made it impossible to write.

We stayed to take on oil. We did not berth in the port but moored to a buoy and a tanker came alongside to transfer the oil. After mooring, we were surrounded by 'bum boats'. These were small boats full of local traders peddling their wares: bolts of silk, silk dressing gowns and pyjamas and porcelain but also cigarette lighters. If you wanted to buy, you lowered a basket down, the boatman put the object into the basket, you hauled it up and haggled with the boatman. If you haggled too hard, he called out 'Hey, you McGregor!' The Scots reputation for miserliness had travelled far. We apprentices were pretty broke at this time, so we didn't buy much but other crew members bought presents to take home.

Suez.

Then up the Red Sea to Port Suez and the Suez Canal. We were painting the white superstructure when a sand storm suddenly developed from the African shore. We couldn't dodge it and the sand stuck to the fresh paint. The bosun would have torn his hair out if he hadn't been bald.

We had to anchor and wait for a convoy to go through the canal. Immediately, more bumboats arrived and one enterprising Arab climbed aboard. He was in Western style clothes: a cheap, cotton tropical suit and a trilby hat. He was a barber. He didn't bother with money and was quite happy to be paid in cigarettes. '50 snouts' was the going rate, which he asked for in a Cockney accent. In fact, whichever crew member he barbered he mimicked exactly the accent they spoke. This was a result of cutting the hair of thousands of British soldiers during the years we had occupied and controlled the Canal Zone.

The Suez Canal runs roughly north to south for about 100 miles from the Mediterranean at Port Said to Port Suez on the Red Sea. It is in three parts: the northern part between Port Said and the Great Bitter Lake, the middle part which is the Great Bitter Lake and the southern part from the Great Bitter Lake to Port Suez. The northern and southern parts are not wide enough for two ships to pass. The north bound convoy waits in the Great Bitter Lake for the south bound convoy to pass. Similar to what happens in the Panama Canal. The Suez Canal passes through desert and there is always sand sliding in down the banks and blown in by the wind. The canal needs constant dredging and there are shifting sand banks. Not an easy navigation.

This time it was made worse because the Canal had been closed since the Six Day War in October 1956. Two years previously, the Egyptian dictator, Colonel Nasser, had come to an agreement with the UK government whereby the UK would withdraw its troops from the Canal Zone. This left the Suez Canal Company without immediate physical protection. The Suez Canal Company was jointly owned by the British and French governments and the British government had administered a zone several miles wide along both sides of the canal. This meant that the UK had the revenues of the canal and effectively governed Egypt with the

Egyptian king, Farouk, as our client (plus a joint government with Egypt in the Sudan). The Egyptian Army overthrew Farouk in 1952 and established a military dictatorship. The new government wanted to build a dam across the Nile at Aswan to control irrigation and provide hydro-electric power. It courted the Russians, the Americans and the UK for funding. The Americans and the UK agreed to fund but when they found out that the Russians were supplying arms to Egypt, the Americans and the UK pulled out of the deal. Colonel Nasser was desperate for funds and cast his eye on the Canal revenues. Hence, he nationalised the Suez Canal Company in July 1956. This was the origin of the infamous Suez Crisis, which signalled the end of the British Empire as it then was.

In the summer of 1956, Israeli intelligence allegedly discovered an Egyptian plan to invade Israel with the newly acquired Russian arms, which included modern war planes. Egypt planned a joint invasion with Jordan and Syria. The Israelis decided on a pre-emptive strike to forestall the Egyptian plan, but they needed support. They turned to Britain and France, still smarting from the loss of the canal. The UK Prime Minister, Anthony Eden, thought he still lived in the time of Lord Palmerston and only needed to send a gunboat to restore order. He persuaded the French to join in an attack on Egypt. The Israelis struck first in the Sinai. France and the UK declared that they would intervene to obtain peace and ensure the continued, unrestricted and peaceful use of the Suez Canal. In October, a joint Anglo-French force invaded the north end of the canal whilst Israeli air planes obliterated the Egyptian air force on the ground. At the same time, Israel occupied northern Sinai, invaded the Golan Heights in southern Syria, defeated the Syrian Army and took the West Bank off the Jordanian Army. Although it was a complete military victory, it was a diplomatic disaster. The Americans refused support and the pound collapsed. We had to pull out, which meant the Israelis had to retreat, although they held on to the Golan Heights and the Jordanian West Bank. It was humiliating for the British and French. It led to Eden's resignation and a constitutional crisis for the French.

We arrived at Port Suez in September 1957 when the canal had only recently been re-opened. The Egyptians had blocked the canal and it took several months to re-dredge. The sand banks had moved and were not accurately charted. The Suez Canal Company had employed only French and British pilots. Nasser had sacked them, so there were no experienced pilots. He recruited from wherever he could, including Russia. Our pilot was a Lieutenant-Commander in the Egyptian Navy. Shortly after we entered the canal, we hit a sandbank at the stern on the port side. It was a severe jolt but we floated off and continued our passage. By this time, Dig Hocken had had enough of the pilot. He asked him what experience he had of piloting in the canal and the answer was none. Dig then asked him what qualifications he had. The pilot said he had a Second Mate's Certificate from Alexandria, which was worthless for these circumstances. So, Dig took over the piloting and used his experience of many years. Experienced seamen can feel how a ship is behaving. A ship handles differently in shallow and confined waters. He brought us safely to Port Said, which was a magnificent achievement. We berthed at Port Said and a diver went down to inspect the hull. He found no damage apart from a few scrapes. We were not allowed ashore, obviously, and we kept a close watch on all comings and goings. We did not want a repeat of the 'Windrush' incident.

During our passage of the canal, we saw hundreds of Egyptian labourers, known as 'fellaheen', moving sand from the canal side and up over the steep bank. They filled straw baskets and scrambled up the bank before depositing the sand on the other side of the bank. It was like a scene from the time of Moses.

The trip home through the Mediterranean, along the Spanish and Portuguese coast and across the Bay of Biscay and up the Irish Sea to Liverpool was uneventful. I did have my first view of the Rock of Gibraltar because we passed it in daylight. You can appreciate its strategic value more from the sea as you pass through the narrow straits.

This trip constituted my first true circumnavigation of the globe i.e. a complete passage from the UK in one direction, in this case, from West to East. On my previous two trips, although I had gone to the furthest point in Australasia and crossed the 180 degrees meridian and the Greenwich meridian several times, they were not a complete round trip. We paid off in Liverpool and went on leave. Monty Banks and Cedric Hufflett went on study leave and I never saw 'Huffie' again.

I travelled home by train, but not by the direct route. The direct route would have been from Lime Street station, Liverpool, to New Street station, Birmingham, then across the city centre to Snowhill station and a train to Stratford. For whatever reason, I decided to travel a slighter longer, and, as it turned out, a more interesting route. I crossed the Mersey by ferry to Birkenhead and took a train from Birkenhead station. This took a more westerly route to Birmingham with stops at Chester, Ruabon, Oswestry, Shrewsbury and Wolverhampton. It was a lovely leisurely journey with interesting scenery and a view of the Marcher country whilst enjoying lunch.

CHAPTER TWENTY

Reflections So far

I was now more than halfway into my Apprenticeship, had circumnavigated the world three times, had visited New Zealand, Australia, Fiji and Panama and spent more than six months all told in those countries. What were my impressions, what had influenced me and had I made the right decision?

Answering the last question first is the easiest to answer. I had enjoyed myself immensely and, I hope, broadened my knowledge. My appetite had been thoroughly whetted and I wanted more. I have often remembered a remark in his column by Henry Longhurst, who was the 'Sunday Times' golf correspondent for many years: 'Find out what you want to do in life and then find someone to pay you to do it.' I felt that I was on the right path, which was only emphasised by a remark from Dig Hocken that his was the only job on board worth having. If I was enjoying what I was doing, how much more enjoyment was awaiting me as I, hopefully, progressed in my career? But at the back of my mind were two questions that I gave no real thought to at the time but became increasingly to the forefront over the next four3 years: could I endure the long, slow sea passages without dying of boredom and did I really want to be in a profession where advancement seemed to be a combination of passing exams and waiting for a vacancy? As far as the first was concerned, I was kept so busy as an Apprentice that the thought did not arise but the second was one I did, occasionally, contemplate.

There was something else that was in my subconscious but had not properly expressed itself. This was the method of training in the Merchant Navy. Was it necessary to spend four years in an Apprenticeship before sitting the first exam? By the time a Deck Officer had obtained his Master's Certificate, he would have been 26 or over. Ten years to obtain a qualification that was later made equivalent to an MSc seems an inordinately long time. By the end of my third trip it was obvious to me that at the end of the formal education at Warsash it would be possible to sit and pass the academic elements of the Second Mate's Certificate i.e. Maths, Chartwork, signals, navigation, meteorology, ship construction, mechanical drawing. I had once expressed this idea to my fellow cadets but was met with derision. Obviously, there were some areas of a Deck Officer's education that could not be taught on shore: seamanship and handling large vessels in different environments and weather, boatwork and lifeboat drill, watchkeeping, maintenance, cargo work. It would be foolish to believe that without practical experience of ship and cargo handling a candidate would be able to satisfy the examiner in the oral. Nevertheless, in my third trip, we were still being instructed in the same syllabus as we were on our first trip. In other words, much of what we were doing in the classroom was revision. In my case, some was necessary, particularly in Maths. Certain aspects of geometry, such as 'Functions of Angles', continued to bewilder me, but I managed to learn parrot fashion and copy out diagrams. What was comforting was that where at school in Warwick, certain mathematical and scientific principles had been difficult for me to comprehend, when I was put in a position where I could see the principles put into practice, the scales dropped from my eyes. Spherical trigonometry and its relationship to navigation became a subject in which I did well. However, I doubt I could now explain to my grandchildren the difference between a tangent and a cosine.

Perhaps I should conclude that four years sea time was necessary for me, personally, to become proficient enough to pass my first exam. Nevertheless, I had spent nearly two years at sea and had still not spent any time on the bridge apart from steering and cleaning the brass. I understand that times have changed and the apprentice regime starts with sea time and then adds academic training. Amongst my contemporaries there was a definite feeling that apprentices, particularly in their early years, were used as cheap labour. We were locked into a centuries' old culture concerning apprenticeships and the time needed to become a Master of your trade, irrespective of the industry concerned. It still persists, for example the insistence that a first degree requires a three year course. Perhaps, the potential loss of income to universities if first degrees could be done in two years is a factor. I contend that this is an issue that needs constant review.

Another issue was the standard of instruction, a word I would use rather than teaching or education. I have mentioned before that I had no evidence that lecturers at Warsash or Instructional Officers on the Durham had any formal training in education. We went through a pre-ordained syllabus without encountering any inspired insights from our instructors. In short, classwork was dull and suited best those who were content with routine and with limited curiosity. The syllabus was also narrow. We had no instruction on the historical context of our trade, the history and geography of the countries we visited or of world trade in general. Here we were in a business that constituted ninety per cent of the carriage trade of the world and yet we were kept ignorant of the economics. Any information that we gained about where we travelled was through our own observations, experience and curiosity. I was finding myself more and more out of tune with the cultural aspirations, or lack of them, of my shipmates.

What is not at issue is that as my Apprenticeship continued, the social constraints became more irksome. I was in my twenty first year when I finished my Apprenticeship, yet I was still shackled by the paternalistic activities of my employer. A Junior Ordinary Seaman just out of school and on his first trip was not subject to the same restrictions as I was and I was nearly five years older. My parents would not have considered restricting me in the same way. This is another reason for considering that a four year Apprenticeship was too long. It may have contributed to the high loss rate of Junior Officers.

I have remarked earlier on the marked differences in personal hygiene between the wharfies in New Zealand and Australia and the UK dockers. This was reflected in their homes, where there was generally more space than found in the UK and the houses were better fitted out with appliances. Here was an interesting dichotomy in that working people had a higher standard of living than equivalent workers in the UK. One of the elements in this disparity was the feeling in Australia and New Zealand that you were as good as the next man.

Australian and New Zealander wharfies presented themselves as more aspirational, not necessarily for themselves but for their children. I often heard talk such as 'My son's going to be an architect' or 'My son's going to be an engineer'. They believed in education. There was a TV science programme in Melbourne presented by a Professor Brown. The wharfies talked about it intelligently and had obviously watched.

Note the emphasis on male children. In male eyes down under, 'Sheilas', i.e. females, were not equal. Pubs were male areas and ladies were only allowed in designated areas or separate rooms. The concept of 'mateship' was very much part of this. If you were 'shouted' in a pub, you were expected to 'shout' back. Being 'shouted' meant somebody doing you a favour or buying you a drink, a cinema ticket or entrance to some occasion or other. Woe betide those who did not respond. People built their homes on this concept. A family would buy a plot and then build on it. Most of the buildings were wooden and could be erected quickly. People would invite their mates round at a weekend, provide food and beer, and they would build the house.

This attitude was aligned with confidence in themselves and their future. They were respectful of the 'Queen' and there was genuine affection for the old country. Our ships were known as 'home boats' and we were the recipients of generous hospitality. Of course, those people with whom I came into most contact were very dependent on trade with the UK, which may have influenced their attitude.

Immigration was beginning to change economic and social life. Both countries were short of manpower if their aspirations for expansion were to be realised. Therefore, immigration was encouraged, witness the Australian Government's subsidising of travel costs, the £10 passage fee for individual immigrants. Immigrants were, generally, welcomed but there was a backlash against so-called 'whingeing Poms'. There were British immigrants who thought that they would be going to a land where everything would be the same as in Clapham or Huddersfield, except that the weather was better. They would be disappointed. There were substantial differences and immigrants needed to accept that and fit in. These migrants did not find it easy on first arrival. Many were settled in poor accommodation, often provided by the Australian or States governments, and took whatever jobs were available, often menial. Some returned to the UK. This treatment and the fact that Australia was not 'Clapham beyond the sea' led to grumbles and consequent labelling of UK immigrants as 'whingeing Poms'. Aussie taxpayers had, after all, paid for the immigrant's passages.

This period was the last one where emigration from the UK exceeded immigration. As well as Australia, UK migrants settled in New Zealand, Canada, South Africa and, even, the USA. This net migration was despite the immigration into the UK of West Indians (the 'Windrush Generation) and South Asians. The West Indians were offered jobs in public transport and the South Asians increasingly provided labour in the textile and clothing industries.

Imperially, the time was one of disaster, particularly in the case of Egypt and the Suez Canal. As we were at sea or on the other side of the world, the view of we Apprentices was one of incomprehension. We felt that the UK was right to invade Egypt. There were also insurgencies in Malaya and East Africa. Not a comfortable time for Imperial administrators.

PART FIVE

At Sea But Not At Sea

CHAPTER TWENTY ONE

Fourth Durham Trip

24th October 1957 to 3rd November 1958

The Galveston Epic

This was known as the 'Galveston Voyage' and became a legend within NZS.

The Prior Events

We were scheduled to sail to New Zealand and be there to unload Christmas booze etc. in time for Christmas. It did not turn out that way.

We had about two week's leave before rejoining Durham in London. She had sailed round from Liverpool to London with a 'coasting crew'. This often happened after a deep sea crew had been paid off. A new crew would join and take the ship round the UK ports until she was ready to go deep sea again. Sometimes, members of the coasting crew would remain as part of the deep sea crew. Apart from those apprentices who had completed their sea time and gone off to take their Second Mate's Certificate, we had other changes to the crew. Des Jones became Second Officer and John Needham was promoted to Instructional Officer. We had a new bosun and carpenter and David Evans was our new Fourth Officer.

One evening, I went to see my sister, She was sharing a flat with two other girls from Stratford in Belsize Park. We had a good night out in the West End with a meal, cinema and a few drinks. There was a problem. London was enveloped in 'smog', which is a mixture of fog and smoke from coal fires. It made visibility very poor and you could taste the atmosphere – unpleasant. Combined with that was a flu epidemic, the Asian Flu. This Asian Flu was world-wide and had arrived in the UK in the autumn of 1957. I was especially vulnerable because I had had no chance of building up immunity. The marine environment is very healthy and there are no viruses. Also, I had been on leave in the healthy countryside. The morning after I had been to see my sister, I felt very lethargic and, later that day, collapsed. I was unconscious for twenty four hours. Several others of us were affected. I convalesced during our voyage from London to the Bristol Channel ports.

By the time we got to Newport, I was OK and taking my full part in ship's activities. I was now a Leading Hand, which meant that I was put in charge of a small gang, say three or four apprentices, to carry out specific tasks. We called at Newport, Cardiff and Swansea to take on steel, wire and tinplate. Then, on to Liverpool, which was our final port before heading for New Zealand.

Liverpool

Although we had paid off in Liverpool at the end of the last trip, this was the first time I had spent any time in Liverpool. At times, it felt like being in a foreign country. The people looked and sounded different to anywhere else in the UK. The Liverpool population is an amalgam of Irish, Lancastrians and Welsh with a smattering of the West Indies. This accounts for the very distinctive accent and 'pudding face' look. Have a look at photos of the Beatles and Jimmy Tarbuck to see what I mean.

We were berthed in one of the docks at the western end of Liverpool, I think it was called Garston Dock. All the Liverpool docks had tidal gates, like London, so that loading and discharge was not affected by the tide. The River Mersey has a high tidal rise and fall. The Liverpool docks were very different to any others we went to, with the exception of Philadelphia. We were accustomed to a considerable working space between the dockside and warehouses, if there were warehouses. This allowed space for cranes and, in some cases, railway lines. The Liverpool docks were very different in that warehouses several stories high came almost to the dock side. There were high arches on the dock side of the warehouses so that cargo could be discharged directly into the warehouses or prepared for loading protected from the weather. Much of the old Liverpool docks have now been transformed into waterside entertainment centres and the old architecture has lent itself well to these new ventures.

Garston Dock is in a suburb called Seaforth – to fans of 'Z Cars', it relates to the fictional suburb of 'Seaport'. This was a rough area. It was then connected to the City Centre by an overhead railway. You could walk underneath the railway, which gave shelter, and was popularly known as the 'Iron Umbrella'. The Liverpool population declined between 1939, when it was 900,000 plus, to about 550,000 in the 1960s. World War Two bombing had caused widespread disruption and the decision was made to move people to better housing in new towns such as Ormskirk and Skelmersdale in Lancashire and Winsford in Cheshire. The drop in population led to a disastrous drop in use of the Iron Umbrella and it was demolished in the late 1950s. I used it and thus have a connection with a slice of railway history.

We had another change of personnel in Liverpool. Frankie Field left and was replaced as Chief Officer by a Mr Rollinson, who proved to be better liked and respected than Frankie.

In Liverpool, I started to learn more about the actual duties of a Deck Officer. I was now classed as a senior apprentice and no longer having to carry out the more menial duties, such as Companion Ladder Quartermaster. I was also in charge of my cabin, which consisted of myself and two others. In port, I worked under the instruction of the Duty Officer, who would be either the Third or Fourth Officer. The duties were related to supervising cargo, keeping the log and recording items such as the draft at 0800 and 1800. Those of us doing this worked watches or shifts. In Liverpool, we had the pleasure of working a two shift system (12 hours on and 12 hours off), which in itself was a portent of things to come. Shipowners were always looking at ways to be more efficient and the most efficient working practices were those that limited time in port. Hence the introduction of shift work, if there was enough labour.

I became friendly with one of the hatch foremen. He was quite a character and had only just got his job back after being caught nicking whisky from the cargo in a Harrison Line ship. This carried no social shame in Liverpool, the home of the 'scallies'. He invited me to join him to see Liverpool play Hibernian at Anfield one evening. The 'hatchie' asked me if I wanted to stop at a pub before the match, but told me he wouldn't go in because he was a teetotaller! Liverpool were then in Division Two of the Football league (now known as The Championship) and Hibernian, or Hibs, were based in Edinburgh and played in the Scottish First Division. Hibernian were named after the Latin name for Ireland and attracted a strong Catholic support, as did and do Glasgow Celtic. It was only a friendly but the ground was packed, which indicates the level of support that Association Football has in Liverpool. Liverpool won and everybody went home happy. It was the first time I had been to a floodlit event.

Alec Guinness was on stage at the Liverpool Everyman Theatre. The play was called 'Ross' by Terence Rattigan and was about the reasons why Lawrence of Arabia turned his back on public life and joined the RAF as an aircraftsman. Guinness was playing Lawrence. The play was on a provincial tour before going to London. It was very different from the epic on a grand scale in David Lean's film 'Lawrence of Arabia'. Guinness was spellbinding, you could not take your eyes off him when he was on stage. I remember vividly how he demonstrated, in his Arab nobleman's costume, how a Skeikh walked differently from other men of inferior rank. I went alone as none of my fellow cadets were interested. I had a drink one evening with some of the cast, whom I bumped into at the Adelphi Hotel, because a couple of them were actors I had known in Stratford.

A Rough Atlantic Crossing.

We set sail for New Zealand in early November. As with my previous trips, I alternated between watch keeping and day work but this time my watch keeping was on the bridge under the supervision and instruction of the Officer of the Watch. The main elements were navigation, chartwork, ship handling, keeping the ship's log (we apprentices had our own log separate from the official log), weather observations and keeping a sharp lookout at all times.

That autumn, the weather in the North Atlantic was particularly severe. In September, there had been a hurricane that precipitated one of the most infamous marine tragedies. The Germans had a sail training ship called the 'Pamir'. It was a four-masted barque, which means that it was powered by the wind and carried square sails on the masts. It had been built in 1904 for the grain trade from South America but was soon obsolete. It was now used as a training ship for the German Merchant Navy, whilst still being used for commercial trade. It had a crew of 85, including 52 cadets. It left a South American port in early September with a cargo of loose and bagged barley. It hit a hurricane on September 21st 1957. By all accounts, the ship had left port in a hurry and the cargo had not been properly stowed and secured. The cargo moved, thus destabilising the vessel. Pamir capsized and only 5 people survived. The Germans thereafter abandoned sail training. I had seen Pamir sometime during my first or second trip and she was beautiful. A terrible event.

Around three to four days out the weather steadily worsened and there was a full gale blowing which soon had the ship hove to with the seas breaking green over the bow. Our course was straight into the wind, but we could not proceed into the wind without incurring damage. It was as much as we could do just to maintain our position. The 4 to 8 watch on this particular morning seemed to be the peak of the weather. It was very alarming, and was the worst I had experienced. Dig Hocken was on the bridge for most of the time, he only left to snatch a couple of hours sleep or to eat. When the weather is bad or the marine traffic is dense, the Master takes over the watch for as long as is necessary. There was a discussion about wind strength and it was estimated that it was Force 12 in gusts. That is hurricane force, which was unusual at that time of the year and was east of the normal trajectory of Atlantic hurricanes, which usually started in the Caribbean and then progressed up the east coast of the USA. The apprentices who had to steer had a hard time and there was some talk about whether we should have two helmsmen on watch.

Why We Ended up in Galveston

Memories after all these years will of course not be wholly accurate, however I seem to think that it was the evening of that day that we were able to move ahead again, after the wind had died down somewhat. Sometime that evening the starboard engine stopped suddenly. We were well used to the engines being stopped from time to time as they were pretty tired and the engineers were always flat out trying to keep them running. This was different, however, as the sound of the starboard propeller ceased suddenly. The next morning it was announced that the starboard engine had suffered a broken crankshaft.

We were south of the Azores, far into the North Atlantic, so what was to be done? Obviously, we had to go somewhere for repairs and could not continue with our planned voyage. Whilst we waited for Head Office to find a suitable port and shipyard, we steamed slowly on the port engine on our original course. One thing was obvious and that was we would not be spending Christmas in New Zealand. Falmouth for repairs was the favourite choice because we could get there with a favourable wind and current and it housed the nearest repair yard. Scot Gilchrist had immediately worked out a course and distance to Falmouth when the full extent of the damage was known. He was obviously looking forward to spending time at home! For some reason we continued on our original course, which took us further away from any UK repair yard. It was a great surprise when we heard that we were to proceed to Galveston, Texas. There was some puzzlement as nobody knew exactly where Galveston was or what facilities it could offer.

We rolled gently along at around 8 knots on the port engine as the engineers nursed it along. We had to steer the ship "hard a port" to "mid-ships" for three or more weeks because the thrust of the port engine tended to push the bow to starboard. The helmsman was forever having to correct this. Lord knows what the condition of the steering gear was like when we finally reached safety. We went through the Leeward Islands to Kingston, Jamaica, where the pilot boat came out with charts of the Gulf Coast of Texas and the approaches to Galveston. Because we did not trade in the Gulf of Mexico, we had no current navigational information of that area. I remember making an entry in the Apprentices' Log that Stetsons and guitars would shortly be issued. Fortunately, the days were warm and sunny. Just over three weeks after the breakdown we arrived off Galveston in the late evening of December 8th 1957, where we immediately hit a difficulty.

Galveston is an island on the Gulf of Mexico fifty miles south of Houston and about midway between New Orleans and the Texas/Mexico border. It is very low lying, the highest point is only fifteen feet above sea level. There is a narrow, shallow channel that separates it from the mainland. The channel is crossed by a causeway and it is the only land connection with the mainland. There is a dredged waterway between Galveston and Houston known as the Houston Ship Canal. This allows deep sea ships to access the oil refinery at Houston, fifty miles north of Galveston. The spoil that was dug out to make the ship canal was deposited in shallow water to the north east of Galveston Island and the resultant island is called Pelican Island. The shipyard, Todds, that was going to carry out the repairs, was situated on Pelican Island. The approach to Pelican Island caused us trouble.

The approach was via a channel between Galveston and Pelican Island. This channel was shallow and Durham was a deep drafted vessel for her length and fully loaded with cargo. The tugs could not get alongside that night because the sea was rough. Next morning all the Galveston tug fleet plus other tugs from Houston swarmed around us and towing lines were made fast. It took 5 hours to work us up the channel into her berth at the Todd's Shipyard. The immediate impression was deflating. Pelican Island is flat, featureless and uninteresting and the shipyard was more a repair and maintenance facility than a place for building ships. Nevertheless, the shipyard workers proved to be efficient, capable and adaptable. Our experience of them compared favourably with UK shipyard workers of that time.

We berthed just in time. As the ship was worked into her berth we lost the port engine, which we thought was cylinder liner trouble again. Also, marine diesel engines are started by compressed air. We carried compressed air in large cylinders, which would be refilled during stays in port. Because of the problems we had faced and the struggle to berth, we only had one 'start' left anyway. Talk about in the nick of time!

A Not So Friendly Welcome

Once alongside we were descended on by the Texas Rangers. They were suspicious of us.

None of us had visas or permits to land in the USA. A few days later, we were issued with permits to stay for 30 days. Despite staying for 6 months, these permits were never renewed and did cause one of our crew members some trouble later on.

Texas Rangers, circa 1960, but not 'ours'

The sight of tall Texans in 10 gallon hats and carrying six shooters was amusing to us. It was like a Western film. However, when one of them demanded that one of us break the seal and open the entrance hatch to No 2 hold, things got interesting. The apprentice politely explained that he could not and referred the Ranger to the Chief Officer. The Ranger became very angry and threatened all kinds of retribution. Capt. Hocken, who was watching from the bridge, took over. "Dig" was not prepared to stand any nonsense, particularly if it impinged on his authority. He advanced on the Ranger and gave him a short and forceful lecture on international law and sovereignty. The Ranger never stood a chance. The hatch stayed shut and sealed. The Texas Rangers stayed on for a few 'heart starters' with the Chief Steward and we had arrived in Galveston Texas. Galveston was the only port in any country that I arrived in where we were immediately confronted with officers of the law. This was our introduction to a country with people who spoke English but who were different to us. The UK and the USA are indeed a people divided by a common language.

CHAPTER TWENTY TWO

Why Did We Stay In Galveston So long?

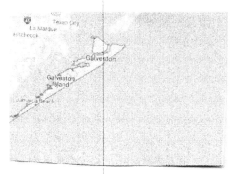

Galveston, Texas.

This chapter is all about two things: repairs and the transhipment of our cargo. It explains the length of our stay. In future chapters, I look at what Galveston had to offer and how we coped in a strange environment.

It was discovered that the port engine had suffered the same fate as the starboard engine i.e. it had a broken crankshaft. We were going nowhere fast. Would we leave the ship to the tender mercies of Todd's Shipyard and go home or would we stay? The repairs were to take 6 months and the job was huge. The entire main machinery had to be removed for the crankshafts to be replaced. Because of the extent of the work, it was decided to take advantage of the enforced stay and carry out other repairs as well as organize several surveys necessary to maintain certificates of seaworthiness, which are essential to getting the best insurance rates.

The crankshafts could not be replaced by local manufacture. If I remember, each crankshaft consisted of two sections. Sulzer, the original Swiss manufacturer, could not provide all the replacements so one section would come from Switzerland and the other three from a firm in Seattle. Provision of new parts would take months. I am reasonably sure that all the main machinery was removed by early January 1958. Removing so much weight from the lower part of the hull altered the ship's stability. We could topple over.

We were not without power. All our lighting, heating, ovens, hobs and machinery were electrically powered. Power generation was provided by an auxiliary diesel engine, called a 'donkey engine'. This stayed in position.

Meanwhile, what was to be done with Durham's cargo? It could not stay with us and had to be transshipped to another vessel. A principal reason was the New Zealand balance of payments issue. There were import controls and high taxes on imported goods. Our cargo was included in the 1957 import quotas and we also carried Christmas 'Goodies'. The delay posed a significant problem for the New Zealand Treasury and our cargo had to be imported to New Zealand without more delay. But there was delay, because the next available company vessel, the 'MV Haparangi', could not arrive until the end of January after discharging elsewhere in the States. Her dimensions were similar to the Durham's, therefore she could take our cargo.

There were no facilities to transship in the shipyard. We were towed across the channel to the town berths. We then started to transfer cargo from the Durham to the Haparangi, which took around 8 to 9 weeks. Haparangi tied up alongside us. We were thus able to discharge onto the wharf and also to the Haparangi. It was a nightmare for Des Jones, the Second Officer in charge of cargo loading and unloading. He had to calculate what to unload and when because Durham was basically top heavy after the engines had been removed. We seemed to lean on the Haparangi at times. First of all, the cargo in the centre of the holds was moved onto the wharf. And then the cargo from the sides of the holds was transferred into the sides of the Haparangi holds. When we had cleared all the hold centres, we swopped positions and Haparangi loaded cargo from the wharf and some from us. It was not simple and required continual adjustment. We seemed to be forever adjusting our mooring lines and derricks. As we rose in the water, Haparangi settled deeper. It was at this time that we realized how much more advanced the Americans were in materials handling. Wherever possible they used mechanical means rather than manual labour. They lowered fork lift trucks into the holds. If they were petrol powered, they rigged pipes to take away the fumes. It was a revelation to us. By the end of March, we finished and Haparangi sailed away.

Haparangi alongside Durham (1)

Haparangi alongside Durham (2)

One of the problems with morale, as always, was the lack of information about our immediate future. For a while after moving back to Pelican Island, we had no news on when the new crankshafts would be ready. The cause of the problem was attributed to the sinking in Gibraltar during the War. When she was built in the early 1930's, all engine bedplates were supported with Lignum Vitae timber chocks. This is a very hard wood from Norway, which has a very high oil content and is very dense. It was ideal for the purpose and was also used in stern tubes of that era because it provided a watertight seal where the prop shaft came out of the hull. When the ship was repaired in Falmouth in early 1943, Norway was occupied by the Germans, so the timber was not available. Steel chocks were used in the damaged area at the aft end of the engines. The official reason for the damage was the very severe weather we had recently encountered in the Atlantic, which caused the chocks to move and put the bedplates out of alignment. The starboard engine was out more than 70 thousandth of an inch over some units. The port engine was not so bad but sufficient to crack the shaft in the end. Given the short amount of time during the hurricane and the minute mis-alignment, it could be argued that this reasoning was faulty. Whatever the official reason, I always believed that hitting the sand bank in the Suez Canal on the previous trip was the principal reason for the problem. There was also the possibility that the engine blocks were not correctly re-aligned after the wartime damage, which could explain the persistent strain on the engines that caused cylinder lining problems.

We were delayed moving back to Pelican Island because another vessel was being repaired. We were towed into an empty berth, called a 'layup berth'. A few days after berthing, a Lykes Line vessel berthing astern of us did not pull up in time. All the Lykes ships were steam turbine, which were not as responsive to manoeuvre as diesel engines. It overshot and whacked us firmly in the stern. The collision set the other vessel's bow back and breached her fore peak causing enough damage to require her to dry dock. We were shifted back into the dockyard around the same time and we were lying alongside the pier with the floating dry dock on the other side of the berth. Late one night a raiding party nipped over to the Lykes Ship and nicked her house flag. The squeal of the halyard block almost gave the game away but all was well.

The floating dock adjacent to the berth was a constant source of interest. Most dry docks are dug out of the land and fitted with gates at the seaward end. This floating dry dock could be moved to wherever it was wanted. I believe its origin was in the Second World War, when the US Navy developed the concept of fleet trains. These fleet trains consisted of large numbers of non-combatant ships and a floating dock providing supply and repair facilities to the US Pacific Fleet. The Pacific Fleet was thus enabled to operate far from shore based facilities and gave it great flexibility in its operations.

The average stay for a ship in the dry dock was about 4 days. T2 oil tankers made up the bulk of the ship repairs, which included descaling and repainting the hull. An exception occurred because of a collision in the Houston Ship Canal one night and a Norwegian freighter was cut right through to the keel aft of the engine room. She was coaxed into the dock and hauled out. She was rebuilt and away in four weeks. They were experts in that yard and although they hardly ever saw a diesel engine, and certainly not one as big as Durham's, they did the repairs very well. Slowly the engine parts vanished from sight back down into the engine room.

Was our time spent productively?

Obviously, we were not able to learn our trade by being at sea. We could not work on deck because it was cluttered. We were not able to paint or carry out normal maintenance work. The cargo transshipment was a once in a lifetime occurrence. We did continue with school work.

The reality was that we spent time on manual activities with no obvious gain for us but what sufficed to keep us occupied. We spent some of our time chipping the after port side of the hull with air guns hired from the yard. These air guns were known as 'jack hammers'. I never walked past the port side of that ship again without a feeling of pride in the job we did. At the time we cursed our luck, mind you! It almost felt like our version of the Burma Railroad, especially as it was now hot! When the ship went into the dry dock before sailing they sandblasted the entire hull except for the bit we had laboured over for weeks! Some of the juniors could not understand why we did this painstaking job in the growing heat of a Texan late Spring. We were perpetually in shorts and bare-chested. Peter Matthews and I, with the benefit of our vast experience (!), explained that we did all these jobs so that when, and if, we ever became Chief Officers, we would know if a job had been done well or badly. I don't think that our explanation was appreciated. To add insult to injury the shipyard 'maties' then spray painted the entire hull, including our lovingly hand painted plates.

Another activity was descaling the anchors and repainting them. They had been lowered onto the dock so they were easy to get at. Not exactly life enhancing.

We could have had extensive training in the operation of a repair yard, which would have greatly helped us should we ever be an officer in charge of repair of a company vessel in the future. Nothing happened. The only 'extra-curricular' education we had was a welding demonstration one day. When he had finished, the welder stepped back and said 'Now that's a purty weld!'. Very Texas.

The company missed out on a wonderful opportunity to extend our general education about shipping and the commercial world. There were no excursions to Houston and its oil refinery, despite the fact that the company was about to enter into the tanker world. The company was also expanding its trade with the USA, yet nobody considered that understanding of the American economy could be of help to us. Another glaring example of the narrow scope of our training and its accompanying lack of imagination. Anything we learnt about our environment was what we found out for ourselves. Situation normal.

Whilst the new crankshafts were awaited, the engine beds had been renewed. By late May, the new crankshafts had been fitted and the main engines lowered back in place. Then the starboard engine was turned over for the first time. At 1220 one day the engine was turned over on air a few times and then the Chief Engineer fed her some fuel. Slowly she picked up each cylinder and ran for about 20 minutes. Then silence. After a while we were stood down thinking it had all gone wrong. However the smiling engineers told us that they were doing a full inspection and that it would be later in the afternoon before they tried again. The looks on their faces said it all. All was going well. In the days that followed the port engine also was started and then for days we ran them without connection to the propeller shafts. The day for sea trials arrived and the old ship took to the sea again for yet another reincarnation.

Broken crankshaft removed

Descaling and painting anchors

CHAPTER TWENTY THREE

What is Galveston?

What did we do that was not maritime related? What was the environment in which we were stranded? Let's first digest information about Galveston and how different our stay was going to be compared with our experiences elsewhere. Galveston is named after an 18ᵗʰ Century pirate, one Galvez. During his time, Galveston became known as a haunt for pirates. One of those based there, Jean Lafitte, assisted the American General Jackson in Jackson's defence of New Orleans during the 1812 War between the UK and the USA. A British force under General Edward (Ned) Pakenham invaded Louisiana in 1814 and laid siege to New Orleans. Partly thanks to Lafitte, the British communications were interrupted. A combination of this and Pakenham's inept leadership led to a British defeat. The Brits left with their tails between their legs. Pakenham, who was Wellington's brother-in law, died in battle. Jackson earned the nickname 'Old Hickory' and became President of the USA ten years later

Galveston was part of the Spanish Empire and then part of the Mexican Empire until 1836. In that year, General Sam Houston, at the head of an army of Texas immigrants from the rest of the USA, defeated the Mexican dictator, Santa Anna, at the Battle of San Jacinto. This was shortly after the Battle of the Alamo, where a small force of Americans, including Davy Crocket and Jim Bowie, held up Santa Anna and sacrificed themselves, which allowed Houston time to gather his army. Thus was the independent state of Texas born. It joined the USA in 1842.

Galveston is an important port for southern Texas. It exports cotton, sulphur and agricultural products. Cattle were bred mainly for domestic consumption. The port area is on the northern side of the island. The southern side on the Gulf is a holiday resort.

Southern Texas is flat. This is a characteristic of all the USA states bordering the Gulf of Mexico: Texas, Louisiana, Alabama and Florida.

FIRST IMPRESSIONS AND EXPERIENCES

We were very surprised to have a TV fitted in our lounge. All the other recreational areas in the ship had one. It appeared that this was standard practice for US shipping agents to arrange. It made us feel that, after the unfortunate experience with the Texas Rangers, we would be better looked after here than in our usual ports. The standard of TV programmes also came as a big shock, and a pleasant one. To start with, there were several channels. All TV and radio in the USA is commercial. There is no equivalent of the BBC. What was obvious was that, in the USA, very large sums of money were spent on the peak time shows. These were shows transmitted nationally. There were three main broadcasters: Columbia Broadcasting System (CBS), National Broadcasting Company (NBC) and American Broadcasting Company (ABC). These companies owned local stations, which broadcast their owners' programmes on a franchised basis. There were also smaller stations that broadcast local programmes and news. The same applied to radio.

Also, there were, and are, no national newspapers in the USA because of the distances and changes in time zones. Therefore, newspapers tended to be local, even those with an international reputation such as the New York Times, the Chicago Herald Tribune and the Wall Street Journal. Journalists and contributors to newspapers augmented their incomes by having their articles syndicated to local newspapers. Americans are also much more commercial in their promotion of goods and services. They embrace advertising, which provided enough income for free TV broadcasts and cheap newspapers. Their newspapers carried several times more advertising pages than news, but Americans consider advertising as news. Some of the advertising was good, much of it was puerile and a lot was too fanciful. I remember a TV ad for a motor vehicle where the presenter eulogised over the styling, describing it as 'sculpturamic'. This was the period when American motor vehicles were plastered in chrome. But, the constant repetition of advertising slogans worked. There was a car dealer called Al Parker, who sold Buick cars. He advertised on the local radio constantly and I can still recall his slogan 'Al Parker, Buick' accompanied by a catchy jingle.

American TV stars were much more closely involved with advertising and marketing than their UK equivalents. 'Sponsors' would pay for programmes to be produced and broadcast, which meant that they had a predominant influence on the programme content. The stars were expected to promote the sponsors, however inappropriate it may sound. The celebrated pianist, Liberace, would introduce the sponsor at the advertising break with 'And now a word from our lovely sponsor'. A noted 'tough guy' actor of the period, Hugh O'Brian, was the star of 'Wyatt Earp', a Western series. He signed off each programme with 'This episode was brought to you by the makers of 'Cheerios''. This was in addition to the usual advertising we knew from commercial TV in the UK.

Whatever your opinion of the commercial aspects of American broadcasting, the result was a variety of programmes that we could only dream about in the UK. On Saturday and Sunday nights, the major channels would compete with big name variety shows. The show titles tended to be linked to an advertiser or sponsor. For instance, there was the Dinah Shore Chevy Show (Chevy = Chevrolet cars) and the Tennessee Ernie Ford 'Ford' Show. Also, Perry Como was the big name on CBS. This compares with the only British equivalent, 'Sunday Night at the London Palladium', which was, at first, compered by Tommy Trinder, a comedian past his best years.

Another example of the difference was how Latin American music was presented. In the UK, there was Edmundo Ros, a Trinidadian via Venezuela, and in the USA, Xavier Cugat, a Spaniard via Cuba. Both were classically trained and were very popular. Both lived to a great age (Cugat 90 and Ros 100). Both ran successful night clubs. Both retired to Spain. So much for the similarities. How they were presented is the contrast. Ros was frequently on BBC Radio and his records sold well. His was essentially a dance band and his music was gentle. He rarely appeared with big bands, spectacular settings and fabulous singers, in contrast to Cugat. He appeared in several films and on TV. He was show business whereas Ros was easy listening. The two styles exemplified to some extent the differences between the British and American approaches to entertainment, until the advent of rock music and large, open air gigs in the 1960s and 1970s.

It was a golden age of TV western series: Have Gun Will Travel, Gunsmoke, Wyatt Earp, Maverick, the Lonesome Gun, Wagon Train. And, TV carried on into the early hours, unlike the UK, where everything stopped before midnight. NBC was also broadcasting its big budget variety programmes in colour, ten years before the BBC

A TV programme that has stuck in my mind was 'American Bandstand'. It was broadcast from Philadelphia at 5 pm EVERY weekday. It played pop music to which an invited audience of teenagers danced. It was hosted by a man called Dick Clark, who was in his early thirties and always dressed in a conservative suit and tie. As well as the dancing, Clark interviewed members of the audience, many of whom were regulars. There was nothing like it in the UK before we had Juke Box Jury in the 1960s and, later, Top of the Pops.

Despite all the above, British TV compared favourably in other respects, especially with its output of drama, sport, documentaries and natural history. The point is that American broadcasting is, first and foremost, entertainment based because it is an advertising medium. It truly represents the element of 'the pursuit of happiness' in the vision of the Founding Fathers of the Republic. Whereas, British TV has successfully restricted the power of advertisers over programme content.

We also had our first taste of how commercialized American life was compared to the UK and elsewhere. In other locations, the ship's garbage was usually taken away by the port or local authority. Not so in Galveston. The shipping agent had to arrange a contract with a commercial waste disposal firm. Not that we noticed any difference. We were also 'visited' by salesmen and promoters. I particularly remember a guy selling Sunbeam electric razors and he was quite successful, although an electric razor did not appeal to me. It was too harsh and my beard was strong. At the time I was still using a Rolls razor that my father had bought me for my fifteenth birthday. This was supposed to be the finest razor that money could buy. The blade was permanent and was attached by a small swivel to the handle. It was sharpened by pulling the blade along a sharpening stone set in the metal carrying box. You then 'stropped' it by running the blade along a piece of leather set in the top of the box. Sharpening was noisy. Eventually, I failed to keep the blade sharp and reverted to an ordinary wet razor with disposable blades.

Another guy came aboard to promote Marlboro cigarettes and gave packets away. There were other salesmen but I can't remember what they had to sell. These people were in such contrast to the UK, where the only salesmen who came on board were insurance salesmen and naval tailors, although the tailors' representatives actually measured us up and advised on cloths. The insurance salesmen could be controversial, particularly if they harassed the apprentices, who had little or no money for the premiums and were not married or had other dependents. One such salesman gloried in the name of Cuthbert Dando and was notorious for his hounding of inappropriate prospects. I heard that he was once thrown into Royal Albert Dock, which was dangerous because the water was highly toxic. Anybody who went in was immediately taken to hospital for observation. Having said that, life insurance with profits was attractive to Officers and older seamen because I am not sure if and when we became eligible to join the company pension scheme and the insurance policy was portable, whereas any pension scheme then was not.

We had our first taste of American hospitality. A local radio station announced that there were 95 Limeys stranded in Galveston on a broken down British cargo liner for Christmas. The ship's phone ran hot for days and soon everyone on board had somewhere to go for Christmas dinner. The generosity of the local people was memorable and the saying "Ya'll come back" was to become part of our vocabulary. It was decreed that because it was not possible to let everyone go ashore at the same time for Christmas Dinner, all would remain on the ship for Christmas Dinner and then we could gratefully accept the invitations afterwards. This was regarded as a very fair move by all.

CHAPTER TWENTY FOUR

Hello and Goodbye

Personnel Changes.

Capt. Dig Hocken was the first to leave during the transshipment process. He went on leave before taking over 'Otaio', the new NZS cadet ship. His replacement, Capt. Keith Barnett had a difficult job. He had to take on a battered old ship with many of the crew demoralised, particularly those married men with families who had no certainty when they would be reunited with their loved ones. He also had to cope with the upcoming substantial changes in personnel. He was naturally cheerful and one of a new breed. Dig Hocken, for all his virtues, was of the old school of ship's master: isolated and aloof. Keith Barnett was much more outgoing and interested in his crew members as individuals. Looking back, he did a good job when morale could have plummeted. Living on a broken down ship in a repair yard in the middle of nowhere was not exactly a holiday camp. However, Peter Matthews found him particularly obdurate on the matter of uniform or appropriate shore going clothes. After Peter became Cadet Captain and the weather grew hotter, he tried to reason with Barnett that it was becoming ever more inappropriate for Apprentices to be forced to go ashore in full uniform or the concession of blazer, flannels and tie. It was ridiculous in the sultry climate of Galveston and bad for morale. Barnett was unmoving and would not use any of his local discretion to override London instructions.

After we had moved back to Pelican Island, news came through that some of the crew were to head home and after leave join the new cadet ship 'Otaio'. Those going included Des Jones (Second Officer), the Third Officer and several engineer officers who now had nothing to do. David Evans was promoted to Third Officer and Monty Banks came out as Fourth Officer, together with a new Second Officer. Several senior apprentices went home to serve on the new cadet ship 'Otaio': 'Jack' Hawkins (the Cadet Captain), 'Dinghy ' Lane, 'Ginger' Eglon, Davey Pounder, Richard Lewis (our fly half), 'Head down' Doyle and Tony Batt. All these were EDH's and had lifeboat certificates.

Earlier, Glenn Smith had gone home and was released from his indentures, but not without a struggle. Glenn was a good friend and a hard worker but he was no longer interested in a career at sea. He could be explosive verbally and we called him 'Boom, Boom' Smith. My view is that he found shipboard life confining. He must have got his father to agree to be released as surety for serving his time. He went home on an NZS ship from New York, I think. He wrote to me later that when the ship docked in the UK, Military Policemen were waiting to take him off for National Service. Merchant seamen were in a reserved occupation and did not do National Service as long as they had spent at least three years at sea. That is what many stewards did by signing on and not doing National Service. Glenn got a commission in the Royal Ulster Rifles and was sent to Cyprus to patrol 'Murder Mile'. Some of the Greek Cypriots were in armed revolt against British rule and wanted union with Greece, which union they called 'Enosis'. From the tone of Glenn's letter, he was in his element.

Glen had also had an unfortunate experience at New Year. He and I were invited to a High School New Year's Eve Party by our girl friends. Mistake Number One was to accept the invitation. Mistake Number Two: we went dressed in our best uniforms. The mother of my girl friend, Elaine, drove us to the hotel after first stopping at a liquor store, where she told us to get a bottle because there would be no bar at the function. When we arrived, there were two or three hundred students there, mostly in casual dress. Glenn and I stood out like ham sandwiches at a Bar Mitzvah. It was very loud and the dance floor was postage stamp size. It was obvious that people had just gone there to hang out and we were ignored. There seemed to be no relationship with the New Year season. Just before midnight, Glenn went to the loo and came back very distressed. Some youths had followed him and beaten him up, including a vicious kick in the balls that drew blood. Just because he looked different and they resented him dating a Texas girl. We left immediately. There was another party in the hotel, which was full of middle-aged people having a good time similar to what we would have wanted. We would have enjoyed ourselves more at that party.

As Monty Banks and 'Huffie' Hufflett, had left us at the end of the last trip, it left only Peter Matthews, Scott Gilchrist, Mackie, Henry McCutchan and myself amongst the apprentices with EDH and lifeboat certificates after we had lost those who had left to join Otaio. That was not enough. Peter became Cadet Captain and Scott and I Watch Captains. It was not possible for the third trippers to take EDH and lifeboat certificates in Galveston. NZS sent four qualified apprentices from Rakaia to make up the numbers. John Tait, an old mate from Warsash was one of them, plus David Harper from Sutton Coldfield and two others, whose names I cannot remember. We five originals were glad to see them as they were needed and it was so good to renew acquaintance with John Tait. David Harper and I hit it off well and enjoyed conversing in mock Brummie. Getting promoted with new responsibilities and the new arrivals meant that any irritation at not being chosen to join the new cadet ship did not last long. According to Mike Smith's memoirs, the other, junior apprentices were dismayed at having to stay in an environment that they did not like. I cannot say that I shared these emotions and I enjoyed my stay in Galveston. I met some strange and remarkable people, as did Peter Matthews.

CHAPTER TWENTY FIVE

Galveston Life

The Galveston population was mostly white with black and Mexican minorities. There was racial segregation. The beaches were segregated into East Beach for the whites and West Beach for the blacks and homosexuals. Blacks did not use white bars and vice versa. Most manual jobs were done by blacks. The dock labourers were predominantly black whereas I did not notice any blacks amongst the skilled workers in the shipyard.

Whilst the people we met were very hospitable, their viewpoints were insular compared to ourselves. The education system did not appear to provide information about countries and cultures outside the southern USA. There was nothing of the cultural and intellectual curiosity that characterized the East Coast and California. Then, as now, half of the American population did not believe in evolution.

This was epitomized in the local newspaper, the 'Galveston News', where it was hard to find news outside Texas, let alone the rest of the world. There was a local dramatic group known as 'The Little Theatre', which put on experimental plays. My girl friend's mother despised them as communist and her view was typical. Peter Matthews was once at a party where he was asked by a middle-aged man how he appreciated the American tradition of free speech. Peter replied that it appeared that you could have free speech provided that what you said was agreed to by whom you spoke to. The man was offended and went off to talk to some friends. They had obviously discussed Peter's reply because the man came back and told Peter that he ought to revise his ideology. Point made, I think. This was 1958, not long after the witch hunts promulgated by Senator McCarthy and the Un-American Activities Committee.

Looking back, it is easier to understand the United States' policy re 'isolationism' despite the experiences of two world wars. This policy fitted, and fits, the views of the mass of Americans who did not live in the political and intellectual milieus on the East and West coasts. This mass is what supports politicians such as Donald Trump. It is allied to a pride in their achievement in establishing and expanding their democratic republic. They are oblivious to the fact that the 'Monroe Doctrine', as stated in 1823 by President Monroe, was unenforceable without the presence of the Royal Navy. It was this presence that deterred any imperial adventures in the American continent by other powers between 1823 and the First World War, thus allowing the USA to expand with little opposition. Most of the population is probably oblivious to the Monroe Doctrine anyway and is steadfast in their belief in the manifest destiny of the United Sates.

To illustrate this insularity, young people of our acquaintance asked if we had bathrooms in our houses. They also thought that Walgreens, a chain of drug stores like Boots, had invented penicillin and that TV was an American invention. The idea that the UK has the highest number of Nobel Prize winners was beyond their comprehension.

Perhaps I am looking at this from too much of a UK perspective. I found that Americans did have a considerable interest in their own country, which was so huge in comparison to most other countries that it could absorb the curiosity of its inhabitants. For instance, Americans travel long distances in their 'vacations', which we call holidays. They do not have as much statutory holiday as we do, just two weeks, although they have ten Public Holidays. These vacations are taken mainly between July 4th (Independence Day) and September 1st (Labor Day). This period has been named 'the driving season' by Irwin Seltzer, in one of his articles for the Sunday Times many years after. An example of this is the vacation taken by my girl friend, Elaine, and her family in the summer before the Durham arrived in Galveston. They travelled to Yosemite National Park in California, a distance of nearly 1,900 miles from Galveston. In other words, half of their vacation would have been on the road. This was not unusual. It partly explains why American motor manufacturers concentrated on large motor cars. If you travelled those distances, you would want a vehicle with a big engine, was well sprung and had a decent radio and air conditioning. Cheap gasoline (petrol) only added to the attraction of long distance driving.

Travelling long distances was not the only matter in Texas to do with magnitude. Everything in Texas had to be bigger than anywhere else. Texas was the state with the largest geographical area in the USA when we arrived. That changed in 1958, when Alaska became a state. Before that Alaska had been a Territory administered directly by the US Secretary of the Interior. Alaska has more square miles of territory than Texas. The Texans were miffed, to say the least. On the site of the Battle of San Jacinto, they built a monument and reflecting pool similar to the Washington monument. But, the monument and the pool were taller and longer than those in Washington DC. Next to the monument was moored a decommissioned battleship, USS Texas, which had been involved in D-Day. This was one of the class of battleships built by the Americans in the First World War that were then the biggest in the world. If it ain't big, they don't want to know.

We got used to seeing men in Western dress even though they had never been near a horse. Big Stetson hat, checked shirt, jeans and cowboy boots. The boots were designed for riding, not walking. They made you mince along, just like John Wayne. Even dressed up, they wore shoe string ties and the backs of their jackets had two seams, one on each side, not like a European suit with one seam. Larry Hagman, who played JR in 'Dallas', dressed like that.

Talking of 'Dallas, brings me to the Moody family. Do not for one moment think that the characters you saw in TV series like Dallas, Dynasty and Knot's Landing, and its modern equivalents, such as Hollywood Wives etc., are fantasy. Peter Matthews and some of the senior apprentices were introduced to a character called Shearn Moody. He was one of the great-grandsons of Colonel William Moody, who had moved from Louisiana to Galveston in 1852.The Colonel originally set out as a cotton trader. His son, William, expanded into insurance and banking, setting up the American National Insurance Company. His son, William Lewis Jr, continued the expansion. The Moody's were fabulously rich. They owned cattle ranches, oil wells, cotton farms, banks and the Galveston newspaper. When we arrived, the Moodys were in dispute with the printing union, who had come out on strike. They employed 'black leg' labour to produce the paper. The result was that photos appeared upside down with the wrong captions, but William Lewis Jr got the paper out and would not give in. The strike had started months before we arrived. The union paid for time on the local radio to promote their cause, It was hilarious, if alarming. Their spokesman said that they were going to smash the 'Mighty, Moody Money Empire'. To do so, he exclaimed that they had so many guns and so much ammunition. It was unbelievable if you had not heard the broadcast. This went on for so long that nobody took any notice of it and there seemed to be no law against incitement of this kind.

Shearn invited Peter and others to a number of parties. At one time, he took them to San

Antonio, where the Alamo Mission is sited. He had a convertible Chevrolet Impala, which he drove badly and inconsiderately. On the way back, the engine blew up. He just ordered a cab to the nearest auto dealer and bought another car. At the time, he was doing his National Service in the Texas National Guard but seemed to spend hardly any time on base. Peter told me that he took them once to his Army base and showed them his office. In the outer office was a desk with an officer sitting behind it. The name plate on the desk said 'Captain So and So'. Behind him was an inner office with a glass door. On the glass was the name 'Pfc Shearn Moody'. Shearn was a Private but he had paid the Captain to sit in the outer office whilst Sean had the inner, whenever he was there.

I met Shearn once or twice and he was a charming playboy. Totally irresponsible. At the time, I did not know that he was gay. His later life was tied up with attempts to defer bankruptcy. After his death in 1996, his lover tried to sue the family for the rights to property and income, which he said that Shearn had passed to him. The courts ruled that any such gifts were inadmissible as they were an attempt to conceal assets in the bankruptcy. Meanwhile, his brother, Bobby, went on managing the 'Mighty Moody Money Empire' with considerable success. I also met the man who ran the Galveston branch of the Moody National Bank. Although he was discreet, he did give the impression that much of his time was spent paying off people. He did tell Peter that Bobby spent too much money.

The other considerable element in the commercial life of the island was the 'Mob'. The 'Mob' had had a hold on Galveston for a couple of generations. I was led to believe that, until shortly before we arrived, that Galveston had been run by the Fertita family. Texas had strict rules on gambling and liquor licences. Gambling was illegal and bars could sell only beer and soft drinks. You could not buy 'liquor' from a liquor store if you were under 21. That did not apply in Galveston. It was notorious for a relaxed lifestyle: prostitution, gambling, bootlegging in the Prohibition era and any kind of booze when and where you wanted it. In Galveston, bars sold everything. Slot machines were everywhere. Just before the Second World War, the Texas Rangers had tried to 'invade' Galveston but, reportedly, old man Fertita, his son, Vic, and their henchmen held them off at gunpoint on the causeway. In the summer of 1957, the Attorney General of Texas had had enough and deployed the Texas Rangers again. This time the Rangers had managed to get in and they shut down most of the notorious establishments. I was shown waste sites that were full of confiscated one armed bandits. Vic Fertita had inherited his 'empire' from his dad and had managed to hold on to much of the property, mostly bars and some retail outlets. I was told that Vic would entertain in his living room with a gun in his shoulder holster plainly in view. The Fertitas were of Sicilian extraction and were linked by marriage to another alleged Texas crime family, the Maceos.

Vic's grandson, Tilman, established one of the most successful restaurant chains in the USA. He has a net worth of $2.5 billion.

There was an odd weather incident one night in January. Being on the coast of the Gulf of Mexico meant that the Galveston climate was sub-tropical. Cold weather was unusual. On this particular night, it snowed, which had not happened for many years. It was only a light snowfall and soon melted, but not before Galveston youngsters had the rare opportunity for snowball fights.

That's the Galveston I knew.

There was another aspect of USA culture that we encountered, which was the national equivalent of the Texas view on size and importance. Shortly before we arrived in Galveston, the USSR had launched the first two space satellites, Sputnik1 and Sputnik 2. As we were at sea, we did not witness the reaction within the USA. But, we were in New York when the USA launched its first satellite, Explorer1, in June 1958. The reaction was one of euphoria that the USA was no longer behind. However, I was in the States when Russia put the first man in space, Yuri Gagarin, in April 1961. People in the streets were apopletic and wanted to nuke Russia. No wonder JF Kennedy had to promise that the USA would be the first country to put a man on the moon, which was not part of the Russian space programme anyway. Their threat was more military.

My Social Life.

The main characteristic of our social life was that we were nearly always broke. A pound was worth two dollars and forty cents then. We never had more than two or three pounds each in our pockets. A cinema ticket and a drink and we were skint. At least we did not have to pay for any transport to get into town. Fortunately, some of us hit it off with the locals. Peter's involvement with the Moodys was exceptional, but shortly after we arrived, the more senior of us were introduced to some families and their daughters, which increased our mobility. Unlike the UK, American teenagers were highly mobile. Car ownership was a given.

Before Christmas, four of us were invited by different families for a meal and were picked up by the daughter of one family at the ferry stage. She had a large car and was accompanied by girls from the other families. Somehow eight of us got squashed in. These girls were either just out of High School or in their last year. They had a quality of clothes and make-up that you did not generally see at home. The girl who was driving asked if any of us had a title. The others looked at me and I decided to play along with it. I said that I was an Earl and that my father was a Duke. 'Ginger' could hardly contain himself, but these girls swallowed it completely. The thing is that they had never met an Englishman before and they were bowled over with our accents. 'Oh, they talk so cute! Just like the movies!' We went to the girl driver's house first and I was introduced to her mother as 'Earl John Ayres'. Her mother wasn't taken in and I told her the truth. She thought it was as hilarious as we did and went along with it for a while.

I was paired off with a girl called Elaine and we clicked, although we never became an 'item'. One thing that I found with American women is that it was easy to talk with them, or maybe they are more inquisitive and outgoing. Americans will very soon divulge their life stories to new acquaintances. They are very sociable. Anyway, before long I had my feet under the table and was driving the family's second car. Her dad was a man of few words but her mother made up for it. They were Catholic but it didn't seem to matter at first that I was Anglican. Elaine was in her last year at High School. High School students got discounts at places like the cinema. If we went to the pictures she would buy the tickets with her discount card. I was still having to go ashore in uniform, so she and her family bought me a couple of shirts and a pair of lightweight cotton trousers. If we were going to get student discounts, then I had to look American. Clothes were inexpensive in America then. One thing I found unusual was that ready to wear men's trousers were all sold in the same length. It was OK if you were tall, but everybody else had to shorten them. Fortunately, I had learnt to cut and sew.

I was introduced to the pleasures of the drive-in. We often pulled in at a drive-in fast food joint. A girl would come out to the car, take your order and deliver it to you, complete with a tray that you could hook on the car door after the window had been wound down. I had never had a hamburger before and I liked them. The meat was excellent, tasty and soft mince, and the burgers would be topped with lettuce, tomato and gherkin. We were also introduced to Mexican food: tamales, enchiladas and tacos, which again was different and enjoyable. The use of tortillas as a wrap for everything was completely new to us. I can't say that I enjoyed everything on the American diet, particularly their dairy products. American milk was homogenized, which is what we are now used to in the UK. At home, then, our milk came with thick cream on the top that my mother used to skim off. American cheese and butter was dreadful and they didn't seem to have any tasty apples. Lamb and pork were non-existent. The beef, particularly steak, was terrific but the steaks were enormous, far too big for one sitting.

Another new experience was the drive-in cinema. You paid as you drove in. The sound was provided by a speaker that was hung on a pillar in the parking space. You unhooked the speaker and hung it on the car door with the window down. The climate in the southern USA was conducive to this activity, even in winter. Looking around, you couldn't see the occupants of some cars. It was obviously where lots of courting couples went.

Elaine's family were friends with a couple in their thirties who had no children. They were very keen on classical music and once I showed an interest, they gave me some old 12 inch 78s. God, they were heavy. They took Elaine and me on trips. We went to San Antonio and the Alamo. I had expected that it would still look like the John Wayne movie, but the Alamo Mission had been swallowed up by the growth of San Antonio and was in the middle of a housing estate. It was hard to envisage what it had been like in 1836. We also went to San Jacinto, the site of the battle that won Texas its freedom from Mexico. The view from the top of the Texas Monument was not awe inspiring but it did demonstrate how low lying Southern Texas is. Miles and miles of flat grassland.

Elaine lived a couple of miles or so away from the port area. It was nothing for me to walk to her house, much to the astonishment of her family and friends. Americans tend to ride rather than walk, even for short distances, There were also no 'sidewalks' (pavements) in her district, so I had to walk in the road. A couple of my colleagues were once picked up by the police in similar circumstances because walking aroused suspicion.

Eventually, my relationship with Elaine faltered, as I was obviously not an American teenager and was always short of cash. The novelty of dating an Englishman did not last. We went to a concert in Houston given by a pop singer who was very famous then, Ricky Nelson. It was just one horrendous noise: girls screaming and shouting, probably wetting their knickers. You could not hear Ricky Nelson. Elaine thought he was 'so fine'. It put me off pop concerts for ever. Her mother started to ask me if was going to settle down and raise Texas kids. I was only nineteen! Elaine didn't turn up for a date one evening and that was that. Bit devastating for my ego, but I soon get over it. Once the novelty had worn off and the local girls realized that we had not got the cash to splash, or cars, all of our female relationships withered.

Group Social Life

On New Year's Day, all the Apprentices were invited to an American football match. These matches are a tradition on New Year's Day throughout America. The Galveston match, known as 'The Shrimp Bowl Game', took place at the local stadium before a crowd of several thousand. It was given that name because the area is noted for seafood. There was a team representing the Navy and one representing the Army. American, or gridiron, football is played on a pitch the size of a football or rugger pitch. There is a white line across the pitch every five yards, hence the name 'gridiron'. Each team consists of eleven players on the pitch but substitutes are allowed for any reason. The big men are forwards or 'line backers', the 'centre' is a sort of scrum half, the 'quarterback' is a sort of fly half and there are runners and a full back. The ball is oval and smaller and lighter than a rugger ball. The aim is to score an 'end' by getting the ball into the opponent's 'end zone' (in goal area) touching down and scoring six points. A conversion is worth one point. The quarter back determines the play. If a kick at goal is taken, a specialist kicker is brought on and he then goes off after the kick.

All the players wear protective chest and back padding, padded shirts, padded knee breeches and helmets. They need this protection because the linebackers can block any other player and shoulder charge whether or not the tackled player has the ball. If your side has the ball, you do it to protect your ball carrier. If your side doesn't have the ball, you do it to disrupt the defence and get at the ball carrier.

The game starts with a coin toss. The winner decides whether to carry the ball or defend. The match is scheduled to last for one hour and is split into four quarters of fifteen minutes each. There is a short break between the first and second and the third and fourth quarters. There is a longer break at halftime. The team that starts the match with the ball has to advance at least ten yards in four plays. If they do, they get another four goes to advance another ten yards and so on. If they don't, it is the other side's turn. A 'play' starts with the centre, who is behind the linebackers, passing the ball backwards beneath his legs to the quarterback. The quarterback then decides whether to run, pass or kick. At the same time his linebackers proceed to take out their opposite numbers in a prearranged sequence and the opponents try to stop them. Once the ball has gone to ground the play is over and they start again. Between each play, the teams go into a huddle to decide what they are going to do on the next play and the coach may or may not substitute players. The coach will substitute as often as he wants. If his team has the ball and is attacking, he will use players who are best at attacking. When his team has to defend, he will bring off his attackers and send on his defence specialists. Consequently, it is unusual for one player to play the whole hour.

At halftime, the cheer leaders come on and entertain and there may be other entertainment. In this match, 'Miss Galveston' appeared and walked slowly across the pitch and back again to the accompaniment of a large brass band. All the time, spectators are going off to buy food and drinks or vendors pass amongst the crowd. You may think that this explanation is taking a long time. Well, it is nothing compared to the time it takes to complete a match. Time outs, huddles, long intervals and advertising over the public address drag it all out to about three hours. We found it boring because you never get more than a minute of flowing play at any one time. As we had no emotional attachment to either team, it was difficult to become interested. What we came to realize is that in the USA, sport is a branch of show business and it is all tied in with commercial profit.

A few days later, the local newspaper asked us to put on a rugger match at the local High

School. We managed to produce two teams from all the crew and performed before a crowd of a few hundred. We were scheduled to play for an hour, just like American football, but with two halves of thirty minutes. Compared to American football, it ended too quickly for the crowd and they didn't seem able to come to grips with the long periods of play before a stoppage for a foul or likewise. They were amazed that we did not play with any protective gear.

A highlight of our stay was a party we gave in our mess room whilst we were unloading. We saved up our beer ration and the cook put on a great buffet with food that was unknown to the Texan girls, like pork pies! We sang naughty songs, danced and played games. Our girl friends were entranced by it all as it was a completely new experience for them.

It was now late February, by which time, as a senior, I was allowed to go ashore in 'civvies': blazer and flannel trousers. By late March or early April, Capt. Barnett got the uniform rule relaxed for everybody whilst we were in Galveston, except for the trippers, who got round it by making arrangements to leave "civvy" gear ashore so that they were able to travel incognito as well. Well sort of, we still stood out like sore thumbs among the locals but that did not matter. It was more freedom of a sort, but as I pointed out earlier, it did not suit the Galveston climate or environment. Unfortunately, this relaxation was withdrawn as soon as we left Galveston. It just shows you how much we had previously circumvented this uniform rule because all of a sudden everybody had civvies to wear.

Making Do

The real problem for us was lack of spending cash. We couldn't sponge off the locals for everything. I sometimes frequented a first floor bar in a side street off the main drag. It was managed by a short, slim, red-haired woman in her late forties. One evening, I was invited by another customer to have a drink, which I had to refuse because I could not buy him one back. This led to a discussion with him and the manageress and an explanation of my circumstances. She said that she was looking for temporary bar help on one or two evenings and would I be interested at five dollars an hour? Would I? One evening's work would be almost as much as my entire monthly pay. Besides which, I was used to bar work. The bar obviously stayed open until much later than my normal shore leave time, but I could get extensions for social invites. For the next few weeks, I put in for more invites than everybody else on board put together and it all worked well. Normally, I would expect to be on duty on board for two to three nights a week. This was for safety reasons to make sure enough crew would be on hand to handle emergencies. Therefore, I had at least four free evenings a week and sometimes five. The bar was doing well and I seemed to be acceptable to the customers. Certainly, I was something of a novelty. If it was quiet, the manageress would put the juke box on and teach me to jive and dance Latin American. She had been a dancer in Hollywood films, but her career never prospered because as she said 'I never slept with the right producer'. All was proceeding splendidly, until one fateful evening when the new Second Officer and the Chief Radio Officer walked in. They were as surprised as I was. There was no doubt that I was in breach of my Indentures that forbade me from frequenting taverns and alehouses. I might also be in breach of employment law in that I was taking unauthorized employment. Anyway, they did not leave and I served them. Next morning, the Second Officer had a quiet word with me. He understood completely why I had taken the job and sympathized with me. He also found out that I had covered my tracks by getting an extension to my shore leave time. If the matter had been taken further, the Chief Officer could have been implicated as an accessory because he had colluded in my deception by granting the time extension. Besides which, I was under-age for such a job. We agreed between us that I would leave the bar job and nothing more would be said, although the word got out and the tale was somewhat embellished to the extent that Mike Smith recorded in his memoir that it was Captain Barnett who walked in the bar whilst I was there and I lost my shore leave. As it happens, my time as a Texas barman would have been limited anyway. The nominal owner of the bar was an Italian-American called Carmelo. At the same time as my little subterfuge was discovered, he had taken up with a new girl friend. I remember Carmelo slobbering all over this girl in the bar one night, oblivious to the other customers. He was fat and odious. His girl friend was unemployed, so he sacked my manageress friend and installed his girl-friend as manager. My arrangement would not have lasted the appointment of the new manageress. My friend later told me that Carmelo was not the ultimate owner. He worked for Vic Fertita, the local Capo Mafioso, who was the real owner. Without knowing it, I had worked for the Mob for a few weeks.

It may be that word about my activities was allowed to filter upwards as evidence of the cash problem we had. Whatever, shortly after my extra-curricular work was uncovered, the Company realized that money was a major problem for us and they gave us a bonus while we were stuck there, which I believe was backdated. These little changes made a big difference to our morale, although with the weather getting warmer, we could spend a lot of time on the beach, provided we knew which was the 'right one'. Peter, Scot, Mackie, Henry and myself plonked ourselves down one afternoon on a nice stretch of beach that was deserted. On the other side of the promenade and a road was a bar and café, where we purchased food and drink. There we were happily ensconced and sun bathing, when I stood up and noticed that four youths in a convertible had pulled up and were staring at us. Now, our haircuts would have given us away as not American, but we were also wearing what later became known as 'budgie smugglers'. Americans were very conservative about beach clothing then. We were obviously the nearest things they had seen to aliens. They continued to stare so I walked over and asked if there was anything the matter. One of them said 'You look like shit, man' and they drove away. It was very sad that at an age when they should have been rebelling in some way, they were acting so conservatively. We later found out that 'our beach' was in the border area between East and West beaches. We were not only inappropriately dressed by local standards but also in the wrong place. Not that it bothered us, but we did seem to end up thereafter in beach parties on East Beach with people we knew.

Looking back now, it was obvious that I and a few others had a fuller and more varied social life than most of the apprentices, particularly the younger ones, who just more or less existed . Four of them did form a "Skiffle Group" which was all the rage in the UK at the time. There was a musician called Lonnie Donnegan who started off his career as a banjo player in Chris Barber's Jazz Band, which was one of the big jazz bands in the UK in the 1950s. Lonnie visited New Orleans in the mid-fifties and came across this type of work song music called 'Skiffle'. Anybody with minimum equipment and skill could take part. All you needed was a guitar and/or banjo player, a wash board, played by scraping thimbles across it, and some kind of instrument to make the sound of a double bass. This could be done with a large plywood box used to pack and transport tea. The box was turned upside down and a piece of string was attached to the middle of the box bottom and to the top of a broom stick. The broom stick was placed upright with the bottom on the side of the now top of the box and the string pulled tight. Plucking the string gave a very satisfactory bass sound. Lonnie formed a skiffle band with himself on guitar, a double bass player and a washboard player. He had immediate success with 'The Rock Island Line' and a naughty song called 'Someone's Digging My Potatoes, Trampling On My Vines'. His most famous song was English, not American. It was 'My Old Man's A Dustman'. Almost every town in the UK could boast a skiffle band and they were ideal for playing at parties and in pubs.

Dave Moorwood (known as 'Mouse') was a second tripper and an accomplished guitar player. He formed the 'Ocean Ramblers' with Dave (Dai) Fenwick on the other guitar, Mike Smith on the tea box base and Dave Sandeberg played the washboard. They were a decent band and attracted the attention of a local radio station, which was looking for unusual news. As a result, they got a session on the radio. Well done them. The 'Ocean Ramblers' stayed together for the rest of the trip.

No danger of breaking this limit!
Peter Snow, Dave Moorwood, Peter Robson and Dave Fenwick

Some of the guys tried their hand at fishing for catfish from the end of the jetty. They had some success. But someone who didn't have success with a new found hobby was the butcher. The butcher was very keen on the Wild West and he procured a highly illegal side arm, together with Stetson, holster and cowboy boots. He used to walk off down the dredge pipeline on his time off shooting snakes. One day he did a fast draw and blew a hole in his foot. He hobbled back to the ship where the Doctor patched him up and he was sent home DBS (Distressed British Seaman). One way of getting out of the place, the more cynical of us remarked.

I do not have much recollection of what the crew members other than the apprentices did in their spare time. I know they went ashore, but most never got further than the nearest dockside bar. Occasionally, I had a drink ashore with the Bosun and the Instructional AB. One crew member who did venture further afield was one of the engineer or electrical officers. He made a coach trip to New Orleans for Mardi Gras. For whatever reason, he was stopped by the police, whereupon it was found that the only ID he had on him was his Seaman's Identity Card and a permit to stay in the USA for thirty days. As I mentioned earlier, that permit was never renewed and he was way over thirty days. Also, the permit had been issued in Texas, not Louisiana. In the end he was returned to us somewhat chastened. During our stay, we apprentices had been lucky in that efforts had been made to provide us with onshore activities. This was not so for the ratings and they were probably completely fed-up by the time we left. We also felt our spirits lift as we realized that our time in 'The Land of the Free' was now coming to an end.

The Last Bar.
Peter Snow, Peter Mathews, Peter Robson, Dave Fenwick and the PTI

As April turned to May, it became hot and humid. There was little or no wind. Our quarters became very uncomfortable at night and sleep was difficult. Unlike the mid-ships superstructure, there was no way for hot air to escape our quarters. The two entrances were above us, which could have allowed hot air to rise if only enough cool air could get in. But each cabin had only one small porthole. Together, these were not big enough to suck in enough cooler air from outside. We had no air-conditioning or effective fans. We had fans but they were linked to a hot air heating system and useless in hot weather.

It was around this time that some of the younger apprentices realized that once the replacement cadets, if any, arrived prior to our departure, then the small band of survivors would not be quite the same. They decided to form a small association that would be open only to those cadets who had made the complete Galveston Voyage. They called it the *Durham Association* and ordered, with Capt. Barnett's permission, a tie from London. The grandmother of one of the apprentices made the arrangements and was responsible for the design on their behalf. The tie was Maroon with the *Durham* crest in gold. Only a limited number of ties were ordered for us, including one for Capt. Barnett. I never received one and was unaware of the formation of the Association until years later. I suspect that the ties were not available until we returned to the UK and after I had left the Durham for the last time.

Durham in Dry Dock

'BRIDGE ON THE RIVER KWAI'

No, there is no river called the River Kwai in Texas, but this film was shown in Galveston sometime near the end of our stay. Its showing provided an example of the differences between British and American humour. Americans, on the whole, don't get irony. In the film, British prisoners of war are shown marching into camp whistling the tune of 'Colonel Bogey', an old military march. Every British schoolboy of the time knew the naughty verse that referred to the genitals of Hitler and senior Nazis:

'They say that Hitler had only got one ball.
Goering had two, but very small.
Himmler was somewhat similar,
But poor old Goebbels had no balls at all!'

I had gone to this showing on my own. As the POWs marched in and sang, I laughed. Absolute silence in the rest of the large audience except for one other laugh. During the interval, I noticed one of my fellow apprentices, Peter Robson, in the audience. He was the other person who had laughed.

'COMMENCEMENT EXERCISES'

About the end of May or the beginning of June, I went to the 'Commencement Exercises' at a local High School. These exercises are actually a ceremony celebrating graduation from High School and the 'commencement' of the students' future life. Originally, these exercises started in the 17th Century at universities such as Harvard. At that time, until they graduated, students were known as Apprentices, thus perpetuating the practice of the old Guilds. On graduation, they became 'Masters' and could commence their adult life. This practice became general throughout the American school system and the ceremony was similar to a University graduation.

Students who graduated from High School receive a certificate similar to our 'A' levels and gaining a certificate is very important as regards University entrance or obtaining a good job. In my time in Galveston, the proportion of students who attended High School was much higher than in the UK, where the school leaving age was 15 and, if you left at 15, you had no qualification. In the USA, you could leave school at 16 provided you had employment, but compulsory education to Grade 12 (the equivalent of our year 13) was made compulsory some 25 years before the UK. This regime has not led to US dominance in international school league tables, quite the opposite in fact.

It was interesting to me to see how the Americans celebrate their children graduating from High School. It was, and is, much more elaborate than what we in the UK do. It struck me as being pretentious and too much celebrating of minor achievement. I realize that this is unfair and subjective because these ceremonies have real meaning for the participants, but I can only state what I felt and experienced. A possible answer could be that people, generally, enjoy ceremony and that we, in the UK, have more than our fair share of public ceremony whereas the USA has a lack of it.

This particular ceremony took place in a large, tiered auditorium with a stage. All the graduates, of whom there were more than a hundred, were arrayed in a medium brown academic gown and a mortar board with a tassel. The graduates formed a line below the stage and then ascended to the stage to receive their certificate from the school Principal. As they left the stage, they moved the mortar board tassel from one side to the other. Somebody made a speech, followed by speeches from whom I perceived to be the Head Girl and Head Boy. Both were very earnest and no doubt worthy on some aspect of education but totally devoid of any wit. I could not help but contrast them with the standard at my old school's debating society, where lack of wit and passion usually attracted derision.

These ceremonies are very much a rite of passage for American High School graduates. They form part of a considerable ritual, which includes the High School Prom, election of the Prom Queen, elections for the most likely to do various illustrious things in later life and a Year Book with all the graduating year students' photographs and a short biography. It contrasted with what happened in the UK at the time where 'O' and 'A' level results were sent to each individual on a postcard. Nowadays, I understand that UK students go back to school to receive their results and we have adopted the American tradition of a Prom. No doubt, more elaborations will follow, but to what end?

A FRATERNITY VISIT

Mackie and I had somehow made the acquaintance of a couple of university students. They invited us once to Sunday lunch at their fraternity house. Students at American universities organize most of their social life via the membership of fraternities, which could be construed as the American equivalent of UK university colleges. Undoubtedly, they provide a sense of identity and belonging that is otherwise lacking on a campus numbering several thousand students. I am not sure how a student becomes a member, presumably it is by invitation or application. Some fraternities carry a higher social status than others. They tend to be known by letters from the Greek alphabet, such as 'Phi Beta Kappa'. I understand that Facebook developed from a fraternity base at Harvard. It was common for fraternities to have their own premises for meetings and socializing. Consequently, Mackie and I felt somewhat honoured to be invited. Everybody was very friendly and the meal was decent enough, pot roast if I remember. There was no alcohol, which was forbidden. Instead we had iced tea, which we endured rather than enjoyed. Americans cannot brew tea and to serve it iced only made it worse. But, I don't think there was much of a meeting of minds and we never met the fraternity again.

NOT SO FRATERNAL OCCASIONS

One weekend afternoon, Bob and I were strolling along the promenade when we were approached by a couple of guys in a large convertible. They offered to take us for a drive, which we accepted, in our ignorance. It turned out they were two gays from Houston out 'cruising' on an away day. They took us to a gay bar and plied us with drink, then to a dance club, literally on the beach. This was on West Beach, which was, apparently by mutual if unexpressed agreement, exclusively for blacks. Gays had taken advantage of the fact that they would be out of sight of any censorious white population and the black population accepted them, possibly because they spent well. Eventually, we felt more and more uncomfortable and, in the time honoured phrase, 'found an excuse to leave'.

West Beach, Galveston. Bob, Peter, AN Other, David Warner.

West Beach, Galveston. Henry and John Tait on left. Others unknown, probably locals.

APPRENTICES SHORE DANCE

It was usual for the apprentices to hold a voyage dance at a shore venue. Normally, this was arranged by people like Melbe Hocken and she would organize a guest list, including available and reputable young ladies and, maybe, one or two local dignatories. Usually the Senior Officers and all available Deck Officers would attend. In Galveston, we had nobody to do such organizing and there wasn't much enthusiasm amongst the officers. Nevertheless, we felt that we had to maintain a tradition and had a go. We hired a function room at the Galvez Hotel, told them our requirements and expected them to come up with a live band, food and drink. We were, or so we thought, just left with the task of making sure that there were enough females to go round. We solved this by contacting the nursing quarters at a local hospital and enough of the nurses accepted. We had not realized that in Texas it was up to us to organise and provide everything. An additional problem was that we were under twenty one, which is the legal age for drinking in Texas. I contacted the hotel a couple of days before to check everything was OK. I was horrified to learn that there would be no live band, only a juke box and no booze. The choice of buffet was limited. Anyway, we decided to carry on and somehow scraped up enough booze from our rations and twisting the Chief Steward's arm. I wish we hadn't bothered. The nurses were a pleasant bunch and eager to enjoy themselves. We turned up in our evening dress uniforms but the venue and the atmosphere were all wrong and the juke box music was inappropriate. The Chief Officer turned up and whispered to me that I had a flop on my hands, to which I could but agree. So, we wound everything up early, apologized to the nurses and took them home. It was just a clash of cultures.

A far more successful event was the Open House evening that Captain Barnett hosted a few days before we left. The open invitation is reproduced below from the 'Galveston News':

MS Durham to Sail Monday

Open House and Buffet To
Show Ship's Gratitude

The owners, crew, and cadets of the English training ship MS "Durham" will show their appreciation for Galveston hospitality during the last six months with an open house aboard ship and a buffet luncheon prior to the ship's sailing on Monday. A buffet luncheon at the Rickshaw Room next Monday noon will be the scene of the public acknowledgement of Galveston's hospitality to the crew and cadets of the "Durham". Representatives of the ship's owners and agents will make the acknowledgement.

From London

Coming from London, England, to offer thanks are J. D. Currie, managing director, and R. Strachan, superintendent engineer of the New Zealand SS Co., owners of the vessel. With them will be Cedric Norton and O. B. Cioli of New York, officials of Norton, Lilley Co., general U. S. agents for the line. Arrangements for their visit and the luncheon are being made by Thomas Phillips, director and vice president of LeBlanc-Parr Inc., Gulf Coast agents. Invitations to the luncheon will be confined necessarily to persons having direct interests in shipping or in restoring the vessel to service.

Open House

Capt. K. Barnett, master of the Durham, will hold open house aboard ship from 6:30 to 8:30 p.m. Thursday and Friday for all others who have extended the hand of friendship to the men of the ship, Phillips said. The Durham is expected to sail Monday almost six months to the day after she limped into port all the way from the Azores with her main crankshaft broken. Ninety-five officers and men including some 30 cadets in training were on board the Durham Dec. 8, 1957, when she tied up at Todd Shipyards. As soon as it was learned they might be here for a protracted period, Galvestonians and Mainlanders opened their homes to the strangers from England, Scotland, North Ireland, Australia, New Zealand and other parts of the far-flung British Commonwealth.

Pleasant Interlude

Instead of bleak holidays that seemed in store for the men far from their native hearths, the season turned out to be a pleasant interlude as the invitations to Christmas dinner poured in from all parts of the city and county. In the ensuing months the men were welcomed and entertained in scores of homes and fast friendships were made. Saturday Captain Barnett will put the ship through a trial run. If no further trouble develops she will sail away on her long delayed voyage with crew and cadets carrying home happy memories of Galveston.

We held what was really a party on the boat deck with an awning over the proceedings that took ages for us to put up and then take down. We didn't have a ready-made awning, so we took the cleanest tarpaulins we had and somehow made them look exotic. The shipboard party was a great success on both days and so many people came, including many of the friends and acquaintances we had made and whom we thought had got fed up with us. An event such as this was an unusual one for the Galveston social calendar and anybody who was anybody turned up, except for Vic Fertita. The cook and his staff excelled themselves with a buffet that would have seldom been seen in Galveston. On both nights, we ran well over the allotted time.

We left Todds Shipyard for the last time in the evening of June 8th 1958. We anchored in Galveston Bay over night whilst the last surveys and inspections were made and farewell drinks were partaken. I was standing the 8-12 watch with David Evans as we looked out over Galveston and its twinkling lights. I remarked that it was my 20th birthday and David said that I could not have had a better present than leaving Galveston. He was right. We had been there too long, but I was being uncharitable to those Texans who had taken us to their hearts and looked after us with kindness and generosity.

'Have a nice day, Texas!'

When I look back on this time, I realize that I was less concerned about not being at sea than the rest of my shipmates. I had not missed being 'at sea'. For the Apprentices, the main concern about staying too long in Galveston was the amount of sea time we thought we might lose. In order to qualify to sit for our Second Mate's Certificates, we had to spend at least three and a quarter years signed on for a deep sea voyage. By no stretch of the imagination could six months in Texas be construed as sea time. Not only were we concerned that we would have to spend more time at sea before we could take our certificates, there was also a problem with our indentures. Because of the delay in Galveston, most of us would have been out of our indentured time before we could sit our exams. This was more of a problem for NZS because they would have had to pay us as Efficient Deck Hands and not apprentices. The difference was an extra £36 pounds a month each plus extra pay for Sundays and Bank Holidays at sea. This especially applied to the senior apprentices, who would be out of time early the next year. NZS made representations about this to the Ministry of Transport. They took the view that there were exceptional circumstances, which NZS had done its best to mitigate. We had carried on with our class work and deck work and seamanship classes. Because of the unusual arrangements that had to be made concerning the transshipment of cargo to the Haparangi, it was also considered that we had gained extraordinary experience, as well as being able to observe at first hand ship repair work. It was ruled that our time in Galveston would be considered as a full contribution to our sea time. This was a great relief all round and a nice tribute to the authorities who exercised common sense.

On June 9th 1958 we sailed for the eastern USA to commence loading for Australia. We were operating under a cargo sharing agreement known as the MANZ Line. This stood for Montreal Australia and New Zealand Line. It was a consortium of the Port Line, NZS and Ellerman Shipping. Trade between Canada, the eastern USA and Australasia was growing and UK shipping companies wanted the lion's share of it. Hence the formation of the MANZ Line in 1936, which was effectively a cartel.

CHAPTER TWENTY SEVEN

NORMAL SERVICE WAS RESUMED

Most of us had not been to the eastern USA before, so everything was a new experience, starting with the passage between Cuba and the Florida Keys known as the Florida Strait. This is where the Gulf Stream leaves the Gulf of Mexico and joins the Atlantic. As the Gulf Stream is squeezed, it increases speed and the current runs at several knots, so we were actually travelling at nearly twenty knots over the ground. We then went through the channel between Florida and the Bahamas and on to Savannah, Georgia.

Savannah

Savannah is several miles up the Savannah River, which river is the boundary between Georgia and Southern Carolina. The river is lined by old style southern plantation mansions, known as ante-bellum, which look as though they are film sets. Their large gardens had oak trees dripping with Spanish moss, which are long green tendrils. It looked very romantic as we glided past. Savannah is where General Sherman's 'March through Georgia' ended in 1864 and split the northern part of the Confederacy from the southern part during the American Civil War.

There was a rather strange episode in our stay. We were visited by English expats who were working in the Tetley Tea factory in Savannah. They had formed the Savannah Cricket Club and invited British visitors to play them. They did not have a ground, so we went to a public park to play. It did not have a mown cricket pitch, so we pitched the stumps where the grass was shortest. Just as we were about to start play, a park keeper appeared and was very alarmed that we were going to play with a hard ball. He was concerned that unsuspecting members of the public might get hit and he forbade us to play. We retired to the nearest bar. I suspected that this happened every time and that the Savannah Cricket Club never played a match. It was just an excuse for lonely expats to meet up with fellow countrymen.

The dock labour was totally black and they spoke in a patois that was very difficult to understand. It seemed that every other sentence ended with 'shhhheet man'.

After we left Savannah, we went north to Newport News in Virginia. We passed close to Fort Sumter, an island at the entrance to Charleston, Southern Carolina. In 1861, Fort Sumter was garrisoned by the Union Army. It was fired on by irregular Confederacy forces, which started the American Civil War.

Newport News, Virginia

This little port in the Chesapeake Estuary is in an area known as the Tidewater Country. It is very low lying. It is near Yorktown, where General Cornwallis surrendered to George Washington in 1781. On the other side of the estuary is a huge American naval base. There wasn't anything to go ashore for and we were only there a couple of days, but a couple of officers went to Williamsburg, which is a living museum. The town has been restored to what it would have been like in the late 18th Century and all the guides, shop and cafe workers are in period dress.

Boston

This was the most northerly stop on our travels. I don't remember much about Boston and I don't think we spent much time ashore. The most noteworthy event was travelling back south through the Cape Cod Canal. Cape Cod Island is to the west of Boston. It is where the passengers in the 'Mayflower' landed in 1620, who later founded the Commonwealth of Massachusetts. The myth about the 'Mayflower' is that it was a planned voyage to take Protestant dissenters from England to the American Colonies. These dissenters had fled from what they considered to be James the First's persecution to Holland some years earlier. Their problem was that their religious practices were too extreme for the Dutch. So, these people looked elsewhere and bought passage on the 'Mayflower'. This vessel's voyage was entirely a commercial venture. Over half of its passengers were ordinary emigrants.

The canal is a dredged and straightened channel between Cape Cod Island and the mainland. It cuts short the passage around Cape Cod Island, but at a price because you have to pay canal tolls. The canal is lined with substantial mansions, many of which were the homes of retired sea captains. They all had flagpoles with the Stars and Stripes flying and several came out to watch us pass.

New York

The seaward entrance to New York is dramatic. The first view of the Manhattan skyline is breathtaking. Then, add Ellis Island, the Statue of Liberty, the view up the Hudson River and the long sweep of Long Island to the right and you understand why so many people have been ecstatic in describing it. On a later visit, I remember one of the shore staff joining us at the entrance and encouraging us to wonder at the sight. It is, indeed, enthralling, but when you have seen Sydney, Wellington and the Clyde, you realise that the entrance to New York is but one of the most marvellous seascapes. This realisation does not diminish the impact of first sight.

NZS ships did not dock in New York City, but on the other side of the Hudson River in Newark, New Jersey. This is the area that produced major show business personalities such as Frank Sinatra, Frankie Valli and the Four Seasons and Joe Pesci. The film 'On the Waterfront' starring Marlon Brando and Rod Steiger and directed by Elia Kazan had been shot in the Newark area a few years before.

There was an efficient bus service into Manhattan that used a tunnel under the Hudson River. The service finished on the first floor of the New York Port Authority bus terminal, which was like Victoria Bus Station in London but much more modern and better organised. It even had noise insulation in the ceiling. You descended via an escalator to the main concourse on the ground floor. Once there, you were right in the centre of Manhattan.

My parents knew people in New York. A couple who used our pub frequently were Joan and Fred Onions. Fred managed a gents outfitters and Joan managed the local branch of Dolcis. I played rugger with their son, Terry. Joan had a sister, Nancy, who had been engaged to a Canadian Air Force pilot in the war. He was shot down. His fellow officers clubbed together and paid for Nancy to emigrate to Canada, where she worked at the British Embassy in Ottawa. She got a transfer to the New York Consulate and met and married Alvah W Burlingame II. Alvah was a Federal District Judge, which means that he presided over important cases. They set up home in Jackson Garden suburb in Jamaica, Long Island. These homes were big, usually bungalows, and all had large basements. My mother arranged for me to get in touch with them. I got a weekend pass and Nancy met me at the bus terminal and we had lunch at a restaurant in the Rockefeller Plaza. This restaurant offered to post a menu home as part of its service. Rockefeller Plaza has fast food restaurants in a sunken area in the middle, which is flooded and frozen in the winter to make an ice rink. I was overwhelmed to start with because of the skyscrapers but deeply impressed. I had a lovely week end at the Burlingame's, including a neighbourhood party. Everybody was so friendly. Nancy took me to a huge discount store at what had been Roosevelt Field. This had been the aerodrome from which Charles Lindbergh had set off on the first solo trans-Atlantic airplane crossing in 1927. Had I arrived a month later, the Burlingames would have been at their summer home at Fire Island just off the eastern tip of Long Island. I liked Al, he had a lovely, dry sense of humour and had the right amount of scepticism to make him an excellent judge. They had a small boy, whom they had named Alvah W Burlingame III. Some Americans have this obsession with creating a dynasty.

David Harper knew of a jazz bar and restaurant just off Times Square called the Metropole. The jazz greats played there. We went there one night. It was on two floors, with a cafe upstairs, where that week's main attraction played. One night a week, the main attraction played downstairs. There was an elevated stage behind the bar. It was only about three feet in depth but ran the length of the bar. That night, we were entertained by two drummers, Zutty Singleton and Cosy Cole, and a trumpeter, Charlie Shavers. They were legends in the jazz world. They were proceeded by a local New York band led by a clarinet player, Tony Pirento. You did not pay to go in, the price of the drinks varied depending on who was playing. Get your glasses filled whilst Pirento was playing and make your drink last while Charlie Shavers was playing. Now, here's the irony. Shavers, Singleton and Cole were black. The Metropole did not serve black customers. It was a warm evening and the front door was open, so that the sound of the music spilled out into the street. Black people were dancing on the sidewalk, but not allowed in the bar. So sad and cruel.

We went to a New York institution called the Radio City Music Hall in the Rockefeller Centre. For two dollars, I think, you got a variety show, a symphony orchestra and a film. It was the home of the 'Rockettes', who boasted that they were the longest chorus line in the world. It was quite an experience.

We had a guided tour of the United Nations Plaza. The original site had been called Lake Success and had been owned by the Rockefeller family. The Rockefeller family had donated the site to the United Nations. Their money came from Standard Oil of New Jersey Inc., which was later altered to ESSO. The guide asked us to guess the height of the entrance hall. This was a favourite question asked of British visitors because the height is 66 feet, the length of a cricket pitch. Iran had donated a huge carpet as a wall tapestry. It was explained that there was one deliberate flaw because the Koran states that nothing made by man can be perfect.

Several of us booked tickets to see a Peter Ustinov comedy called 'Romanoff and Juliet', which took the mickey out of the spying by Russia and the USA during the Cold War. Ustinov was marvellous. We were a bit put out that there was no bar in the interval. I believe that this is common in American theatres.

Merchant Marine Academy, King's Point, Long Island.

The visit to the American Merchant Marine Academy was a highlight of our New York stay and left us gob-smacked. The opulence of the establishment was way out of our experience. There was, and is, no UK equivalent.

I understand that the origins of this establishment between the wars was the result of political interest in the highest quarters, not least from Franklin D Roosevelt. Consequently, the MMA was publicly funded and lavishly so. It is also closely attached to the US Department of Defence and is regarded as a source of officer recruiting to the military, particularly the US Navy. The importance of the Academy is further emphasised by the Academy Superintendent holding the rank of Rear-Admiral in the US Navy. It carried the same status as West Point (the US Military Academy) and Annapolis (the US Navy Academy).

The campus was very large with imposing buildings and situated on the northern shore of Long Island. The cadet establishment was 2,700. Cadets join between 17 and 25, in other words they have to be High School graduates. On induction, they immediately become enrolled in the US Navy Reserve and their training is almost indistinguishable from a Navy establishment. They embark on a four year degree programme, where most of their studying is done at King's Point. It is only during part of their second or third years that they actually get any deep sea experience. Their curriculum was somewhat broader than ours and would better equip them for a non-seagoing career. Additionally, sport was an important and integral part of the training, with several sports involved in the US competitive college programmes, known as 'Conferences'. On graduation, they receive a certificate entitling them to serve as a Third Officer at sea. They are also awarded a BSc and a commission in the US Navy Reserve. About a third of graduates join the American Merchant Marine, another third join the Navy and the remaining third take up civilian employment which usually has some connection to the maritime world i.e. insurance, banking and port authorities.

We were intrigued that deep sea training formed such a small part of the programme, in stark contrast to the UK tradition. Whether or not, the US system produced equivalent or better seamen, it was obvious that the career opportunities for graduates of the AMA were significantly higher than for UK Merchant Navy Apprentices. The awarding of a recognisable qualification (a BSc) in itself made the American system infinitely superior to the UK system, particularly for those who left the Merchant Navy and struggled to find a shore job commensurate with their abilities and experience, as I was to find out. The Americans had status, we did not.

Our stay in New York was eye-opening, exhilarating and enjoyable. All too soon we had to leave. But, I would return.

We proceeded through the Caribbean and across the Pacific with no problems at a steady 14 knots. No engine breakdowns.

Noumea

Noumea is the capital of New Caledonia, which is a French colony. It is a large island about 500 or 600 miles off the coast of North Queensland. Noumea is more primitive than Suva in Fiji. It had an open drain running the length of the main street. We had a small amount of cargo to unload and did not stay long, but we were entertained to a dance on a Sunday afternoon. The atmosphere was weird. Although someone had rustled up a bevy of local talent, they were exclusively the daughters of French officials and their mothers were present as chaperones. No locals and no daughters of other French settlers. The dance ended about six and we asked what the girls would be doing for the rest of the evening. Without exception, they said that they were going home and would not accept any invitations. Their fathers arrived with transport and we went back to the ship with our tails beneath our legs. It wasn't as if there was any other kind of entertainment available. It was very Victorian. It was with relief that we left.

On reflection, this attitude was not surprising considering the recent French experience. The French had been kicked out of Indo-China (Laos, Cambodia, Vietnam) in 1954, there had been the debacle of Suez in 1956, there was an insurrection in Algeria, with brutality on both sides, and the Third Republic was plagued with political insecurity. A degree of paranoia and insecurity was only to be expected amongst settlers and officials within the French Empire. Whatever, it contrasted unfavourably with neighbouring Fiji.

Brisbane

Thank God for Brisbane and a taste of freedom, although 'Cloudlands' was not open. Four of us went to the theatre, which was showing 'Salad Days', a whimsical musical that was popular at the time. We enjoyed it.

Sydney

I can't remember anything about this trip to Sydney, other than we completed unloading and went on to Melbourne to start loading for home.

Melbourne

It was now mid-winter in Melbourne and I remember ice on the puddles. We played our only rugger game on this trip against a local team and lost, although it was close. Considering how little practice time we had, we did well. The Third Officer, David Evans, had to be drafted in to make up the numbers and it was strange, as the team captain, to tell him what I wanted. On this trip, all my previous social contacts were not around, so a bit dull.

If I remember correctly, our lives were diminished at this time because Henry had to leave us. He suffered a detached retina and had an operation in Aussie. That was the end of his sea career and I did not catch up with him until 2021. He was the first apprentice I had met in NZS and we had spent so much time together over nearly three years. He went back to farming and lived on the farm where he had been born. All those journeys around the world and, in the end, it must have seemed that he had never left.

Port Pirie

This place is at the northern end of the Spencer Gulf. It is at the finish of a railway line from Broken Hill, where there is considerable mining for precious metals, including gold. The railway runs through the main street. And there is no platform. You buy tickets at a pink railway station and have to climb aboard from the street. It was like a Wild West town. Port Pirie also has the largest lead smelter in the world.

Adelaide

We had a good time here. Dave Harper knew some girls from a previous visit and four of us arranged to meet at one of the girl's homes in the evening on a Saturday, after we had been to the races. The girl's name was Rosetta Angus Parsons and she lived in an expensive area near the racecourse. Adelaide was originally built with a large cleared area all round the town. The width of the area was a cannon shot, so any hostile forces would be within visible cannon fire before they got to the main defences. This cleared area became an attractive park area and nowadays includes the racecourse and the Adelaide cricket ground. The most expensive houses are near the racecourse. Rosetta had organised a party of people from a background of mixed interests and it was good fun. Her dad, Geoff, was a bit miffed that he had not known we were going to the races as he had gone and would have 'shouted' us i.e. paid for everything as his guests as he was a member. I met a girl called Gill McLachlan and we remained pen pals for a while. She was as keen on cricket and rugger as I was.

These people were all well known to Melbe Downer, who organised our voyage dance for us. We enjoyed ourselves so much at the dance that Rosetta and Gill suggested that several of us go on to a night club afterwards. First of all, we had to report back on board and then sneak off. Monty Banks was the Duty Officer and he knew all our tricks. The girls were waiting in a car for us at the back of a warehouse. I had got everybody else off the ship without anybody noticing and was half way down the companion ladder myself. Monty appeared at the top of the ladder and we looked at each other for a while. Eventually, I said 'May as well be hung for a sheep as for a lamb'. Monty replied 'Trog, make sure you let me know when you get back'. So, off we went to this night club. We had something to eat and whisky from tea cups, poured out of a tea pot. This wasn't a gimmick. Night clubs couldn't get a licence in those days and everything had to be disguised. They had a 'gipsy' violinist, all dressed up with a bandana round his head and a pencil moustache. He went round the tables playing gipsy melodies. He wouldn't leave us alone. So we had to pay him to go away.

That was the highlight of our stay in Aussie.

The survivors of Galveston. Note lack of formality. We did look like a 'Band of Brothers'

Albany

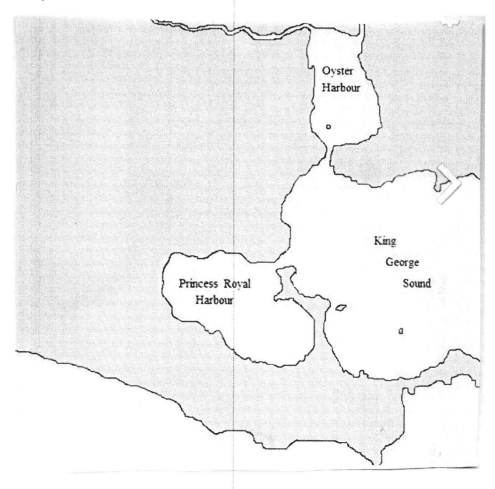

Albany is a tiny place in Western Australia, several hundred miles south-east of Perth. It was in King George Sound, which was entered through a narrow strait. King George Sound is almost round. The whole place is isolated, which just about sums it up. Until 1897, Albany was the only deep water port in Western Australia, so to get to Perth was a long journey overland from Albany.

Fremantle

Fremantle was established in the 1890s as the port of Perth and is at the seaward end of the Swan River. We finished loading here. Perth lies several miles up the Swan River and large ships cannot navigate the Swan River. This is where black swans come from. Perth became popular with Dutch settlers after World War 2 and the whole of Western Australia is different to the rest of Australia. It is the biggest state, but much of it is desert. Calgoorlie is a centre of mining and there was a big gold strike there in the nineteenth century, but Calgoorlie is hundreds of miles from anywhere. Perth is further away from Sydney than Moscow is from London.

David Harper and I had dinner one night in Perth and decided to have a brandy in a bar on the way back. The barmaid brought the brandy out of the fridge.

And so, we sailed home, through Suez and the Med, without incident. On the trip home, Monty went out of his way whenever we were sharing a watch to teach me about navigation and tested me continuously. It paid off later, for which I am eternally grateful.

Antwerp, Hull and London

We paid short visits to Antwerp and Hull before berthing in London. The senior apprentices paid off in London on November 3rd 1958. We had been away nearly 13 months. Monty was on deck to wave us off and I remember us yelling 'Goodbye, Monty' through the taxi window as we pulled away. John Tait and David Harper had completed their sea time and went off on study leave. I only saw each of them once again, David during my next leave and John at an exhibition in the 1970s. John had a job related to Merchant Navy equipment. One of the sad things about my life after the Merchant Navy was that I lost contact with so many people I had sailed with. I have recently made contact, electronically, with Bunny Hayward and Charles Hufflett, but it is obvious that most of have been scattered to the four winds and a number will no longer be with us. Recently, Peter Matthews' wife, Carolyn, found out how to contact me via 'Ancestry' and I have since met Mackie, Henry, Peter and Scot through that contact.

It was goodbye to Durham forever but not the end of my apprenticeship. My indentures were scheduled to end on March 29th 1959. Had I stayed on the Durham for her next voyage, my indentures would have ended before the completion of that voyage. I could not have been signed on as an apprentice for the period of the voyage after my indentures had ended. I would have had to be signed on as an Efficient Deck Hand whilst still living in the apprentices' quarters. I would not have been subjected to the same discipline as the other apprentices and my pay would have increased by £27 per month. Not only that, but I would have completed enough sea time to sit my Second Mate's Exam. My sitting for this exam would have been delayed, which would have been unfair. This applied to six of the eight apprentices in the Senior Class. The answer was to assign us to other vessels destined for shorter voyages. Peter Matthews, Scott Gilchrist and myself were assigned to a new ship, 'SS Lincoln'. She was a parcel tanker, which means that she could carry different sorts of refined petroleum products in different tanks at the same time. P&O had decided to get into the oil carrying trade and had commissioned and built several such tankers. They were not large but would carry cargo that was worth more per ton than crude oil.

Firstly, I had a long leave and my first Christmas at home since 1955.

CHAPTER TWENTY EIGHT

SS Lincoln: Time Filling

29th December 1958 to 20th February 1959

Greenock

We signed on at Greenock in the river Clyde, west of Glasgow. Lincoln had been built at John Brown's Shipyard and had just finished sea trials. Her first trip was to Houston for a cargo of 'gas oil', which is like a dirty paraffin. We sailed on December 31st with a largely Scottish crew, who were thus denied Hogmanay. We immediately hit bad weather and damage. Lincoln carried what was called a 'Suez Canal searchlight' in order to traverse the Suez Canal and other enclosed waterways at night. It was housed in the bow. A round door opened in the bow when the searchlight was in use. The bad weather damaged the door and we shipped water. We limped into Harland and Wolff, Belfast, for repairs, which lasted about two days and we didn't bother to go ashore.

Off we went again and an experience with living conditions that was a novelty to those of us who had endured the Durham. We were berthed on the Officer's deck and shared their lounge and saloon. Lincoln was equipped with air conditioning because she would be sailing in very hot and humid areas such as the Persian Gulf. There was a problem to start with. Air conditioning not only lowers the temperature but also reduces humidity. If the humidity is reduced too much the air becomes very cold. The settings were not right and we endured a day's discomfort in the Atlantic midwinter before the engineers got it right. Until they did, it was, literally, warmer out than in.

Yet another accident befell us. We were about a day's sailing off Bermuda in a roughish sea. The Chief Officer and Peter Matthews went on to the foredeck to inspect a pipe or a hatch coaming. The decks of tankers tend to be lower than for conventional cargo ships and they have less protection in the way of bulwarks. Not much more than a chain fence actually, because little work is done on deck at sea. There is a central, elevated gangway the length of the deck to provide access from the main superstructure to the forecastle and bow. The deck itself is covered in pipes and raised entrances into the cargo tanks, called coamings. Suddenly, a large wave swept over the deck. It hit Peter and flung him on to the Chief Officer, who was driven on to one of the supports of the gangway. The Chief Officer was badly hurt with internal bruising and needed urgent hospital treatment. We steamed as fast as possible towards Bermuda, where there was a US Coastguard patrol vessel. She came out to take the Chief Officer away as she was faster than us. The Coastguard vessel came alongside and the Chief Officer was lowered into her via a cradle. It was a superb piece of seamanship as the Coastguard vessel was pitching up and down and we had to be so careful that the Chief Officer did not suffer further damage. This was a reminder that a sea career is commensurate with danger.

NZS was trying to train as many officers as possible in tanker work and Lincoln carried a 'spare' Chief Officer, known as a First Officer. He took over as Chief Officer and proved very competent, although he was eccentric. He used to go ashore in a cape instead of a raincoat. He actually made notes on the back of a fag packet. We apprentices did not get on with him at first, but eventually there was mutual respect, which we earned.

We went into Bermuda, for what reason I do not know.

Bermuda

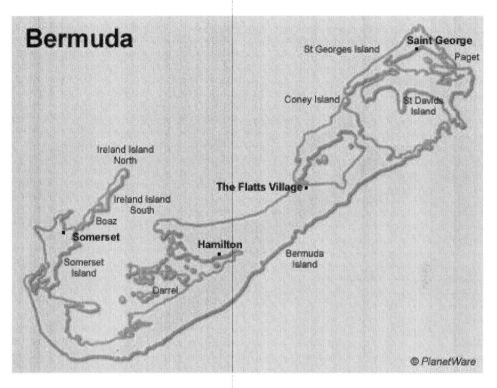

Bermuda is the oldest English colony, founded in the reign of Elizabeth 1st. It is in the middle of the North Atlantic between the USA and North Africa. It lies in roughly the same latitude as the Canary Islands and has a similar, attractive, all year round climate. It is very popular with affluent Americans for winter holidays. Tourism is the island's biggest earner. Bermuda is actually several islands, low lying and seemingly made up of pink stone. They are pretty with good sandy beaches.

There was no berth for us in the main harbour, Hamilton. We were berthed a few miles away alongside a vessel that had been impounded. This is like a house being re-possessed because the occupants cannot pay their mortgage or their bills. It meant that we could not cross this vessel in order to get ashore. The only way ashore was by boat. There was inadequate provision of harbour craft to provide a service for us. We apprentices came up with a wheeze. Lincoln, in common with all NZS ships by this time, was equipped with a crash boat, the prototype of which had been tested on the Durham. We approached the First Officer with a scheme to use the crash boat as a ferry service. We would run a time tabled service after working hours for a fee of one shilling per passenger. To our surprise, the First Officer said yes on one condition: if any passenger was on official business or it was within working hours, we could not charge. We ran the service for three or four days from six in the evening to midnight and we became the most popular members of the crew. I think it went some way to weld the crew into one unit as we were a completely new crew with most of us being strangers to one another. The takings enabled us to have a run ashore ourselves and I went up to see the injured Chief Officer in hospital. He was astonished to see me.

Because we were English, the Bermudans looked on us as second best citizens because we had not got the same spending money as the Americans. The dollar is king in Bermuda.

There was one amusing incident during our ferry service. We dropped off and picked up at two points and we had a time table for when we would be at each point. The First Officer did not understand this and was waiting to be picked up from one point at about 10.30 one night and watched us as we sailed by. Our schedule was to pick up from that point at 11.30 pm. He had to wait an hour for us to pick him up and was not amused.

Just after we left Bermuda, Scot's Indentures came to an end and the company had to pay him as an EDH. NZS had not calculated on this and expected that we would be back in the UK before his Indentures ran out. But the delays at the start of the voyage and the stay in Bermuda put paid to that expectation. Peter and I protested that we were carrying out the duties of an EDH and more, we had been apprentices for the same length of time as Scott and should be entitled to an EDH's pay but to no avail. NZS stuck to the letter of the law rather than considering morale and whether or not we would return to them as Officers after our examinations. Typical of shipping companies and I should have taken more notice of the attitude.

We sailed from Bermuda in late January for Houston, Texas, up the ship canal from our old stamping ground, Galveston. Whilst sailing there, we stood watches on the bridge. The First Officer also instructed us on how a tanker operated when taking on cargo and unloading. I expect that nowadays everything is measured electronically and computer controlled. We measured how much cargo was in each tank manually. In the hold coaming was a little hatch about a foot across, which you opened whilst loading. Into the hole, you thrust a measuring stick several feet long. The stick was marked off in inches and feet and you rubbed chalk on it before thrusting it in the hole. The chalk was discoloured by the oil, so that when you pulled the stick up, you could tell how much distance there was between the surface of the oil and the top of the tank. Lincoln had about two dozen of these measuring holes, so if all the tanks were being loaded at the same time, you had to rush around to make sure no tank was over loaded.

The Fourth Officer was a Geordie and this was his first trip as a Deck Officer. He had not been an NZS cadet, in fact he had spent his apprenticeship on tankers. He got married whilst he was studying for his Second Mate's, which astonished us. It must have been hard financially for them. He told us that they existed on cauliflower cheese. He was a nice bloke and I hope he did well.

Houston

We had a couple of days loading in Houston. Peter and I went ashore one afternoon and stopped for a drink on the way back. In this bar was a salesman from Anheuser-Busch, one of the biggest brewers in the States. Their main product was, and is, Budweiser. The salesman was there to promote a new product called 'Busch Bavarian', which was a kind of sweet stout. He worked the bar for all the time we were there, which was about an hour. He told jokes, tried to get us to buy this new product and was the all-American guy. We had never seen anything like it before, even with my experience in the trade. If Anheuser-Busch were employing people all over the country to do this, there wouldn't be much profit. Still, that's the American way and you can't convince them otherwise.

We had an uneventful journey home and berthed at the Isle of Grain, near Dartford in Kent. An awful place. A jetty on the edge of marshland in the middle of nowhere.

The whole trip was so different from our time on the Durham and none of us could envisage being a tanker man: sea journey, load in an isolated spot, off in 48 hours, unload in another isolated spot. No thanks. We signed off here and the Marine Superintendent, Captain Moncrieff, asked if we had been converted to tankers. We responded with a resounding 'NO'. I now had enough sea time and my indentures were cancelled a month early by mutual consent. Technically, I was unemployed, but I was free to make my own decisions for the first time in over four years.

CHAPTER TWENTY NINE

Study Leave: Cardiff, MV Cornwall and Warsash

March 1959 to October 1959

I was in a dilemma. My dad had had his second heart attack and I was torn between helping him with the business or going to Warsash for study. I opted for a compromise, which did not work. The University College of Wales, Cardiff (UCoW), ran Merchant Navy exam courses. There was a direct rail connection between Stratford and Cardiff, so I could catch a train at any time to get home in an emergency. Also, I could go home on Friday afternoons and return to Cardiff early on Monday mornings.

The UCoW campus was on Cathays Park, to the north of Cardiff Castle. South of the Castle, St Mary Street ran to the railway station. Near to the railway station was a hotel called the 'Merchant Navy Hotel' which was exclusively for Merchant Navy personnel, in particular those on study leave. It all seemed a perfect set-up for me when I joined in March 1959. A condition of study was that I had to join the Students Union, which I suppose meant that I was a bone fide university student. Not that it was of any importance.

There is a fundamental problem with all Merchant Navy courses. The courses are run on the equivalent of an endless tape. Once a course has been completed, the instructor starts again from the beginning. It is impossible for the students to coincide their arrival with the start of a course. Therefore, most students find themselves finishing a course before beginning it and then having to go back to the start and work until the course arrived at the point where the student started. Consequently, each student has to decide himself when to finish studying and take the exam. Exams take place every month, except August and December. Availability of funds is also an issue, especially for those taking their Second Mate's. We were unemployed and reliant on savings from our meagre pay and Unemployment Benefit of two pounds twelve and sixpence a week, which we got in cash every week from the Labour Exchange (now called 'The Job Centre'). We had to pay our course fees and hotel fees. Most of those taking the higher exams would have been subsidised by their shipping companies. Even so, many who were taking their Extra Masters had to take unpaid leave and that course of study could take a year. There was no compunction to attend lectures and submit course work. Everything relied on our self-discipline and most of us coped.

But, we were a convivial lot. There was one gang, who only worked in the morning and spent their lunch hours playing darts in a pub. They were mostly locals who were living at home. I remember being with some of them in a pub in St Marys Street one evening when a little fellow in a drab raincoat and cloth cap entered. The locals knew who he was and he was greeted with 'Hello, Jimmy! How are you? Have a drink!' His name was Jimmy Wilde and he was a drunk, both drink and punch. He had been flyweight boxing champion of the world but was now on his last legs. He died shortly afterwards and the whole of Cardiff lined the streets for his funeral.

I went home every weekend and helped my dad, although I played rugger for Stratford on Saturday afternoons. One Saturday, Cardiff Rugby Football Club was playing Coventry RFC. Cardiff was then one of the leading rugby clubs in the world and Coventry laid claim to being the leading club in England. The Cardiff team was staying at the Red Horse Hotel across the street from our pub. I thought that they would need somewhere more convivial, so went over and invited them to dad's pub. They accepted and I had some of my mates from the Stratford club there. You could not move in our Smoke Room. Cardiff had beaten Coventry and were in a celebratory mood. Despite my mother's protest that we hadn't got a singing licence, they sang their hearts out. Many of the team were internationals, including Alun Priday, the full back. I mentioned that I was studying in Cardiff and he asked where I was doing my training. I told him I had nowhere, to which he replied 'Oh, you'd better come and train with us then'. Wow, just like that! That's the rugger world, a player is a player and we're all mates. I did go once, but I couldn't keep it up as you would have expected. Their captain, C D (Derek) Williams, played wing forward (flanker). His boast was that he was the only Cardiff forward without a Welsh cap. I met him a couple of times in Cardiff and he always had time for a chat. He worked for Shell, who gave him all the time he needed to promote Cardiff RFC. Rugby Union was supposedly amateur then, but top clubs always found employment for their top players that allowed them unlimited time for training and playing. On match days, Derek carried a wad of notes given to him by the club treasurer. The players never paid for their drinks or other expenses. Also at that time, Newport Athletic Club was an umbrella organisation that included Newport RFC. If you were a member of that club and aspired to play for the first team, you knew that you had been picked for the first team when the club secretary gave you a chit to get fitted out with a blazer and flannels and a club tie at the local Burtons, a nationwide tailoring chain and gents outfitter of the time. It was necessary to be well turned out if you represented the club. It worked well for many years until it became impossible for leading players to remain amateurs and train and play at the top level.

My problem was that I had started my course in March, then there was an Easter break and I felt I could not spend all week in Cardiff. During Easter and for a couple of months after, I boosted my funds by driving one of Sonny Rose's pleasure launches on the river. I decided to use my books and study at home, help Dad and take my exams in July. Looking back, it is obvious that my interest in a sea career was starting to wane and that my real interest was making sure that I had a piece of paper to show for my time at sea. I also had my 21st Birthday, which was a very boozy party in our living room and all organised at short notice. I was going to have a river party but it rained all that week.

I passed my written exams, signals and Radar Operator's Certificate easily and it was all credit to the instruction I had had on Durham. If you look at my reports from Durham, they are not entirely complimentary, even though I ended up second out of eight in the Senior Class and I was awarded the prize for Best Cadet of the Year. I realised that we had been judged more strictly on the Durham than the Ministry of Transport examiners did. The problem was the oral exam, known as 'viva voce' in University terms. Each candidate would be examined individually by an examiner, who could ask any questions he liked on any relevant subject. The questions mostly covered ship handling, seamanship, cargo handling and stowage and 'The International Rules for the Avoidance of Collision at Sea'. There were thirty two of these Rules and you had to learn them off by heart. The exam room had a large table, on which there were models of ships and buoys marking channels. The examiner manoeuvres the models around into various situations and ask you how you would cope. That part was OK, but then he asked me a series of questions that were totally beyond my experience. I froze and failed. That meant that I had failed everything and had to take all the exams again. Had there been exams in August, I could just have taken the oral again as the written results lasted for a couple of months. He told me to get some more sea time and come back in October. I was devastated.

The only consolation was that my dad was better and did not need me.

With some trepidation, I contacted NZS and told them the sorry story. I need not have worried. I was told that it happened to lots of people and that I would get a berth as an Uncertificated Fourth Officer. In truth, NZSC gained a short term officer for 'coasting', which they needed.

MV Cornwall
8th August 1959 to 29th August 1959

London

The Cornwall was 'coasting', which means that it was loading and unloading in UK and Continental ports before setting off for Australasia. During this trip, the Chief Officer took me under his wing. He started by getting me to explain why I had not passed the oral. His view was that I had come up against an examiner who was prejudiced against candidates who came from 'prestigious' shipping companies and who delight in devising questions that are far out of the candidate's experience and which he is unlikely to experience if he returns to the shipping company where he passed his apprenticeship. He then spent a lot of time when we were sharing watches on preparing me for the oral. This was invaluable.

Hamburg

Hamburg is on the Elbe estuary and is the biggest port in Germany. It had been largely demolished by Allied bombing in the war. A series of incendiary raids in 1943 caused more fatalities than the atom bomb dropped on Hiroshima. There had been considerable rebuilding but the scars were very visible. Because of its position on the Elbe and connections to canals, Hamburg linked the North Sea to much of Germany right up to the Czech and Austrian borders.

The commercial docks are on the south side of the river, whilst the main city is on the northern bank. There is a large pedestrian tunnel under the river. You get to the tunnel by a lift at each end.

Hamburg is famous, or infamous, for an entertainment district known as the 'Reeperbahn' in the St Pauli area. One of the streets, called Herbert Strasse, is where licenced prostitutes ply their trade. It is similar to an area in Amsterdam. They sit, in their lingerie, in front rooms with coloured lighting and the curtains drawn back. 'Clients' press the door bell, go in and the curtains are drawn. The street attracts sight-seers, including couples. One of the women was doing her knitting! It was weird and impersonal and seemed about as much fun as buying fruit and veg from a High Street shop. Actually, buying fruit and veg seemed more fun.

There was better entertainment at an establishment called the 'Zillertal'. This was a huge drinking hall with a brass band. The band were dressed in Lederhosen. It was all 'oompah' music and the audience joined in on certain songs by linking arms, singing and swaying from side to side to side. You could go up to the band leader, who looked like Hermann Goering, and ask to conduct the band. He only accepted about one request in five, and I was one of those he accepted. You had to buy the all the musicians a drink. The drink came in 'steins', which are large tankards holding a litre, that's nearly two pints. You drank either 'helles' or 'dunkles'. Helles beer was light in colour and Dunkles was dark. You could understand why the band leader only let a few members of the audience conduct the band, otherwise his musicians would have been too pissed. As it was, they all had large beer guts. It was very convivial and great fun.

Antwerp

By contrast, Antwerp was quaint and the old town still had medieval and Renaissance houses. It is a long way up the Scheldt estuary. Like Hamburg, its position provides water-borne connections into the country's hinterland. There are rivers and canals everywhere in Belgium and all are connected.

During this voyage I experienced, for the first time, the joys of 'watch and watch'. In Northern European waters, the combination of bad weather and sea traffic meant that especial care had to be taken by Deck Officers. NZS insisted that Deck Officers keep watch for four hours on and four hours off whilst navigating around the UK and the near continent. In practice we doubled up e.g. the 2nd and 3rd Officers kept watch together as did the Chief and 4th Officers. In bad weather that affected visibility e.g. fog, snow, heavy rain etc, the Master would also spend long hours on the bridge. Hence the need for the Master's chair. As Deck Officers also had to keep abreast of their extra-curricular duties, these periods were very fatiguing. We often did not go to bed between watches but dozed in arm chairs in the Officers Lounge. You can imagine that it was not pleasant to do 'watch on watch' and then go immediately to 12 hours on and 12 hours off for cargo work in the next port.

London

Back to London, signed off and with my confidence restored. The Chief Officer advised me to go back to Warsash to finish my study leave and take my exam in Southampton. My parents also had the same opinion.

Study Leave: Warsash

I did not need long in Warsash and made no attempt to go home at weekends. Consequently, I had no problem with taking my exams this time and became a qualified Deck Officer.

'Bunny' Hayward was studying there at the same time. He had been my junior when I was a Junior Leading Cadet in my second term at Warsash. He lived at Hillhead, just a few miles away and had acquired a pre-war Standard 8 Saloon. One Friday, we arranged to meet some of his friends who worked in London but were coming down for a sailing weekend. One of them was a guy called Mike LaHaye, who worked in a ship broking business i.e. they arranged for ships to be chartered, which is renting them out to third parties. We became great friends and I stayed with him sometimes in London, including a flat he used to share with his sister in Carlton Mansions, Maida Vale.

We had arranged to meet at the 'West Meon Hut' for drinks and had a riotous evening. This was long before the pub became a carvery. On the way back, as we were coming down a steep hill into West Meon village, the brakes failed and we went through a brick wall and bounced off a house front back onto the road. My head went through the windscreen, no safety glass in those days, which caused a bad cut near my right eye. I came to lying in the road. There was so much blood that a local inhabitant asked if I was dead. I was conscious enough to assure him in old Anglo-Saxon that I was very much alive. We were taken to Southampton Hospital, where I was stitched up and put to bed. When I woke, there was somebody with their head over me. There was a light behind this head, which created a halo. At first, I thought it was an angel, but it was a nurse. Poor old Bunny had come off worst with a back trauma. Nothing broken, but he was in pain for some time afterwards.

After we were discharged, Bunny's father took us back over the route to see if we could remember anything, but we couldn't. The owner of the house where we had knocked down the wall had put up a sign 'West Meon Welcomes Careful Drivers'. He had only just rebuilt the wall after a previous accident.

Bunny had had an alarming incident in Shanghai on his last trip. He served his time with P&O and on this trip they were loading rice in bags. Rice is very susceptible to moisture, so great care has to be taken to shield the bags from anything metallic that might cause condensation. Special mats are placed around any metal structures in the cargo hold. Bunny heard a 'wharfie' asking, in perfect English, if he would like more rice mats installed. Bunny was very surprised to hear a Chinese talking in a perfect Home Counties accent. He got into conversation with the man, who turned out to be a doctor trained in England. As such he was suspect to the Chinese Communist Party, consequently he was not allowed to practice but had to undertake manual work. He and Bunny got into conversation and Bunny invited the man to his cabin for a drink. The man accepted, but as he left he said 'I must now run the gauntlet'. As he went along the quay, Bunny heard gunfire and never saw the man again.

My study time at Warsash coincided with the General Election of 1959. Harold Macmillan, the then Prime Minister, coined the motto: 'You've never had it so good', which was not an exaggeration. The Conservatives were returned in a landslide on October 8th. I went up to London that evening and met the usual suspects in the 'Antelope' near Sloane Square. The suspects included Mike LaHaye and G Mackenzie Wylie, the captain of London Scottish RFC. Having consumed large amounts of Benskin's Best Bitter, we found ourselves outside the Junior Carlton Club, a bastion of Tory privilege. The club was holding open house, which included a free buffet and drinks. We made full use of the offerings. The club was full of members in evening dress. I cannot conceive what they thought of we gatecrashers but it seemed to be a night when all was possible.

PART SEVEN

Life As A Deck Officer

CHAPTER THIRTY

A New Deck Officer

A new Deck Officer

SS Hororata

31st October 1959 to 4th May 1960

SS Hororata

Falmouth.

I joined the Hororata in Falmouth as a very raw Deck Officer. I had signed a contract with NZS for two years. Not many men of my age then would have had such a length of contract. It would cover the 'sea time' I needed before I took my First Mate's Certificate. It indicated that NZS wanted me to stay with them for the rest of my working life.

The Hororata was a steam ship and had been built in 1942. Together with the Tongariro and the Tekoa, they were the only steamships left in the NZS fleet. Steam ships are more comfortable than diesel engine ships because of the lack of vibration. But, whereas diesel engines can be started immediately, steam engines have to have the water in the boilers heated hours in advance and it takes longer to stop and start the engines when manoeuvring. Thus, they fell out of favour.

Most of the engine room crew had qualified as steam engineers, so they did not get moves around the company's ships much. This produced an engine room crew who had known and worked with each other for several years. They were more like a family, which created a relaxed, happy atmosphere. I felt really wanted all my time on her and have a great affection for this trip. It was helped because I knew the Chief Officer and the Third Officer from my time in the Durham. The Chief was Dick Hannah and the Third was David Evans. David welcomed me warmly as 'John', which was strange at first because I had been accustomed to being addressed by my surname. When I told him about my problems with the Cardiff examiner, he confirmed everything I had been told, even though David was Welsh and proud of it

The 'Horror' was in Falmouth for repairs and had just come out of dry dock. This gave me a few days to get to know the ship's layout before real work started.

Avon mouth, Newport, Cardiff, Glasgow, Liverpool

The above were our loading ports. We worked twenty four hour shifts, twelve hours at a time, which was a foretaste of how our working lives were changing, with the consequent loss of free time. The most momentous event was buying a sextant. Glasgow had a marine instrument shop that was famous worldwide for new and second hand gear. I was so pleased to get a first class sextant for the price of a week's wages. In Liverpool, I collected a new uniform, for which I had sent my measurements on ahead to Miller Rayner. Before I was fitted, I had a talk with the salesman about 'doeskin' and how unsuited it was for a working environment. He looked through his samples and advised me to select a cloth called 'Corkscrew Venetian'. It was lighter than doeskin, more easily cleaned and difficult to tell the difference, except close up. It turned out to be an excellent choice. I also bought more white shirts and shorts. We wore whites in the tropics all the time. Although obviously cooler than our blue uniforms, you were continually washing them and could not have enough. White clothing is impractical in a working environment. Nowadays, the Merchant Navy has copied the Americans and has khaki kit except for formal occasions.

Before we sailed for New Zealand, David and I produced the cargo plan, in triplicate. There were no photocopiers then. We kept one plan, one went to head office and one went somewhere to be copied for each of the ports where we were going to unload. The plan showed the holds in plan and elevated views and was about A2 in size. Every item had to be shown where it had been stowed. It took hours and our writing was done with very fine nibs because the writing had to be small. As the nibs were so fine, we used 'dip-in- pens, which required a lot of blotting. Also we coloured in sections to differentiate one type of cargo from another.

The first couple of weeks at sea, I was on 'probation'. The Fourth Officer traditionally keeps the 4 to 8 Watch, morning and evening. A brand new Fourth is never trusted to be on his own at first. Whilst an Officer is on watch he is responsible for the safety of millions of pounds worth of ship and cargo plus the lives of sixty people. Initially, the Chief Officer stands watch with the Fourth and mentors him. The Fourth does all the duties: watching the course steered, lookout, navigation, keeping records. Gradually, the Fourth is left on his own. Firstly, the Chief Officer comes on watch later and then reduces the amount of time he is on watch to nothing. By the time we were in the Caribbean, I was considered 'safe'.

Apart from being on watch, I had also to take morning sun sights with the Second and Third Officers, work out a dead reckoning for the noon sight and then do the noon sight with the Captain on the bridge. After which, we worked out our noon position and calculated the course and distance we had done since yesterday's noon. The Master and Second Officer then decided on the course, or courses, to steer until the next noon and how many minutes to alter the clocks at midnight. The actual moment that the sun appears at its highest (the zenith) at noon varies by several minutes anyway, but you have to alter the clocks to allow for how much your longitude is expected to change over the next twenty four hours. In addition, the Fourth Officer had administrative duties: making out lists for lifeboat and fire drill, keeping the weather log, extracting events from the log likely to affect insurance. These activities meant that I had to learn to use a manual typewriter, including making stencils for producing copies of reports and lists on a Roneo machine. This machine was a screen printer. It used liquid ink and was messy. I had never typed before and had to teach myself, one finger on each hand. God, it was slow and laborious! Plus, relieving the Second Officer for an hour so that he can have his lunch. There is no such thing as an eight hour day at sea.

David Evans and I hit it off immediately. We shared a love of cricket and rugger. David was also keen on classical music, particularly piano works. He had a collection of LPs and a record player. We could play them at sea because there was no engine vibration. He told me that, when he was Fourth and Third Officer on the Durham, he knew all about my exploits but saw no point in exposing me. He had been through the same experiences when he was an apprentice on the 'Rakaia'. During one stay in Sydney, Rakaia was berthed in Rushcutters Bay opposite the naval base. A Japanese ship was also berthed there. It had the shipping company's name painted on both sides of the hull. The name was 'Yamashita Line'. The night before the Jap ship was due to sail, several of the apprentices got together with a Midshipman from one of the Aussie Navy ships. The 'Middie' provided a motor launch and David and some others 'acquired' black paint and brushes. The docks were not solid structures but were built with a steel frame supporting a concrete deck. You could just get a small boat underneath the deck and alongside the ship. They painted out the first three letters and the last letter of the shipping company name, Their handiwork would not be noticed until the ship drew away from the berth. Next morning, the Jap ship left the berth and sailed across Port Jackson to the heads and the Pacific Ocean. This was a distance of several miles and took about an hour. 'A SHIT LINE' was in full view of half of Sydney for that time. There was no love lost between the Aussies and the Japs in the 1950s and the Sydneysiders revelled in the sight. It soon got out who was responsible and the 'Rakaia' apprentices were the toast of Sydney for the rest of their stay.

Panama

We docked in Cristobal at the north end of the canal and I went ashore in Panama for the first time since my first trip. Cristobal is poor and depressing. It is very humid and the house walls run with damp. Not somewhere you want to spend any time in.

Christmas at Sea in the Pacific.

This was my first Christmas at sea, for which we received an additional day's pay. We had a turkey lunch. Otherwise, it was an ordinary day but for an incident on my watch in the evening. One of the stewards pestered me to let him have a go at steering. He kept on and on until the helmsman, from Stornaway in the Outer Hebrides, joined in on the steward's side. They wore me down and I, reluctantly, said he could have ten minutes but the helmsman must stay with him. There were no other ships or land in sight, so it was relatively safe. We gave him instructions about what to do and how to watch the gyro compass bearing. I then needed to go into the chartroom to work out what time to take my star sights and which stars to use. When I came back on to the bridge, I discovered to my horror that we had gone through a one hundred and eighty degrees turn and were heading back where we came from. I told Mac, the helmsman, who had a big grin on his face, to take over immediately and get us back on course. At the same time, the Old Man (Captain Roberts) was playing a game of deck quoits on the boat deck with the Chief Engineer. He noticed what was going on and I expected a right rocket. But his reaction was 'Well, it's Christmas' and got on with his game. I did notice that, from then on, I was treated with greater respect by the crew. Officers could be human.

This seems like an appropriate time to describe the formality of the life of an Officer in the NZS. There was a considerable degree of regimentation and routine, in addition to the watch system. Deck Officers and Radio Officers wore uniform at all times except for the night watches between 8 at night and 7 in the morning, when we could wear casual clothes.

Although we could choose whether or not to wear uniform caps on bridge watch, we had to wear them for 'noon sights'. In port and on cargo duty, Officers always wore uniform caps. This was to distinguish us from other workers and enable us to be identified easily by stevedores etc. The Duty Officer wore full uniform for morning and evening colours i.e. when flags were raised or lowered.

All the above was OK, but it was at mealtimes that formality became irksome, particularly for the Engineer Officers and for any Deck Officer who was wearing his boiler suit if he was involved in any messy work, i.e. moving items in a hold.. All Officers ate in the Saloon, where there was one round table in the middle and a rectangular table on each side. The round table was the Captain's table. He sat at the forward end facing the stern. His senior Officers sat at this table: Chief Engineer, Chief Officer, Second Engineer, Chief Radio Officer and Chief Steward. On the port side table sat the middle ranking Officers with the Second Officer at its head. These Officers were: 3rd Engineer, Chief Electrician, Chief Refrigeration Engineer. On the Starboard table sat the junior Officers with the Third Officer at its head. Officers even had their allotted seats at the table. This seating plan was rigidly adhered to. Officers had to wear uniform for all meals. This was very irksome for the engine room staff, who usually worked in overalls, and had to clean up and change before meals and then change into working clothes afterwards.

All the cutlery and tableware was silver and we had silver service. Each table had its own steward. The Captain was always served first. There were never less than four courses at each meal.

Officers and Petty Officers were always referred to by their rank by their seniors. If an Officer was senior to you, you referred to him as 'sir', at least in public. You never spoke to the Captain unless he spoke to you first or you had an official message.

The Merchant Navy is, essentially, a civilian service and this formality became more and more irksome and out of tune with the times. Nowadays, meals are served on a cafeteria basis and all the crew eat together.

In the midst of this formality, there is always some humour. All NZS ships recorded weather details at regular intervals throughout the day. We noted the air temperature, the sea temperature, wind speed and direction, cloud formation and the state of the sea. Much of this was formalised i.e. wind speeds were recorded on a scale of 0 (calm) to 12 (hurricane). The duty Radio Officer then turned it into Morse code and sent it off to the nearest Meteorological station. The Met Office still uses information from ships to make our weather forecasts. We also recorded these details in a special weather log, which could include unusual items. One day, David Evans recorded: Observed one turtle, swimming in a south-westerly direction.

In the Pacific, we were often accompanied by dolphins, who delighted in playing games by jumping in front of the bow. Occasionally, we saw a whale.

Working Hours in New Zealand

Whilst other parts of the maritime world were already working, or moving towards, 24 hour cargo working, New Zealand still adhered, mostly, to the working hours that were in place on my first trip: Monday to Friday, 8 to 5 and occasional working on Saturday mornings. This was probably due to lack of dock labour but also to a reluctance on the part of the Kiwis to change working practices when they saw no need. As it was, this was my last trip when I was able to enjoy the time made available.

The Master had no set working hours. His time was, for the most part, his to decide how to spend it. He would need to liaise with shipping agents, shipping company representatives and port authorities, particularly with regard to sailing times. He would also receive reports from his Heads of Departments and discuss incoming cargo with the Second Officer. Otherwise, he could do what he liked. My last Master, Captain Allen, once wore civvies whilst we were docking in Port Adelaide and had his golf clubs waiting at the companion ladder. My first Master on the Durham, Dig Hocken, was also a keen golfer and he and his wife, Melbe, had a full social life.

The Chief Officer worked days and was responsible for ship's maintenance and safety with the Bosun and any shore based workmen reporting directly to him. He also supervised boat and fire drills.

The Second Officer was principally concerned with cargo discharge and loading. He supervised the 3rd and 4th Officers and allocated them tasks as necessary. It was his job to ensure that the vessel was stable at all times. Technically, this means ensuring that the 'metacentre' is always above the centre of gravity. The metacentre will vary depending on how much cargo is on board and where it is stowed together with the amount of fuel and water in the tanks. The distance between the centre of gravity and the metacentre is known as the GM. What he needed to do was make sure this distance was neither too big nor too small. Too big and the ship would be very stable but would roll violently. Too small and the ship would roll slowly but would take a long time to return to the upright position. The time between the extent of the roll and beginning to return to the upright position is known as the moment of inertia.

It was part of his job to see that the ship was on an even keel i.e. the draft at the bow was the same as the draft at the stern.

The Second's cabin had a model of the ship which was about four feet long and had all the hatches and tanks accessible so that he could place different weights in each space. The model was placed on a movable platform, which reacted to the weights. This enabled him to experiment with different cargo loads to find the optimum loading. He would be supplied with information on cargo to be loaded in advance of any arriving. He then allocated cargo to the various decks in each hold and sent instructions accordingly to the stevedore company and to the 3rd and 4th Officers. Besides ensuring that the ship remained stable, he also had to be aware of the cargo destinations so that cargo for Port A was not stowed underneath or to the side of cargo for Port B. It took time to work this out and he had to do it manually. There were no computer algorithms to help him.

We also had a formula to work out the changes in draft at sea because of water and fuel consumption. We calculated this every Sunday morning at sea and the 2nd Engineer made whatever alterations were needed by pumping water and fuel around the tanks.

The Second Officer was responsible for producing cargo plans, which were then filed and sent ashore for forwarding to all the ports where we would discharge. Actually, the 3rd and 4th Officers produced the plans.

The Second Officer liaised with the stevedore companies, who then worked out which holds would be worked on particular days, arranged for deliveries from warehouses and freezer works and allocated the wharfies required.

Daily, he would receive the loading and discharging reports from the 3rd and 4th Officers and the stevedore company and adjust his working plans.

Nominally, the Second Officer worked days but his workload often meant that he worked into the evenings. The Master would also keep in close contact with him, not only to understand what was happening daily but also to know when cargo was likely to be finished and the ship could sail.

3rd and 4th Officers.

These two Junior Officers worked whatever hours were needed. The extreme was when there was 24 hour working and they would work 12 hours on and 12 hours off. Usually, the 3rd would work the daylight hours, meaning that the 4th rarely got an evening ashore during that time. Any other duties that they had such as drills and paperwork had to be fitted in.

These two Officers supervised the actual cargo work and ensured that the correct cargo was loaded in the correct places. Where bonded or valuable cargo was being loaded or discharged, they supervised the work closely in the appropriate compartment. Each carried a notebook and wrote down what they observed being loaded and discharged. All cargo would have labels indicating not only the destination but the consignee and, sometimes, the shipper. Noting this was particularly important for frozen cargo. The meat carcasses would be wrapped in muslim gauze with the name of the consignee or its logo printed on the gauze. The 2nd Officer checked these notebooks daily against the stevedore's reports. It was not unusual for there to be discrepancies, which were usually the fault of the stevedore who had not given such close attention to what was happening as the Officers did.

When unloading in the UK, the dockers did not often discriminate between consignees. One carcass looked just like another and as long as the consignee received the correct number, nobody seemed to bother

At end of the working day, the Duty Officer made rounds of the hatches to check that all were properly covered and secured. He locked the access hatches. During the day, the Duty Officer kept an eye on the mooring lines. During discharge, the lines would tighten as the ship rose in the water. The reverse was true when loading. He would organise loosening or tightening the mooring lines as necessary with the Bosun. This discipline also applied to the Companion Ladder so that wharfies, crew and visitors had safe access to the ship at all times.

Every morning and evening, the Duty Officer noted the fore and aft drafts and reported them to the 2nd Officer. The Duty Officer was responsible for flag ceremonies at 8 am and at sunset. The necessary flags were raised at 8 am and hauled down at sunset.

The 3rd and 4th Officers produced the cargo plans. We had A2 or A3 plans of all the holds. As we loaded, we filled in the plans with the information we had gathered. Cargo was shown in coloured sections with descriptions in ink. We had to use very fine nibs and liquid ink. This required copious amounts of blotting paper and there were no margins for error. We produced a master and three copies, all by hand. We kept the master. One copy went to NZS and the others for copying and forwarding to the ports where we were to discharge. These plans were produced in our own time. Each hatch would have three compartments; upper, middle and lower and sometimes lockers for secure cargo. Therefore a 6 hatch ship could have 20 compartments.

As I mentioned above, on this trip we worked a five day week and 8 to 5. The 3rd and 4th Officers would be the Duty Officer on a daily rotation. The Duty Officer started duty at 8 am with the flag ceremony and reading the drafts. He remained on duty until 8 am the next day. The other Officer would work from 8 am to midday and was then nominally free until he took over as Duty Officer at 8am the next day. However, there was always some paperwork or other duties not related to cargo that needed to be done. Also, although we had a Cabin Steward who cleaned our cabins, changed bedding, cleaned the lounge, surrounding areas and bathrooms, he did not wash or iron our clothes. We had a washing machine in the ablutions for our own use and an iron and board. Given that we changed our shirts, shorts and underwear on a daily basis, we were always washing and ironing.

However, it did mean that you could get ashore three or four evenings a week and sometimes in the afternoon. If you knew people ashore, then you could have a good social life and see something of the country. A problem was that you did not always know if you could accept an invitation because the ship may or may not sail on that particular day.

Wellington

It was now mid-summer and the weather was pleasant but not overly warm. The dreaded Wellington wind did not make an appearance. It was quite strange to arrive here and not immediately be bombarded with social invitations. I was no longer a rather nice and well-mannered (YES!) young Englishman, who was a bit of a novelty. There were no organised trips and no organised sport. I telephoned a few of my old contacts and met them for drinks.

Then I started the first, serious romantic attachment of my life. I don't know how it came about but Dick Hannah knew, or met, a girl from Hawkes Bay, which is an agricultural province on the east side of the North Island. Her father owned a sheep station and she had just left school and come to Wellington on a trip with her best friend. Dick said he would organise a blind date for the best friend. His first thought was to take David Evans, but David had other ideas. He was saving up to go to Oriel College, Oxford University, where his father, now a Church of Wales vicar, had been a student. David rarely went ashore. He was studying for his 'A' levels via a correspondence course. He sat his exams on board later in the trip under the Chief Officer's supervision. Dick asked me if I would like to join him on the date and I accepted.

We met the girls in the Wellington Hotel, where they were staying and I was introduced to Jann Giblin. I could not believe my luck. She was very attractive, short with tight, black curly hair. I remember she had a dress with a sticky out skirt that was very fashionable at the time. I think she was pleasantly surprised that I was halfway good looking. We went off to dinner in a restaurant, where we had to take our own booze. We hit it off straightaway.

If I remember rightly, we were six in the party, with the other couple being a friend of Dick's and his girl friend. It was a Friday night. The next day, Dick's friend took all six of us to Paraparaumu, where we lit a bonfire on the beach and stayed until the early hours. On Sunday, the girls went home and we promised to keep in touch. Then it was more difficult than it would be today to communicate. Mobile phones were then over twenty years away. We had a telephone in the ship's office, which the quartermaster on the companion ladder was supposed to answer. We were not supposed to use it for outgoing calls. Jann's people were 'graziers', that is they grazed livestock, mostly sheep. Cattle were bred to keep the grass down and manure the land. Jann's father, John Giblin, had about 1,500 acres in the middle of Hawkes Bay, about 10 miles from a town called Waipukurau. In Maori, that means 'water from many bellies'. They had a phone, but it was what is known as a party line. If you shared a party line, you had your own number but other numbers shared the line. Somebody else might be using the phone line when you rang. Sometimes, you had to book a call. The post was regular but it took too long. Somehow, we coped.

By now, there was a worrying trend concerning drink on the Hororata. This was a real problem in those days on board when people could get isolated and drink was cheap. A bottle of duty free gin was £0.43 on board. Dick was slightly drunk every day and this became worse as the trip went on. He drank on watch, he drank every lunch time and he drank every night. The Chief Engineer was on his last trip before retiring. He was devoted to 'pink gin' (Plymouth Gin with a dash of Angostura and diluted (perhaps) with water). 'Pinkers' was a favourite in Royal Navy Officers' messes. As well as drinking on board, the Chief went on parties everywhere to say goodbye to all the Kiwis he had known over forty years. On top of that, we had an Irish carpenter, who had been on the Durham with me. He was on his last trip and was partying ashore as well. Before we got back to England, all three were relieved of their duties and confined to their quarters because their drinking had got so bad. The Chief Engineer was carried off on a stretcher when we arrived back in London. You can imagine that it increased the work load on those junior to the alcoholics.

Lyttelton for Christchurch

It was hot in Christchurch, although it is further south than Wellington. I remember going to a cricket match and being roasted. The Chief Engineer and the Chief Radio officer went to a motor racing meeting and came back with blistered faces. There was no shade at the track.

We had arrived in New Zealand the summer after the British Lions tour of 1959. The series against the All Blacks had been close. Although the Lions lost the series 3-1, they had come close to winning the first test in Dunedin. They scored four tries to none for New Zealand. Why did they not win? The Lions did not have a reliable goal kicker and only one of their tries were converted. That plus a penalty made it 17 points to the Lions. New Zealand had, on the other hand, a world-class kicker in Don Clarke, their full back. Tries were then only worth three points, the same as a penalty. Clarke kicked six penalties -18 points. This was a pattern that continued throughout the series and the Lions were very popular wherever they played because of the attractive rugger they played. Anyway, just as we docked at Lyttelton, a shore chippie who knew David Evans came aboard. He was an Irish immigrant to New Zealand. His first words to David were 'We were robbed' and then he burst into tears.

Talking of this Lions tour, the Chief Radio Officer told me another story concerning the Lions. Just before the Lions played New Zealand at Auckland in the final test, an NZS ship was approaching Auckland from Panama. The NZS senior staff in the Auckland office had assembled one morning for a berthing conference. Ships do not arrive in port willy-nilly and just berth. There is much organising to do. Reserving available berths, organising labour and transport, re-supply of food etc. The meeting was anxiously awaiting news from the approaching ship about her ETA (Estimated Time of Arrival) so that all the necessary arrangements could be made in good time. A telegram from the ship was delivered and read eagerly. Here is the gist of the telegram: 'Please obtain four tickets for the Lions test'.

Wellington

And so back to Wellington and a reunion with Jann. She and her friend were coming back to Wellington for a few days to shop, only this time they were to be chaperoned by their mothers. Jann's mother was lovely with beautiful, lustrous curly hair, although it was white. I learned later that the hair was a legacy of her grandfather's marriage to a Maori. Jann obviously had that hair gene. We had a few precious days together and it was obvious that we had strong feelings for each other. I remember telling her so on our last evening when we were on Mount Victoria looking out over Wellington Harbour. It was very romantic and I had picked the best spot. Her mother decided that I should visit them for a few days. Easier said than done. It was not usually possible to get several days' leave during a voyage unless you were married and your wife and/or family lived in the country. However, I first had to get Dick's permission and he squared the Old Man. So it was arranged that I would have a few days off after we reached Napier in Hawkes Bay and rejoin in Auckland.

Before I left Wellington, I paid a visit to a family I had met on my second trip. The daughter had gone out with one of my fellow apprentices, Jack Hawkins, and she had arranged our trip to Pararaparaumu to surf on my second trip as an Apprentice. I mentioned that I had met a girl from Hawkes Bay and was going to spend a few days on the station. Immediate interest aroused. 'What's her name?' 'Jann Giblin'. ' I was at school with Jann, she was a couple of years below me'. The mother chimed in with 'I know her mother'. You can't be too careful in New Zealand with what you say about people. The country may be big, but the population is small and in any town you visit somebody will know your acquaintances in another town.

Napier

This is the main port of Hawkes Bay. There is always a swell from the Pacific here so it is difficult to get in and tie up. Whilst in port, a constant watch has to be kept on the mooring lines in case you have to adjust them. But, I was spared all that because I was picked up by Jann and her mother almost immediately and off we went. Waipukurau is about a two hours drive south of Napier and on the way we passed through Hastings, the main town in Hawkes Bay. Hastings is about the same size as Alton and Waipukurau is a village.

We had a stop for a drink just outside Hastings. Mrs Giblin asked if I wanted a drink, so I said yes, fully expecting that I would go into the pub alone, as it was still not usual for women to drinks in pubs in New Zealand. And Jann was underage. Not a bit of it, they came in with me and it was a great relief to know that the Giblins were liberal in their outlook.

We passed through Waipukurau and after a few miles turned off onto a dirt road. A quarter of an hour later, we reached the Giblin station and I was introduced to the rest of the family: John (Jann's father), her younger sister 'Bubbles' and her elder brother David. Meeting David for the first time was another indication that this was a family that did as it pleased and did not stand on ceremony. David had his quarters separate from the main house and had his own bathroom. The bathroom had a door open to the yard and David was having a bath. In I walked and David said hello and shook my hand.

The main house was an elongated, L-shaped bungalow with a number of extensions. I gathered that John Giblin was the third generation of his family on that land. I had a bedroom in an extension, as did Jann, so the family seemed to live almost separately. The roof was corrugated iron, painted red. There was a practical reason for this because rain runs easily off corrugated iron and can be channelled through drain pipes into a tank underneath the house. They had no mains water but had recently been connected to mains electricity. Whilst I was there, John and David and a hired hand painted the roof. My offer of help was turned down on the basis that I might not be insured if I fell. This was a bit ironic because I was allowed to saddle and ride a horse and explore the paddocks on my own, out of sight of the house.

They had several dogs for sheep herding. Jann said that they were exclusively her dad's and if he left the station they barked until he returned.

John Giblin told me a story about a shearing gang leader called Bill Smith. Bill Smith is a quintessentially English name, but this Bill Smith was a Maori. He ran a shearing gang and turned up annually to shear John Giblin's flock. At the end of the shearing, the Giblins always threw a party for the shearers and a few friends. Bill liked his beer and loved parties. One year, he abstained from the jollification. John asked him why and he said that he had become a Mormon. Next year, Bill was once more the life and soul of the party. John asked him why he was no longer a Mormon. 'I lost all my mates' was the reply.

Shearing sheds make splendid dance venues. They have the space and lovely polished floors from the lanolin off the fleeces. Wool was the principal source of income for a grazier but the development of synthetic materials collapsed the wool market in years to come.

It was a magical few days and during them there was no doubt that Jann and I were in love. She arranged a trip to the local cinema. It did not have seats but wooden benches with wooden back supports. I suspected that the benches had been made locally. Jann made sure that all her friends were there so that she could show me off.

Jann wanted to be a Karitane nurse. This was a peculiarly Kiwi institution that supplied paediatric trained nurses for families with new born babies. The nurses could live in or call on a pre-arranged time table. It was so popular that there were four hospitals that trained such nurses. Jann had applied to Auckland General Hospital and was due to go there for an interview. We decided to fly up there together, where I would rejoin Hororata. Looking back at this time, it is amazing that so much clicked.

Auckland

We flew from Hastings Airport. The terminal was like a large bus station and the runway was a grass strip. New Zealand Airways operated from such places all over the country. Our aircraft was a Dakota, known also as a DC3. It is the most successful commercial aircraft ever built and is very sturdy, reliable and economical. It was the mainstay of Allied air transport in the Second World War and some DC3s are still flying today. But, it had its limitations. It was powered by two piston engines that struggled at altitudes over 5,000 feet. It was not pressurised and was slow. The cruising speed was about 180 mph. If the headwind was strong enough, the plane might make no progress.

The PA rather grandly announced that our 'Douglas airliner' was ready for boarding. After take-off, our route took us over the central mountains of North Island, over Mount Tangariro

(6,500 feet high) and Rotorua. We had a head wind so we had plenty of time to see the sights. We arrived late in Auckland to find Jann's aunt waiting for us. Peggy Moss was Jann's mother's sister. She was married to a dentist, Ken Moss. Ken had served in the New Zealand Division in North Africa in the Second World War. They were both in their late forties and had married late. They had two children under four, a boy and a girl. I took to her straightaway and I think she liked me. She did question me pretty strongly about my feelings for Jann and about my future. She probably then telephoned her sister afterwards because she made a proposition that Jann and I should consider ourselves unofficially engaged and formalise everything once Jann had done her training and I could make a decision about my future. It was eminently sensible and both of us were over the moon that I had been accepted into the family. I do not believe that there was any other motive because of the way I was received and both sisters' reactions to subsequent events.

Auckland Main Berths 1950s. Leading straight off Queen Street.

Whilst we were in Auckland, the Chief Engineer introduced me to a new development that changed my shaving regime for the better. I had mentioned above that during our stay in Galveston, I had abandoned my Rolls Razor for disposable blade razors. These disposable, double edged blades, which had been invented by King Gillette in 1901, were a huge advance on the cut throat razor and were promoted as a safety razor. The problem was that the blades were made of mild steel, blunted quickly and liable to rust if stored long enough, particularly in the Tropics. Most men were lucky to get two shaves per blade. Often, I would only get one shave. Consequently, it was necessary to lay in a large stock before a long sea voyage. Although the Gillette Company continued to be the largest and best known makers of safety razors and blades, there were competitors, who mostly tried to compete on price, often with inferior products. I remember one blade with the name of 'Seven O'clock, Cock'.

Unbeknownst to me, a company called Wilkinson Sword had been developing stainless steel blades that provided a better, smoother shave and the blades lasted for several shaves before blunting. As the name implies, Wilkinson Sword had been a maker of military and naval swords since the 18th Century and had experience with stainless steel products. At that time, these new blades were not generally available, and certainly not in New Zealand. The Chief Engineer had, somehow, got his hands on a supply before we had left the UK and he offered me a couple. The blades fitted the Gillette Safety Razor. I was blown away with the change and the two blades lasted until we reached the UK. I have used stainless steel blades since then. Despite many changes to the actual razor handle, the invention of disposable razors and the advent of rivals to Wilkinson Sword and Gillette, the principle of a blade made from stainless steel remains.

I left Auckland for home a very happy bunny with heightened expectations of a letter at very port.

Except that we were not going straight home but were taking a little diversion via...

Venezuela.

This was to be our introduction to South American politics. There had been a political coup in Venezuela that had brought to power a party opposed to big business. The business party included the big cattle ranchers amongst its numbers. Venezuela has the largest oil reserves in the world and rich agricultural land. It was self-sufficient in food and exported beef.

In retaliation against the coup, the cattle ranchers had stopped sending cattle to market and there was no meat in the shops. The government used its oil revenues to purchase chilled beef wherever it could find it. The problem with chilled beef is that there is a finite time between slaughter and consumption, say about five or six weeks. Beyond that time, the meat has to be frozen. Venezuela had bought chilled beef in New Zealand and we loaded 1,500 tons in Auckland. It was just our luck that not only were we available in the right time scale but also we were going in the right direction.

Consequently, we arrived at the port of La Guaira in mid-March 1960. La Guaira is the port of Caracas,the capital of Venezuela. During our passage to Venezuela, there had been a counter coup and the big business party was in power again. The ranchers had sent cattle to market and the chilled warehouses and shops were full. Nobody had thought to advise NZS of the changed situation. If so, we would have been diverted.

Nobody knew what to do with us and we waited two or three days for something to happen. I believe that the UK government used its diplomatic channels to resolve the matter but Venezuela had to locate chilled warehouses with spare capacity before we could be unloaded. La Guaira is a strange place. It is not a natural harbour, just a stretch of beach at the northern end of a mountain chain. The mountains rise straight from the beach. The harbour is entirely man-made. It is only there because Caracas, the Venezuelan capital, needs an outlet to the sea. Caracas is about thirty miles inland over the mountains and is itself in an elevated basin in the mountains. I have never understood why the Spanish made it the capital because it was so isolated. Until shortly before we arrived, the only way to reach Caracas was by mule track. Now there was a mountain road, partly through a tunnel. The journey which used to take days now took an hour.

The La Guaira mountainside was dotted with shanty towns. The government had built apartment blocks down by the sea as a social improvement, moved the inhabitants of the shanty towns into them and then bulldozed the shanties. But there was nowhere in the new buildings for chickens and goats, so the inhabitants moved back to the mountainside and rebuilt the shanty towns, leaving the apartment blocks empty.

Whilst we were waiting for something to happen, Brian Boys and I made a trip to Caracas. Brian was a Kiwi and his father was a grazier in Hawkes Bay. Brian had decided to join the Merchant Navy and had been accepted by NZS as an apprentice. NZS decided that it would be better for him to join a cadet ship in the UK at the start of a voyage, alongside other trippers, rather than halfway through in NZ or Australia. We were giving him a passage to the UK. He worked it as an apprentice. He was a couple of years older than normal for starting his indentures and I never got to the bottom of his decision then, but did so partially, later. Anyway, it was good to have another person similar to me in age and interest on board.

We visited Caracas on a Sunday. To get there we hailed a cab. We asked how much, accepted the driver's price and climbed in. What we did not realise was that the taxi operated like a bus. Anybody could hail a taxi until it was full. The price you paid depended on how many people were in the taxi. The more people in the taxi, the lower would be the price per person. He had quoted us a price on the assumption that he would pick up more passengers en route, but we did not realise that. When the driver pulled over to pick up a woman with a couple of chickens, we told him not to pick her up and carry on. He replied with a rapid speech in Spanish, which we did not understand. At last, he shrugged his shoulders and drove on. We arrived in the centre of Caracas, got out and paid what we thought was the fare, only for the driver to start shouting and gesticulating. These Latins do get worked up. We did not understand him. Eventually, a well dressed old gentleman came up and apparently asked what was the matter. The taxi driver then turned to him and shouted and waved his arms about. Soon, a small crowd gathered and they all started shouting and waving their arms. We walked away and left them to it.

Caracas is in a bowl surrounded by mountains. The mountains were a vermillion red after recent rains and made a spectacular contrast with the white buildings, which were a mixture of old colonial Spanish and modern. Somehow, we found ourselves at the race track. It being Sunday, there was a meeting. The track was not grass but dirt, as are many in the Americas. The grandstand had comfortable seats and was better fitted out than many race courses I had been to in England, Australia or New Zealand. We bought a race card and were wondering what to have a bet on when this unsavoury looking character accosted us. He had greasy hair and needed a shave. He grabbed the card from us and jabbed his finger on the name of a horse. We guessed that he was some sort of tipster but did not want anything to do with him. As it happened, we backed that horse, it won and he came looking for us, obviously wanting a share of our winnings. We just kept saying 'non comprehendo'. He went off after a while, much to our relief. Anyway, our winnings paid for our day out, although we had done nothing to help Anglo-Venezuelan relations. They don't speak the lingo, you see!

We caught a cab back having made sure what price we would pay. Fortunately, this driver spoke some English.

After that weekend, wharfies and lorries appeared to start unloading. The lorries were just open trucks with tarpaulins to cover the contents. It was hot and the meat would not last long if the journey was long, which we believed was the most likely event. Unloading was slow, not helped by the lack of suitable clothing for the wharfies. They turned up in thin cotton clothes and had to work in chilled lockers, which were at less than five degrees Celsius. Their foreman came up to me and said 'Piloto, Piloto, es frido!'. Of course it is, I replied. He wanted us to provide warm clothing but he was told to find some himself. That was another delay, added to which was the irregularity of the lorries turning up. We were there about ten days for a stop initially scheduled for two. NZS would have made a loss.

During our passage from Caracas to the UK, both the Chief Engineer and Dick Hannah were relieved of their duties and confined to quarters. Dick had DTs. The chippie also had to be relieved of his duties. This reminds me of a funny event when we were in New Zealand. The chippie had brought a charge against a Junior Ordinary Seaman for insubordination and abusive language. The custom in the Merchant Navy is for the Chief Officer to hear the charge, assess the evidence and decide on punishment, usually loss of pay. I was asked to attend the hearing as a witness. I have mentioned before that the chippie was Irish, short and with a lovely Cork accent. When asked to provide his evidence he did so and finished with 'he called me an f.....g old c...'. It was the way he said it that made it difficult for Dick Hannah and myself to keep a straight face. Two days loss of pay. This same seaman, age about 18, had also run foul of others including me. He lost another two day's pay for running off to answer the telephone in the ship's office when I had ordered him to adjust the companion way ladder. The Bosun had a hard time with him.

London, Cardiff

It was a relief to get back to England. We unloaded partly in London and then in Cardiff. David Evans left us in London and I only ever saw him once again at Iffley Road, Oxford, when the University played the 1963 All Blacks. He just happened to be in the stand next to the BBC television camera stand, where I was viewing the game. But that's another story. David was in his last year at Oriel.

Nearly all the crew paid off in London and I was retained to coast round to the Welsh ports, as was Brian Boys. Whilst in London, David and I were interviewed together by Captain Moncrieff, the Chief Marine Superintendent. This was by way of an appraisal and to ask us about future ambitions. I thought that it was out of order to interview us together and not separately. David had by now been assured of his place at Oriel and was let go immediately. Moncrieff thought that I was a bit old to be a Fourth Officer at twenty one, which David and I thought was irrelevant. Moncrieff asked me about my views on 'Wh' ships. I will expand more later on, but my reply was as neutral as I could make it, just saying that we all had to do a stint on those ships at some time. In my innocence, I did not realise that I had in effect volunteered, which I regretted thereafter. This was an example of how NZS managed the expectations of its Officers. I was never asked what my ultimate ambition at sea was, nor what I thought about the recent voyage or the state of the ship. Communications were oblique, to say the least. There were instances of Officers being told that their next trip would be a single outward and return voyage i.e. six months or less. This information was important for married men. Once at sea, the news was given out that the voyage would be a 'double header' i.e. UK to Australasia then USA East coast then Australasia then home, up to a year away.

The Chief Engineer and Dick Hannah were paid off. The Chief was taken ashore on a stretcher. Dick left NZS and took over a pub.

When we got to Cardiff, I had a moan about not going on leave and wangled a weekend off. I took Brian Boys with me for a long weekend from Friday afternoon to Monday morning. Brian expressed surprise at how green the countryside was as we looked out of the train. No sooner had we got back to Cardiff than we were paid off. Whilst in Cardiff, much to my surprise, the old Chief Engineer and his wife paid us a visit. She had got him on the wagon and he looked so well and nothing like the pathetic creature he had been just a couple of weeks beforehand.

The old Chief had a fund of stories and here are a few of them:

Ruapehu and hot water

Between the wars, NZS operated a passenger liner called the 'Ruapehu'. She was steam driven. At the time of this story, the 'Hororata' Chief Engineer was then the Second Engineer on the 'Ruapehu'. In those days, on a long ocean voyage, there was no fresh water for washing, even for passengers. The ship's water tanks were not big enough. You washed in sea water pumped out of the ocean and water was heated by transferring heat from the waste water that came from the engine room boiler. The washing water was on the same circuit as the water used for lavatory flushing. There were complaints that the water was not hot enough. The Second Engineer and one other bypassed the heating pipe so that it got hotter water from the boiler. All very satisfactory. However, on this trip there was a lady who enjoyed the sensation of warm water on her bottom after flushing the lavatory. Nobody knew this. The next time she used the lavatory, there were howls of pain from her cabin. Her bottom had got burned by the now scalding hot water.

Bill 'Groaner' Davis and the Heavy Derrick

This concerns an incident in 1940 when the Chief was serving on an NZS ship whose master was Captain Robertson. Robertson had a daughter, Anna Neagle, who became a very famous film star in the 1940s and 1950s.

I cannot remember the name of the ship but the incident occurred on its passage from Panama to Auckland, New Zealand. The ship was carrying a passenger, one Captain William Davis RN, otherwise known as Bill 'Groaner' Davis. Davis had a reputation for fierce efficiency and discipline. He was being sent out to take command of 'HMNZS Achilles'. The Achilles had taken part in the Battle of the River Plate in October 1939 when three heavily out-gunned British cruisers had taken on a German battleship, the Graf Spee, and won. When the Achilles returned to Auckland, the crew were heavily feted and they thought they had won the war. Discipline wavered and Davis had been sent out to re-instate it.

The ship was sailing alone. In 1940, the Pacific was out of reach of the German Navy and the Japanese had not entered the war. There was no need for convoys.

Cargo ships carry what is known as a 'heavy derrick'. It is a boom attached to the bottom of one of the masts and is used to load and unload cargo that is too heavy for the normal derricks. Usually, the heavy derrick is secured upright against the mast or across a hatch when on voyage. It is unusual for it to be 'raised' at sea. i.e. in the working position. One morning before breakfast, Robertson and Davis are on the bridge together. Robertson sees another vessel on the horizon and raises his binoculars for a closer look. He is somewhat perplexed at what he sees. He handed the binoculars to Davis and invited him to have a look and tell him what he saw. Davis looked, handed the binoculars back and said 'I don't know that there is anything strange?' Robertson asked him if he had not seen that the other vessel had its heavy derrick raised. 'So what?' replied Davis. Robertson kept on about it until Davis said 'Well, isn't your 'heavy derrick' raised in the morning?'

'Chocolate'

On one trip, his ship had docked at Lyttelton to unload. Lyttelton had dockside cranes and the crane driver had to climb a long steel ladder to reach his cabin. The ship had a small cargo of chocolate in one of the lockers. No matter how vigilant the ship's officers are, dockers always find a way to broach cases containing alcohol, tobacco, chocolate or other valuable cargo. This day was no exception. The chocolate was unloaded in the morning and, as normal, some of the dockers went to the pub at lunchtime. Chocolate was probably sold or handed out in the pub. What the dockers did not know was that the chocolate was laxative chocolate. One of the crane drivers had had a couple of beers and some chocolate. After lunch, he climbed up to his cabin, but soon afterwards he was seen frantically scrambling down the ladder. Unfortunately, he did not make the bottom. He was seen to stop suddenly.

CHAPTER THIRTY TWO

Purgatory

10th June 1960 to 6th Sept 1961

To Canada

I had a month at home in lovely weather for May. I have added what happened during this leave to Volume Two of my master chronicle. My parents were lukewarm about my relationship with Jann and were more concerned with the possibility that I might leave England and them than my happiness or desires. Natural, I suppose.

David Harper visited whilst we were both on leave. He had not rejoined NZS after obtaining his Second Mate's Certificate, but had joined the China Steam Navigation Company. This company was based in Hong Kong and had been involved in the opium wars in the 1840s, which led to the UK gaining Hong Kong as a colony and entry port for Chinese trade. China Steam paid better than other companies and David had gone for the money. He was more flush than I was and had a more extensive wardrobe. He had taken full advantage of the ability of Hong Kong tailors to make a suit in twenty four hours at ridiculously cheap prices. David had suits made with light weight materials that were more comfortable in hot climates and did not become commonplace in the UK until some years later. That was our last meeting.

After about three weeks, I was ordered to report to London on June 8th and be prepared to travel to Montreal, Canada, to join the 'Whangaroa'. Six of us left London by boat train for Liverpool on June 9th to take passage on the 'Empress of Canada'. The six of us were: David Le Cornu (Third Officer), a Chief and Second Electrician, two Junior Ordinary Seamen on their first trip and myself. We ordered copious amounts of drink on the train. When the time came to pay, we convinced the train steward that we were on official expenses and that British Rail should invoice NZS. We never heard what the outcome was but presumed NZS paid up. The invoice probably got 'lost' amongst many others.

The 'Empress of Canada' was a trans-Atlantic passenger liner owned by the Canadian Pacific Railway. They had several liners all called 'Empress of somewhere or other' and they carried passengers between the UK and Canada. The officers travelled first class and the seamen second class. I shared a cabin with David Le Cornu, who came from Jersey and had been an apprentice on the Rakaia. We had two double beds, wardrobes, a sofa and armchair, a desk and en suite. It was very luxurious. We sailed on June 10th and had nothing to do on the passage which took about five days. It was quite boring and you just followed a routine. Cocktails with the Captain on the first evening. You dressed for dinner every night except the last one. There was dancing every night, but the band was no good and we did not find any suitable partners. There was a cinema and a swimming pool, but the pool was down in the bowels of the ship. It is too cold on a North Atlantic crossing to have an outdoor pool. One night we went to Second Class to see how the two young seamen were getting on. They were having the time of their lives. Sixteen, just left home and plenty of girls, it was a great adventure for them. David took one of the Second Class passengers to bed and caught a dose of crabs. Fortunately, none of my clothes got caught up with his.

The most interesting part of the voyage was dodging icebergs off Newfoundland. The summer months are the most prolific for them. Going up the St Lawrence River for the first time was also an experience. It is several hundred miles from the start of the St Lawrence Estuary to Montreal and was quite weird to travel for more than a day up a river in an ocean going ship.

Montreal.

The Whangaroa had not arrived in Montreal. David and I and the Electricians were put up in a first class hotel. The seamen had to make do with the Seamen's Mission. We went down to the Mission and played table tennis. One of the young guys from the shipping agent took us out on the town. It was a bit weird. Montreal was once in 'Nouvelle France' until Wolfe won the Battle of the Heights of Abraham in 1759 in the Seven Years War. The Peace Treaty of Paris after that war gave us control of what is now known as Canada. What is now called Quebec Province is French speaking and can be hostile to English speakers. The French they speak is old French with sometimes different words to modern French. For instance, Montreal is two words joined together Mont and Real. It means Royal Mountain but Real is old French, whereas Royale is modern French. In one bar we called at, David Le Cornu, who spoke good French, ordered drinks but the locals glared at us and we beat a retreat.

A weekend approached and I decided to go to Ottawa. We had met a couple and their teen-aged daughter on the Empress boat. I think their name was Cunningham. The daughter was returning from finishing school in Switzerland. Mr Cunningham was a travel agent, based in Ottawa. I wanted to get in contact with an old RAF colleague of my dad, who was called Andre Seneca and came from Ottawa. He and dad had exchanged Christmas cards after the war and I vaguely remembered him. I had discussed this with the travel agent and he and his wife invited me to visit them if I had the chance. This seemed an ideal time and I phoned them and was invited for the weekend. I caught a train on Saturday morning, which took about an hour, and was given the Grand Tour. Once you've done the Parliament buildings, that is about it but the countryside is pleasant in the summer. We got hold of all the Senecas in the Ottawa phone book and called all the numbers, but no success. I was surprised at how many there were but it was explained to me that there was a Seneca tribe of North American people, so it was no wonder we couldn't find Andre. He had probably moved away. The Cunninghams were very Anglophile. He drank imported Bass. I had a nice weekend and went back to Montreal on Sunday evening.

On Monday, we had to leave the hotel and doss down in the Seamens' Mission. Whangaroa was late and NZS did not want to spend more on hotel bills.

MV Whangaroa

MV Whangaroa

Around the end of June, Whangaroa arrived and we went on board and relieved those of the crew we had been sent to replace. Whangaroa was named after a small harbour at the northern end of North Island, New Zealand.

This ship was one of three, whose names all began with a 'Wh', hence the name 'Wh boats'. The other names were 'Whakatane' and 'Wharanui'. They were built between 1954 and 1956 in Glasgow specifically for a trading route between Australia, New Zealand and the east coast of Canada and the United States. Australia and New Zealand were actively looking for new customers for agricultural products and reducing their dependence on the UK. Both countries were in what was known as the 'Sterling Zone'. This meant that their currencies were interchangeable with UK Sterling and their denominations were in pounds, shillings and pence. The NZ pound was of almost equal value to the UK pound, but the Aussie was worth about 60% of the UK pound. Whilst the UK was the dominant world trader and creditor, this worked well for the UK dominions. But, once UK dominance ended and the British Empire declined, this produced adverse trade conditions for British Dominions. Australia and New Zealand found it difficult to buy American products because they had no dollar reserves and did not sell enough to the USA and Canada in order to build up reserves. After World War 2, this began to change and more and more product from down under was going to North America. This coincided with a change in the relationship between the UK and Australia and New Zealand, which was worsened by the UK's attempts to join the European Economic Community. Success in this would have meant tariffs on goods imported from the Commonwealth. Those who had fought for Britain and the Commonwealth felt betrayed and they looked elsewhere for trade and support.

As a result of these new trading opportunities, three UK shipping companies formed a cartel in 1936, euphemistically called a 'conference line', to carry this trade. They were NZS, Port Line and Ellerman Shipping. They called their arrangement the 'MANZ Line' (Montreal, Australia and New Zealand). Initially, the companies used existing ships, but NZS built three 'Wh' ships specifically for this trade. They were of slightly different construction to the standard NZS ships. They were shorter and shallower in order to access ports that could not take the larger boats. They had five instead of six holds, although all were refrigerated.

The superstructure was designed to allow six passenger cabins on the boat deck. The Deck Officers had their cabins on the boat deck, as was the forward Officers' Lounge, which meant that the Master's quarters were built on its own deck between the Officers' Lounge and the Bridge. The saloon was on the main Officer's accommodation deck and not on the main deck, so that food had to be sent via a dumb waiter from the galley.

These ships were not scheduled to make visits to the UK, so crew changes were usually made in Canada. NZS crews did three round trips lasting about fifteen months before being relieved. It was a bone of contention because Port Line rotated their crews after two round trips. Assignment to a 'Wh' ship was not a popular one, particularly for married men.

My new captain was called Lampbrick. He was in his late thirties, thin and pernickety. He was not liked. He had eccentric ideas about ship handling in traffic, which most of us found alarming. The Chief Officer was 'Nibbie' Niblock, and the Second Officer was called Eddie. He was the only Deck Officer who had not served his time as an apprentice with NZS.

We loaded in Montreal and then went to Quebec, where we were only there overnight. I had wanted a look at the Chateau Frontenac, then the biggest hotel in the world, and take a walk up to the Heights of Abraham. I never got the chance.

Boston

This was the next stop and some people from our agents took us on a pub crawl around the supposedly dangerous areas, including one called 'Scully Square, which had been notorious but had been cleaned up.

New York

We did not berth in Newark, as usual, but just next to the Brooklyn Naval Yard. I did not get to see the Burlingames, this time around. I did go to the Metropole again and saw Gene Krupa. He was then the most celebrated jazz drummer in the world. He gave us a rendition of 'Bolero' that had me spellbound.

One of the people who worked in our agent's office arranged a trip into the Catskills one Sunday. It was a lovely summer's day and very enjoyable. Up until then, I had not realised how accessible mountainous areas were to the New England coast. Such a contrast to the mostly flat environment of America's East Coast.

We took on three middle aged couples as passengers in New York. Two were American on a retirement trip and one was Australian returning home after their retirement trip.

Philadelphia

The birthplace of the United States and where the Declaration of Independence was signed. There is the Liberty Bell in the building where it all happened. The building looks insignificant now with all the skyscrapers around it.

Looking back, it is obvious that there was little time whilst on the American and Canadian coasts for much social life, hence the paucity of description and stories. Life was very much confined to docksides and their immediate environs.

Then through Panama and we arrived in Sydney in their mid-winter, although it was not cold.

The Pacific passage was largely notable for the disruption of our routine by the passengers. Each couple was allocated a different table in the Saloon. The Captain had the Aussie couple, and the American couples were shared out between the other two tables. The couple on our table shared my surname and were very pleasant. He had been a head teacher in Florida. His family originally came from the West Country and were amongst the earliest emigrants to America in the early sixteenth century. We were probably very distantly related.

The other American couple were a different kettle of fish altogether. She had terrible table manners and could never get to grips with English table etiquette. I don't think she could be bothered to try. She used to put marmalade on her corn flakes. However, her husband was interested in sport, particularly golf, which provided a topic of conversation.

It wasn't so much the meal times that were the problem, it was the demands on the Officers' time, particularly the Deck Officers, that were irritating. I can understand the passengers' need to be engaged with us because we were not a normal passenger liner. No band, no dances, no entertainment. We were the entertainment. They had their own section of our lounge, which could be separated by closing a door, but it was always open. Often, when I came off watch at 8 in the evening, I wanted to go to bed because I would be up at quarter to four. The passengers would have none of it. I had to pass the lounge to get to my cabin. 'Have a drink', 'Come and play cards'. It was hard to continually refuse without being rude. They would be up until eleven or later and several nights of this was knackering, especially as you could not make it up in the day. The poor old Second was even worse off as he went on watch at midnight. Eventually, as the voyage wore on, they began to realise that they were being unreasonable and slackened their demand for our time. The Australian and the Florida couples were, however, very pleasant people and, at times, provided a bit of welcome relief, particularly with deck games such as shuffle board and deck quoits.

During the Pacific crossing, Captain Lampbrick got obsessed with the phenomenon known as the 'Green Flash' and was keen on the passengers witnessing it. This could happen immediately after sunset and could only be seen at sea. In certain conditions, the very last rays of sunlight could be refracted and appear green. It only occurred for two or three seconds and you had to concentrate to see it. Because of Lampbrick's obsession, I, as Fourth Officer, who would be on watch at sunset, had to be particularly careful to calculate correctly the time of sunset. I would have done this anyway, because I needed to plot which stars I would use for evening star sights, which I would take at the end of twilight when it was dark enough to see the stars but still light enough to see the horizon through my sextant telescope. Lampbrick would usher the passengers up to the bridge at the appropriate time and hope that there would be a green flash. We did see one a couple of times but it got a bit aggravating for me to have 'my bridge' occupied, evening after evening, by too many people, who tended to get in the way of my duties. Yet another instance of passengers being a bloody nuisance.

When we got to Sydney in the Aussie late winter, they left. Relief all round and we never carried any more passengers during my time on board, Thank God!

There was an unusual event in Sydney. This was the first organised strike by the National Union of Seaman that affected every British ship in any port in the world. Obviously, it could not affect ships at sea, because a strike at sea would be classed as mutiny under the Merchant Shipping Act. On one nominated day, all the ratings went on strike, after breakfast, for twenty four hours. That meant that the ship could not be worked, including cooking and the engine room. The striking crew had to leave the ship for twenty four hours and fend for themselves. Their demands were reasonable and most of the officers were in sympathy because what the ratings wanted was, in the main, wanted by all UK seafarers. I can't remember exactly what the demands were but they centred on rates of pay, more pay for weekends at sea and payment for holidays. So far as I remember, most of the demands were met and they eventually led to better terms for all UK seafarers. It was a remarkable piece of organisation by the NUS.

As the officers had no cooks and the dockers' union supported the NUS, there was no work and no food on board. All the officers were put in a coach and whisked off to a first class hotel for lunch and dinner. It was a day off for us. The only sour note was that one of the seamen produced a nasty cartoon of the Chief Officer, Nibby Niblock. It depicted him as Hitler, which was highly offensive. Even his mates did not like it. He had committed an offence under the Merchant Shipping Act and was fined two or three day's pay.

The rest of trip was largely uneventful (Brisbane, Melbourne, Geelong and back across the Pacific) except for two items.

In the first, David LeCornu and I played golf at the Geelong Golf Club and were invited to stay for a club evening. One of their members, Herb Elliot, was the current Olympic 1500 metres champion and, at that time, held the World record for the distance, but he was not able to come to the meeting. In true Ausssie style he was described as having 'just shot through'. By this time, I started to play golf at least once in each port. Golf was one of those games that it was possible to play at any time. Most clubs were hospitable and allowed us to play for the payment of a 'green fee' and there was often a member looking for a partner or partners for a round.

The second concerned unauthorised female visits on board. Visits by females were strictly controlled. Officers could entertain guests and hold parties, but all visitors had to be ashore by midnight. All crew members could have visitors during daylight hours at weekends. Otherwise, ratings were not allowed visitors after dark, especially female. I think that it was on this trip that I was Duty Officer one night in Melbourne. I had gone to bed and was awakened by the Quartermaster in the early hours. He was accompanied by a police constable. I got out of bed and the officer explained that he was looking for a woman who might be on board with one of the engine room crew. I dismissed the Quartermaster with the hope that he would have the sense to find the woman and get her ashore whilst I groped my way around the accommodation areas with the policeman. I took my time to put on my dressing gown, find a torch and question the copper for more of the story. It turned out that a neighbour had reported a woman missing. She had been away from home for two or three days and the neighbour was concerned because there were children left alone in the property. The Police established that the woman concerned had last been seen in the company of a crew member of the 'Whangaroa' in a bar. I am not sure how it was also established that the crew member was an engine room rating. Together with the copper, I made the rounds and established that there was no missing female on board. The Quartermaster had done what I hoped he would do. The policeman said goodbye and apologised for disturbing me, but we both understood what had been going on. I surmised that this was a common occurrence. I made no official report but had a word with the senior engine room rating, the donkeyman, and made it clear that I did not want my beauty sleep disturbed again.

On another occasion, when I was on the 'Whangaroa', we were in a port which I cannot remember and I was Duty Officer on a Sunday afternoon. I heard some noise outside my cabin. One of the young stewards was about to take a young woman up to the bridge. He looked startled to see me and dragged the young lady back down towards his quarters. I suppose he wanted to show her over the ship. However, he was in the Officers' quarters without good reason. By the same token, Officers would not go into the crew's quarters without good reason. I had a word with his immediate superior, the Second Steward, and nothing more was heard. I suspect that another Officer might have made a bit of a song and dance about it, the steward would have been fined a couple of day's pay and morale would have suffered.

All the time I was missing Jann. I found myself pacing up and down the bridge on my watch talking to myself out of frustration. One evening, the Quartermaster, an experienced AB from Stornaway on the Isle of Lewis, asked me if I knew I was talking to myself. That started off a conversation about our respective love lives. He was married, but his wedding day was highly unusual. He was Best Man at a wedding and was waiting in the kirk but the groom did not turn up. So he married the bride instead. Apparently, they were making a go of it.

I was now starting to have problems with my tummy. Sometimes, I could not keep food down and vomited. It did not help that I felt that I could do no right as far as Captain Lampbrick was concerned. He picked on me for so many minor things, like not wearing a shirt in view of the passengers. I could not be reassured by others that I was treated no differently to the rest of us. I felt that it was personal.

Jamaica

On our way back from Australia to the United States and Canada, we called at Kingston, Jamaica, to load Tia Maria and tobacco, which were secured in lockers in Number Three hold. This cargo was for Australia. We paid a visit to the Myrtlebank Hotel, which was then the only decent hotel in Kingston. It had a lovely swimming pool and we were served drinks around it. It felt as though we were on an expensive holiday. The hotel was first built in the 1870s but was destroyed by earthquake in 1907. It was rebuilt and featured as 'the club' in the first James Bond film 'Doctor No'. Three years later in February 1966, it was gutted by fire and never rebuilt. The fire was just a few days before the Queen and Duke of Edinburgh were to attend a Gala Ball fundraiser for the Commonwealth Games due to be held in Jamaica. So, I was lucky to have experienced a bastion of colonial splendour.

Greetings from Jamaica, B. W. I.

The Swimming Pool, Myrtle Bank Hotel

We worked day and night shifts and I was on duty loading the last of the tobacco during the night. We were due to sail before breakfast the next morning. Because I had been on shift all night, I was excused duties for leaving port and went to bed. Ordinarily, I would do a search for stowaways, but this time David LeCornu was supposed to do it. More came of this later.

We called at Sunny Point, North Carolina, to load heavy calibre ammunition for the Aussie Army. Sunny Point is a major supply base for the American Army. The Aussies had decided that it would be better if their military equipment was aligned with the Americans because of common interests in the Pacific. This was one of the reasons they needed to earn dollars. We loaded the ammunition in Number One hold. It was bitterly cold. A North wind blew straight from the Arctic, heralding an early start to winter.

Next port of call was Montreal. But there was a strange happening on the way. One morning, a black man, dressed only in a thin cotton 'Shell' company overall, appeared on the foredeck. He had stowed away in Jamaica believing that we were calling at New York. He had a girl friend in New York, with whom he had four children. He was an illegal immigrant and had already been deported twice from the USA. He had climbed the ladder inside the foremast as a hiding place. As the days passed and we were not in New York and it got colder and he was hungry and thirsty, he revealed himself. We accommodated him in the sick bay and provided him with meals and warm clothing. When the police arrived in Montreal to arrest him, he asked Nibbie if he would give him a suitcase to carry his 'new' clothes. He was given some wrapping paper.

Another strange sight was 'sea smoke'. As we left the Gulf Stream and entered the Labrador current, there was this collision between warm and cold water. The warm water condensed and rose in translucent tendrils almost like the smoke from many small bonfires.

The temperature had changed at Montreal. It was unseasonably warm and humid for early November. It reached 70 degrees Fahrenheit and we were in shirt sleeves in November. Very unusual. But it soon turned cold again as we headed down the St Lawrence and down to Newark, New Jersey, on the Hudson opposite New York. Nibbie left us here. I cannot remember who replaced him as Chief Officer. Nibbie was amongst a number of crew members who had done their three trips. So, we had several new crew members to get to know. This changeover was dated November 29th 1960 and was officially the commencement of a new voyage, which meant the commencement of a new logbook. This entailed more admin work for me because all the ship's details, including the names and ranks of the ship's crew and their rates of pay, had to be noted in the new logbook.

In Newark I had a surprise promotion. I had now done over twelve months as a Fourth Officer. If I had not been sent to the Wh boats, I would have been starting my third trip as an officer, probably as Third Officer. Consequently, I was now losing seniority, which was essential because promotion from now on was very much stepping into dead man's shoes. Lampbrick told me that he had recommended me for promotion because I had deserved it. Surprise, surprise! I was now a Third Officer and earning more, although I still carried out the duties of Fourth Officer. I was known as Supernumary Third Officer, shortened to 'Super 3O'. David LeCornu and I were now of equal rank although he had seniority. There was an amusing consequence. I was now entitled to wear a thick gold stripe instead of a thin gold stripe, but where to find new stripes in Newark? A couple of the engineers had spare stripes, but they came with red rings. So, I had to carefully separate the red from the gold before sewing them on to my blue uniforms and my tropical epaulets.

Otherwise, this was not a time I was enjoying. It was only made bearable by frequent letters from Jann. I had a long talk with Eddie, the Second Officer. He was hoping to get married in New Zealand but did not know when he would get leave. Knowing his predicament helped. After an uncertain start, he and I began to get along well and I learned a lot from hm. He was very particular on accuracy and presentation, the benefits of which I appreciated. He had previously been employed on the South Asia trade. He had had a bad time in East Pakistan, in what later became Bangladesh. For some reason, they were delayed at the port of Dacca and were running out of provisions. It was impossible to buy provisions ashore, probably because of problems with the shipping agent, hence the delay in port. When they finally got away, they were on the point of starvation. This experience convinced him to find a better berth.

Off we went through Panama back to Australia and more months away from the light of my life. We celebrated Christmas in the Pacific, although it had nothing I remember. Just another day at the office.

CHAPTER THIRTY THREE

Relief

However at Sydney, life seemed more worthwhile. The weather was glorious and we had the news that we would be going to New Zealand to load after finishing unloading in Melbourne. Chance to see Jann? Eddie would take leave and get married. NZS had arranged a temporary Second Officer as soon as we got to Kiwiland.

We unloaded the ammunition in Sydney. We could not go alongside a berth as it was considered too dangerous. We were anchored in Port Jackson near Rose Bay and unloaded onto barges. This was going to take several days. Although we were at anchor, we kept sea watches. This worked out well for me. Australia had just started a Test Match against the West Indies. It was the third of five matches to be played. The first match in Brisbane had resulted in a tie, which was very, very unusual. A tie is where both sides score the same number of runs and both sides lose all their wickets. Australia had won the next Test at Melbourne over Christmas. There was great interest in the Sydney match. I thought that I will never get another chance like this and made a proposition to David le Cornu to swap my evening watch for his. That meant that I was free from 8 in the morning until 8 at night. Play began at 1100 and was scheduled to finish at 6. Plenty of time to get back. David and the Second Officer, Eddie, agreed.

The third morning of the match was the first day I attended. I was at a tram stop and unsure which tram to catch. I asked another bloke at the stop and he said that he was going to the game. We travelled and spent the day together. We bought tickets at the turnstile and settled on the 'Hill'. This was an open mound that has since had a stand built on it. It was a favourite spot for Sydneysiders to heckle the players and anybody else who caught their fancy. We stood there all day and watched a fascinating day. The West Indies were batting and Frank Worral, their captain, played Alan Davidson, the Ausssie fast bowler, for a four through cover that brought 'Oohs' from the crowd. The ball was over the boundary line before you knew it. One of the best shots I have ever seen. Davidson was a noted hypochondriac and was always moaning about some ailment or other or rubbing his joints and muscles. Richie Benaud, one of my heroes, was the Aussie captain and had to keep cajoling Davidson to keep going. By the way, Davidson was a magnificent bowler and carried the Aussie bowling for a long time.

We went to the bar at lunchtime and had to blow dust off our glasses. Then I bumped into someone I never thought I would see. Dr Emrys Roberts had been a partner in the GP practice we used in Stratford and had treated my father for his first heart attack. Well, there he was, large as life. He had emigrated to Aussie. I couldn't help myself and said 'Dr Roberts, I presume?' He was as astonished as I was. What a memorable day. I went to the last two days and saw the West Indies beat Australia for the first time, to my delight. One of the West Indies bowlers, Lance Gibbs, was playing in his first Test match. He got three wickets in four balls. This was one of my most memorable occasions.

Less memorable was a sailing experience. We carried two whalers and a dinghy. Some of the Engineers kept badgering me to take them out for an afternoon's sailing in one of the whalers. It was blowing a brisk wind and I doubted their ability to cope. The boats had been lowered into the water as soon as we anchored and were tied up to a boom. Against my better judgement, I agreed to give it a go. It was bad enough getting everything ready and the sails hoisted. An utter shambles and I wanted to call it off then. We sailed off down wind and after about a mile I tried to instruct my crew in the mechanics of turning round and going back against the wind. It didn't work and the wind caught the mainsail in the wrong position and split it. We only had the foresail left, which was not enough to get us back. Fortunately, a motor boat saw our predicament and gave us a tow back. My crew never wanted to repeat the experience.

When we finally docked, somebody organised a party which went on almost until breakfast time. I seem to recall that one of the Engineers was friendly with a girl in the shipping agent's office and she organised her mates. It turned out that they were a gang that went everywhere together. I got paired off with a girl whose dad was a DJ with a local radio station, Radio Macquarie, but I can't remember her name. All I can remember is that she was in this group and they asked us to join them in going to a dance, the pictures or the beach. Strangely enough we went everywhere by bus. It was the first time I had been to the northern suburbs of Sydney and been on Manley Beach, which had better surf than Bondi. Shortly after we left Sydney for a port south of Sydney called Port Kembla. Previously, the girls had asked us if we could make it to Sydney for the next Sunday. I was the only one who could make it and spent a lovely family Sunday. We had traditional roast lunch on the hottest day of the year and then went to Bondi, where the temperature reached 105 degrees Fahrenheit. Then I caught a late night train back to Port Kembla. It never ceased to amaze me how hospitable people were to me wherever I went and never wanted anything in return.

We finished unloading at Melbourne and Captain Lampbrick went on leave. He had married an Australian and they lived just outside Melbourne. So the MANZ Line worked for him in terms of his family life. His wife picked him up and she seemed really nice and friendly. Too good for him. His temporary replacement, Captain Allen, also lived in Aussie. He was getting near retirement and was quite content to do relief duties rather than go deep sea. He kept himself to himself and didn't bother us, which was a nice change from Lampbrick. He was more interested in golf and was off playing as often as he could. It was a game I found myself playing more as you could play anytime it was convenient and there was always somebody at a golf club to share a round with.

Whilst we were in Melbourne, the final Test in the Australia/West Indies series took place at the Melbourne Cricket Ground (MCG). At the start of the match, the series was level with each side having won one match (the Fourth Test at Adelaide had been a draw). This was the deciding match. On the third day of the match, a Saturday, a world record number of spectators watched –over 90,000. I did not manage to make that day but I did get to see some of the last day, which was more dramatic. The Aussies needed to bowl out the West Indies to win and looked like doing it. A West Indian batsman, Joe Solomon, was doing his best to delay matters. Richie Benaud bowled to him and Solomon swept the ball round to square leg, but in doing so he lost his balance and his cap fell onto the wicket and knocked a bail off. Benaud appealed and Solomon was out 'hit wicket'. Game over but many people thought that Benaud had been unsporting. Not so, the rules were clear about any part of the batsman's apparel striking the wicket.

What I did not know until some years later was that Graham (can't remember his surname) , the captain of Stratford on Avon Cricket Club, and his new wife Joy Eborall, were on honeymoon in Melbourne and had been to the match on Saturday. Some years later, we were having a drink after a match at Stratford and he produced an aerial photo of the stadium taken on that day. None of us knew that we were all in Melbourne at the same time. I had known

Joy since school days. She had travelled on the same bus to school as I did. Her parents, Ted and Joyce Eborall, kept the Garrick Inn and were old and great friends of our family.

My stomach was playing up and the shipping agent arranged for me to have a hospital check up. I had a barium meal drink and an X-ray. This was the first of three similar examinations over the next few months and none of them found anything. But I kept on being sick on occasions.

Before we left Melbourne, I had organised a couple of weeks' leave when we got to New Zealand on 'compassionate' grounds.

From Melbourne, we sailed to The Bluff, where I was able to telephone Jann on a pre-booked call and hear her voice for the first time in months. We started loading here and some of the cargo was frozen crayfish. New Zealand crayfish are large and were being sold to fancy restaurants in the States, where they were served up as Lobster Thermidor at exorbitant prices. Crayfish are cheap as chips in Southland, New Zealand. Before we left Bluff, we got an invite to the Mayor's Dance. It was very pretentious because all the available single girls were 'presented' to the Mayor and his wife as though it was a debutantes' ball at Buckingham Palace. This sort of thing went on all over New Zealand and Australia. One girl I danced with asked me if I was a professional dancer.

C: Compassionate Leave

Next stop, Timaru, and the start of my leave. I took a plane from Timaru to Christchurch, where I got another to Auckland. The plane from Timaru was a Vickers Viscount. It was a four engine turbo prop, which means that a jet engine drove a turbine that turned a propeller. Much smoother and a great improvement on the old DC3. I was the only passenger.

Auckland

Jann's Aunty Peggy wanted me to stay with them but I thought it was not fair on them with very young children, so I booked into a hotel and Jann and I had our first meeting. We were slightly awkward with each other at first, but everything went OK by the end of the day. I felt a bit strange being perfectly at liberty in a strange city. Jann was studying for her first year exams so we had to arrange our time together carefully. Eventually, I succumbed to Peggy's entreaties and ended up staying with them. Ken and Peggy's kids liked us as we took them down to the beach as though we were an old married couple. But, it felt absolutely right. Besides that we did what all courting couples did and went out and had a good time dining at the 'Peter Pan' restaurant, drinking, cinema, days on the beach. I took her to Eden Park one Saturday to see the Governor General's XI play a visiting young MCC side. The Governor-General was Lord Cobham, who had played for Worcestershire before the war. My dad had known him slightly. He was a very sociable man and well liked. This was to be his last first class match and he made 46 before being caught. Everybody was willing him to get 50, but you don't have fairy tales every day. Ray Lindwall opened the bowling for the Governor-General. He had been a fearsome fast bowler in the 1940s and early 1950s. This was also his swansong but he still had the most beautiful fluent action. He had the MCC opening batsmen tied up in knots. It was a great pleasure to see him in action again. Jann went to sleep in the sunshine!

Auckland is an attractive city. It sits on a narrow neck of land with one foot in the Tasman Sea to the west and the other in the Pacific to the east. The harbour is on the Pacific side and is guarded by Rangitoto Island, an extinct volcano. The beaches are lovely and safe. It has a good climate, although Hawkes Bay people say it is too damp for them because of the nearness to two oceans. The docks are an extension of the main drag, Queen Street. There used to be a department store called Whitcombe and Toombs in Queen Street, locally known as Titcombe and Wombs. Although Auckland had over a million inhabitants, everything seemed well spaced out and it was not far to go to be in rural surroundings.

After just over a week, Jann needed more time to study and was worried about her exams. She even took her books with her when we went on a day out. At this time, I told her that I was prepared to leave the Merchant Navy and move to New Zealand. The Moss's immediately began looking at the Auckland Herald for jobs for me. A bit premature as it would be almost a year before I could complete my contract, pass my next exam and emigrate. Obviously, Peggy rang her sister with my news and she and John wanted to see me, so I flew over to Waipukurau for a few days. What the Giblins did was take me around to a few events where their friends could see me. I remember going to an agricultural show where there was a new type of power boat on display. This had been designed by a New Zealander to be used in shallow rivers and was a world first. It did not have a conventional motor and a propeller. It had a motor driven pump that sucked in water at the bow and spewed it out at the stern. It operated like a jet engine and was brilliant. This was the genesis of the jet ski. This invention was part of the glimmerings of a tourist trade for New Zealand, made possible by the growth of jet travel. You could now fly to Australia and New Zealand by jet from Europe and America. The Giblins also wanted to make sure that the neighbours knew of me and approved. They arranged a dinner party for a dozen or so people. One guy had an English wife and she asked me what I thought about English TV, there being, at that time, no TV in New Zealand. Given my life style and absences from home, I could only give her a vague reply. The main course was mutton, standard fare amongst graziers. They did not eat lamb because it was too valuable. John Giblin had killed and butchered a ram for the meal. I like mutton but realise it is a bit strong for most tastes. Another test passed.

Whilst at Waipukurau, I mentioned that we had given passage to Brian Boys in the 'Hororata'. Mrs Giblin said they knew his parents and David chimed in saying that they had been at Wanganui Collegiate together. He asked if Brian had explained why he left Wanganui suddenly, but I didn't know. That partly explained why Brian was with NZS. I suspect that he'd been sent to sea to get him out of the way over some misdemeanour.

Mrs Giblin loved to play cards. She taught me how to play gin rummy, which she said I would need when I settled in NZ. She also tried to teach me 'bezique', which is complicated. It was a favourite of Winston Churchill. I never played it again.

The Giblin's house was on a rise with a view over their land to the north. Given the Hawkes Bay climate and soil quality, the area between their large garden and the front paddocks would have been ideal for a vineyard. As it was, Mrs Giblin complained that she was like all other graziers' wives in that gardens were the last thing on their husbands' minds. I have often wondered if vines were ever planted there once New Zealand obtained a reputation for fine wine and Hawkes Bay proved ideal for the growing of Pinot Noir grapes.

Then I flew back to Auckland with Mrs Giblin and rejoined the Whangaroa. Mrs Giblin had come to spend time with her sister. Whangaroa was in Auckland for another ten days or so, so Jann and I had more time together.

I had an interesting encounter at this time that was separate from my work and Jann. Despite the strict import quotas, none of the New Zealand ports were enclosed, apart from Auckland. Open wharves were the norm, and even in Auckland I was never stopped for a search as I went through the gates. This contrasted strongly with the UK, particularly in London, where we would be routinely stopped and searched if we left the dock area with baggage. HM Customs and Excise regularly searched vessels, even if they had arrived at a UK port from another UK port. On arrival in the UK from abroad, we had to declare any purchases made abroad. This was in the era of rigid exchange controls. I don't recall ever seeing a New Zealand Customs Officer and I don't know if smuggling was a problem for the New Zealand authorities. One afternoon in Auckland, I walked up to the top of Queen Street and went into the 'Steineker Bar'. 'Steineker was a brand of strong lager. The bar had few customers. The barman noticed my English accent and got into conversation with me. As soon as he found out that I was a merchant seaman, he lost no time in telling me that he was interested in any consumer goods I could smuggle in, particularly radios. What surprised me was that the barman assumed that I might be interested and that I was not a 'police stooge'. I expressed no interest. It was the first and only time I was ever approached for this purpose in either New Zealand or Australia.

Jann had now finished her exams and she and her classmates had organised a dinner at a restaurant called 'The Man in the Moon' about half an hour's drive outside Auckland. We were worried that I might sail before the dinner. We needn't have worried. I had invited Peggy and her kids to tea one afternoon and to look over the ship. The kids were fascinated. The Chief Refrigeration Engineer assured Peggy that there was no way we would be able to leave before the dinner.

So we went to the 'Man in the Moon' and it was our last night together. We went in a VW Beetle owned by a boy friend of one of Jann's student colleagues. One of the tyres developed a puncture and there was no jack to raise the car in order to change the wheel. We had to lift the car at one corner and find a stone to hold it up. Then, the car wouldn't start and needed a push start. Although the girls were in their finery, they lifted and pushed with the best of them. Typically Kiwi! After the dinner, Jann and I spent our last hours together on the beach. I took Jann back to Peggy's in the early hours to find everybody up. They had stayed up to say goodbye as Whangaroa was leaving that afternoon. Much hugging and kissing and tears.

D: The Crunch Time

Back into the old routine across the Pacific, through the Panama and up to New York via the Florida Strait, where I had an alarming experience. This is the sea passage between Florida and the Bahamas. It is mostly shallow with shoals and sand banks, so you have to be careful. It was near the end of my evening watch and it was pitch black. I was looking out for the lights of other ships and lighthouses, but there was nothing. We did not have our radar on. All of a sudden there were the navigation lights of several ships coming towards me, and fast. They had only switched on their lights at the last moment. As they swept past I could see that they were warships, including an aircraft carrier. This was the American navy on patrol. It was only two years before the Cuban missile crisis and tension was high in this part of the world.

I went to see the Burlingames in New York and it proved to be my last visit. I knew that I would be finishing my stint on the Wh boats before the end of the year and wanted to make sure that I said farewell. We went for drinks to neighbours across the road. It was nearly Spring and people were talking about their heating bills for the past winter. One woman couldn't understand why the Burlingame's heating bill was lower than anybody else's. Another woman said it was because she's English and they don't heat their houses as Americans do. It was true, Most American houses are over-heated by our standards.

I had an ulterior motive for visiting the Burlingames. I wanted a present from the USA for Jann and for Peggy Moss's kids. Mrs Burlingame took me to this discount store on Roosevelt Field, which was amazing. I bought some pedal pushers for Jann, which she couldn't get in NZ, and a top, and a toy each for the kids. For Jonathan Moss I bought a robot man with an electric motor and an animated doll for his sister, again not available in NZ. All in all, I did well.

Montreal

We were not sure if we would make Montreal because the ice had not melted everywhere, but it was OK, although still cold. After which we went to Port Alfred about 50 miles up the Saguenay River on the north side of the St Lawrence Estuary. The snow and ice had just melted and everything looked a sickly grey/green. It did not help that there was low cloud and no sun. But, Whangaroa had been built to access small ports like Port Alfred and bigger ships would not have made it.

Eddie, the Second Officer, left us here to go home and start married life. David LeCornu was promoted to Second Officer and I became Third Officer in my own right. A new Fourth Officer had been flown out to take over from me. Flying out replacement crews now became the norm rather than taking the sea passage. As Third Officer, I was now the senior Junior Officer and head of our table in the Saloon. I was also the senior Duty Officer in port supervising cargo and also responsible for all the bridge and chartroom equipment, for which I had to keep a record and make a regular inventory. The new Fourth was a really nice guy and we got on well.

We next went to Corner Point, Newfoundland, to load newsprint. Once again, the landscape was grey/green. A miserable looking place. 'Newsprint' was paper produced from conifers for the newspaper industry. It came in large rolls about twelve feet long and four feet wide. Corner Brook had a factory, owned by Bowaters, that produced the newsprint. We were shown around and I found it very interesting to see how quickly a pine tree could be made into paper.

We did have an unfortunate experience in the local club, where some of us had been invited for drinks. When we arrived, there was a group of men in their forties and fifties who clearly resented us. One of them came over and started ranting about 'Tommies' who ran away in the war. Obviously, they had seen service in the Second World War and something unfortunate had happened that involved British soldiers. We were an easy target. Needless to say, we did not overstay our welcome.

We were supposed to load in a port on Prince Edward Island or Nova Scotia, I can't remember where. Anyway, we couldn't get in because of ice and sailed away without being fully loaded. I was so glad to leave Canada, hopefully for the last time.

CHAPTER THIRTY FOUR

HEARTBREAK

There was no letter from Jann in Panama, but I was not unduly worried. I had no mail from home either. It was not unusual for mail to chase us round the world. I was more worried when I received nothing from Jann when we got to Melbourne and sent her a telegram for news. In Adelaide, I received a post card which just said 'Bad news in Sydney, I'm afraid'.

I did not know what to do and there was nobody I felt able to talk to. I applied for a week's compassionate leave and got it starting from when we got to Sydney. I knew that we would not be going to NZ this trip, indeed after Adelaide the second time around we were going home through Suez. Whangaroa was due a refit. Swarbrick also left us for extended leave and Captain Allen took over to take us home.

What happened next in Adelaide was bizarre. I got in touch with Rosetta Angus Parsons, mainly because I was certain that I was going to leave the Merchant Navy and wanted to say good bye to my friends. By this time, Gill McLachlan had got married to an Englishman and was living in Highgate, London. Rosetta organised a lavish dinner party at her house. I met a GP and his wife there and we had a discussion about the differences between the NHS and the Aussie Health Service, which was a mixture of public funding and compulsory private health insurance. I found the GP's argument very persuasive and have remained convinced that we should have followed the Aussie arrangement. Anyway, I could not finish my food and felt very poorly. I arranged my third hospital appointment about my insides and again there was nothing. The consultant suggested that the cause was likely to be psychological, with which I was inclined to agree.

Meanwhile, Rosetta had sensed that I was in turmoil and turned up one morning to take me away for the day. I would have been free from midday but persuaded my colleagues to let me go a couple of hours early. She was driving a Mercedes 600 and off we went up country. We had lunch with some friends who had a station in a hilly area. I remember that I was grilled pretty hard about what I wanted to do with my life. Afterwards, we went further inland to the Parsons station in a district called Pewsey Vale. Their house was a large mansion, but was hardly used and we had to remove dust sheets. Rosetta's mother preferred to live in Adelaide. We had a look round the home paddocks and the stables. Rosetta used to ride to school from here. Then she made tea and biscuits. Without any warning, she asked me if I had to go to New Zealand. I didn't know what to make of that. Was she propositioning me? We hardly knew each other. I think I replied that I didn't have to but I wanted to if everything turned out OK. I think that she sensed my indecision, which was based on uncertainty. Did she know something that I didn't? As I have mentioned, it can be a small world out there.

We went out to a night club, met some friends of Rosetta's, and for the first time in a long time, I felt relaxed and comfortable. Rosetta was very attractive. We had a big hug when she dropped me off and I sensed that she wanted to develop our relationship. She even talked about following me to Melbourne but I demurred, if only because it would not have looked right.

We had an enforced day off in Adelaide. It was our turn around port and it was decided to fumigate the holds. This was in case there were any rats on board. Rats are very tenacious animals and can survive the extreme cold of a freezer hold. I had heard apocryphal tales of rats turning white because their bodies told them it was winter. Buckets containing formaldehyde were lowered into the hold. The fumes would kill any life. For safety reasons we had to vacate the ship for twenty four hours and were put up in a hotel. We did not return until it was considered that there were no more fumes.

We sailed for Sydney, where there was a message for me from the shipping agent that there was a package waiting for me in the office. When I got there, I was given a parcel wrapped in brown paper with a broken corner. . It was obvious what was in the package. The chap who handed it over asked if I still wanted to take leave. Inside were my letters to Jann and a photo I had given her. No letter of explanation. But my mother had forwarded to me a letter Jann had written to her. Jann explained that she was accustomed to a certain life style and that I would not be able to offer her that for some time, if ever. My mother was extremely angry and I was devastated that Jann could not have written to me. It was very cruel.

Nevertheless, I was determined to see if I could make something of moving to New Zealand. In retrospect, it was probably bloody mindedness that drove me. I'll show them. I flew to Auckland, where the Moss family welcomed me with open arms. Peggy advised me not to act like a knight in shining armour and sweep Jann off her feet. She said that she is not the same girl that I knew six months ago and that she may be seeing someone else. Whatever, I had bought her some presents and arranged to see her to hand them over. She was very cool with me and said that I should have given the presents to Peggy. Bloody hell, talk about putting the boot in.

In retrospect, one or other of us would have called it off at some time. In the eighteen months since we had met, we had spent only about a month together all told, and that was not a continuous month. I had met Jann when she was fresh out of school. I doubt that she had had much contact with males of my age, given the isolation of the station and that she had attended a girl's boarding school. I would have been a novelty, and attractive because of that. A year or so in Auckland would have broadened her horizons and I would have paled by comparison. Although I was devastated, I never had my stomach problem again, so maybe I had, unconsciously, doubt or indecision which manifested itself in a digestive problem.

Peggy Moss also had a long talk with me about how I presented myself. As with many English people, I was accustomed to being ironic in my speech, which was a defence mechanism in some respects as it allowed us to be self-deprecatory as a means of being polite and not assuming superiority. It was made clear to me that, as far as New Zealanders were concerned, it only confirmed them in their opinion that the Poms were too damned superior in their attitude. I was very grateful to her for being so helpful and so frank. Up until then, I had not realised that I could be capable of such behaviour, even if it was unconscious. It does show that if travel does not actually broaden your mind, you must be careful to understand the point of view of others with a different background and act accordingly.

Auckland and Hawkes Bay

I had arranged an appointment with a firm called Watties, who were based in Hastings. They had a canning and freezer factory and sold frozen and canned vegetables under their own brand. The General Manager gave me an extensive tour of their facilities and then we had an hour or so in his office. I think I made an impression because he could see that I was sincere about coming ashore. Also, I had operational management experience and was OK with shift work. The result was that he indicated to me that once I had come back to New Zealand, then they would most likely take me on as a trainee manager. I felt that I could take him at his word and went off feeling that I had achieved something in difficult circumstances.

I had booked into a pub/ hotel in Hastings and went to a cinema across the road that evening. I did not know that the publican and his wife had also been to the cinema. He told me that had he known, he would have 'shouted' me. Another example of Kiwi hospitality. Similarly with Mr and Mrs Giblin, who had invited me to stay a night and picked me up in Hastings and drove me back to the airport the next day. It illustrated again to me how kind New Zealanders are and reinforced my desire to live there.

When I got back to Auckland, I booked into a hotel rather than go back to the Moss's. The Rangitoto was in and my brother was serving on her as an Ordinary Seaman. We had an evening out together, which was the first opportunity I had had to talk to someone I really trusted. I said goodbye to the Moss family and flew to Melbourne.

I arrived in Melbourne on a Saturday to find that Whangaroa was not in port. I could not find out more because the shipping agent's office was closed until Monday. I booked into a small hotel and had just enough money to pay in advance for two nights. I went to the office on Monday and was told that Whangaroa was not expected for a couple of days. Anyway, the office gave me money to cover my hotel bill because it was a legitimate expense plus cash for meals etc. I found out that another Wh boat, the 'Whakatane', had docked over the weekend. I took a tram to Port Melbourne to see if there was anybody on board that I knew. I was delighted to find Scot Gilchrist there as Third Officer plus the Fourth Officer who had been on the Durham a couple of trips below me. It was rather a boozy reunion. Scot was saving up to get married and stayed on board when I invited him out for a night. The Fourth and I proceeded to 'beat up' the town. We started off at the first floor bar of the Elizabeth Hotel with Fosters Lager served in silver tankards and ended up with a champagne dinner. It was a big tonic for me.

Whangaroa finally arrived, we loaded and left for Adelaide, our last port before sailing.

At Adelaide, I wrote a resignation letter and gave it to Captain Allen to forward to London. I went to say goodbye to Rosetta and she was tearful. I had not realised that she had such feelings for me. But, much as I liked her, I could not reciprocate. She married about a year later. Her husband, Alastair McLachlan, was a cousin of Gill McLachlan. I believe that they were related to Ian McLachlan, who opened the batting for Australia at the time.

We had an uneventful journey home apart from three alarming incidents whilst I was on watch.

The first occurred when I had relieved the Second Officer for lunch one day in the Red Sea. There is always a lot of traffic here and, although there are no designated channels, the convention is that vessels will pass vessels going the other way on the right hand side – port to port as the saying goes. Also, don't get close. A ship displaces its weight in water all the time as it moves, which means that it can create a vacuum. If two ships get too close, the vacuum can suck them in and cause a collision. There was a ship going the other way and it would not keep clear, even though I altered course. We passed about fifty yards apart and the people on the other ship were laughing, waving and cheering. They were playing a nautical form of 'chicken'. The Old Man came up to the bridge in a very bad temper, especially as his lunch had been interrupted. Anyway, no blame to me.

Secondly, I was on watch about ten o'clock at night just before we reached Port Suez. I noticed that the steaming lights of a vessel ahead of us and coming towards us did not appear to change bearing. I took several bearings of this vessel over the next ten minutes and concluded that it was on a collision course. I needed to take evasion action, so I altered course to starboard and kept starboard helm on until we had gone through three hundred and sixty degrees and back on our original course. The vessel I was concerned about had gone towards the Sinai shore and was no longer a problem. The manoeuvre I took is known as' taking a round turn out of your course'. It is used infrequently. I did it so smoothly that only the quartermaster, the lookout and myself were aware of it, although I had to enter it in the log.

The third incident occurred off the north coast of Malta, east of Valetta. Again, I was on watch about ten o'clock when I observed lights coming towards me from the direction of Valetta. I took regular bearings and concluded that this other vessel would hit us if it did not alter course. According to the collision regulations, she had to alter course and I had to maintain course and speed. She kept on coming until she was less than a mile away. I needed to alert her because it appeared obvious that nobody on her was on watch or keeping a lookout. I took out our Aldis signalling light. You can use this light to send Morse code messages or shine a constant beam. I shone the beam on to her bridge, which I could now make out. All of a sudden, she altered course to starboard and passed our stern. This was gross negligence on the part of the other vessel and lives could have been lost.

All the above incidents show that not all countries observe the rule of the road. We had it drummed into us so hard that it became second nature to be careful. Thank God, otherwise I might not have survived.

As soon as we got to Liverpool, I was told that my resignation had been accepted. I was paid off and caught the next train home. First of all, I had to pay customs duty on the items I had bought at Port Said: a couple of silk dressing gowns, a silk chongsam dress for my mother and some china. I think I paid seven shillings and sixpence duty (thirty seven and half pence in decimal currency). I presented my purchases to a couple of Customs Officers, who were ensconced in the Chief Steward's office with drinks and in jovial mood. Duty on silk should have meant that I paid several pounds in duty, but the Customs Officers declared that my goods were Hong Kong cotton and therefore subject to lesser duty. This was a common occurrence and HM Customs and the Merchant Navy had a convivial relationship, which was strengthened by the hospitality that Chief Stewards offered.

Thus, on September 6th 1961, I ended my career with NZS. Not a word of thanks or regret, no asking me if there was anything NZS could do to change my mind. Just a throw away remark from Captain Moncrieff that my decision was because of petticoat government. Fifteen months on one voyage was more than enough reason to leave, let alone any other considerations. NZS had spent several years and money to train me to where I had got so far. It did not appear that they wanted to keep me, but perhaps I had not proven myself good enough. However, when they learnt that I was taking study leave, they offered to put me on salary straightaway if I was to return to sea. Why did not Moncrieff offer that at our interview together with advice that I should take my First Mate's Certificate before any final decision?

It was fraught when I got home. I immediately booked a passage to New Zealand to leave in early October on the Rangitata. My parents never accepted that I wanted to live in New

Zealand and pressure was put on me to stay in England. I remember we went on a car trip one day and my dad stopped the car on Bromyard Common. He got out alone and walked off for a few minutes. When he returned, he said 'I don't know how you can live anywhere else but in this country'. My parents had never been abroad.

My dad did want to make sure that I did have a position to go to. I had not heard from Watties, although I had written to them with my expected arrival date. Dad suggested I telephone them and we booked a call. Just as well. Watties had received my letter but the factory had burnt down and they had no idea what they could offer when I arrived. I cancelled my ticket and got a full refund. I could make no long term decision.

Friends and family suggested that at least I should go to Warsash and study for my First Mate's Certificate. I would at least have another qualification should I remain ashore. Looking back on it, I am sure that my parents thought that I would go back to NZS. The reality was that I had, as my Careers Master had indicated would happen, got the sea out of my system.

CHAPTER THIRTY FOUR

Final Decision

Study Leave: Warsash.

I returned to Warsash in mid-October and met up again with David Gardner. He was an Old Warwickian and had also been at Warsash with me as a cadet. He had served his time with Shaw Savill. Like me, he wanted to come ashore and had also decided to get his First Mate's Certificate first. His dad had given him the old family car, which was a Ford Popular, so he went home every weekend. I joined him a couple of times, but decided it wasn't worth doing it every weekend. I needed to concentrate. In any case, winter was coming on and the Ford Popular had no heating. It also had no windscreen washers, so frequent stops had to be made to wipe the windscreen.

Having spent the Christmas holidays at home, I took my exams in early February 1962 and passed. I knew that I had passed the oral on the day I took it but had to wait a week or two to get the results of the written exams. When the result arrived in the post, my father's immediate reaction was 'When are you going back to sea?' I said I wasn't. He said nothing, walked away and did not speak to me for the rest of that day. My mother was away on a jolly with the Ladies Licenced Victuallers. When she came back next day, my dad made sure that he spoke to her first. The first words she said to me were 'Got yourself a job yet?' This reaction was wholly in keeping with how she voiced her emotions about my achievements or lack of them. I sat the '11 Plus' exam before my 11th birthday. The results showed that I had come third in my area or district. There were maybe several hundred children in that area who had taken the exam. All my mother could say was 'There were two others in front of you.' Not one word of praise. My sister and I often felt that what my mother wanted was something to boast about within her social circle and, by doing so, advance her own esteem.

To be fair to my parents, my news could not have come at a worse time. Flower's Brewery had, at last, produced plans to refurbish the Anchor. Having been taken over by Whitbread, Flower's had access to funds to improve its estate. It involved cancelling the lease of the news agents next door and substantial rebuilding of the property. Our living quarters were to become a restaurant and the bar area was to be restructured downstairs. Twenty years beforehand, my father would have been delighted. Now, he was too old (58) and in ill health. Besides which, the brewery had decided it wanted to install a manager. In this way, the brewery would get all the profits. Consequently, my dad had been given twelve months' notice of the termination of his tenancy. This was after forty years in the business and twenty five years as a Flowers tenant. And he had no savings. The brewery made things worse by trying to get building work done whilst my parents were still in occupation. My dad had to employ a solicitor to stop this on the grounds that his tenancy gave him 'occupation without let or hindrance'.

They needed my concerns like a hole in the head. Nevertheless, I was made to feel ungrateful for all the sacrifices they had made, which was unfair because my parents had never stinted themselves. It was not my fault that my father was a bad business man. At the time, I should have taken more account of my mother's mental health. When I was in Galveston, she had become severely depressed and suffered a breakdown. In retrospect, her condition could have been made worse by an early and precipitate menopause. She told me once that she went through the change in a couple of days. In those days, nobody talked about menopause, still less its potential for causing mental ill health. Her treatment involved electrotherapy, which is very unpleasant. She was declared recovered, but she remained very sensitive to anything that reflected badly on her self esteem. I had obviously let her down in respect of how she saw herself in her social circle and I was never forgiven. Perhaps, I should have been more pro-active in explaining my action, but as time went on it became increasingly difficult to have any realistic conversation on the matter, although my dad became reconciled to the reality and supported me mentally, if not with deeds.

But initially, everybody my dad knew who might make me change my mind was drafted in to do so, including Do and Nipper, his sister and brother. Chris Rookes, Dad's oldest friend, was the chief offender. He arranged for me to meet a man in charge of a management training centre for the Birwell Group, an engineering and specialist welding company. Eventually, this company became part of GKN. The training centre was just outside Stratford in a country house, Caldicott House. Dad, 'Rooker' and I had a pleasant lunch with the trainees. I was then sequestered with the Principal, who turned out to be a retired captain in the Royal Navy. I was under the impression that this man was going to give me guidance on furthering a career ashore. I had a nasty shock. He proceeded to grill me hard why I did not want to stay at sea and implied that he had come ashore with great reluctance. Meanwhile, my dad and Rooker were reclining before an open log fire with a large glass of brandy each. I had been conned and was angry, although I held my peace. Assuming that my father and Rooker had my best interests at heart, they made a fundamental mistake in assuming that the Royal Navy and the Merchant Navy were compatible. Quite the reverse. RN ships tend to be attached to a 'home port' and spend considerable amounts of time in port. RN crews also take courses at shore establishments. They often live with their families. By contrast, Merchant Navy crew are wanderers of the sea, spend long periods away from their families and work long hours. This retired captain was entirely the wrong person to advise me. It would have been better to find someone who was a senior Merchant Navy officer, preferably one who had come ashore. The nearest person who could have done so was a man who was Staff Captain on the 'Queen Mary' and living in Stratford. But even he was still serving.

I cannot help but contrast my parents' behaviour with their behaviour when my brother decided to come ashore. I believe that his principal reason for going to sea was to follow me. He realised that a seaman's life was not for him and came ashore after about two years. He expressed a desire to become a chef and my parents used all their contacts to help him get a position. My father obtained an interview with Ind Coope and Allsop, a major brewer based in Burton on Trent. Ind Coope owned a number of hotels. My father drove my brother to the interview, after which my brother was offered an apprenticeship. He was assigned to the Leofric Hotel in Coventry, which was conveniently near home. The fact that my brother was six years younger than me may have been a factor in the differences of support, or lack of it. But it cannot have been the whole reason. I don't think that my mother ever came to terms with my decision. I think that she felt that I had let her down and that she had lost esteem amongst her friends. She could no longer boast about my achievements. Whatever, I felt that I could not live my life to satisfy the expectations of my parents. That I can write in this vein sixty years later indicates the extent of my alienation from my parents and the lack of healing and reconciliation.

I was looking for a job and was signed on to the Management and Executive Register at the Labour Exchange. This meant that the Exchange would look out for management opportunities for me. I did get several interviews and John Gray, who played rugger for Stratford, was very keen for me to join his sales team selling knitwear yarn. But the pressure to go back to sea continued until one Sunday when my parents and I had gone over to the Red Horse Hotel for a drink. An old friend of my dad's was there, one Ted Thompson. Ted had known dad when they were both in Worcester and Ted was a member of the famous, or infamous, Thompson family. Ted had built up a substantial wholesale and auction business in West Bromwich, specialising in fish. I had never met him before, but he made a point of sitting next to me. He must have heard something of what was going on and sensed what I was going through. He just said' If you don't want to do it, don't'. I have been eternally grateful to him for that advice. I felt that, at last, somebody had bothered to consider what I wanted and how I felt. My parents never sat down with me and asked me to explain why I had made the decision to leave the Merchant Navy and what I would really like to do.

One of the issues I faced in obtaining a job ashore was that shore-based employers had no concept of sea going qualifications and whether or not they bore any relationship to qualifications that they recognised i.e. 'A' levels, degrees and other professional qualifications such as accountants, solicitors and architects would acquire. The fact that I had exercised authority and responsibility beyond what most people of my age would have experienced apparently carried no weight. This was a situation that plagued me until the end of my career. Looking back, the truth was that I was confused and floundering. I knew what I did not want to do, but not what I wanted to do. It took me nearly twenty years to find a job that really interested me and made use of what abilities and experience I had. Even then, I did not get the recognition I felt I had earned, and I suspect it was because I was not a member of the 'club' where admission was limited to university graduates.

I am sure that I contributed to this situation, initially, because I did not know how best to present myself and received no instruction or training in that respect. Looking back on the time and reflecting, I realised that it took me some twenty years to realise what I was best at. I had several jobs involving marketing and selling and, although I had some success and applied myself, the day to day act of selling, particularly the selling of an article, was stressful. Marketing a different way of doing things was more interesting and I eventually developed skills in market analysis and presentation that enabled me to do this. Had I not gone to sea and, instead, gone to Birmingham University and taken a business degree, as my Careers Master had offered as a consideration, perhaps these skills would have arrived earlier and I might have made a different fist of my so-called 'career'.

Returning to what I was to do in the future, I felt under a compulsion to accept the first seemingly reasonable offer and show my parents that I was not going to stagnate but had some purpose in life. A company called Thames Board Mills was a leading company in the production of paper board for packaging and packaging cases. They had factories in Purfleet, Essex, and Warrington. They offered me a job as a management trainee at a salary above my Merchant Navy salary, although I now had to pay for my own board and lodging. I joined them in April 1962 and, had I not done so, I would not have met Gill Beswick, who became my wife and has given me love, children and great happiness ever since. I would not have changed that and have never regretted leaving the Merchant Navy. I am a blessed and rich man.

PART SEVEN

Was It Worth It?

CHAPTER THIRTY FIVE

RETROSPECTIVE THOUGHTS

All my training and experience as a salesman has confirmed to me that human beings make decisions for emotional reasons. We rationalise those decisions later. How else to explain why different people presented with the same circumstances that require a decision will not universally make the most logically correct decision? My decision to leave the sea was no different. I was no longer emotionally involved in a life at sea. I went for a job in the 1970s where the interviewer had himself been in the Merchant Navy. After I had outlined my career so far, he observed of the Merchant Navy 'the best thing about being at sea, is being ashore'. It is probable that, in my case, the main attraction had been travel to and experiences in other countries rather than the time spent at sea. I have the same attitude now to any form of transport. It is a means to an end. The interesting things are what happen at each end of the journey or chance events during it. As I began to spend, proportionately, more time both at sea and working in port, with consequently less free time for my own enjoyment, it proportionately decreased the attraction of a sea career. All those eager beaver apprentices, who joined NZS at the same time as I had, left the sea during the 1960s.

In producing this chronicle, it became obvious that there were external and highly logical reasons why none of us stayed. They were mostly connected with changes over which we had no control. The salient fact is that probably none of us were conscious of how these changing circumstances shaped our decisions. I would like to examine them in more detail now because I strongly believe that they are part of our social history.

Looking back on this after so many years, I have realised for the first time that the system needed Junior Officers to walk away. Once you became a Master, you might serve as a Master for twenty five or thirty years or even longer. That was several times longer than it took to obtain a Master's Certificate. If nobody left after obtaining the qualifications, there would be a block on promotions except for death or retirement. Eventually, there would be no places for Apprentices because there would be too many qualified Officers, many without a berth, There appeared to be no middle course, such as in the Armed Services. There was no provision for Short Service Commissions, which would allow young men to satisfy a need to travel with the added benefit of management experience that the outside world would recognise. If an Army Officer wishes to progress beyond junior rank, he or she has to pass an examination to become a Major, usually in his or her early thirties. If he or she does not advance beyond that rank by the time he or she is in the early forties, he or she is retired, with a pension. Similar decisions are taken if regular promotions do not follow, so that only the best suited become Generals. I believe that the same system applies in the Royal Navy and Royal Air Force. It makes the most of the abilities of Officers to the limit of their capabilities, after which there is a pension. There was no such system in the Merchant Navy, although there were similarities in the life style. It would appear that shipping companies relied on a variant of natural selection over which they had no control. For a young man leaving the sea, there was no provision to prepare him for an entry into a life style that would prove foreign and difficult to adapt to. Shipping companies were cynically using us and content for us to go because it suited their purpose.

I had earlier mentioned that, when I first visited New Zealand, the Kiwi working week was almost universally a five day week, 8 until 5. Only essential services and retail operated on Saturdays and Sundays, indeed the shops closed at midday on Saturday and the pubs did not open on Sunday. This did not last, although the changes came more gradually in New Zealand than they did in the rest of the world. It was a relaxed life style that allowed plenty of time for home grown leisure, most of it outdoors. Time in port was leisurely and allowed time for seeing the country and developing relationships.

In 1955, my year at Warsash, the UK still had one of the largest merchant fleets in the world. You could find UK registered vessels in every major port. But it was changing. The UK had thrived on a policy of buying raw materials in the cheapest markets and selling manufactured goods in the dearest markets. This worked well when the British Empire was effectively controlled from Whitehall and the dominions and colonies sold their raw materials to the 'Mother Country'. It did lead to imbalances so long as sterling was the dominant world currency. New Zealand, for example, had a chronic balance of payments problem after World War 2. The sterling dominance declined after the Second World War and the dollar became paramount. Countries in the Sterling area became restless. Not only did they want political independence but economic independence as well. They wanted to trade with the USA, none more so than Australia and New Zealand, who had begun to alter their trading partners from 1936 with the opening of trade links to the USA and Canada. This was manifested most forcibly to me by the operation of the MANZ Line, which had been a major element in my decision to leave the Merchant Navy. Not the least of the reasons was the overlong appointment to the Wh boats. I have mentioned before that Port Line only required their crews to do two voyages whereas NZS required three. I was not in a positive mental state at the end of my Wh time. It could be argued that I was mentally exhausted.

Other countries began to expand their merchant fleets and shipbuilding. The UK fell behind. This was partly due to geography. UK shipyards did not have the width and depth in their rivers to build and launch the new, super sized vessels, particularly oil tankers. The USA, Japan, Korea and Spain and a few others cornered this market.

Restrictive practices and blindness to new construction methods were big factors. In the UK, the unions, under the post-war Labour government, had pursued a policy of full employment partly by restricting the areas in which particular trades could work. It helped to achieve full employment, but we paid an awful price with the collapse of our heavy industries in the 1970s and 1980s. Here is an example: it is the start of my fourth trip and we have workmen on board in Royal Albert Dock carrying out a variety of repairs. One repair needed was to stop a leak in the deckhead (ceiling) of one of our cabins. The deckhead was steel with a covering of teak on the deck above. The solution was to make a steel tray and fasten it to the deckhead. A tap was fitted on the tray to drain it. The tray had been made by sheet metal workers and a sheet metal worker and his mate arrived to fit the tray. They found that the deckhead is made of steel that is too thick for a sheet metal worker to work. All they needed were four holes drilled to take the securing bolts, but the holes had to be drilled by a boiler maker. Restrictive practices limited the thickness of metal that the sheet metal workers could work on. There was no available boiler maker. Two days go by and the sheet metal workers sat on their arses. A boiler maker and TWO mates arrived, they drilled the holes in about an hour and the tray was then fitted. Thus, because of restrictive practices, it had taken three days and five men to fit a tray about two feet by three feet in size.

This was standard practice throughout British industry as I found out later when I worked in newspapers and witnessed at first-hand how the printing unions held back new technology and working practices. It was rife in the motor industry and eventually led to the demise of British owned volume car manufacturing.

We should have adapted to new ways of training people. Our system of apprenticeship decreed that an apprenticeship lasted four years. You had to do that time to become a journeyman welder, carpenter, electrician, what have you. The Japanese were turning out a skilled welder in less than a month.

By the 1960s, the UK had lost its lead in shipbuilding. The examples I have given could be replicated in every industry in the UK: railways, vehicle manufacture, generating power, communications, printing, road building. We had only ourselves to blame that our share of world trade declined.

World trade was also expanding and the countries with whom the UK had traditionally traded wanted their share of the expansion and payment in US dollars. New Zealand and Australia had been selling their agricultural produce to the USA and Canada since the 1930s. New Zealand was always hampered in its expansion by the lack of mineral wealth and the capacity to produce goods with added value. As time went on, synthetic materials began to eat into the textile markets that had previously been dominated by wool. By contrast, Australia was, and is, rich in minerals: coal, gold, lead, diamonds, iron ore, opals. It also exported wheat in large quantities. Consequently, Australia has always attracted more inward investment. Eventually, tourism could be said to have saved the New Zealand economy.

Both countries also looked to Asia for trade expansion. Before I left NZS, trade had increased between Australia and New Zealand and Japan to the extent that NZS was building ships designed for that trade.

There were profound changes in Europe too. In the early 1950s, France and Germany formed the Coal and Steel Confederation. This was a bi-lateral treaty designed to protect German manufacture and French agriculture. In 1956, France and Germany expanded this treaty by bringing in Italy, Belgium, the Netherlands and Luxembourg to create a new trading bloc enshrined in a new treaty, the Treaty of Rome. It explicitly envisaged a political, economic and monetary union. Thus was born a new trading bloc with an internal market three times the size of the UK. It appeared to be very attractive to many in the UK, especially the politicians. Here was an established market, access to which could, maybe, solve many of the UK's economic problems. The UK was no longer the dominant financial and economic country. Where it had been the world's banker in 1914 with extensive investments around the world, it was now one of the world's biggest debtors. Two World Wars fighting for the right side had bankrupted the UK as an Imperial power. It is easy to understand how the European market looked so attractive. But, it would come at a price. Membership of the European Community involved tariffs against imports from non-member countries and meant abandoning most of the old British Imperial free trade ethos. This was foreseen by other members of the now British Commonwealth and they resented it. This was another reason for them to look for other trading partners. The UK could have developed its Commonwealth links to better advantage. 53 countries with about 25% of the world's population and abundant opportunities to expand food production, manufacturing and mining. These resources would have been backed by the UK's expertise in financial services and experience of managing transport and distribution on a world-wide basis. There remained considerable good will and a genuine regard for British values and its system of government. It has taken nearly 50 years to reverse this decision and free the UK to pursue a course that suits its geographical position and the desires of its inhabitants.

I can understand the attraction of joining an economic community, the GDP of which, overall, was growing faster than the UK and whose markets were on our doorsteps. By contrast, it appeared that our other markets did not contain the same potential. However, the majority of the countries that formed the then European Economic Community had forms of government and law dissimilar to the UK's. Besides, the EEC had originally been formed to protect the industry of Germany and the agriculture of France. Eventually, these differences proved too much for the majority of the UK electorate and we have now left what eventually became the European Union – not a concept we had signed up for.

Whatever the decision that may or may not have been made to the contrary, there was then the problem of low productivity in the UK economy, which has still not been solved. The attitudes of the UK population, which still had something of a superiority complex, are the main obstacle to a solution. These attitudes have included a reluctance to change.

I believe that it is apposite to look at this period because the decision of the United Kingdom electorate to leave the European Union has now provided an opportunity to develop an economic community based on the Commonwealth.

Equally apposite is the situation as I have been writing (2020/23). We have been labouring in the grip of the Covid-19 pandemic. The country had been in lockdown for many months with people confined to home, limited outdoor activity, schools closed, industry shut downs and the issue of a major recession. All appeared very necessary to preserve the nation's health, but there are strong arguments that the restrictions went too far with adverse effects on the economy and education.

The interesting aspect of this pandemic, if we can see beyond the personal tragedies that so many deaths have brought about, is its commonality with other calamities in accelerating change. Changes that would have happened over a longer period of time are occurring sooner i.e. the changes in shopping habits from physical to online and the increasing reliance on information technology. Of particular interest is the speed with which vaccines have been produced to combat the pandemic. It is confidently expected that the techniques developed to produce these vaccines will be adapted and used in other medical areas to produce success in combating other diseases, particularly cancer. Creative destruction has been taking place and the future lies with those who are best placed and willing to take advantage.

Unfortunately, rather than acknowledging that we have to move on, the reaction of the unions involved in nationalised monopolies (schools and the NHS) has been largely negative. The management of the National Education Union (NEU) is wholly left wing and it would appear it has sought to tussle with the government's advisers rather than getting on with the job of furthering education. This is a reaction that has echoed throughout my life. Similarly, the British Medical Association's stance re school re-opening and pay follows its traditional standpoint. It has, historically, appeared to be more interested in the narrow interest of its members than the national interest. It should not be forgotten that the BMA were the strongest opponents of the NHS at the NHS's foundation, far stronger than the Conservative Party, many of whose members saw the advantages of the NHS. It is worthy of note that such attitudes are largely confined to organisations associated with public monopolies, where it has been noted before that they exist to further the interests of their own members at the expense of those whom they are expected to serve.

I am reminded of Churchill's attitude to the solving of difficult problems: 'never mind the difficulties. The difficulties will argue for themselves. Let me know on half a sheet of paper how you propose to deal with the problem'. If only we had more people with that attitude.

Reverting to my earlier paragraphs, the evolving trading patterns and the resultant expansion in the 1950s and 1960s could not be sustained with existing work patterns and designs of ships. Business required ever faster methods of delivering manufactured goods and raw materials. The old days of a leisurely working week Down Under and time to savour the delights of those countries were beginning to disappear. Ship owners needed to make their existing vessels work harder. Hence, cargo began to be worked on a two or three shifts a day basis in the UK, USA, Canada, Australia and New Zealand. Having worked four hours on and eight hours off plus administrative and statutory work, say a ten or twelve hour day, for three or four weeks at sea, Duty Officers in port were working twelve hours on and twelve hours off, seven days a week. The Second Officer also had to work harder and longer to cope with the faster turn-around.

The change was only going to accelerate. An American had already formed a company called Seaborne Containers to carry cargo in a new way in specially designed ships. These ships were not loaded in the old way. Forty foot containers were preloaded at the point of manufacture or in special freight forwarding depots, then delivered to the docks and loaded onto specially built ships. This was a revolution and meant that time in port would be drastically reduced. Also, these ships could only load or discharge in ports with the necessarily expensive infrastructure and transport links to handle large containers. No more spending a couple of weeks in a turn round port and a couple of months on the New Zealand coast. Ships in the future would be turned round in days. Although the large scale roll-out of these ships and the necessary changes in port infrastructure was in the future, NZS was already planning for this. Some of my contemporaries had already been allocated to a research team by the time I left. By 1970, P&O had merged all its cargo companies into P&O General Cargo Division. Ships no longer plied their trade exclusively between the UK and Australasia. All of the NZS ships of my time had been scrapped or sold within ten years of my leaving.

I had mentioned to New Zealanders of my acquaintance that their future lay in the tourist trade. Very few people could see that. It was one of my reasons for considering New Zealand as my home. New Zealand has an enormous variety to offer in terms of climate, geography and opportunity for enjoyment such as skiing, mountaineering, trekking, sailing, surfing, beaches, food, space. The jet age had arrived and long range jets could now reach the farthest corners of the globe. My friend, Tom Pargetter, was in the England Rugby team that toured NZ and Australia in 1963. They flew by jet via America and Fiji to Auckland. There were regular flights to Australia via Bahrain and Singapore. It was not long before the first intrepid tourist arrived. New Zealand became a pioneer in extreme sports e.g. bungee jumping. The jet age made ocean going passenger liners obsolete. Ten years after I left, NZS sold or scrapped its liners. The world I had started out on, no longer existed by the time I left.

The attitude of the Transport and General Workers Union(TGWU) at this time bears examination. It was the union to which the dockers and stevedores belonged. It was obvious even in my time that changes would have to be made. Because of the formation of the National Dock Labour Board after the war, the old casual employment of dockers had gone. And a good thing too. It was, socially, a bad and demeaning practice. The new regime brought its own problem: one of over-employment, leading to unsustainable costs. After the formation of the National Dock Labour Board, anybody who wanted work in the docks had to sign on with the Board, which virtually guaranteed work, even if none was available. The result was over-employment. Ships in London had to employ shore workers to carry out work that was done by the crew in other countries. We even had shore based quartermasters to man the companion ladder. That was three men per ship, each doing an eight hour shift. There were often too many stevedores for the work needed and it was not uncommon to see stevedores playing cards in the holds. Over time, the costs became too high and, in the late 1960s, ship owners, the port owners and stevedoring companies tried to rationalise working practices. They were also trying to develop Tilbury as a major container port. Up stepped one Jack Dash, a Communist and self styled leader of the stevedores, who would have none of this. He organised a series of 'wild cat' strikes, and the TGWU proved either useless or unwilling to discipline him. This was trading suicide. At the same time, Rotterdam had developed what they called 'Europoort'. It was a state of the art port capable of handling container traffic and the largest ships then in existence. It was also, because it was at the mouth of the Rhine, ideally placed to transfer cargoes from the large European canal barges to ocean going ships and vice-versa. Europoort became, and remains, the largest port in Europe. London used to have a lot of this trade. It was now out-of-date, bedevilled by restrictive practices and too expensive. Jack Dash and the TGWU took no account of this. London Docks never recovered.

I could see that my experience with the MANZ line operation was going to be the pattern. Less time in port and consequently more time at sea. I had already experienced the mental anguish of being isolated during my first serious female relationship. It happened to others, frequently. Did I want to stay at sea and become an eccentric, perhaps embittered, captain? I would have become a captain because I only needed to pass one more exam and continue to illustrate my competence. Merit and ability had little to do with promotion. Captains retired or died and other officers left the service before reaching that rank. Thus were places for promotions made available. It merely became a matter of being in the right place at the right time. On my last trip, David LeCornu became Second Officer because Eddie, the incumbent Second Officer, was moved to another ship. I took David's place as Third Officer. These promotions came because we were available to take them, nothing more. An ambitious man could go mad with frustration because of that career pattern.

I don't suppose that, at the time, I thought exactly on these lines and my decision to leave was an emotional one. I just no longer wanted to do it. But, what I had seen, had experienced, had discussed with my colleagues and what I had thought about the future must have had an influence on my decision, even if I was not consciously aware of those factors.

There have been changes to working conditions since I left. Had they been in place before I left, would I have stayed? These are the changes as I understand them:

Trade patterns. Ninety per cent of physical world trade is transported by sea. Consequently, the demand is there but the concentration on 'just in time' and reduced stockholding of raw materials has increased the demand for swift delivery. Add to that the reluctance of consumers to wait coupled with a demand for non-indigenous products, particularly food, means that ships are worked harder.

Working conditions. Merchant Navy Officers are now entitled to 186 days leave a year. Do they get it? Is the demand so great that employers are forced to commute leave for extra payment? Very possibly. Crew members are now allowed to take their wives. But, how many can take advantage of a free cruise if they have children?

In my day, the Merchant Navy was exclusively male, but has become open to both sexes and there are female Masters. This change must have enriched everybody's working life.

Technology has reduced the size of crews. Where I was accustomed to a crew of sixty or more, larger ships now have twenty or thirty. What does that mean in terms of work load?

Navigation and communication. This is undoubtedly an area where innovation has produced the most benefit, principally through satellite technology. Satellites were beginning to be used in the marine world when I left but mainly for military use. In the early 1970s a system called MarinSat was in wide use. Navigators could now plot their position through GPS with an accuracy that was only dreamed about before. And it could be done quickly and without laborious calculation. This did not relieve the Watchkeeper of his or her responsibilities to keep a good lookout or take extra care in bad weather.

Radar has developed as well. It was not a precise tool in my day and there were collisions where the Watchkeeper had relied too much on Radar. These became known as RACs or Radar Assisted Collisions. We only used radar when we were in a busy shipping lane, close to land or in fog. Most of the time it was switched off. Nowadays, it is more precise and has greater range.

Perhaps the greatest change so far as individual crew members are considered has been the development of the WorldWideWeb, personal computers and mobile phones. This has enabled crew members not only to keep in constant touch with family and friends in private but also to have access to news and entertainment as it happens. Mental, if not physical, isolation has been almost eliminated.

These changes had not happened in 1962, so it is purely hypothetical to take them into consideration so far as my decision was concerned. I have never regretted that decision to come ashore. It has taken me sixty years to delve into my memory in writing this memoir and I am surprised that my assessments of the events of that time still have resonance with me. I submit that they have proved to be well-judged.

One issue that I do regret is not keeping up contact with old shipmates or contacts ashore. I should have joined the New Zealand Association and the Durham Association when I came ashore. Who knows what differences it might have made to my life if I had maintained old friendships? I have made some attempts recently and have managed to contact Bunny Hayward and Charles Hufflett. However, one lives in Australia and the other in New Zealand and time has virtually eliminated our common experiences.

There has been one successful attempt to re-contact old shipmates, but it had nothing to do with my efforts. Unbeknownst to me, Peter Matthews and his wife, Carolyn, had managed several years ago to re-establish contact with Scott Gilchrist, Hugh Perks, Henry McCutcheon and Bob McGregor. They had all joined 'Durham' at the same time as myself. Peter lives in

Canada, Hugh and Henry in England, Bob in Australia and Scott in New Zealand. A reunion had taken place when all were in England at the same time. I, apparently, was invisible until Carolyn tried Ancestry. One summer day in 2021, I was very surprised to take a telephone call from Peter. It was emotional and humbling to realise that people thought enough about me to want to get in touch again. Since then, Bob, Henry and myself have met twice. Hugh, unfortunately, died before Peter called me. Covid had prevented all five of us meeting until Peter and Carloyn, Scott and Robin, Bob and Kathy and Henry and myself had a couple of days in a hotel in Keynsham, near Bristol in May 2022. What has surprised me at our meetings is that I still feel anger at my treatment by NZS. Peter is even angrier despite having left NZS at the end of his apprenticeship. Peter told me that, when he was Cadet Captain, he had conversations with Captain Barnet about improving our training and conditions. All to no avail. Bob and Peter joined China Steam Navigation Company and did not regret it. The atmosphere was, according to them, more relaxed. David Harper went to Butterfield and Swire. Scott went back to NZS but left for China Steam after his marriage in 1962. Thus NZS lost all its March 1956 Apprenticeship intake within 6 years. No further comment necessary.

Survivors Reunion, Keynsham, May 2022
Please see Page 129 for original pose.

CHAPTER THIRTY SIX

My Brief View of British History with Regard to the European Question

In the Preface, I stated that I would expand my thoughts on the European issue. This had not been my initial intention but, as I wrote, I could not help but realise that my thoughts and ideas about British history had relevance. The principal issue of British history has been what has been called the 'Continental Imperative'. Walter Bagehot wrote: 'to wash its hands of Europe would be a betrayal of Britain's past and future'. It is impossible for the UK to ignore Europe because of geography. However, Sir Winston Churchill also stated in 1946 'we are with Europe, but not of it.' His view was no doubt coloured by his experiences as a member of the 'Big Three (the USA, USSR and the UK) during the Second World War, but it acknowledged the reality that the UK faces the open sea more than it does Europe.

It can be argued that whenever the British Isles have been closely connected with Europe, either as a subordinate country or in close alliance, the best interests of the country have not been served.

My narrative and opinions are principally concerned with England and its relationship with Europe rather than the British Isles as a whole, although England's interests morphed with overall UK interests over time. My views can be challenged because of my, necessarily, brief exposition, but the drift of what I express carries legitimacy.

The first instance to support the argument occurred when the Roman Empire occupied Britain. It did so to satisfy the vanity of the Emperor Claudius, who was thus able to add the honorific 'Britannicus' to his name. Rome then exploited Britain for nearly four hundred years. After it had evacuated Britannia, it left no organisation or system of law and the infrastructure it had built was in decline. There was no central power, just a collection of tribes. There is little evidence that the British economy benefited from the Roman occupation. The evidence suggests that the Romans had to send money to Britain to maintain its army, thus there was an imbalance of currency movements. The reality was that the Roman ruler of Britain (Dux Britannica) was suffering from Saxon probing at the end of the 4th Century AD and had appointed a subordinate (the Count of the Saxon Shore) to deal with this threat. The Saxon threat imposed an additional financial burden. The Romans probably left more because they could no longer afford to occupy Britain than for any other reason.

By contrast, the immigrants from Northern Germany and Scandinavia would appear to have had a lasting and more beneficial effect. The arrival of the Anglo-Saxons was part of a great westward migration of peoples. It was probably largely peaceful. There is no strong evidence of an armed clash between the Germanic tribes and the Celtic tribes. The Saxons were great timber fellers and preferred to populate river valleys, which they could cultivate with their heavier ploughs. The Celts cultivated the higher ground, which required less clearance and easier ploughing. Over time, the Celts retreated westwards and northwards and fault lines can be demonstrated which equate to the linguistic characteristics of place names, but DNA suggests that there was considerable intermingling.

The Saxons brought a culture that is immediately recognisable in the day to day activities within the UK today. They were self governing and self policing. Rulers, although increasingly from powerful families, went through forms of election on the demise of a previous ruler. The kings, particularly those of Wessex, ruled through an advisory council called a Witan. The Witan preserved the principle of the ruler being elected by approving the claims of the sons of the previous ruler. The Witan was principally made up of landowners and leading clergymen. This principle has been maintained in recent coronations where the sovereign is presented to all sides of the congregation for the acclamation of his or her crowning. Villages and towns held their own courts of law, where a system of fines (wergild) was applied to transgressions, including murder. They had a system of land ownership that was not dependent on service to a superior, although cultivation was on a communal basis.

For over four hundred years, what we now know as England had no overall ruler. It was a collection of separate kingdoms, whose fortunes and lands fluctuated during its time. The Saxons had no standing army. Rulers relied on the provision that able bodied men owed 30 days military service a year, a system known as the *fyrd*. Consequently, no army could be sustained in the field for a full campaigning season. The land was fertile and people prospered. After the Saxons' conversion to Christianity in the 7th Century AD, many religious foundations were established and accumulated valuable objects in precious metals. There were no fortified locations of note. The country was ripe for attack. And attack came from Scandinavia.

The Scandinavians, principally Danes, originally came as raiders but over time increasingly as immigrants, who were prepared to fight for land. They overran and wiped out the eastern Saxon Kingdoms leaving only Mercia in the Midlands and Wessex in the South and West as independent Saxon kingdoms. Gradually, the House of Wessex established an ascendancy through war and diplomacy. The Danes were settled in the eastern and north-eastern part of England (the Danelaw) and accepted the suzerainty of the House of Wessex. Wessex, under Athelstan, unified what we know as England in the early part of the 10th Century AD and the House of Wessex became Kings of England. The Danish settlers brought with them ideas of individual freedom and land ownership that were to have a profound effect on English politics in the English Civil War (1642 to 1651).

Thus, the rulers of England were not autocrats and there was an element of democracy in their governance.

Unfortunately, the Wessex line foundered with the death of Ethelred the Unready and the assassination of his son, Edmund Ironside, in the same year, 1016. Their successor was a Danish invader. He was Canute, who married Ethelred's widow, Emma of Normandy, and although he was also King of Denmark and Norway, he ruled England as a Saxon king. Saxon institutions survived.

The British Isles, particularly that part we know as England were, and are, fertile. The Saxons prospered. Its powerful, landowning families were content to live in their traditional manor houses. There were no castles because there was no need. However, the last of the Saxon kings from a legitimate background, Edward the Confessor, the son of Ethelred, was childless. He had spent his early years as an exile in Normandy and brought some Norman culture to his realm, particularly architecture. He began the building of Westminster Abbey. On his death, England was amongst the most prosperous lands in Europe, if not the most prosperous. This was a situation immensely attractive to a foreign invader. Edward had married Edith of Wessex, a daughter of the Godwin family, who became Earls of Wessex. On Edward's death, Harold Godwinson, Earl of Wessex, used his power to be acclaimed King of England. He was undoubtedly English with English manners and dress. He wore his hair long in the English fashion, in contrast to the cropped hair favoured in Europe. England was an independent kingdom with no ties to Europe.

This was disputed by two European rulers, Harold Hardrada of Norway and William , Duke of Normandy. Harold claimed the crown through his relationship with Canute's family. William because he claimed that Edward had promised him the crown and that Harold Godwinson had sworn on oath to support him. The legitimacy of that oath is doubtful as it may have been obtained through trickery. Whatever, both Hardrada and William prepared for conquest. Hardrada struck first and landed in Yorkshire. King Harold Godwinson assembled his army and surprised Hardrada at Stamford Bridge near York. Hardrada was killed and what remained of his army fled back to Norway. Meanwhile, William had been waiting, increasingly frustrated, in Lower Normandy. The usual prevailing south westerly winds were not present and north easterlies had been predominant. These weather conditions had enabled Hardrada to strike first. The wind changed to south westerly whilst King Harold was in Yorkshire, William set sail and landed in Pevensey Bay. His army consisted of armoured and mounted warriors from various lands along the English Channel coast. William had bribed these followers with promises of land in the most prosperous part of Northern Europe. The temptation was too great to resist and these armoured raiders considered themselves superior to the English, who fought on foot.

William had a problem. It was autumn and he could not rely on seaborne supplies. As well as men, he had several thousand horses to feed and he was confined to a narrow strip of land between the sea and an escarpment. He needed a quick victory. Harold had not wasted time. He made a forced march with his personal retinue, assembled the local fyrd and prepared to deny William the opportunity to advance by taking up a strong position on a ridge overlooking William's camp. William had to attack up a steep incline and the English shield wall held firm for a considerable time. William pretended to retreat, whereupon the western wing of Harold's army advanced without orders and exposed itself to a cavalry counter-attack. It was all over soon after and Harold was killed. The English were now leaderless and the country's interior was open for advance. William seized London, was crowned on Christmas Day, proceeded to claim all the land for himself and established a military dictatorship.

He ruled via awarding land to his followers on condition that they render him military service as required. Nearly all the Saxon landholdings were seized and redistributed. This was the era of the warrior elite, which had become established in Europe during the turmoil following the demise of the Roman Empire. A large landholder, conventionally known as a 'baron', would then subdivide his holdings amongst his followers on condition that they render him service as required. Those Saxons who lived on the land became 'serfs' and were virtually the property of the landholder. They were allowed to till their fields on condition of tilling those parts of the communal fields held exclusively for the landholder's benefit. Serfs were not allowed to leave the landholders' property. Thus was established what is known as the 'feudal system' in England. It overturned centuries of the steady growth of a proto-democracy. I acknowledge that this is something of a simplicity because at least 20% of the Saxon population were slaves. However, my observations remain valid for the other 80%.

The Anglo-Saxon legal culture never entirely died, there are strong echoes throughout subsequent history and the Anglo-Saxon political concept eventually triumphed. It was even used by the descendants of William's baronage in their dispute with King John. The idea of judgement by one's peers and no imprisonment without just cause are Anglo-Saxon in concept and not Norman French. Henry IV was declared king by Act of Parliament. The Grand Remonstrance of 1641, presented to Charles 1st by his parliament, referred specifically to legal precedent from the time of Alfred the Great. The Bill of Rights, 1689, formally ensured that an autocratic monarchy could no longer exist in England.

The cultural divide between Saxons and the Norman overlords was enormous. The Normans spoke French and were largely illiterate, whereas literacy was common amongst the Saxon ruling class. Consequently, written business and administration became almost a monopoly amongst the only body of Norman French that had been educated – the clergy. The clergy owed their allegiance to the Pope, the Bishop of Rome, who was also a temporal ruler - the Papacy had substantial landholdings in central Italy. Initially, the senior clergy (the bishops) were French in origin. Documents were in Latin or French. It was not until the advent of Henry IV in 1399 that there was an English king who spoke English as his first language.

The Norman landholders built fortified strongholds, known as castles, in order to house their garrisons and to overawe the populace. From the king downwards, landholders also had land in Europe. The maintenance and expansion of those properties dominated the lives of landholders. Consequently, England expended blood and treasure over five hundred years in pursuit of dynastic and land ambitions that had nothing to do with domestic English issues. England, for the first time in its history, was 'of Europe'. It was not to its advantage.

It can be argued that subsequent English and Welsh battlefield triumphs e.g. Crecy, Poitiers and Agincourt, were irrelevant to purely English interests. So long as the rulers and their adherents had land and dynastic interests in Europe, England was used as a reservoir of soldiers and funding. It was not until English kings no longer had landholdings in Europe that domestic issues assumed equal prominence with foreign policy. This developed in the 15th Century AD. Whereas Henry V campaigned in France for dynastic reasons, Edward IV campaigned to protect and increase trade and used his army as a bargaining power rather than a war winning weapon. In England, the balance between a military ruling class and a subservient peasantry was gradually changing. Businessmen, principally of English stock, started to be politically prominent and the Lord Mayor of London was important in state affairs. There was also considerable intermarriage between the lower orders of landholders and the English.

The first substantial change came with the break from Rome. As well as its attraction to Henry VIII in resolving his dynastic problem i.e. finding a wife who would provide a male heir, independence from Rome was very attractive to powerful elements within the English political classes. English politics could proceed without foreign religious or temporal interests, which was a theme that had bedevilled relations between the English monarchy and the Papacy since the Conqueror's time. It suited a growing middle class who were now well represented in Parliament. By the time that Mary 1st had lost Calais, England was no longer concerned with European dynastic issues, but Scotland was because its queen, Mary, had also been Queen of France until the death of her first husband. Scotland had always valued what it called the 'auld alliance' with France and this had been a continuous source of friction between England and Scotland, particularly along the borders, until the crowns were unified under one sovereign, who was simultaneously James VI of Scotland and James 1st of England.

In the late 16th Century AD, England was an insignificant island off the north-west coast of Europe. It was fertile and there were rich fisheries in the surrounding seas. But it had little to offer the outside world beyond wool, which continued to be the chief export. This was the age of mercantilism which meant that there was a belief that the produce of the known world was limited. If you wanted more, then the only recourse was to take what you wanted from another party and make them poorer as a consequence. Consequently, the English method was to raid the possessions of other countries, principally Spain. Encouragement came to adventurers such as Francis Drake from the monarch, Elizabeth 1st, principally by her buying shares in these piratical enterprises.

This was a hand to mouth existence and English finances were never on a par with Spain, which itself was denuding its American possessions of precious metals in order to support its dynastic position in Europe. However, without the Elizabethans realising what they were doing, they set England on a path of pursuing its own interests and establishing the largest empire in history. The late Tudor era saw the establishment of the first English colonies abroad and the development of warships and their armament that led to predominance in naval affairs until the First World War. It was this predominance allied to a monetary system adopted from the Dutch example that enabled English, Welsh, Scottish and Irish emigrants and traders to create a world-wide empire. In the process, the United Kingdom of Great Britain and Ireland, as it became in 1801,prevailed against formidable rivals, not only because of naval dominance but because its monetary system was superior. In 1914, the UK was the largest creditor in the world and its overseas revenues enabled it to import more than it exported. It is difficult to believe that this could have occurred if England had still been tied to Europe in some form or other.

The UK, in concert with its Imperial partners, expended its capital and revenues fighting for the right causes in two world wars in the 20th Century, but at the cost of becoming bankrupt in 1945. It survived via a massive loan from the USA, which had become the inheritor of the UK's position as the champion of the Western world. Europe, principally Germany, France and Italy recovered and prospered. By the late 1950s the GDP of the six countries that had founded the European Economic Community exceeded that of the UK. The attraction of joining such a community gained ground in UK political circles, especially within the Conservative and Liberal parties. Only the then leader of the Labour Party, Hugh Gaitskell, opposed this move, but he could not carry the senior members of his party with him despite the support of ordinary members. Subsequent events proved right his opinion that we were throwing away a thousand years of history.

I feel that it is useful here to digress into a consideration of the foreign policy of the USA and its consequences. In 1973, the UK joined the European Economic Community, with the approval of the USA. The foreign policy of the United States throughout the twentieth century has been opposed to the continuation of the British Empire and had actively sought its destruction. Given that the UK was in hock to its most powerful ally, it is not surprising that British politicians pursued a policy that the USA approved. It suited the USA for the UK to be enmeshed in a group that was essentially inward looking and no potential threat to American interests. The reaction of Barrack Obama, then the US president, after the UK referendum in 2016, illustrates this USA policy perfectly. As far as he was concerned, the UK would be at the back of the queue when it came to negotiating a new trade treaty.

The USA's policy throws up a paradox. The USA had become an imperial power but without the will to accept the attendant responsibilities. This was partly due to the USA being an importer of both capital and migrants. This was the reverse of the manner in which the UK had acquired an empire. From the time when the nascent USA consisted of thirteen colonies before independence, the drive to acquire territory was paramount. It continued apace after independence. The USA purchased much of the territory along and to the west of the Mississippi from France in 1804. Its government actively encouraged westward migration via land grants. It attempted to invade and conquer Canada in the War of 1812 against the UK. It bought Alaska from the Russians in the 1870s. After its war against Spain in 1898, it acquired Puerto Rico, Cuba (temporarily), the Philippines, Guam and Wake Island. It also acquired Hawaia. There is no question that the USA is not adverse to expansion.

It will also intervene where it considers its interests endangered, which throws up further paradoxes re Suez. The USA was partly responsible for the nationalisation of the Suez Canal by the Egyptians because it withdrew funds for the Aswan Dam. However, it could not condone an Anglo-French control of the Canal Zone, and by implication Egypt, because it would mean the re-establishment of Anglo-French domination in the Middle East. Hence, it opposed, vigorously, the Suez Canal invasion. Four years earlier, there had been a coup in Iran. A political leader, Mossadeq, had thrown out the Shah and nationalised the Anglo-Iranian Oil Company (part of BP). The Americans intervened and re-instated the Shah. BP regained its interests. The Americans had not acted to save UK interests but to prevent Iran passing into the sphere of influence of the USSR. Similarly, the intervention in Vietnam, which was influenced by the 'Domino Theory'. If one country fell to Communism, surrounding countries would follow suit. The initial American error was to intervene in a civil war. The second error was not to appreciate that the Vietnamese were not going to exchange French rule for American. The third error was to fail to understand that they could not prevail without annexation. Interestingly, the USA asked for UK military support. Fortunately, Harold Wilson's government refused.

It has been a characteristic of USA foreign policy that where they have successfully intervened, they have not stayed or put in place an adequate regime to sustain their victory. This is despite two outstanding examples where they did so: Japan and West Germany after World War II. In Japan, the Americans were fortunate in having a Commander-in-Chief, Macarthur, who had extensive experience of Asian politics and realised that the Japanese Government had to be re-organised on democratic lines. In Germany, a combination of British diplomacy and the Russian threat persuaded the Americans to stay and contribute to the establishment of a democratic regime.

Otherwise, their instinct has been to get in and get out with as little involvement in local politics as possible. In the case of Germany, the US Treasury Secretary (Henry Morgenthau) had put forward a serious post war policy of dismantling all German industrial capacity and returning the country to an agricultural state. Americans do not seem to understand that as a world power and to protect their interests, benign annexation, perhaps for a defined period, is the best answer. The result has often been a prolongation of conflict. The prime example was the retreat into isolationism after the First World War and the refusal to join the League of Nations. Thus, the principal democratic power played no part in restricting the rise of totalitarian regimes, particularly in Germany and Italy. Its policies in the Middle East and Afghanistan are cast in the same vein.

The ironic paradox is that the USA pursued an expansionist policy in the 17th, 18th and 19th Centuries that led to its dominance as a world power today. Now that we are negotiating a trade treaty with the USA we must beware that internal politics within the USA does not override our best interests.

Returning to the European question, the EEC became the European Union following the 1992 Maastricht Treaty, which was in furtherance of the clause in the 1956 Treaty of Rome that envisaged a political union. The UK electorate had acquiesced in joining the EEC because it had been convinced that the EEC was essentially a common market without becoming a political union. As a nation, the UK had not understood that the Napoleonic vision of a united Europe had endured and looked as if it was to become reality. A reality that the UK had, in the past, expended blood and treasure to ensure did not happen. In 2002, Andrew Roberts published his book 'Napoleon and Wellington', a brilliant exposition of the characters and actions of the two men. It is worthwhile considering the final paragraph of his book:

Napoleon's programme of a politically united Europe controlled by a centralised (French-led) bureaucracy, of careers open to talent and a written body of laws, has defeated Wellington's assumptions of British sovereign independence, class distinctions and the supremacy of English common law based upon established, sometimes ancient, precedent. 'I wished to found a European system, a European code law, a European judiciary' wrote Napoleon on St Helena. 'There would be but one people in Europe'. There is some irony in the fact that Waterloo was fought a mere twelve miles from Brussels, the capital of today's European Union. For, although Wellington won the battle, it is Napoleon's dream that is coming true.

Fortunately, for the UK, his conclusion was erroneous. The Maastricht Treaty and the subsequent Treaty of Lisbon opened the eyes of the British people and over the next twenty years they began to understand that they had been conned. The political, social and legal attitudes of the EU and the UK are contradictory. The people of the UK have reverted to their traditional, and successful, policy.

I am indebted to Peter Padfield, in his books 'Maritime Power' and 'Maritime Supremacy', for explaining the differences between a land-based power and a maritime power. The UK had achieved its high commercial and imperial status because it became a maritime power. The EU is, essentially, a land power and looks inward rather than outwards, hence the tariff barriers against our Commonwealth partners. It was inevitable that tensions would grow between the aspirations of the EU and the UK. These tensions could not be reconciled and the UK elected to leave the EU in 2016 and revert to its previous status that had brought it success over a period of nearly four hundred years.

Throughout this turmoil, the British Commonwealth of Nations endured and grew. It owes it survival and growth principally to the efforts of Queen Elizabeth II, the Duke of Edinburgh and, now, their heir, King Charles III. Queen Elizabeth II was the titular head of the Commonwealth and, by agreement with the Commonwealth members, Charles III has succeeded her. It now numbers 55 nations, four of which (Mozambique, Rwanda, Togo and) were never part of the British Empire. This voluntary organisation represents 2.5 billion people, a third of the world's population. Its Heads of Government meet annually to discuss matters of mutual interest. Its representatives in the UK gather together each year on Remembrance Sunday to lay wreaths at the Cenotaph in Whitehall.

This Commonwealth represents an opportunity for the UK to become a major participant in a voluntary grouping that has enormous potential. We, in the UK, will be able to converse and trade with people who are more like minded to us than any other country, with the exception of the USA. We have a shared language, legal systems, existing commonalities in trade and a wealth of agriculture and minerals. There appears to be a willingness to forgive the UK's abandonment of these opportunities.

There is also the Chinese question. There is no doubt that China has embarked on a policy of world supremacy and is a threat to our most cherished ideals. It is adept at advancing the philosophy that prosperity is not the consequence of democracy. The EU appeared to have no policy other than appeasement, until its hand was forces by Putin's invasion of Ukraine, whereas Commonwealth countries such as India and Australia are prepared to challenge China. Therefore, politically as well as commercially, our future lies with developing the British Commonwealth as a powerful bloc of independent nations. This was envisaged by Disraeli a hundred and fifty years ago. It has taken us a long time to get to this position and it may not yet be generally recognised as our future, although Boris Johnson has declared that our future is in the open sea. The 2020 Defence Review indicated that the Johnson Government understood this historical concept. The chance to be a maritime power again beckons us.

APPENDICES

These appendices cover subjects and items that would clog up the narrative with having to explain them. The Appendices are:

Appendix One: Glossary of Naval Terms, in Alphabetical Order.
Appendix Two: Ranks and Responsibilities in the Merchant Navy
Appendix Three: Navigation

APPENDIX ONE

A Glossary of Naval Terms in Alphabetical Order.

These are not intended to be comprehensive. A comprehensive list would be another book.

Cargo Ship Structure

Essentially, a cargo ship of my time at sea could be divided into three parts:

The cargo carrying part, known as holds (see below).
The engine room, which would be in the middle part of the ship (amidships) and below the main deck.
Superstructure, usually amidships. Superstructure is that part of the ship built above the main deck. It is usually on four levels. The lower is at main deck level and held the crew's quarters, the galley, ship's stores, ship's and steward's office and the officers' saloon. The second level was the officers' cabins and lounge. The third level was the boat deck, captain's quarters, radio shack and radio officers' cabins. The fourth level was the bridge, which spanned the width of the vessel above the captain's quarters. The bridge contained a wheel house, 'wings' on either side (which gave views along both sides), chartroom behind the wheel house and a pilot's cabin.

Parts of a ship.

Afterdeck: the part of the deck between the superstructure and the stern.

After part: any part that is in the stern end of the ship or in the back end of any part of the ship.

Ahead: anything that is in front of the ship. Verb: to go ahead = to go forward.

Aloft: above the deck, usually if you are on the mast or rigging. Verb: to go aloft.

Astern: anything that is behind the ship. Verb: to go astern = going backwards or in reverse.

Below: any part of the ship below you at that moment. Verb: to go below.

Bilges: located along the sides of the ship at the very bottom of the holds. A series of sumps to collect surplus water from the holds, especially from condensation.

Bitts. These were short, vertical, metal posts and placed in pairs on either side of the bow and stern. Used to secure the hawsers once the ship was docked.

Boat Deck or Top Deck. The Captain's Quarters were built across the full width of the top deck at the fore end. Behind his quarters was the top part of the engine room structure, the 'empty square', on top of which was the funnel (the engine exhaust) and the vents. On the port side of the square was the radio shack and radio officers' quarters. The ship's sick bay was on the starboard side. There were four lifeboats slung two on each side of the boat deck. The boat deck had sufficient space for deck games such as deck quoits or shuffle board.

Bow: the 'front end'. Also known as the 'stem'.

Bridge: this was the highest part of the superstructure and at the front or forepart of the superstructure. It spanned the full width of the ship. This was the 'command area' of the ship. It contained the ship's wheel, magnetic compass, gyro compass master and a repeater, radar monitor and signalling equipment. Officers kept their watches on the bridge. The bridge had a central, closed area with windows at the fore part. Underneath the windows was a long bench with cupboards underneath. These housed items such as signalling flags and flags of the nations the ship expected to visit. On each side of the enclosed section was a sliding door that led on to a bridge wing. Each bridge wing had a ship's telegraph. This was used to pass commands from the bridge to the engine room. It was made of solid brass on a brass pillar. It had a dial on each side a bit like a clock but marked out as follows : Full Speed Ahead, Slow Ahead, Stop, Slow Astern and Full Speed Astern. There was a double handle on a swivel that could be moved to whatever command the Master, Pilot or Officer of the Watch wished to pass to the engine room. When the handle was moved, it moved a handle on an identical telegraph in the engine room and set off a sound signal in the engine room. There was also a sound tube by which the engine room and the bridge could communicate by voice. At each end of the bridge wing was a gyro compass repeater that was used to take bearings. On top of the bridge structure was a flat, open area surrounded by railings. It contained a magnetic compass. If the gyro compass was not working, bearings could be taken from the magnetic compass, which did not use electricity. If the weather was too bad to station a lookout in the bow, the lookout would stand his watch here.

Bulk head = Wall.

Bulwark. The metal wall that ran from the bow to the stern along both sides of the ship along the lower deck. It was about three feet high and prevented crew members from falling off the deck into the sea. Alongside Nos. 2 and 3 holds, the bulwark would normally be metal railings. The bulwark was pivoted at the bottom so that it could be folded down flat when working cargo.

Capstan. A large winch at the bow. It has two purposes. Firstly, to haul up the anchor and chain, secondly as a winch for hauling in the hawser.

Cargo holds; always referred to as No 1, No 2 and so on with No 1 always at the fore end of the ship i.e. the foremost hold. Normally, Holds 1, 2 and 3 would be on the fore deck and holds 4, 5 and 6 (if fitted) on the after deck.

Chart Room: Immediately behind the bridge was the chartroom. This had a large work bench on top of which was the current chart in use and other kinds of navigational equipment, including the chronometer. The chronometer was the most accurate way of telling the time and was based on the revolutionary design originally produced by William Harrison in about 1735. It was always kept to Greenwich Mean Time. It was housed in a special watertight and airtight box that was kept at a constant temperature to avoid discrepancies. The chronometer was slung on 'gimbals', a pivoting system that kept the chronometer as near horizontal as possible to avoid inaccuracies that could be caused by the ship's movement. It had a glass top so that you could read the time. Charts not in use were stored in drawers in the work bench. We used the chartroom to brew up cocoa and coffee during the night watches. The chartroom and the chronometer, in particular, were the responsibility of the Second Officer, who was responsible for navigation and loading cargo.

Companion Way. Essentially a staircase. Each deck had access to the next deck, above and below, via external and interior companionways.

Companion Ladder. The principal means of access to the ship's lower deck from the dockside. It looked like a narrow, wooden staircase with rope rails. It could be raised up and down depending on how low or high the ship was in the water. It was raised and stowed in a special place when at sea.

Deck = Flat open space or a floor.

Deckhead = Ceiling.

Deck houses: structures between each hold that housed winches and acted as store rooms. The ship's carpenter (the 'Chippy') had his workshop in a deckhouse between Nos. 4 and 5 hatches on the after deck.

Engine Room. In cargo ships the engine room was situated in the hull between Nos 3 and 4 holds. It contained the main engines, auxiliary engines, storerooms and workshops.

Fore deck: the part of the deck between the superstructure and the bow.

Fore part: any part that is in the forward (front) end of the ship or the front end of any part of the ship.

Funnel. Essentially the engine's exhaust system. It is always placed on the highest point of the superstructure and is connected to the engine exhaust pipes. The exhaust pipes are contained within the funnel. The higher the funnel, the greater the draught and the more effective the exhaust. Companies generally paint their funnels in company colours.

The engine room had to be ventilated. It was done so by huge fans that drew the hot air upwards and then out through vents on top of the radio 'shack'. This meant that the middle of the superstructure was an empty square above the engine room and was surrounded by a steel wall or bulkhead.

Galley: the area on the main deck where the ship's cook and his staff worked. It contained ovens, butchery, prep benches, store rooms, fridges and freezers. It was in front of the top part of the engine room compartment.

Gunwale. The top of the bulwark or the top 'strake' of an open boat.

Hatches: rectangular openings in the deck that allowed access to the cargo holds. These hatches were surrounded by a 'coaming', a steel wall about two feet high that stopped you from falling in. These hatches would be covered by boards and tarpaulins when the ship was at sea.

Hull: the main bulk of the ship that contained the cargo holds and engine spaces.

Locker. A walled-off section of a hold that was used for secure cargo (alcohol and tobacco) and chilled cargo that had to be separate from frozen cargo. Lockers could be locked.

Mast. An upright, hollow, metal post. The foremast was positioned between Nos. 1 and 2 hold and the aftermast between Nos. 4 and 5 hold. The radio aerial was slung between the foremast and the aftermast. The heavy derrick for heavier cargoes was attached to the foremast. Masts were also used to carry flags (see 'halliards'below).

Officers' deck. This was immediately above the crew's quarters. There were cabins on each side of the engine room 'empty square' with a lounge at both the fore and aft end. A corridor ran round the 'empty square'. There was a covered open deck that ran round the outside of the cabins. The ablutions and washing machine area were immediately forward of the 'empty square'.

Scuppers. Essentially gutters along the side of a deck that allowed rain and storm water to run off the decks and into the sea.

Stern: the 'back end'.

Strake. Originally, a line of horizontal wooden planks that made up the hull. In a metal hulled ship, a strake is a line of horizontal metal plates from bow to stern. The strake next to the keel is known as the garboard strake.

Superstructure: that part of the ship that was built on top of the hull. It usually consisted of four 'decks' (i.e. floors or storeys). The bottom deck held the crew's quarters, galley, ship's office and Officers' saloon (dining room). The second deck held the Officers' quarters and two lounges. The third deck held the Captain's quarters, the radio office ('radio shack) and the Radio Officers' quarters. The fourth deck was the bridge. The bridge was over the Captain's quarters. The boat deck, where the lifeboats were stored, was on the third deck of the superstructure.

Working alleyway: a covered walkway on each side of the lower superstructure that allowed access between the fore and after decks. The crew's quarters, the galley, the ship's office, entrance to the engine room and the Officer's saloon led off this alleyway.

Equipment names.

B.1
Rope: There are no such things as rope or string at sea. A length of rope or string would be known by its function.

Hawser. A thick rope, the thickness of a man's thigh, used to secure a ship to the shore. Usually made of sisal. Also known as a forward or stern line. These were attached to a winch barrel on the capstan in the bow to haul in or slacken off. The stern lines were attached to the aftermost winch barrel at hold No 5 or 6 for hauling. A hawser would also be used for towing by a tug.

Heaving line. A long length of cotton or nylon line with the free end woven into a tight hard knot. The standing end would be tied to a hawser or spring. The heaving line was then coiled and thrown from the ship to shore. The shore party hauled on the heaving line and then the hawser or spring so that the hawser or spring could be attached to a shore bollard. A heaving line could be used to pass a hawser between two vessels.

Knot
  A method for fastening rope or twine to an object.
  A method for securing one length of rope or twine to another. Different knots would be used for different thicknesses and where one length is thicker than another.
  A decorative way of stopping a length of rope or twine from fraying.
  Measurement of speed: one knot = one nautical mile per hour.

Line. Any length of rope, small in diameter, used for a variety of purposes.

Painter. A line connected to the bow of a boat that is used to secure the boat to a jetty, another boat or the dock.

Sheet: a line fastened to the bottom corner of a sail and then to a cleat on deck to keep the sail in place. Hence 'three sheets in the wind' means out of control, or drunk.

Spring. A wire rope. Either a forward or stern spring. The forward spring went from near the bow on the ship to a shore bollard that was further aft. The stern spring went from near the stern of the ship to a shore bollard further forward. Springs are used to dampen the effect of tidal movement in harbour so that the ship is maintained in a stationary position. Otherwise cranes and derricks would have to be continually adjusted.

Splice. A method for joining one length of wire or rope to another by intertwining. Or a means of stopping one end from fraying by intertwining.

Twine. Thinner lengths of line.

B2. Lifting Equipment

Block and tackle (pronounced 'takel'). A block is a metal or wood block that surrounds one or more grooved wheels on a spindle. You reeve (thread) rope or wire over the wheel so that the grooves around the wheel grip the rope or wire and keep the rope or wire in constant touch with the wheel. On derricks, the cargo block has one wheel. A full block and tackle has the rope or wire riven (threaded) through two blocks so that when you pull on the rope, it can haul a greater weight. See 'A Lift' below.

Halliard. A length of line used to hoist flags and other small items. The halliard would be rove through a block on the mast. The flag is fastened to the halliard and then hoisted up.

A Lift. Block and tackle used to raise or lower a derrick. One block was fastened to the top end of the derrick, the other to the top of the derrick post. You hauled on the 'free' end of the wire to raise the derrick by winding the wire around a winch and applying power to the winch.

B3. Miscellaneous Terms

Fleet: a section of hull, bulkhead or other vertical surface that is to be painted and is within a man's reach to the left or right.

Greenwich Mean Time (GMT). All time is regulated by the moment when the sun crosses the Prime Meridian. That time is expressed as 1200 GMT. Unless your position is on the Greenwich Meridian, all other positions on the globe are either forward of GMT (O to 180 Degrees East) or behind GMT (0 to 180 degrees west).

Holiday: where a man painting has 'missed a bit'.

Knot: a means of expressing speed. A knot is one nautical mile per hour (see below). Thus 10 knots per hour = 10 nautical miles per hour. A nautical mile is longer than a land mile.

Latitude;

The globe that is our Earth is, for navigational purposes, encircled by imaginary parallel lines between the North and South Poles and the Equator. The distances between these lines are measured in degrees. Thus, the Equator is always 0 degrees and the North Pole is 90 degrees north and the South Pole is 90 degrees south. Each degree is further subdivided into minutes where 60 minutes of latitude equals one degree of latitude.

The earth is what is known as an oblate spheroid. It is slightly flattened at the poles. Thus, a minute of latitude at the poles is longer than a minute of latitude at the equator. The charts used by navigators allow for this.

Longitude:

Similarly, there are imaginary lines of Longitude. These are all at right angles to lines of latitude. All lines of longitude come together at the Poles. Longitude is expressed as so many degrees west or east of Greenwich. Greenwich is 0 degrees longitude and this line is known as the Prime Meridian. The furthest west or east of Greenwich is the 180 degree meridian and it is located in the Pacific Ocean. It is either 12 hours in front of Greenwich Mean Time or 12 hours behind, depending on whether you cross that meridian going east or west. If travelling eastward, then you would be 12 hours in front of Greenwich and would have to put your clocks back 24 hours on crossing the 180 degree meridian as you would then be 12 hours behind GMT. If travelling westward, then you would be 12 hours behind GMT and would have to advance your clocks 24 hours on crossing the 180 degree meridian as you would then be 12 hours in front of GMT.

As with latitude, a degree of longitude is divided into 60 minutes. This means that a minute of longitude at the Poles is nothing. The length of a minute increases the further you are from the Poles until it is at its maximum at the Equator. Navigators' charts allow for this.

At sea, a vessels position is determined by working out which line of latitude it is on and which line of longitude it is on. Where the lines coincide is the vessel's position.

Merchant Shipping Act

This act had laid down the regulations for operating UK merchant ships and the maintenance of discipline.

Mercator Projection:

The earth is a globe, but navigators need a map on a flat surface. A man called Mercator worked out a way to portray this without too much distortion several hundred years ago. His projection is still used today.

Money System. The pay of Merchant Navy crew is expressed as a monthly amount. However, ships do not carry money for wages and salaries. No money is paid at sea but you could 'buy' items such as work clothing, alcohol and cigarettes every week at sea and in port. Ratings and Apprentices were only allowed beer. Officers could buy spirits. Cigarettes were sold in boxes or tins of 200. Alcohol and cigarettes were duty free, which made them very cheap and many saved their fags for taking home on leave. However, the Customs regulations only allowed us so much a week and we could only take 200 cigarettes on leave without paying duty. The cost of these was deducted from your accumulated pay at the end of the voyage. Petty Officers and ratings could earn 'overtime', and this was essential for the married lower paid. Without overtime, ship's maintenance such as painting would not have been done. Being at sea is a seven day a week job, but this went unrecognised for years, Shortly after I joined, the regulations on pay changed. All crew members were paid extra for Sundays and Bank Holidays at sea. When we were in port, we could 'sub' each week. You put in a request to the Steward's Office for what you wanted to draw that week and the Second Steward paid out that amount at Friday lunchtime. On 'Signing Off' all crew members, contracted and un-contracted, were 'paid off. We received the accumulation of our monthly pay, overtime and Sundays at sea less what was 'subbed', spent on board and remittances. A crew member could sign a Remittance Order that authorised a relative, usually wife or mother, to apply to the ship owner for a portion of the crew member's pay every month. In this way, a married crew member could ensure that his wife and family had regular money. For all of us, it was a way of saving.

Nautical Mile;

This is a standard measurement. It is measured in two ways. Firstly it is one minute of latitude at 45 degrees latitude North or South. Secondly, it is 1,000 fathoms long. A fathom is 6 feet, so a Nautical Mile is 6,000 feet or 2,000 yards. One nautical mile = one knot in speed. Thus one knot is faster than one mph.

Ship's Log.

The official record of the voyage. It is a statutory obligation under the Merchant Shipping Act to maintain a ship's log. Each voyage had a separate log. The log was a book larger than A4 but smaller than A3. The size was what used to be known as 'Foolscap'. It was leather bound.

The first page contained the name of the ship and the number of the voyage. On the next page was a list of all the crew members and their rates of pay, except for the master, whose rate of pay was listed as 'salaried'.

Each day was then allocated two adjacent pages. The left hand page recorded the course and speed for each four hour watch and any changes therein. It also recorded the wind direction and speed and the sea state. If in port, it was left blank. If the ship was manoeuvring to the orders of a pilot, i.e. when entering or leaving port, the left hand page had this entry 'To Commander's Orders and Pilot's advice' for whatever time was appropriate. If the Master was manoeuvring and there were constant changes of course and/or speed, it was recorded as 'To Commander's Orders'. On the right hand page was recorded any significant incidents during each four hour watch i.e. sightings of land or other ships, changes of course, and, particularly, bad weather. After each watch, the Officer of the Watch signed the right hand page. In practice, this log never left the ship. A fair copy would be made at the end of the voyage and sent to the shipping company for their records. I daresay that such records are now recorded electronically.

I remember that we were not allowed to use ball point pens. For many years after Mr Biro invented the ball point pen, documents written with a ball point pen were considered inadmissible in law. We had to use liquid ink using an old fashioned nib that you 'dipped' into the ink or a fountain pen. Also, the space we had was small and writing had to be small. Then it had to be blotted and could be messy. It was considered that writing in ball point ink could be altered after the event i.e. it was open to fraud.

See also 'Ship's log' in Navigation below (Appendix Three).

Shipping Agent. These were companies who contracted to look after a shipping company's interests in foreign ports. They arranged the berthing i.e. where and when you docked, organised wharf labour, delivered supplies, acted as our 'Post Office' and banker (they delivered our 'subs') and any other business the ship needed seeing to. In Australia and New Zealand, NZS had bought a number of agents and these operated as subsidiaries of NZS whilst retaining their old names. In other countries, NZS contracted with independent agents.

'Signing On and 'Signing Off'. This is an old tradition. Seamen, unless contracted for a specific period to a shipping company, were only paid for the duration of a voyage. Each un-contracted member of the crew signed the Muster Book at the beginning of the voyage. This recorded his rank and rate of pay. At the end of the voyage, un-contracted crew members 'Signed Off' and were given what pay was owed them (see Money System above).

Trip: a colloquial name for a voyage.

Vessel: this is the official name for any waterborne craft. I have often used the colloquial name 'ship' because it is more easily understood by non-seafarers. Hence the Durham is MV Durham (Motor Vessel Durham).

Voyage: This is an official term. It covers the period of time between the crew 'signing on' and 'signing off'.

Appendix Two

Ranks and Responsibilities in the Merchant Navy

Traditionally, there were taboos about who socialised with whom. The Master usually only conversed socially with the Chief Engineer and the Chief Officer. Otherwise his contacts were mostly on a business basis with the Second Officer, Chief Radio Officer and Chief Steward. I never once set foot in the Master's quarters. Officers did not socialise with ratings, a situation that was emphasised by the physical separation of the Officers' quarters from the ratings' and that Officers were served by stewards at meal times. Generally, nobody socialised with the apprentices. An Officer did not go ashore with ratings.

Only Officers were required by their employers to wear uniforms, except for Stewards, who wore uniforms when serving in the Officers' saloon. In reality, the uniforms, although indistinguishable in design from the Royal Navy, were company liveries and each company had its own distinctive cap badge. There was no legal obligation to wear uniform. All crew members paid for their working clothes.

A: The Master.

The ship's master has four gold stripes on his uniform. In NZS (and all P&O ships) stripes were sewn onto each shoulder of our blue uniform. Stripes were carried on epaulettes on white, or tropical, uniform. The master was the commander of the ship and everybody was responsible to him and he was responsible for the total operation of the ship and carried the can if things went wrong. The master determined what course the vessel steered in order to get from A to B. Usually referred to as 'The Old Man' irrespective of his age and, sometimes, as 'God'.

On entering or leaving port, anchoring or in bad weather, the Master took command on the bridge.

B. Deck Officers.

Chief Officer: the Chief Officer had three gold stripes. He was responsible for all operations on deck i.e. outside the engine room and the galley, which included ship's safety, maintenance (including lifeboat stores and condition) and watch keeping. At sea, if there was no Fourth Officer, he would stand watch on the bridge from four to eight in the morning and evening, but generally his working day, either in port or at sea, was from breakfast to dinner and he could take evenings off in port i.e. go ashore. In the event that the Master died or was indisposed, the Chief Officer assumed the responsibilities of the Master, always assuming that he had obtained his Master's Certificate.

On entering or leaving port and anchoring, the Chief Officer was in command of the fore party.

The Second Officer. He wore two gold stripes. He was usually known as 'Second'. His main responsibilities were navigation, cargo stowage and ship's stability. He organised the midday sun sight and determined the ship's noon position and advised the master on which course or courses to steer. He was responsible for the chartroom and maintaining the chart library, updating charts and looking after the chronometer. He had to make sure that the ship maintained an even keel and was not top heavy by ensuring the accurate stowage of cargo. He also liaised with the Second Engineer concerning the stowage of fuel and water. At sea, he kept watch between midnight and four in the morning (the graveyard watch) and midday to four in the afternoon (the afternoon watch). In port, he worked breakfast to dinner and could take evenings off i.e. go ashore.

On entering or leaving port, the Second Officer was in command of the after party.

The Third Officer. He had one gold stripe. He was usually known as Third. In port, his responsibilities were to support the Second Officer and to act as the senior officer of the team consisting of himself and the Fourth Officer. He was responsible for overseeing the cargo operation: loading and unloading and the securing of hatches after work. He and the Fourth Officer rotated their hours because there always had to be an officer on duty. If cargo was being worked on a day basis, that is if work ceased at approximately 5pm, then the Duty Officer would be on duty from 8 am until 8 am the next day. The Officer not on duty was, theoretically, free from midday until 8 am the next day. This also applied at weekends. If cargo was being worked in shifts, then the 3rd and 4th Officers would share the shifts i.e. on 24 hour working, the 3rd would work 8 am until 8 pm and the 4th would work 8 pm until 8 am. Thus, the Third and Fourth Officers had less time off than other Officers. Together with the Fourth Officer he would record all items of cargo being loaded and note where each item of cargo was stowed. He and the Fourth Officer would produce a plan showing where all the cargo was stowed. At sea, he kept watch from eight in the morning to midday (the forenoon watch) and from eight in the evening to midnight (the evening watch). He was responsible for the ship's signalling equipment: lamps and flags plus flags used for ceremonial and ornamental use and any other portable equipment on the bridge.

On entering or leaving port, the Third Officer assisted the Master and Pilot and transmitted messages to the engine room via the ship's telegraph or voice pipe.

The Fourth Officer. He had one, thin, gold stripe, which was half the width of the Third Officer's. He was usually known as 'Four O'. In port, he supported the Second and Third Officers. At sea, he kept watch from four in the morning until eight in the morning (the morning watch) and from four in the evening to eight in the evening (the dog watches). He would try and plot the ship's position by star sights at sunrise and sunset. This was more complicated than determining the ship's position by sun sight at noon, therefore Masters and Seconds relied more on the noon sight and their own experience. Four O would also have clerical duties thrust on him as the junior officer. These were mostly typing out various lists and extracts from the ship's log for insurance purposes.

On entering or leaving port, the Fourth Officer maintained the movement book, which recorded all engine room movements, course changes and passing of significant landmarks or buoys.

Lifeboats. Each Deck Officer had charge of one lifeboat. At lifeboat drill, he was responsible for checking the muster, allocating lifeboat crew to various duties, lowering and raising and, where appropriate, pulling and sailing.

C. Engineer Officers

The Engineers' Department was the largest department on the ship in terms of numbers of people. It was usual for Engineer Officers to have served an apprenticeship in a shipyard or with one of the major marine engine manufacturers. In order to progress, they had to pass a series of examinations.

Chief Engineer: he wore four gold stripes with red piping in between the stripes. This red piping was worn by all engineer officers. He was responsible to the Master for all ship's machinery. He did not stand watches but worked only in the day. As with the Master, much of his responsibilities were to do with paperwork and reporting.

Second Engineer: he wore three gold stripes and was of equivalent rank to the Chief Officer. He organised the engine room crew and reported to the Chief Engineer. His duties were very much 'hands on' and he was a watch keeper (four to eight), although he often delegated that responsibility.

Third Engineer: He wore two gold stripes and was of equivalent rank to the Second Officer. He kept the same watch as the Second Officer,

Fourth Engineer: He wore one gold stripe and was of equivalent rank to the Third Officer. He kept the eight to twelve watch.

Fifth, Sixth, Seventh, Eighth, Ninth, Tenth Engineer and Junior Engineer (i.e. not yet qualified): They wore a thin gold stripe and were allocated duties and watch keeping by the Second Engineer. The Fourth Officer was considered superior in rank to these engineers.

Chief Electrical Engineer: equivalent rank to Third Engineer. Responsible for electricity supply. If he had an assistant he would be known as Second Electrical Engineer and equivalent to the Fourth Engineer. Rarely worked watches.

Chief Refrigeration Engineer: equivalent rank to Third Engineer. Responsible for refrigeration machinery and maintenance of appropriate hold temperatures.

In port, Engineer officers mostly worked days on maintenance and any other required work. They would work shifts as required by the ship's cargo working.

D. Radio Officers

Most ships carried two radio officers. The senior was known as Chief Radio Officer and carried two gold stripes. The junior carried one gold stripe. The radio shack was on the boat deck and the radio officers had their cabins next door so that there would be no delay in reaching the radio should an emergency arise. The Chief Radio Officer reported directly to the Master. Radio Officers were obliged to keep.radio watch at designated times, otherwise they kept watch as they and the Master determined. Radio Officers were usually trained by the Marconi Company and were often retained, after training, by Marconi, who then leased them out to shipping companies. NZS preferred to employ Radio Officers directly and paid them better. Communication was usually by wireless telegraphy in Morse code. This was because radio signals were weak over long distances and Morse could be sent via weaker signals. Radio conversations were rare and only took place if we were close enough to shore based maritime radio stations.

The Marconi Company was by this time a subsidiary of the General Electric Company. It had been started by Gullielmo Marconi, an Italian domiciled in England. In the early 1900s he successfully made the first trans-Atlantic wireless telegraphy transmission from Lands End to Newfoundland, and thus the wireless age began. The Marconi Company also pioneered the first electronic TV system in the 1930s.

The development of digital technology and satellites has rendered Radio Officers redundant. Communications are now the responsibility of Deck Officers.

E. Steward Officers

Chief Steward or Steward in Charge. A Chief Steward on a passenger liner had much more responsibility than one on a cargo ship. Hence, the Chief Steward on a passenger liner ranked with the Chief Officer and wore three white stripes. On cargo ships, the Chief Steward would wear two white stripes and would mess with other officers. The shipping company may, at its discretion, have only appointed a Steward in Charge. He wore two white stripes but his position was ambivalent as he was neither an Officer nor a rating. He tended to take his meals alone. Whatever their ranks, these stewards were responsible for the ship's catering, relevant stores and hygiene i.e. laundry. The Ship's cook and Second Steward (see below) reported to him. His job included liaising with the master on legal matters, dealing with customs officials, keeping the records of all crew members and paying 'subs'.

F. Petty Officers.

The following are what is known as Petty Officers. With the exception of the Second Steward, they did not wear uniform and supplied their own working clothes. They had their own mess at the after end of the crew's quarters on the starboard side. All Petty Officers had their own cabins. It is unusual for a Petty Officer not to have been in a lower rank i.e. AB or cabin steward before promotion.

Bosun (short for Boatswain). He was the senior deck rating. His rank was equivalent to a Chief Petty Officer in the Royal Navy. His main responsibilities were maintenance of deck and cargo equipment, lifeboats and paintwork. He worked very closely with the Chief Officer. He was also responsible for deck ratings watch rotas i.e. who was on watch and when. In a normal cargo ship, ratings were divided into watches. Some senior ratings only did day work, which was carried out on the Durham by the apprentices. The senior ratings were usually on day work and the juniors on watch. When the apprentices were working 'on deck', the apprentices worked directly under the Bosun. On entering or leaving port, the Bosun was in charge of the forward berthing party, under the Chief Officer.

Lamptrimmer (Lamps). He was the senior deck rating after the Bosun. His main job was to look after the deck stores (paint, rope, canvas, cleaning equipment etc.) and allocate supplies as necessary. On entering or leaving port, he was in charge of the after berthing party, under the Second Officer.

Instructional AB. This was a special rank for an Able Seaman with many years of experience and the establishment of good character. His job was to support the Bosun in training the apprentices on a cadet ship in the duties and responsibilities of deck ratings. Specifically, he would instruct us in rope and wire work (knots, splices) and help the Bosun to supervise our work. He would also work 'overtime' to supplement his pay.

Ship's carpenter. Of all the deck ratings, the 'chippie' had the most independent role. He worked directly for the Chief Officer on maintenance and mending of anything to do with woodwork. He was also responsible for measuring the amount of water in the hold bilges and scuppers. He would take 'soundings' every morning by lowering a weighted line through holes in the deck and then down a tube into the bilges. These holes were located all round the main deck. He recorded his soundings and reported any anomalies. Chippies would always have served an apprenticeship in a shipyard before going to sea.

Donkeyman. The senior engine room rating, who reported to the Chief Engineer. His function re work in the engine room mirrored the Bosun's on deck.

Ship's Cook. Responsible for feeding all the crew. The catering staff prepared and cooked all meals. The cook was responsible to the Chief Steward for all the stores under his control. So, if food went mouldy or was not properly stowed, it was the cook's fault. Under him, he had a butcher (or second cook), baker, perhaps a pantryman and pantry boys (who did the donkey work).

Second Steward. He wore a uniform with one white stripe. He was responsible for the stewards and reported directly to the Chief Steward. He was responsible for the ship's laundry (mostly bedding, towels, napkins, tablecloths, tea towels) and handing out subs.

Stewards were allocated as follows:

Steward Ratings:

Captain's Steward, Senior Officers' Steward and Junior Officers' Stewards. These people served the officers at meals, cleaned cabins and changed Officers' bed linen and towels. They wore uniforms at meal times: black trousers, white shirt and tie, short white jacket.

Butcher and baker: responsible to the Cook. As their names suggest, mainly dealt with meat and baking elements in the ship's menu. Would be known as a 'sous chef' in a shore establishment.

Pantry Man: any person employed in the Ship's Cook's department who had served for several trips and would be given responsible for a particular function i.e. vegetables and fruit or frozen produce and the preparation of them.

Pantry Boy ('Peggy'): a young person on his first or second trip and allocated to duties at the discretion of the Cook.

A proportion of Stewards had elected to serve in the Merchant Navy rather than do National Service. Until 1960, all males over the age of 18 were required to serve two years of National Service, and most were recruited into the Army. The Royal Navy and Royal Air Force preferred volunteers for longer service because of the longer training that was needed to produce skilled sailors and airmen. Provided that a Steward did three years in the Merchant Navy, he was exempt from National Service. This suited ship owners because it made it easier to recruit Stewards for jobs that entailed long and repetitive hours. I doubt that the somewhat rigid social hierarchy on board endeared many Stewards to their 'calling'.

G. Deck Ratings

Able Seaman (AB): a seaman with several years' service whom the shipping company recognised as valuable and, accordingly, paid him more. An AB had to have an Efficient Deck Hand Certificate (see Efficient Deck Hand below). There is no officially recognised rank of AB in the Merchant Navy.

Efficient Deck Hand (EDH): each UK Merchant Ship had to carry a statutory number of Efficient Deck Hands. To become an EDH, an Ordinary Seaman would present himself for a practical examination in seamanship: rope and wire work, splicing, knowledge of nautical terms, basic health and safety. On the Durham, there were not enough EDHs, therefore apprentices on their third trip took the EDH exam to ensure that there were enough qualified seamen to satisfy the regulations.

Ordinary Seaman: an un-certificated rating who had some experience.

All the above would take their turn as quartermasters at sea i.e. manning the ship's wheel. On entering or leaving port, it was usual for the senior ABs to act as quartermasters

Junior Ordinary Seaman (a 'Peggy'): a young seaman on his first and second trip. Often assigned to menial tasks such as cleaning the quarters of more senior ratings and washing-up.

H. Engineer Rating

Greaser: any man employed to work in the engine room of a diesel-powered ship. In a steam ship, he would be known as a 'stoker'.

I.Pilot.

The pilot is not a member of the ship's crew. In certain coastal waters and entering or leaving port, regulations and insurance requirements state that it is mandatory to employ a 'Pilot'. The pilot's job is to advise the Master when navigating difficult waters. Close inshore, in river estuaries and harbours, conditions change. Currents change with the tide and weather. Sand banks come and go. 'Shoals', which are areas of shallow water, change shape and size. Navigational marks change or there are temporary marks. The deep water channel fluctuates. Local knowledge is required to manoeuvre the ship safely. The Pilot always operates in a defined geographical area and has extensive local knowledge and experience.

The Pilot will first and foremost be an experienced sea officer with at least a Master's Certificate. Most will have an Extra Master's Certificate. Before being allowed to operate on his own, a Pilot has to serve a probationary period where he 'shadows' another Pilot and then is gradually allowed to perform all the Pilot's duties under the supervision of his mentor.

The Pilot would board at sea from a small, covered vessel called a Pilot Cutter. He would board the ship via a rope ladder hung over the ship's side adjacent to No 3 hold. The rope ladder had strips of wood attached a few feet apart. These strips were wider than the rope ladder and are called 'stretchers'. They stop the ladder from twisting. In calm weather, it is still a hazardous climb for a middle-aged man, but even worse in bad weather and at night. He has to jump from the cutter, which is moving up and down, onto the ladder.

Whilst he is on duty, the Pilot gives orders directly to the quartermaster and the Officer manning the engine room telegraph. The law states that he has to advise the Master what to do and the Master then passes on the order. This is cumbersome and could cause delay in an emergency. In practice, the Pilot gives orders directly. These orders are not generally logged and the ship's log is annotated 'To Commander's Orders and Pilot's Advice'. The Master retains absolute authority and responsibility at all times and it is he who has to answer in case of accidents or misadventures, although legal history provides for responsibility and obligations on the Pilot's part. When the ship is in an estuary or manoeuvring in port, the 3rd or 4th Officer maintains a log of all engine movements (slow, stop, half ahead, half astern etc) and the time when navigational marks are passed. This is recorded in a small pocket book called the movement book and is a legal document i.e. it can be referred to in court.

In the UK, Pilots belong either to Trinity House or the local Port Authority, depending on who has the legal authority in the area. In London, the Port of London Authority starts at Gravesend and extends upriver to Richmond Lock. If a vessel is headed for London and is proceeding up the Channel, the Trinity House pilot is usually picked up at Dover and hands over to the river pilot at Gravesend. Trinity House is one of the oldest establishments in the UK, perhaps the world. The organisation takes its name from its headquarters, Trinity House, which is situated between the Tower of London and Tower Bridge. Trinity House also has responsibilities for lighthouses and lightships. Although it gets revenue from the pilotage fees, there are also dues that ship owners have to pay for operating in waters where it maintains lighthouses and lightships.

Why become a Pilot? Mainly because a Pilot can make use of his seafaring abilities and spend more time sleeping in his own bed.

Appendix Three

Navigation

In the deep oceans, navigation had not significantly changed since the time of Captain Cook in the 1770s. On reflection, I am aware that I have followed the wake of Captain Cook. He produced the first accurate maritime charts, which were still being used in my day: Newfoundland, the St Lawrence River, Pacific Islands, New Zealand, Australia, Antarctica and the American Pacific coast. His charts were astonishingly accurate, which accuracy has been proved by comparison with satellite images. He was one of the great explorers and navigators, perhaps the greatest. He opened up a third of the world to us.

Navigation is essentially the ability to know where you start from, where you want to go, what course, or courses, to steer to get there and how you check that you are on the right course. We used a compass, a chronometer, a sextant, charts (ocean maps), logarithms, knowledge of the movements of the sun and stars. If Cook or Nelson were alive in the 1950s, they would have recognised all the equipment we had.

That is not to say that there had not been advances: gyro compasses, radar, radio. But these only helped us to be more accurate in using traditional methods. In European coastal waters there was an electronic system called Decca Navigator, but its range was limited. The Americans had a longer range system called Loran, but it was not accurate. Some lighthouses sent out a radio beam which you could tune into and, when it was at its strongest, you took a bearing which told you that you were somewhere on that line of bearing but you could not determine the distance. Radar was only useful if you could get a signal bouncing off land. As most marine radar sets only had a range of ten to fifteen miles, it was no good if you were well out to sea. There were no satellites. The Americans had developed a system called SINS – Ship's Inertial Navigation System. It measured the ship's speed, course and attitude i.e. is the hull going up or down and at what angle. It was designed to be used on nuclear submarines, which remained submerged for weeks or months and had no physical means of checking their position. The US Navy did not make it generally available for obvious reasons.

Here is a list of the equipment we used and how we used them.

Admiralty Handbooks:

These were published by the Admiralty and illustrated items of navigational interest in different parts of the world. They included written descriptions and accounts from Admiralty navigators plus photographs and sketches. Until recently, Naval and Military Officers were required to make sketches. Some of the handbooks we used had sketches made by Captain Cook and other 18th and 19th Century navigators. They were amazingly accurate. The written parts often contained items of general and historical interest. These handbooks were invaluable if you had never been to that part of the world the handbook covered.

Celestial Sphere:

This was an imaginary transparent sphere surrounding the Earth on which all objects used for navigation were presumed to exist. A geographical position for stars was determined by this method. It assumed that the Earth was the centre of the universe and in doing so reversed all that Copernicus had determined. However, it was merely a device to aid navigation and was very successful.

Charts:

The name comes from the Latin 'Carta'. Hence cartography, the science or art of map-making. Charts are used to plot (mark) the ship's position, the course so far steered ('made good') and the course to steer towards the destination. The globe is divided into easily managed sections and a chart of that section is drawn and printed. Charts show lines of latitude and longitude, the coastlines and islands (if any), landmarks such as light houses, water depth and any items of interest or danger i.e. shipwrecks above the water or just below, rocks and the nature of the sea bottom, for instance 's' = sand.

Chronometer and ship's clock:

Until the late 18th Century, navigators had no method of accurately determining longitude at sea. Latitude is easy because you can measure the height of the sun above the horizon at noon. This is known as the Zenith. Using this height and the date, the navigator can work out how far is the distance between the vessel and the imaginary position of the sun on the Celestial Sphere. You then take away or add the known latitude of the sun and you have your latitude. This method has been known for thousands of years.

Calculating longitude is not so easy. Each minute and degree of longitude east or west of Greenwich is equivalent to a period of time. How do you calculate that period of time? You need an accurate timepiece that will always tell you what time it is at Greenwich. Essentially, provided that you have accurately determined how many hours and minutes you are in front of or behind Greenwich time, you are able to translate the time difference into degrees and minutes of longitude. There were no accurate timepieces until the late 18th Century. In 1720, Parliament passed an Act offering a large sum of money to anybody who could design an effective timepiece that could be used on board. Several tried and failed. There were clocks but they were too big and cumbersome. In the 1730s, a Mr Harrison presented his invention. It was just a few inches across and similar in depth. It had a waterproof case and could be mounted in a gimbal. A gimbal is a device that moves with the ship's motion and keeps the object in the middle stable. It is two concentric rings with the inner ring joined to the outer by a swivel joint. The outer ring is similarly joined to the chronometer case. The device worked and was commissioned by the Admiralty, after decades of delay. This gave the Royal Navy an enormous advantage in navigation. One model was installed in Captain Cook's first ship and fully proved its worth. Chronometers are an essential part of a ship's navigational equipment today.

You start to determine your longitude at noon by using a sun sight taken at about 8 am. This provides a height in degrees and minutes of the sun above the horizon. You also take a bearing of the sun. This enables you to determine how far away the ship is from the sun assuming you are both on the celestial sphere. You draw a line on the chart at right angles to the bearing at the point of distance from the Sun. The ship will be somewhere on that line. You then calculate where you expect the ship to be at noon by using the ship's course and the expected distance travelled in the time until you take the noon sight. You then transfer the bearing of the morning sight to the expected noon position. At noon, the sight provides an accurate estimate of latitude. This 'noon' is not necessarily 1200. It will be the time at which the Second Officer has calculated that the sun will be at its zenith, i.e. the highest point above the horizon. This 'noon' will be a minute or minutes before or after 1200 on the ship's master clock. You can calculate the expected angle of sight beforehand. If there is a difference between the actual sight and the calculated sight, you just adjust the distance along transferred bearing originally taken at 8 am. A line at right angles to that bearing will 'cut' the exact line of latitude. This is your noon position and is accurate to within a mile or so.

Star sights could also be taken at sunset and sunrise. However, although potentially more accurate, they were dependent on taking at least three star sights within two to three minutes and accurately recording the times of sights using the chronometer. The weather and clarity of horizon were also important. As these sights would be taken by the most junior of the officers, the 4th, during his watch and were not corroborated, they were not used by the Second Officer. Nevertheless, 4th Officers were encouraged to take star sights as often as possible as an alternative.

Compass;

This is a device that always points to North and allows a vessel to determine in what direction it is heading. For centuries, magnetic compasses were the main form. Unfortunately, they cannot point to true north. The earth's magnetic field is not aligned with a true north to south line. The magnetic North Pole is some distance away from the North Pole and its position is not constant. This distance is known as Variation and is measured in degrees east or west. Variation itself varies depending on the ship's geographical position. Metal ships also have their own magnetic field, which affects the compass. This is known as Deviation and the amount of deviation depends on which direction the ship is heading.

Thus, to know true north and the true course to steer, the navigator has to allow for Variation and Deviation.

In the 1930's, the Sperry Corporation invented the gyro compass. This has a disc that spins at high speed and its needle will always point to true north. You can attach remote repeaters to the central mechanism so that you have a replica compass wherever you need it. We had a repeater on the bridge that the quartermaster used and repeaters on each side of the bridge. These repeaters were used to take bearings of landmarks and other ships. It was probably the most important nautical invention of the 20th Century until satellite navigation.

Knot: A measure of speed. One knot = one nautical mile. A nautical mile is one degree of latitude at 45 degrees North or South. Hence, a nautical mile is longer at the North or South Pole than at the Equator because the earth is not a perfect sphere. It is an oblate spheroid i.e. it flattens slightly at the poles.

Navigation tables:

These tables were in a book that enabled the navigator to translate his sights and other calculations into mathematical figures called logarithms. It meant that instead of lengthy and inaccurate calculations, these calculations could be done simply and accurately using simple arithmetic.

The tables also allowed calculations for determining speed and distance covered.

Sextant:

An instrument used to measure the height of a star or the sun above the horizon. It used a series of mirrors and a telescope to bring the image of the sun or star down to the horizon line. A lever attached to the mirrors is aligned with a scale at the bottom of the sextant and you read off the angular height on the scale. The lever swung through one sixth of a circle, hence the name 'sextant'.

Ship's log' :

A mechanism to indicate the ship's speed. From time immemorial, a length of wood, called 'the log', was attached to a line and lowered over the side at regular intervals in time. The line was divided into regular lengths by a 'knot'. As the ship moved forward, the line was gradually fed out and the number of knots counted for a specified time. This gave a rough estimate of how fast the ship was travelling. This was how Nelson and Captain Cook calculated speed and distance.

In the nineteenth century there were improvements. The Admiralty, or streamed, log was the most common used. It was a little propeller attached to a couple of hundred feet of line. The other end of the line was attached to a recorder with a clock face rather like the speedometer in a car. The face showed the actual speed and the distance travelled. It was 'streamed' by lowering the propeller over the stern and allowing it to be towed behind the ship at the extent of the attached line. The propeller was turned by the action of the water as the ship moved. The propeller then turned the line, which in turn activated the 'speedometer'. It was not very accurate because of the energy lost in turning the line. The readings would also vary dependant on the sea state. More often than not, we did not stream the log and relied on the engine revolutions to give us an indication of speed. Also, these logs and the engine revolutions only measured speed 'through the water' and not 'over the ground' as you get from a car's speedometer. Sea water is constantly on the move and is affected by wind, waves and currents. Consequently, the actual speed and distance varied significantly from that indicated by the log.

There were no significant improvements until the invention of the Chernikeeff Log before the First World War. Captain Chernikeeff was an Officer in the Imperial Russian Navy and worked in the Hydrological Department. He devised an impeller log that was suspended at the end of a short tube attached to the hull. When the vessel was travelling at a speed in excess of one knot, the impeller was turned by the water flowing past and sent an electrical signal to a receiver on board, which translated this signal into speed. It was more accurate than any other log then in use. After Chernikeeeff escaped from Russia in 1917, he established a company in the UK that sold the log to several navies throughout the world, including the Royal Navy. Its usefulness was enhanced because its information could be utilised in weapons control systems. However, it still only measured speed through the water and the protrusion of the impeller and tube meant that it was susceptible to damage.

In the 1960s and 1970s, several companies developed the electromagnetic log. This projected an electrical signal into the water, which signal was reflected back by ions in the water. The signal was transmitted to a receiver on board similar to the signal from the Chernikeeff log. Thus it overcame the problem of underwater damage but, because it transmitted an electrical signal, it could be detected by enemy warships. Its main disadvantage was that it only recorded speed through the water.

At the same time, the Doppler log emerged. This sent a sound signal to the sea bed, which bounced back to a receiver further aft. The difference in frequency between the transmitted signal and received signal can be represented as the speed of the vessel. Its principle advantage over other logs is that it provides speed over the ground. However, the Doppler log does not work when the seabed is deeper than 300 feet. When that is the case, the log can be used to bounce off a dense layer of sea water at depths of 20 to 30 fathoms, but this only provides speed over the water. The received signal is also liable to other errors, although it is generally more accurate than other logs.

Nowadays, the position of any moving object on land, sea and air can be calculated to within metres at any given time via satellite. In my day, as we travelled at bicycle pace, such accuracy was not essential.

Star charts:

These were transparent, plastic circles on which were shown the positions on the celestial sphere of prominent stars. You had a different chart for whatever latitude you were in. It enabled the navigator to determine which stars he was most likely to be able to 'shoot' on a given day and time.

APPENDIX FOUR

MAPS RELEVANT TO MY VOYAGES

World Map

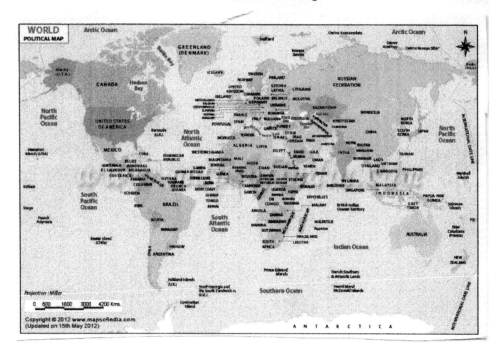

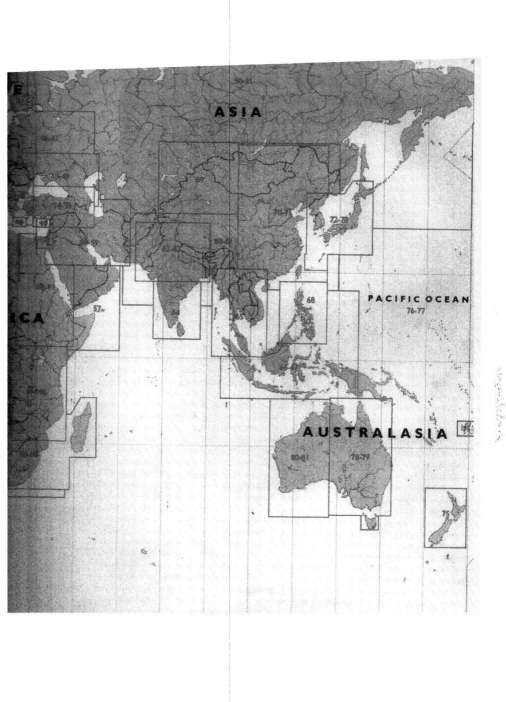

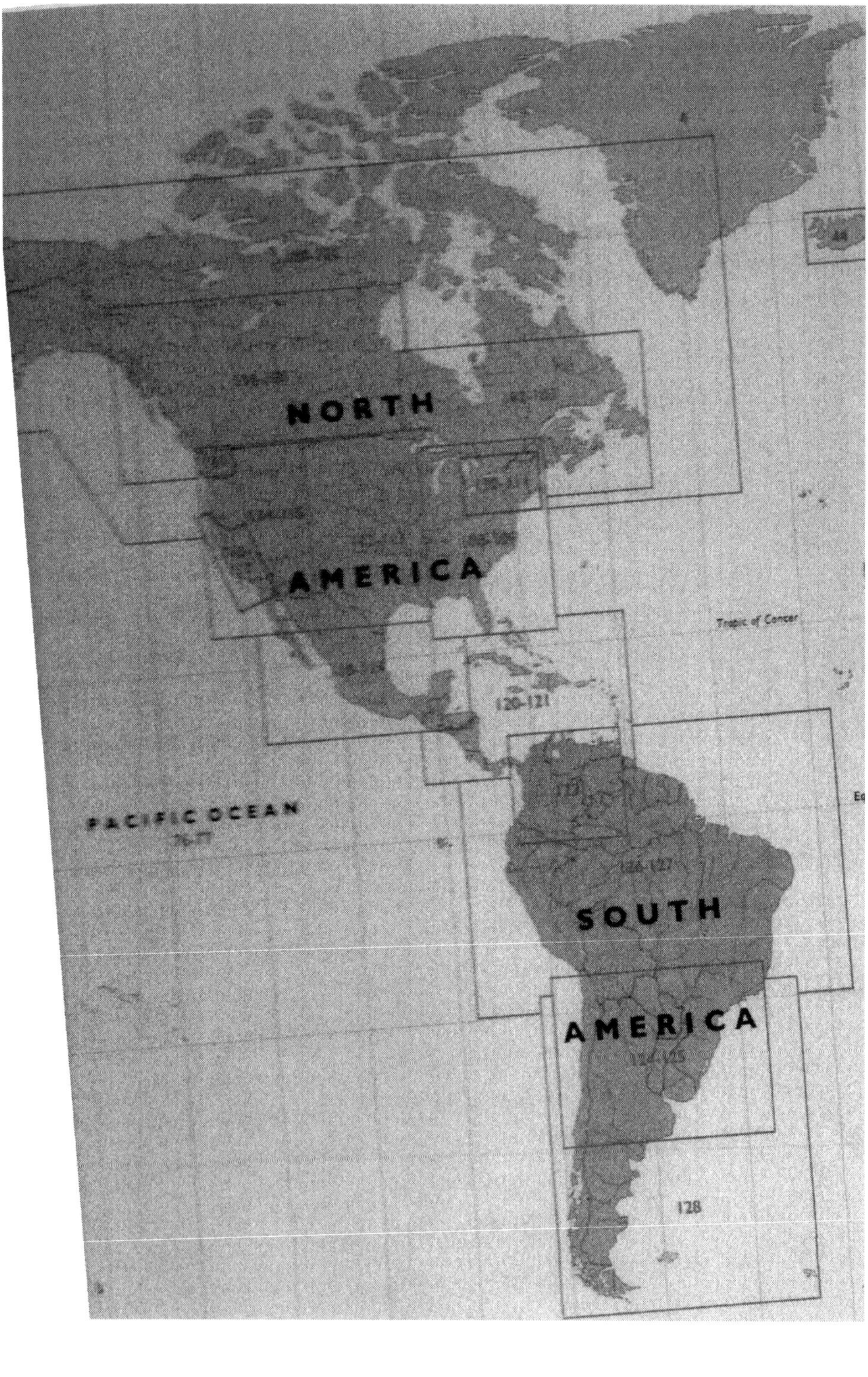
NORTH
AMERICA
Tropic of Cancer
120-121
PACIFIC OCEAN
SOUTH
AMERICA
128

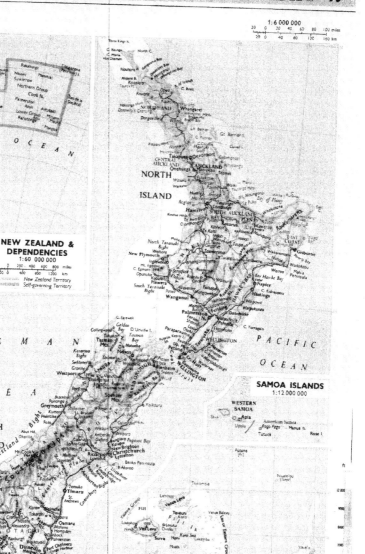

1:6 000 000

NORTH
ISLAND

NEW ZEALAND &
DEPENDENCIES
1:60 000 000

New Zealand Territory
Self-governing Territory

SOUTH
ISLAND

SAMOA ISLANDS
1:12 000 000

WESTERN
SAMOA

FIJI AND TONGA
ISLANDS
1:12 000 000

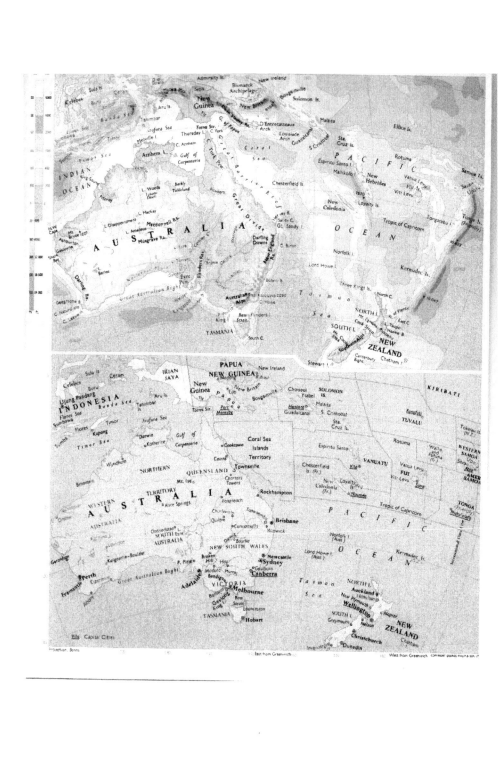

NORTH AMERICA 99

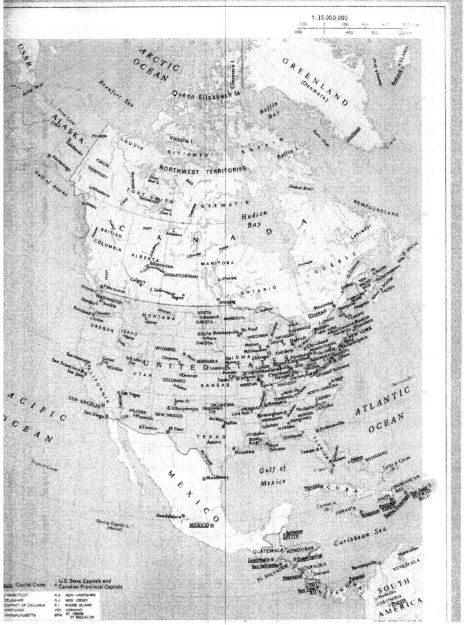

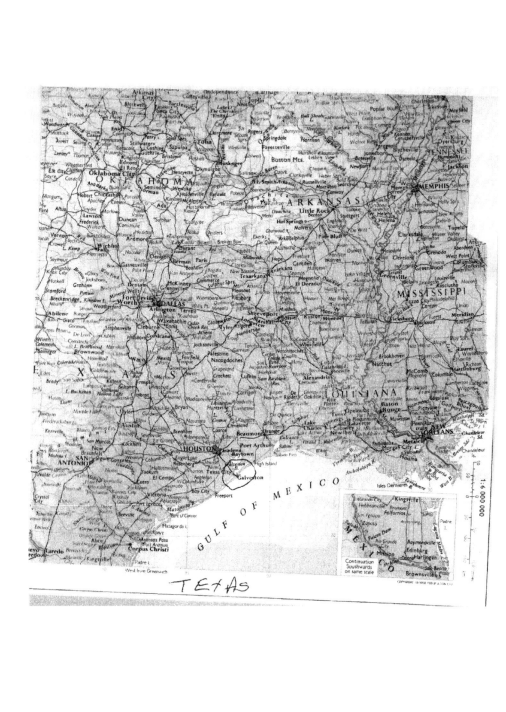

TEXAS

Printed in Great Britain
by Amazon